ISBN 978-0-266-82565-4
PIBN 10083651

THE
FEDERAL SYSTEMS

OF THE

UNITED STATES

AND THE

BRITISH EMPIRE

THEIR ORIGIN, NATURE, AND
DEVELOPMENT

BY

ARTHUR P. POLEY, B.A.

OF THE INNER TEMPLE AND MIDLAND CIRCUIT, BARRISTER-AT-LAW,
FORMERLY EXHIBITIONER OF MERCHANT TAYLORS' SCHOOL AND
SCHOLAR OF ST. JOHN'S COLLEGE, OXFORD

" The crimson thread of kinship runs through us all "
SIR HENRY PARKES

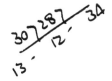

LONDON: SIR ISAAC PITMAN & SONS, LTD.
No. 1 AMEN CORNER, E.C.   .   .   .   1913

Printed by Sir Isaac Pitman
& Sons, Ltd., London, Bath,
and New York . . 1913

PREFACE

In this book an attempt has been made to give an account of the four great systems of Government of the United States, Canada, Australia, and South Africa, and to explain their nature, origin, and development. In covering such a wide field it has only been possible without defeating the object the Author has had in view—the presentation of a lucid statement in a reasonable compass of space—to deal but briefly with many matters which deserve ampler treatment. If fuller knowledge is desired the reader is referred to the histories and excellent treatises which have been written by distinguished writers on the several Constitutions.

It is believed that no attempt has hitherto been made to bring the four Constitutions together for the purposes of comparison, and in this respect the present work may perhaps claim to break new ground and to be of general Imperial interest.

The scheme adopted has been to trace the origin and development of Colonial Government from the establishment of the American plantations down to the present time. The formation of the United States and the creation of the three Imperial systems have marked stages in the History of the Empire.

To explain the Constitution of the United States without referring to the reasons that actuated its framers in its construction would be as unprofitable as it would be to describe it without relation to its indebtedness to the Constitution of Great Britain. In the same way each Constitution in turn, as it throws light on its predecessor, lends itself to the object of comparison and to a proper understanding of the value of federal systems.

In the last chapter of the work a suggestion is made for a closer union of the Empire. If this chapter be read in conjunction with the first chapter its historical meaning will be better appreciated.

In treating of the Union of South Africa, it has been termed for the purposes of comparison a federal system, notwithstanding that it is described in the Constitution Act as a legislative union. The Author's apology is that it exhibits so many of the features of federalism that it would be impossible to omit it.

During the progress of this work through the Press two amendments have been made to the Constitution of the United States. It has been possible to deal with the one relating to Income Tax, but the other substituting direct election of senators by the people of the States in place of election by State Legislatures has been so recently passed that it has been impossible to do more than mention it here.

Most of the well-known authorities to whose works recourse has been had are referred to in the notes to the text. Particular mention, however, must be made of Lefroy's *Legislative Power in Canada*, the works of Sir J. C. Bourinot, Quick and Garran's *Annotated Constitution of the Australian Commonwealth*, Professor Harrison Moore's *Commonwealth of Australia*, and last, but not least, Mr. Keith's recently published great work on Responsible Government.

In the laborious task of preparing the work for the Press, the Author has received much help and many valuable suggestions on the United States' Constitution from Mr. John Foreman, F.R.G.S., Barrister-at-Law, the well-known author of *The Philippine Islands*, and on the Canadian Constitution from Mr. Horace J. Douglas, Barrister-at-Law, whose knowledge of this Constitution has been of considerable value.

In the labour of preparing the index he gratefully acknowledges his obligations to Mr. Geoffry L. Hardy, Barrister-at-Law.

A. P. P.

3 PLOWDEN BUILDINGS,
TEMPLE,
April 28, 1913.

CONTENTS

viii CONTENTS

The Federal Systems of the United States and the British Empire

Their Origin, Nature and Development

CHAPTER I

ERRATA

On page 389, line 5, omit the words " for each " ;
on page 390, line 12, substitute 40 for 64 ; and on
line 15, " South Africa " for " Australia."

of a State or Provincial authority. A distinct feature of a Federal Constitution is the continuance of two Governments in the same country distinct in their organisation and action, and independent of each other in their authority. Mr. Bryce considers that " the most striking and pervading characteristic of Federation is the existence of a double government, a double allegiance, a double patriotism."

In all Federal Constitutions the powers and functions of the Central or Federal authority and the State or Provincial

Character-istics.

Apportion-ment of functions.

¹ Dicey's *Law of the Constitution*, 6th Edition, p. 139.

viii   CONTENTS

The Federal Systems of the United States and the British Empire

Their Origin, Nature and Development

CHAPTER I

GREAT BRITAIN AND HER COLONIES

FEDERAL Constitutions are not of modern origin. They A Federal Constitution defined. are found existing in the later periods of ancient Grecian history, generally owing their inception to the necessities of a common defence. Sometimes these necessities resulted in a Confederation, which differed from a Federation in that it was more in the nature of an alliance of States bonded together for a particular purpose. A Federal State, on the other hand, has been defined as " a political contrivance to reconcile national unity and power with the maintenance of States rights where the central authority operates directly on the people of the States and not indirectly through the medium of the States."[1] A Federal Constitution, therefore, recognises the existence of a National - sovereignty and at the same time acknowledges the existence of a State or Provincial authority. A distinct feature of Characteristics. a Federal Constitution is the continuance of two Governments in the same country distinct in their organisation and action, and independent of each other in their authority. Mr. Bryce considers that " the most striking and pervading characteristic of Federation is the existence of a double government, a double allegiance, a double patriotism."

In all Federal Constitutions the powers and functions of Apportionment of functions. the Central or Federal authority and the State or Provincial

[1] Dicey's *Law of the Constitution*, 6th Edition, p. 139.

‑authorities require apportionment. The methods of distribution vary in different constitutions and, accordingly as a preponderating proportion of the powers is assigned to the Central or Federal authority or given to the States or Provinces, the constitution is described as a more or less unified one.

A Federal Constitution may endow the Central or Federal authority with such limited powers that it may be but little more than a Confederation. On the other hand, the Central or Federal power may be so enriched that the States or Provinces may possess such minor functions that they are but one degree removed from local authorities.

General Character-istics of.

In all Federal Constitutions there are certain special characteristics. Among them will be found an elaborate distribution of powers for the most part capable of exercise directly on the citizens of the Federation by the Federal or State authorities independently of each other ; a recognition of the part played by the States in creating the Union acknowledged as a rule in the composition of one branch of the Federal Legislature; the Establishment of a Judiciary to decide the extent of the Federal and State powers and the State powers *inter se ;* and a Supreme Law embodied in a written constitution giving effect to these principles.

Fo ir constitutions.

In the pages of this work an attempt will be made to examine the nature of four constitutions of Anglo-Saxon or mainly of Anglo-Saxon origin, which were based upon and embodied the spirit of the British Constitution. Of these

Three Subordinate.

Constitutions three may be termed subordinate, for although created by the people of the country over which they are the supreme law, they were sanctioned by the legislation of the Imperial Parliament. The other and eldest of the Constitutions was fashioned independently of British

United States Constitution Sovereign.

authority a great Sovereign Constitution providing for the government of the people of the United States. The three British Imperial Constitutions acknowledge the same Sovereign, but are otherwise bound by few political ties to the United Kingdom. Invisible links, however, unite them. The peoples who dwell under their protection are mainly descendants of inhabitants of the British Isles, inheriting the language and literature, the laws, and the political institutions of their Motherland. Even those of their peoples who are not of the same race subscribe to political institutions, whose beneficence they have enjoyed, and whose wisdom has been demonstrated by experience.

The rise and development of these Federal systems mark a stage in the history of British colonisation. Properly to appreciate this, it is necessary to show how the British system of colonisation was distinguishable from others. The history of Greek colonisation tells how from the Mother States of Greece many colonies sprang and spread themselves over the lands that border the Mediterranean. Through the mists of legends may be seen the Ionian cities, rising by the waters of the Ægean Sea, from Phocæa to Miletus, and ultimately forming themselves into one league under the title of the Ionic Confederation. *Stage in the History of British colonisation.* *Greek colonisation.*

Sailing from their parent States of Thessaly and Bœotia, the Æolians built new cities along the northern parts of Asia Minor and the northern isles of the Ægean Sea. Following the setting sun, some of the pioneers of Greek civilisation spread Westward to Sicily and Italy, others settled on the southern portion of Asia and the west coast of Asia Minor. The Southern Islands knew the Dorians, who, like the Æolians and Ionians, formed Confederations amongst themselves or loose alliances.

From their ancient homes the Greek colonists brought a common religion and common customs, and the sentiment of a common origin. Bound by no political ties to the land they had left, it was yet not forgotten. In their new homes they copied the institutions of their Motherland, and became independent self-governing communities, opulent and democratic, till democracy ran wild and the government of the tyrant succeeded to that of the people, the foreign invader to that of the despot ; last of all in many instances ruin and decay crumbled their tottering walls, and dust and desolation shrouded the streets of long-forgotten splendours. In the hey-day of their glory, from time to time, something like *Greek citizenship.*

an attempt was made to create a bond of union. It stopped short, however, at defensive leagues such as the Confederation of Delos made between the Ionian cities and Athens.

Yet the Greek colonist was always a Greek wherever he went. He carried with him his old Hellenic fellowship, his passionate love to his Mother City, his metropolis, but no political ties bound him. No statesman, no missionary of Empire, rose to preach the gospel of unity to him. His imagination halted at a dream of a pan-Hellenic Federalism. No steamship bridged the seas ; no telegraph annihilated space. Seers and poets alike were silent. The Delphic oracle gave forth no message of warning. A Mediterranean Empire was not even in the palmy days of Greece a dream.

The Greek, in later years, under the pressure of external danger, formed the Achaian League that preserved for a time, but was unable to perpetuate, a Grecian unity. Federation came at last, but Federation came too late.

The Roman colonies. The Roman colonies were essentially different from the separate States of Greece ; for they were not autonomous. The strength of Rome lay in her unity. Wherever her eagles triumphed she imposed the Roman yoke, the Roman language, and the Roman civilisation upon the subjugated peoples ; till, over centralised, she fell asunder a prey to internal convulsions and the rude shocks of more virile races. Like the Greek, the Roman failed to understand the principle of Federation which might have combined the Grecian idea of autonomy with his own idea of the value of unity.

Anglo-Saxon. The Anglo-Saxon conqueror of Great Britain knew nothing of Federation. In his opinion a neighbouring State required to be subjugated because it was a neighbouring State, or else to remain a source of permanent danger. The Anglo-Saxon understood a united country ; he also understood local self-government, but he never dreamed of a Federated heptarchy.

Hundreds of years were to pass before his descendants were destined to establish in a new world a Federal system.

The four Governments of the United States, Canada, Australia, and South Africa, unite three races : the British and French in Canada, and the British and Dutch in South Africa. The Constitutions of the United States and Australia are wholly the work of men of British race, particularly may it be said with regard to the whole of the people of Australia that the people whom its Constitution unites are a people whose kinsfolk are traceable in the cities, towns, and villages of the United Kingdom. As the Greek colonists who left their motherland to found new colonies and in turn, when they had become established, formed yet other colonies, so the descendants of the Anglo-Saxons, Danes and Normans, who had crossed the stormy seas to find homes in Great Britain after many centuries of rest again started wandering to seek new dwelling-places beyond the oceans. *Four Federal systems unite three races.* *Constitutions of United States and Australia wholly British.*

At the commencement of the oversea emigration, all the Plantations, as the Colonies were then termed, were settled by the King's licence and grants. The Englishman settled in North America under Constitutions and powers of government framed by the King's charters and commissions. The colonist understood himself as removed out of the realm, but both in the executive and legislative capacity of government, as in immediate connection and subordinate to the King. *Formation of Plantations.*

The North American Colonies were all in the true spirit and meaning of the thing counties palatine, and some of them were actually and expressly created such. *Originally Counties Palatine.*

Thus, the grant of the lands now called Louisiana in 1630 to Sir Robert Heath, and his heirs ran : " We erect the same into a province and incorporate it by the name of Carolanea or the province Carolanea with all singular such like and as ample rights, jurisdictions, privileges, prerogatives, royalties, liberties, immunities, and franchises as well by sea as land within the regions, territories, islands, and limits aforesaid to have exercise, use and enjoy the same as Bishop of Duresme in the bishoprick or County Palatine of Duresme," etc., etc. *Grant of Louisiana.*

Maryland
and Maine.

To similar effect were the charters of Maryland and Maine.

Limitations
of the feudal
Constitution
of England.

The Constitution of England as it stood at the time of the foundation of early colonisation had been founded upon or built up with the feudal system, a system which could not extend beyond the realm. Nothing in it had provided for colonies or provinces outside the realm. Lands which were outside the realm were not the property of the realm, but since all the colonists were the King's subjects, the King as their sovereign lord assumed rights of property and government ; as the colonists were freemen who had left the country with the King's consent, " the King, by his Commission of Government or the Charters which he gave them, established these colonies as free states, but subordinate according to such precedents and examples as his

County
Palatine of
Durham
taken as
example.

Ministry thought suitable. The Constitution of the County Palatine of Durham was considered a precedent to be followed, and the model of this Constitution was taken as to their regalia."

Plantations
compared
with the
Duchies of
Gascoigne and
Normandy.

The Plantations, however, were further compared to the duchies of Gascoigne or Normandy. Consequently it was assumed that they should be treated as Jersey was, which was part of the duchy of Normandy. The methods of administration which exist on that island were therefore

Appeal to
the King
in Council.

applied to the Plantations. Appeals on matters of law were brought to the King in Council as appeals had been brought from the Courts of Normandy to the King as their Duke in Council, according to the ancient custom of Normandy,

Appeal to
Lords in
England.

and not to the House of Lords in accordance with the custom of England.

Constitution
of Jersey,
by analogy
followed.

Jersey was governed (1) by the ancient custom of Normandy prior to its severance from the duchy ; (2) by municipal or local usages and Constitutions ; (3) and by ordinances made by the King or his Commissioners Royal. Charles I adopted by analogy the theory that the Plantations were his desmesnes in his foreign dominion. As it was, in accordance with the Constitution of Jersey, to hold meetings and Conventions of the three orders or estates

to raise money for public necessities subject to the negative
of the Royal Governors, so the Colonies received similar
rights.

Parliament at first did not seriously contest the King's
claim to dominion. In 1612 when the House of Commons
endeavoured to pass a bill for establishing a free right of
fishery on the coasts of Virginia, New England, and Newfoundland, they were told in the House by the King's
ministers that it was not fit to pass laws here for those
countries which were not yet annexed to the Crown. From
1624 to the outbreak of the Civil War the King's claims over
the colonies were unchallenged.

After the Restoration the Plantations ceased to be treated
as desmesnes of the King, and were deemed to be part of
the territories or dominions of England.

The government of the Plantations by the King in Council
during the reigns of James I and Charles I shows an administration actuated by a constant desire to improve and
promote colonial prosperity.

At first the King in Council appointed temporary committees to examine into single questions, as in 1618 when a
committee was appointed to enquire into the grievances of
the Western Ports against the Newfoundland Company.
Such committees often included members not of the Privy
Council itself. On Dec. 19th, 1632, the first committee of
Council for Plantations was appointed under the title of
the Committee on the New England Plantations. It was
reappointed in 1633, and then comprised the Archbishops
of Canterbury and York, the Lord Keeper, the Lord Treasurer, the Lord Privy Seal, the Earl Marshall, Earl of Dorset,
Lord Cottington, Mr. Treasurer, Mr. Comptroller, Mr.
Secretary Coke, and Mr. Secretary Windebanck. In 1635
the Committee for Foreign Plantations was established
and remained in existence till 1641.

After the Restoration in 1660 a committee was appointed
to sit twice a week to receive, hear and examine, and
deliberate upon any petitions, propositions, memorials, or
other addresses presented by any person concerning the

King's claims
originally
not contested.

Change after
the
Restoration.

Desire for
the good
government
of the
Plantations.

Committees of
Privy Council.

Appointment
of.

1660-1696.

Plantations. This committee was directed from time to time to make its report to the Board. It ultimately assumed entire control of Colonial affairs until 1696. For a time, however, its control of Colonial affairs was shared by a Council of Trade and a Council of Plantations, both of which had been appointed in 1668. The Privy Council, however, still continued its former policy of appointing special committees to deal with special questions. The Council of Plantations came to an end in 1665. In 1668 a Council of Trade was appointed, and in 1670 a Council of Plantations. The two bodies were united in 1672 by letters patent, but their commission was shortly afterwards revoked by the King. To this united body was due the instructions for colonial governors which were prepared under the guidance of Shaftesbury and Locke.

Instructions for colonial governors.

The government of the Plantations during this period was managed with much wisdom, and very great care was taken in arriving at conclusions. All the great officers of the House were from time to time consulted, as were ambassadors abroad and Colonial officials.

From 1675 to 1696 the administration of the Plantations was carried on by the Lords of the Committee for Trade and Plantations. This body, with some alteration, continued to exist until 1782.

Course of business.

The regular method of dealing with Colonial business from 1675 to 1696 was first to refer all matters for consideration to the Committee for Trade and Plantations, and after the Committee had made a report, to make orders more or less in accordance with its recommendations.

In addition to regulating matters of trade, the Privy Council, in its appellate jurisdiction, exercised those functions with reference to the Plantations which it still exercises through the Judicial Committee.

Committee for Hearing Appeals.

In 1696 a standing committee known as the Lords of Committee for Hearing Appeals was appointed. The range of business that came within its jurisdiction was even then very considerable. The Committee dealt with such matters as complaints as to the conduct of Governors and boundary disputes; they also entertained appeals from Colonial courts. The majority of the cases heard consisted of appeals brought from Colonial Governors and their Councils sitting as courts of appeal or courts of chancery in the colonies.

The jurisdiction of the Privy Council, however, was occa- Defiance of jurisdiction of sionally defied. Massachusetts Bay required to be warned Privy Council. not to endanger her charter by passing an Annual Act of a very extraordinary nature, which laid discouragements on the shipping and manufacture of the home country. Massachusetts Bay, it appeared, allowed the free importation of wines and commodities from the place of their growth but charged double duties on their importation from the United Kingdom, the only place from which they could at the time be legally imported. The proprietors of Carolina on another occasion were ordered to disallow a duty of 10 per cent. which they had imposed upon all British manufactured goods imported into that province from Great Britain.

During the whole of the earlier portions of the eighteenth Growth of North century the North American Colonies grew in importance. American Colonies. Many of them found it necessary to appoint agents in England to look after their commercial interests. South Carolina passed an Act for appointing an agent to solicit First appointment the affairs of the province in the kingdom of Great Britain. of agent for The agency thus established became subsequently of great South Carolina. consequence. The Hon. Abel Ketellby, of the Inner Temple, London, was the first agent, and received for his services at the expiration of two years an allowance of two hundred pounds a year.

The Parliament of Great Britain took an increasing interest Appointment of Colonial in their progress. In 1768 a Secretary of State for the Secretary. American or Colonial department was appointed.

The position of affairs when the American Rebellion Outbreak of American broke out may be briefly summarised. Great tracts of Rebellion. country had been settled by British immigrants and communities had risen with rights of self-government, fully conscious of their growing power. At the head of each colony was the Governor at this period mostly appointed by the King, some colonies, however, still possessed the right to choose their own Governor. The laws enacted by the respective legislatures of the Colonies, if not repugnant to the laws of Great Britain, were valid. Once a bill received the assent of the Governor, it became operative until a notice was given of its disallowance by the Sovereign in Council with whom the power of disallowance remained. During the existence of government by the King in Council and the Committee of Trade and Plantations, the North

Political changes in Plantations.

American Colonies underwent considerable political changes in relation to the Motherland.

Royal or Provincial establishments generally established.

The Proprietary and Chartered Governments originally established had mostly yielded to Royal or Provincial Establishments whose officers were appointed by the King or by the Governor as his representative. [1]

At the outbreak of the Civil War the only Proprietary Governments remaining were the Governments of Hudson's Bay called New Britain, and the Provinces of Pennsylvania, Delaware, and Maryland ; the only Charter Governments that continued were Massachusetts Bay, Rhode Island, Providence Plantation, and Connecticut. [2]

Parliament's desire to exercise a greater control.

The appointment of the first Colonial Secretary coincided with one of the periods of Great Britain's commercial activities, with a consequent desire of Parliament to assume a closer control over Plantation affairs. The interest of Parliament was seen during the earlier portion of the reign of George III, when a number of oppressive Acts were passed by the British Legislature in support of Parliament's claim to tax the Colonies. Thus, the legislature of New York was suspended ; the Charter of Massachusetts Bay declared void, and trade with the harbour of Boston prohibited ; and the Act to apply stamp duties passed. This, however, was repealed the year after its enactment. A catastrophe likely to overwhelm British supremacy in the most populous portions of North America seemed to many thoughtful men to be rapidly approaching.

[1] *Stokes on the Colonies*, p. 19.
[2] *Ibid.*, p. 21.

Among those who offered their counsel at this time to the Government was Thomas Pownall, who at one time had been Governor of Massachusetts Bay and South Carolina, and Lieutenant-Governor of New Jersey. In 1764 he published his opinions. He clearly stated his view that there must be either an American or a British Union. There was no other alternative. George Grenville, with whom he was in correspondence, admitted the force of his argument that the Colonies should have representation in the House of Commons. He said further that should such an application be properly made by the Colonies to Parliament in the same manner as applications had been made from Chester and Durham, and probably from Wales, it would in his opinion be entitled to the most serious and favourable consideration. "I shall continue in the same sentiment," he writes, "but I am much afraid that neither the people of Great Britain nor those of America are sufficiently apprised of the danger which threatens both, from the present state of things to adopt a measure to which both the one and the other seem indisposed." *Opinions of Thomas Pownall. Views of Grenville.*

Pownall's ideas, so far as a union was concerned, were those of Benjamin Franklin. In a letter to Governor Shirley in 1750, Franklin says that he should hope, too, that by such an union the people of Great Britain and the people of the Colonies would learn to consider themselves not as belonging to different communities with different interests, but to one community with one interest. *Benjamin Franklin.*

"Now I look on the Colonies," he continues, "as so many counties gained to Great Britain, and more advantageous to it than if they had been gained out of the sea around its coasts and joined to its land ; for being in different climates they afford greater variety of produce and materials for more manufactures ; and being separated by the ocean they increase much more its shipping and seamen. And since they are all included in the British Empire (which has only extended itself by their means, and the strength and wealth of the parts is the strength and wealth of the whole), what imports it to the general State whether a merchant, a smith, or a hatter grew rich in Old or in New England ! "

The imagination of Pownall and Franklin conceived such a union as had been the union of Wales with England, completed as it had been by representation in Parliament.

Capital of Empire to be shifted to most populous centre.

Pownall was prepared to shift the seat of Government to the most populous centre of the Empire, and wherever that was found to be, to that he was ready to advocate removal. As Chester and Durham, palatine counties, had at one time been parts of England without representation in Parliament, in like position were the British North American Colonies.

No notion of Federated Empire.

No idea of a Federated Empire occurred to Pownall or Franklin. In fact, no such scheme could have been carried out having regard to the one-sided commercial system that then existed between Great Britain and her Colonies.

Pownall, as he says, meant his book as a caution against laying the foundation of an American Imperium separate and distinct from the kingdom of Great Britain.

The disaster he predicted came to pass.

Influence of American War on Great Britain.

The war of American Independence broke out and severed thirteen of her colonies from Great Britain. It produced another result. It formed the American Confederation which in turn led to the establishment of the Federation of the United States. Its influence on the Government of Great Britain was seen in the abolition of the office of Secretary of State for the Colonies and the Committee for Trade and Plantations in 1782. What need was there, argued Burke, of expensive administrative machinery when the greatest of Great Britain's colonies was gone. Canada as yet was but a small struggling community. Possession had only been taken of a portion of Australia twelve years before. Great Britain held no portion of South Africa now comprised in the great legislative Union. The changes

Administration of the Empire by King in Council ceased.

effected in 1782 by Burke left the Royal prerogative unimpaired, but the administration of the Empire by the King in Council ceased. Parliament had usurped its place, and for a time failed.   Nevertheless Parliamentary Government Administration by continued.   A Secretary of State, responsible to Parliament, Colonial Office and succeeded the Committee for Trade and Plantations.   Acts Parliament. of Parliament began to take the place of orders of the Privy Council, and orders of Council became mere executive Acts promulgated on the advice of the Colonial Office.   Severance was a great disaster, but it might have been otherwise.

THE UNITED STATES

CHAPTER II

THE CONFEDERATION OF THE UNITED STATES

Constitution preceded by Articles of Confederation, 1777.

THE present Constitution of the United States was preceded by Articles of Confederation, assented to on the 15th of November, 1777, in the second year of the Independence of America, and agreed to by the States of New Hampshire, Massachusetts Bay, Rhode Island, and Providence Plantations, Connecticut, New York, New Jersey, Pennsylvania, Delaware, Maryland, Virginia, North Carolina, South Carolina, and Georgia. These articles, forming a loose Confederation, proved unworkable, and early threatened from their inherent defects to break up that union of the States which the framers of them had fondly hoped to make perpetual.

Defects in Confederation.

An examination of some of their defects explains the necessity for the alterations which took place, and the modifications which at once transmuted a Confederation into a Federal Government, and breathed a spirit of national life into the infant American Republic.

Causes of American Rebellion.

The American Rebellion was due to many causes. The commercial policy of Great Britain, which regarded her colonies as created for the special benefit of the home manufactures, and lack of knowledge of their affairs which caused Parliament to stumble into lamentable mistakes, are credited with being main contributory factors, but there were others. The authority of laws passed by the British Parliament once discontent was aroused was questioned. It was argued that none of the American Plantations had been created by Acts of Parliament but all either by grant or charter from the King. The controlling government of the Colonies was the King in Council. To the King in Council either directly or indirectly through the medium of the

14

Committee of Foreign Plantations their grievances had hitherto been brought. The Constitutional doctrine that there should be no taxation without representation, learned by the colonists from the Mother Country and accepted as part of their constitutional life was said to have no application to them, otherwise why should the British Parliament tax them without their consent.

Taxation without representation and the existence of many other grievances led to the assembly of a great Congress of the States at Philadelphia in 1773. Of the thirteen North American Colonies all but Georgia were there represented. Amongst the delegates who met in council were men subsequently to become famous, but who were then little known beyond the boundaries of their own States : the two Adamses from Massachusetts, Patrick Henry, the orator ; George Washington from Virginia ; Dickinson, the author of the once famous letters from a farmer in Pennsylvania ; Peyton and Randolph, Quincy and Jefferson. This Congress drew up a Declaration of American Rights which they directed to their fellow-colonists, to the King, and the people of England. It was couched in studiously moderate language, and won the highest praise from the aged Lord Chatham, but neither King George nor the people of England received it favourably. They regarded the American colonist as a discontented individual to be coerced into obedience rather than pacified by concession. Military preparations proceeded feverishly on both sides, till the rifles of Lexington sounded the outbreak of civil war in April, 1775.

Congress then assumed the functions of sovereignty. The delegates declared that the provinces they represented should thenceforth be styled the United Colonies of America; they required all persons to abjure the British Government and swear allegiance to the Congress.

In 1776 Congress published the Declaration of Independence, an abstract proposition of civil government which had been copied substantially from the Declaration of the Assembly of Virginia, compiled from Tom Paine's celebrated

Congress of 1773 at Philadelphia.

Declaration of American Rights.

Outbreak of civil war, 1775.

Declaration of Independence.

formula of the Rights of Man. This Declaration declared
that the colonies were free and independent States with all
powers belonging to a sovereign people.

Articles of Confederation. In the following year Articles of Confederation were
agreed to by the delegates of the thirteen States and curi-
ously enough the Articles were thirteen in number. The

Subsequent ratification. Articles, however, do not appear to have been ratified by
all the States until 1781, in which year the delegates of
Maryland, the last of the States to ratify, signed on her
behalf.

The United States and American Articles of Confederation. By the Articles, the Confederacy was styled the United
States of America. It was declared that each State should
retain its sovereignty, freedom, and every power, jurisdiction
and right which was not by the Confederation expressly
delegated to the United States in Congress assembled. It
was made clear by the express words of the Article that
unless a power was in actual terms given to the States in
Congress assembled, the States in Congress assembled had
no express authority to act. The Articles further declared

Nature of Articles. that delegates should be appointed annually not less than
two in number nor more than seven from each State. No
person should be capable of being a delegate for more than
three years in any term of six years. Moreover each State
was to appoint delegates as its Legislature directed, and
each Legislature had power to recall and appoint others

Disqualification of delegates. in their stead at any time. No delegate could hold office
under the United States for which he or another for his
benefit received salary, fees, or emolument of any kind.
Each State was required to maintain its own delegates
during meetings of the States and whilst the delegates were
acting as members of Committees.

Votes of States. In determining questions in Congress each State had one
vote. Freedom of speech and debate in Congress were
declared to be absolutely privileged, and the persons of the
Members of Congress immune from arrest and imprisonment during the time of their going to and from and
attendance on Congress, except in cases of treason, felony,
or breach of the peace.

The control of the States over their delegates was supreme, through their delegates they directed and controlled all the powers that they had delegated to the United States in Congress. The Confederation was therefore little more than a firm league of friendship entered into by the States with each other for their common defence, the security of their liberties, and their mutual and general welfare ; they bound themselves to assist each other against all force offered to or attacks made upon them or any of them on account of religion, sovereignty, trade, or any pretence whatever. The better to secure and perpetuate this mutual friendship, the free inhabitants of each State, paupers, vagabonds, and fugitives from justice excepted, were declared entitled to all the privileges and immunities of free citizens in the several States, including all privileges of trade and commerce, but subject to the same duties, impositions and restrictions, that bound the inhabitants. No restrictions, however, extended so far as to prevent removal of property imported into any State to any other State of which the owner was an inhabitant. It was also expressly declared that no impositions, duties, or restrictions should be laid by any State on the property of the United States or either of them. In order to assist in effecting freedom of intercourse and freedom of trade, full faith and credit was required to be given in each of the States to the records, acts, and judicial proceedings of the court and magistrates of every other State.

Fugitives from justice in respect of the crimes of treason, felony, or other high misdemeanour, wherever they might be found in the United States, were to be delivered up on demand of the Government or executive power of the State to the State from which they had fled.

In matters where one authority must act for the whole, the States assented to prohibitions on their sovereign authority. They agreed that no State should without the consent of the United States in Congress assembled send or receive embassies, or enter into conferences, agreements, alliances, or treaties with any kings, princes, or states.

2— (2125)

They prohibited persons holding any office of profit or trust under the United States from accepting offices, emolument, or title of any kind whatever from kings, princes, or foreign states, and affirmed the democratic basis of their existence by forbidding the United States to grant titles of nobility.

Treaties *inter se*.

As between themselves they consented that two or more of their number should not enter into any treaty or alliance whatever between them without the consent of the United States, and if any treaty or alliance should be formed its purposes and its proposed duration were required to be accurately specified prior to the request for such assent.

Treaty power left to United States in Congress.

The power of making treaties with foreign powers was left to the United States in Congress assembled and the States agreed not to lay any imposts or duties which would interfere with any stipulations in treaties entered into in pursuance of any treaties already proposed by Congress to the Courts of France and Spain.

Vessels of war and standing armies.

No State was permitted in times of peace to maintain vessels of war except such number only as Congress should deem necessary for the defence of the State or its trade; a somewhat similar provision applied to the keeping of a standing army for only such force was allowed as in the judgment of Congress was requisite to garrison the forts necessary for the defence of the State. The duty, however, of each State to keep up a well-regulated and disciplined

Militia.

militia and to provide for its equipment so that when called upon it might be ready to take the field was expressly asserted. When land forces were raised by any State for the purpose of common defence, the State Legislature was empowered to appoint all its officers of or under the rank of colonel, should a vacancy occur the State filled the vacancy.

War.

States were forbidden to engage in war without the consent of Congress unless their territory was actually invaded, or unless they had received definite advice of a danger of an Indian invasion so imminent as not to admit of Congress being consulted. The prohibition against war extended to the commissioning of naval forces and granting letters of marque or reprisal except after a declaration of war by Congress, and then a State was only empowered to act against the kingdom against which the war had been declared and subject to the regulations of the United States: an exception was made in the case of a State infested with pirates.

War charges and all other expenses incurred for the common defence or general welfare allowed by Congress, were made defrayable out of a common treasury. The funds for providing the treasury were supplied by the States in proportion to the value of all land within each State granted to or surveyed for any person, as such land and the buildings and improvements thereon should be estimated according to the manner directed by Congress from time to time. *Expenses of common defence.*

The United States possessed no power of direct taxation. The taxes for paying the proportion due from each State were directed to be laid and levied by the authority and direction of the State Legislatures within the time agreed upon by Congress. *No powers of direct taxation.*

The following powers are enumerated as having been expressly conferred upon the United States in Congress assembled— *Expressly enumerated powers.*

The sole and exclusive right and power of determining on peace and war subject to the exception already mentioned of an invasion of a State.

The power to send and receive ambassadors and to enter into treaties and alliances, with the exception that no treaty of commerce might be made which interfered with the State legislative power to impose such imposts and duties on foreigners as their own people were subject to, or prohibited the exportation or importation of any species of goods or commodities whatsoever.

The United States further had the express power of deciding in all cases what captures on sea or land were legal, and how prizes taken by the land or sea forces of the United States should be divided or appropriated. Power was conferred of granting letters of marque and reprisal in times of peace, and authority was given for the establishment of courts for the trial of piracies and felonies, and for finally determining appeals in all cases of capture, but no Member of Congress was eligible to sit as a judge in any such courts.

Disputes between States.

In disputes between States the Congress were declared to be sole judges whether the difference were one concerning boundary jurisdiction or arose from any cause whatever. The method of determination was for Congress on the petition of a State stating the matter in question and praying for a hearing to give notice by order to the other State to the controversy, and assign a day for the appearance of the parties by their lawful agents. The parties on appearance were entitled by joint consent to appoint com-

Court of Hearing.

missioners or judges to constitute a Court of Hearing, but failing agreement, Congress had the power to name three persons out of each of the United States, each party then had the liberty to strike out alternately one till the number was reduced to thirteen, out of that number not less than seven nor more than nine names as Congress directed were selected in the presence of Congress by lot. These persons or any five of them constituted the commissioners or judges. A majority was sufficient to determine finally the controversy. Where either party neglected to attend without strong reasons on the day appointed by Congress, or refused to strike out names, Congress thereupon nominated three persons out of each State, and the Secretary of Congress struck out names on behalf of the defaulting party. If either party refused to submit to the authority of the Court or declined to appear or defend their case, the Court proceeded to pronounce sentence or judgment in his absence. The judgment or sentence was transmitted to Congress and lodged amongst the Acts of Congress for the security of the parties concerned.

The commissioners before trial were sworn on oath to well and truly hear and determine the matter according to the best of their judgment without favour, affection, or hope of reward.

Controversies concerning the private right of soil claimed under different grants of two or more States whose jurisdiction was in question were determinable in the same manner.

This curious Court of Appeal thus created for settling Character of Court. interstate disputes was probably the only court that the States at the time would have sanctioned. Its manner of selection and composition rather suggests trial by jury than the establishment of a solemn judicial tribunal. It is very possible that except for the urgent necessity of the case no tribunal would have been established; at this time, however, there were numerous boundary disputes pending and pressing for immediate settlement. The States no longer having the right of recourse to the Privy Council, could devise no more satisfactory court for settling their differences.

The powers the States conceded as proper to be solely and exclusively dealt with by Congress were powers to regulate the alloy and value of the coin struck by their authority or that of the respective States, to fix the standard of weights and measures, to regulate the trade and management of Indian affairs, although in regard to this latter power the legislative right of a State within its own limits was guarded from infringement or violation. Powers to establish and regulate post offices, and to exact such postage as might be necessary to defray all the expenses of the office, to appoint all officers of the land forces, excepting regimental officers and all naval officers, and to make rules for the government and regulation of the land and naval forces and direction of their operations completed the delegation.

When Congress was not sitting a Committee of the States Committee of States when Congress not sitting. sat in the recess. This committee was composed of one delegate from each State. Congress, however, was at liberty to appoint other committees and civil officers for the management of the affairs of the United States under its direction. It had also power to appoint one of its number to preside in Congress, but no person was eligible to serve more than one year in any term of three years.

Since Congress was required to ascertain the sums required Borrowing powers. for the public services and to appropriate and apply them, it was necessarily armed with a borrowing power, and a right to issue bills on the credit of the United States, but every half-year the States were entitled to be acquainted with the amount borrowed.

Power was given to build a navy, to agree upon the number of land forces, and to requisition each State for its quota in proportion to its number of white inhabitants. The requisitions of Congress were declared to be binding on all the States and the State Legislatures, who were Requisitions on States. directed to raise the forces required by the demand and equip them at the expense of the United States. Some discretion, however, was given to Congress to reduce the quota from a State or to exempt it from its military obligation ; it could even increase a quota demanded from any State unless the State Legislature objected by adjudging that the extra number could not be spared.

Even in matters dealing with its own internal management Congress was greatly fettered. Every question except a question of its adjournment from day to day was required to be carried by the votes of a majority of the States. In the exercise of the most important of its powers the assent Assent of nine States when required. of nine of the States was required. Thus, even in matters of great urgency, such as the appointment of a commander-in-chief during the war, such assent was necessary.

Congress had power to adjourn to any time within the year or to any place, but not for longer than six months. Journal of proceedings. It was authorised to publish a journal of its proceedings, but could except from publication matters where secrecy was desirable, such as discussions on treaties, alliances, or military operations. The yeas and nays of the delegates of each State on any question were required to be entered in the journal on the desire of any delegate, and any delegate was entitled to a transcript of the journal, except the excepted parts, to lay before the Legislature of his State.

The committee of the States or any nine of them could execute during recess such powers of Congress as Congress by the consent of the nine States had vested in them, but none of the important powers which required the assent of nine States could be delegated.

Congress by the Articles of Constitution assumed the liability for all bills of credit, borrowed money, and debts contracted by or under the authority of Congress prior to the assembling of the United States in Confederation and all liabilities so incurred were charged on the United States. The United States and its good faith were solemnly pledged for their satisfaction. *Liability of Congress for bills and borrowed money.*

Should Canada accede to the Confederation and join in the measures of the United States, it was provided that she should be entitled to all the advantages of the Union, but no other colony was entitled to admission unless admission were agreed to by nine States. *Canada entitled to join Union.*

Lastly, the States agreed to abide by the determinations of Congress on all questions which by the Confederation were submitted to them ; they agreed that the Articles of Confederation should be inviolably observed, and that the Union should be perpetual, and they further declared that the Articles should not be altered unless such alterations were agreed to by a Congress of the United States and afterwards confirmed by the legislatures of every State. *Agreement to abide by determinations of Congress.*

Such was the first Constitution of the United States, born of necessity and nursed in the nation's conflict with Great Britain. With every favouring circumstance to support it—a people drawn almost wholly from the same stock, professing, with the exception of Maryland, the same religion, it failed not from lack of respect to the laws or impatience of forms of government by the people, but because it could not weld in one harmonious whole the United States or form a suitable framework for future development. If particular attention has been drawn to it it is because the people of the United States condemned it.   In the light of its defects they constructed their present Constitution.   The existence of this in turn has served as a model for the Imperial Federal Constitutions, notably that of Australia.   The demonstration of its working has also shown what are the powers that can be properly conceded to a Federal, and what should be left to a State or Provincial authority. *Failure of Constitution.*

CHAPTER III

THE ORIGIN OF THE SECOND CONSTITUTION

WITH the fall of Lord North's Administration in 1782 and the resolution of the British Government to discontinue the war, the Independence of the United States was secured. Meantime so low had Congress fallen in public estimation

Washington asked to assume supreme power.

that many of George Washington's officers urged him to terminate its pale shadow of authority and assume the supreme executive power. Washington dismissed these counsellors in so peremptory a manner that they made no

Discontent of Army.

further attempt to renew them. The discontent of the Army with Congress may be easily accounted for. During the progress of the war it proved itself impotent to cope energetically with the situation. For instance, after the battle of Long Island, whilst the English forces extended their lines from New York, and battalions of troops were urgently demanded, Congress thought fit to discuss as an abstract proposition the danger of standing armies. Throughout the progress of military operations the generals of the new Republic found it difficult to obtain either pay or clothing for their soldiers. Congress, however, was only in part to blame. It had but limited powers to obtain quotas of men and money from the States, and it met with but little encouragement from the State Legislatures. Congress, con-

Insufficient powers of Congress.

scious of its limitations, ultimately sought to extend its powers. On April 18th, 1783, when the question of the settlement of the debt due to the war became pressing, it recommended to the several States that it was indispensably necessary for the restoration of public credit that Congress

Claim to levy duties on imported goods.

should possess power to levy certain duties upon goods imported solely for the purpose of discharging the interest on the principal of the debts contracted for supporting the war. As an inducement to the States they were offered the power of appointing their own collectors, although the

24

collectors were to be amenable to and removable by Congress alone. The power of levying duties was to be limited to a period of twenty-five years. A further resolution was passed by Congress for an amendment of the constitution altering the existing system of raising money.

In the opinion of many outside Congress further drastic changes in the Constitution were required. On September 11th, 1786, commissioners from the States of New York, New Jersey, Pennsylvania, Delaware, and Virginia, met at Annapolis, and reported that there were important defects in their system of Federal government. They recommended that a general Convention of deputies from the different States should be summoned for the sole purpose of investigating and suggesting a plan for supplying such defects as should be discovered to exist and for rendering the Constitution of the Federal Government adequate to the exigencies of the Union. On this resolution, which was transmitted to Congress, duly coming before it, Congress resolved on the motion of one of the deputies from Massachusetts "that a Convention should be summoned to meet on the second Monday at Philadelphia for the sole and express purpose of revising the Articles of Confederation and reporting to Congress and the several Legislatures of the States such alterations as were agreed, which when agreed to by Congress and confirmed by the States should render the Federal Constitution adequate to the exigencies of government and the preservation of the Union."

Although the second Monday in May, 1787, was fixed as the appointed day for the Convention to meet it did not sit until the 25th of the month owing to an insufficiency of members arriving to constitute a representation of a majority of the States.

Twelve States ultimately were represented, at first seven only. The delegates elected George Washington to the chair, and chose William Jackson as secretary to the Convention. The sessions were held in private. They closed on Monday, Sept. 17th, 1787, after the Convention had

Meeting of Commissioners at Annapolis.

Recommendation by.

Resolution for Convention at Philadelphia.

Washington chairman, 1787.

unanimously resolved upon a Constitution which was signed by thirty-nine out of the fifty-five delegates.

Nature of Constitution.

The Constitution agreed upon by the Convention exceeded the limits of their authority. During their deliberations the delegates came to the conclusion that no mere alteration of the Articles of the Confederation would meet the circumstances of the case. " It was asked," said Madison, in " The Federalist," No. xxxix, " what authority had the Convention ! They ought to have preserved the Federal form, which regarded the Union as a confederacy of sovereign States instead of which they framed a National government which regards the Union as a consolidation of the States." His answer was that " the proposed Constitution was to be founded on the assent and ratification of the people of America, given by deputies elected for the special purpose, but the assent and ratification was not to be given by the people as individuals, but as composing the distinct and independent States to which they belonged. Therefore, it was the assent and ratification of the States derived from the supreme authority of the people themselves. It followed that the establishment of the Constitution could not be a National but must be a Federal Act, resulting neither from a majority of the people of the Union, nor from that of a majority of the States, but from the unanimous assent of the several States that were parties, differing no otherwise from their ordinary assent than in its being expressed not by the legislative authority, but by that of the people."

Defence of "The Federalist."

Reception by Congress.

Congress received the report of the Convention on the 28th of September, 1787, and resolved that the report of the Convention with its resolutions and the letter which accompanied them, should be transmitted to the State Legislatures, in accordance with the resolution of the Convention.

State Conventions.

On receiving the report and resolutions of the Convention, the several States summoned Conventions, and the subsequent ratifications of the new Constitution by these were forwarded as they were obtained to Congress.

Ratification of the ninth State.

On the 2nd of July, 1788, after the ratification of New Hampshire, the ninth State in order to ratify, had been received, Congress became entitled to proceed with the new Constitution.   Congress accordingly resolved that the ratifications of the Constitution of the United States transmitted to Congress, should be referred to a committee to report an Act to Congress for putting the Constitution in operation in pursuance of the resolutions of the late Federal Convention.

The report of the Committee was received on the 14th Resolution of Congress. of July, 1788.   On the 13th September Congress resolved that " the first Wednesday in January, 1789, should be the day for appointing elections in the several States, which had, prior to that day, ratified the Constitution ; that the first Wednesday in February should be the day for the electors to assemble in their respective States and vote for a President, and that the first Wednesday in March should be the time and the present seat of Congress the place for commencing proceedings under the Constitution."

It has been already stated that the deliberations of the Two schemes before Convention. Convention that framed the Constitution were held in secret. Although the Constitution had been approved by Congress, it may be asked how was the serious and doubtful task of procuring its ratification by the State Conventions obtained. The Convention had considered two schemes, one known as the Virginian scheme ultimately the basis of that adopted, and the other the New Jersey scheme which contemplated little more than what the Convention had been summoned to do that was to make amendments in the Articles of Confederation.   Those who favoured the New Jersey scheme threatened a determined opposition.   An enlightened public opinion was necessary if the Constitution were to be ratified by the State.

It fell to three men to explain to the people the nature Hamilton, Madison, and Jay. of and the reasons for the new Constitution.   Of these Alexander Hamilton and James Madison had been members of the Convention, but Jay, the third, had not.

The general Convention dissolved on 17th September, " The Federalist." and on the 27th October, there appeared in the columns of a New York journal the first of a series of papers called

" The Federalist." These papers, eighty-five in number, were continued till the following June, they were then rapidly republished throughout the States, attracting by their language and reasoning extraordinary popular interest. Hamilton contributed sixty-three and three he wrote in conjunction with Madison ; Madison contributed four-teen, and Jay five. In a great measure owing to their arguments the Constitution was finally ratified. The reasonings of " The Federalist " have such general applica-tion to Federal government that a survey of Federal systems would be incomplete without reference to them. It would seem more appropriate, however, to discuss them, when considering the details of the Constitution.

Elliot's debates on the Conventions.

The debates in the Conventions of the several States that took place prior to the ratification of the Constitution have been collected and revised from contemporary publications and other sources by Jonathan Elliot, whose work was published in 1830. The debates are of the greatest value ; as clearly showing the opposition encountered. Never-theless the ability and wisdom of the men who composed the State Conventions and the arguments of leaders of public thought ultimately triumphed, and the new Constitution received ratification.

Late ratification of Virginia and New York.

Refusal by Rhode Island and North Carolina.

Virginia and New York did not assent till after nine others had assented. Rhode Island, which had stood aloof from the Federal Convention, refused at first to ratify it, as did North Carolina, and their assent was only attained later, when the new Constitution had been some time in existence. Some of the States, indeed, ratified it subject to alterations, which afterwards formed the first amendment to the Constitution.

Before explaining the Constitution, it is necessary to examine what was the position of the States at this time.

Position of States.

Nature of Constitutions.

The thirteen original States stretching along the eastern seaboard of America had all been subject to the British dominion. They consisted, according to Blackstone, of (1) proprietary governments such as Pennsylvania, New Jersey, and Maryland, granted by the Crown to individuals in the nature of feudatory principalities with all the inferior regalities and subordinate powers of legislation, which had formerly belonged to the owners of counties palatine, yet still with these express conditions that the ends for which the grant had been made should be substantially pursued, and that nothing should be attempted which might derogate from the sovereignty of the Mother Country. (ii) Charter governments, such as Virginia, in the nature of civil corporations with the power of making bye-laws for their interior regulation and with such rights and authorities as were specially given them in their several charters of incorporation.

Most of these colonies or plantations possessed a Governor and General Assembly, corresponding to the British House of Commons, together with a Council of State, which found its counterpart in the British Upper House. These Assemblies possessed the power of making laws suitable for themselves, but with the concurrence of the Governor, and then subject to subsequent disallowance by the King in Council.

The constitutional changes that took place in England with the accession of William of Orange vested greater power in the British Parliament, and Parliament soon used its power to declare its supremacy over the Colonies by enacting a statute[1] that any laws, bye-laws, usages, and customs in practice in the Plantations which were repugnant to any law made or to be made in Great Britain should be utterly void and of no effect; some years later the Statute 6 Geo. III, c. 12, was passed; this expressly declared that all " His Majesty's Colonies and Plantations in America have been are and of right ought to be subordinate to and dependent upon the imperial Crown and Parliament of Great Britain who have full power and authority to make laws and statutes of sufficient validity to bind the Colonies and the people of America subjects of the Crown of Great Britain in all cases whatsoever."

It is not difficult to conceive what the descendants of the

[1] 7 and 8 Will. III, c. 27.

men who left England in the *Mayflower* to escape the oppressive legislation of Parliament thought of such legislation as this.

New Constitutions on Declaration of Independence. New Jersey. On the Declaration of Independence, when the States adopted new Constitutions they placed their views on record. The first Constitution of New Jersey, which may be quoted as a typical instance, repudiated the authority of the British Parliament, and recited that whereas all the constitutional authority ever possessed by the Kings of Great Britain over these Colonies or their other dominions was by compact derived from the people, and held of them for the common interest of the whole Society: allegiance and protection were in the nature of things reciprocal ties, each equally depending upon the other, and whereas George the Third, King of Great Britain, had refused protection to the good people of these Colonies and by assenting to sundry Acts of the British Parliament had attempted to subject them to the absolute dominion of that body and also made war upon them in the most cruel and unnatural manner for no other cause than asserting their just rights. All civil authority under him was necessarily at an end, and a dissolution of government in each Colony had consequently taken place.

" And whereas in the present deplorable situation of these Colonies exposed to the fury of a cruel and relentless enemy some form of Government is absolutely necessary not only for the preservation of good order but also the more effectually to unite the people and enable them to exert their whole force in their own necessary defence and as the honorable the Continental Congress the Supreme Council of the American Colonies has advised such of the Colonies as have not yet gone into the measure to adopt for themselves such government as should best conduce to their own happiness and safety and the well being of America we the representatives of the Colony of New Jersey having been elected by all the counties in the freest manner and in Congress assembled have after mature deliberation agreed upon a set of charter rights and the form of a Constitution."

It will be seen by comparing the legislation passed in Great Britain with the preamble of the first Constitution of New Jersey that the gist of the complaint was that the King had assented both to Acts of the British Parliament and had usurped authority by waging war against the people.

Therefore the people of New Jersey declared that the King had forfeited all his rights by such acts, and consequently the people of the State were entitled to assume sovereign functions, including all royal rights, such as the right to make peace and war, and treaties which had hitherto been vested in the Sovereign ; and thereupon New Jersey became a sovereign state.

The position adopted by New Jersey was adopted by the other States, and they framed constitutions upon the same model. *Position of New Jersey generally adopted.*

Georgia, in the preamble to her Constitutional Act, went further in her assertion of grievances than New Jersey. *Georgia.* She complained of the King's veto and the denial of the Governor's powers to pass laws of immediate and pressing importance unless suspended in their operation for the King's assent, and when suspended neglecting to attend to them for many years. She also asserted that the King had combined with others to subject them to a foreign jurisdiction by giving his assent to its pretended Acts of legislation, which had, by suspending their Legislature, declared itself invested with power to legislate for us in all cases whatsoever.

The Sovereignty of the States was declared to exist from the date of the Declaration of Independence. The language of the Declaration, asserted " that these United Colonies are and of right ought to be free and independent States," " and that as free and independent States they had full power to levy war, conclude peace, contract alliances, and to do all other acts and things which independent States might of right do."

Holding strongly to this position, the States were unwilling to surrender any of their rights or derogate one jot from their sovereignty. Some portion had been jettisoned during the War under the Articles of Confederation, but a further encroachment on their powers was not to be conceded lightly.

It will be seen that the Convention framing the Constitution had had no easy task.   They considered all the material at the time available.   They sought both ancient and modern precedents, and adopted such of them to their particular purpose, as seemed suitable to their circumstances.   The nature of the solution will be shown when the Constitution itself is considered.

CHAPTER IV

FEDERAL CONSTITUTIONS, ANCIENT AND MODERN

AMONG former Confederations, whose history and constitution were more or less known to the Convention which framed the United States Constitution, was the Amphictyonic Council. Madison remarks[1] "that from the best accounts transmitted of this celebrated institution, it bore a very instructive analogy to the Confederation of the American States. The members retained the character of independent and sovereign States, and had equal votes in the Federal Council. This Council had a general authority to propose and resolve what it judged necessary for the common welfare of Greece ; to declare and carry on war ; to decide, in the last resort, all controversies between the members ; to fine the aggressing party ; to employ the whole force of the confederacy against the disobedient ; to admit new members. The Amphictyons were the guardians of religion and the immense riches belonging to the Temple of Delphi, where they had the right of jurisdiction in controversies between those who came to consult the oracle. As a further provision for the efficacy of the Federal powers they took an oath mutually to defend and protect the United Cities, to punish the violators of this oath, and to inflict vengeance on sacrilegious despoilers of the temple. In theory and upon paper," continues Madison, " this apparatus of power seems amply sufficient for all general purposes. In several materials they exceed the powers enumerated in the Articles of Confederation. The Amphictyons had in their hands the superstition of the times, one of the principal engines by which government was then maintained : they had a declared authority to use coercion against refractory cities, and were bound by oath to exert this authority on necessary occasions."

Amphictyonic Council.

[1] "The Federalist," No. xviii.

Modern opinion has not countenanced the views expressed by Madison that this council was ever a Confederated government except in the very laxest sense of the word. " It was not a political but a religious body. If it had any claim to the title of a General Council of Greece it was wholly in the sense in which we speak of General Councils in modern Europe. The Amphictyonic Council represented Greece as an ecclesiastical synod represented Western Christendom, not as a Swiss Diet or an American Congress represents the Federation of which it is the common legislature." [1]

Madison, however, dwells on the defects of the Amphictyonic Council, its weakness, its disorders, and the destruction of the Confederacy. " Had the Greeks," says the Abbé Milot, " been as wise as they were courageous they would have been admonished by experience of the necessity of a closer union and would have availed themselves of the peace which followed their success against the Persian arms to establish such a reformation."

The Achaian League.

Of the Achaian League another of the celebrated classical instances referred to in " The Federalist," Madison says : " Could the interior structure and regular operation of the Achaian League be ascertained it is probable that more light might be thrown by it on the science of Federal Government than by any of the like experiments with which we are acquainted." [2]

Likeness between Achaian League and United States Constitution.

Modern research has shown the striking resemblance that exists between the older union and the younger union, with a difference of two thousand years between the two.

De Mably.

Such knowledge of the Greek Federal systems as the framers of the American Constitution possessed was almost entirely derived from the works of Gabriel Bonnot de Mably, a French publicist, who was born in 1709 and died in Paris, on the 23rd April, 1785. In 1749 Mably published *Observations sur les Grecs, Entretiens de Phocion, Observations sur l'histoire de France, De la législation*. In 1771 he visited Poland at the request of its Government, to prepare for

[1] Freeman's *History of Federal Government*, pp. 126, 127.
[2] " The Federalist," No. xviii.

them a code of laws. In 1781 he published a work, *Du* Consulted by American Congress.
gouvernement de la Pologne. In 1783 he was consulted by
the American Congress on the preparation of their Constitution, and embodied his ideas in his *Observations sur le*
gouvernement et les lois des États-Unis d'Amérique (1784).

It may be well conjectured that Mably's account of the
Federal Leagues of Greece would be accepted as authoritative.

Assuming its correctness, the authors of " The Federalist "
drew striking and valuable lessons from historical precedent,
and wherever possible they delighted in referring to precedent
and so they turned to the Achaian Federation.

This famous Federation flourished in the later days of Nature of Achaian League, B.C. 281-146.
Ancient Greece, from B.C. 281-146. It gave a measure of
freedom, unity, and general good government which might
well atone for the lack of the dazzling glory of the Old
Athenian democracy. For all practical purposes it ended
with the battle of Lenkopetra and the sack of Corinth,
B.C. 146.

In its later or federal days Achaia probably owned a Federal Assembly.
written Constitution. It possessed a Federal Assembly,
in which the sovereign power was vested, and in which
every citizen had a right to be heard. As the system of
representative government was wholly unknown in Ancient
Greece, every citizen in theory had the right to be present
whenever the General Assembly met ; whilst in Athens there
was no physical difficulty in every citizen attending the
deliberations of the Assembly, in the Achaian Federation
it was otherwise ; there were long distances to travel and
prohibitory expenses. It was impossible to provide for
payment of members when every member of the
Confederation was a member of the Assembly.

The General Assembly legislated, elected magistrates, Functions of General Assembly.
and declared peace and war. It met twice a year. Occa-
sionally extraordinary meetings were summoned when special
necessities arose. It probably assumed, from the reason
already explained, the character of an assembly of well-
to-do classes. Poorer members of the community were Voting of cities.
hardly likely to attend. Voting took place by cities in the

same way that voting took place by States in the early American Confederation. Indeed, if it had been otherwise, and voting had taken place by counting heads the people of the city in which the Assembly met would always have had the preponderating influence. The original meeting-

The Capital. place of the Assembly was at Aigion, at first the most important city of the League. At a later period the accession of powerful cities caused it to become one of the least important. The claims of contending cities for the seat of government ultimately caused the League to be without a recognised meeting-place. The possibility of such a rivalry amongst the States of America led the framers of the United States, and the Australian Constitution, to make special provisions for the establishment of a situation to belong solely to the Federal power as a site for the capital.

Power of magistrates. The General Assembly of Achaia, since it met regularly only twice a year, and then for a short session of only three days, of necessity had to endow its magistrates with great powers. The magistrates resembled ministers of Great Britain, who initiate measures and explain and defend their policy in Parliament.

The magistrates appeared personally before the General Assembly and were accustomed to explain their proposals. Since they were annually elected, it may be assumed that they were rarely out of touch with their constituents. If they were they could not be removed till the expiration of their year of office.

The Senate. In addition to the General Assembly, as in all the other Greek Commonwealths, there was a senate which was essentially a Committee of the Assembly. It consisted of 120 members. It is probable that the Government first laid its proposals before this committee or senate before they submitted them to the General Assembly.

Heads of Government. At early times there were two heads to the Government, but in later times there was only one. Since the League originated in the necessity of self-defence and co-operation for mutual purposes, the chief or president bore the military

The General. title of General. In civil matters he was advised by a council of ten, but in military matters he acted as a dictator, having sole command of the armies in the field, and subject only to having his conduct called into question by the General Assembly. He was not eligible for election for two successive years, but could be chosen each alternate year. The office of General was unpaid and so was one that could only be supported by a citizen of means. *Chosen each alternate year.*

Of the Council of Ten, who were likewise unpaid, it is thought that they originally represented the ten Achaian towns of the Federation. In civil matters they advised the General, and were elected at the same time as he was, and held office for one year only. Although the General's Council was chosen for him, they were probably men of the same way of thinking, for there are indications that they were adopted by a caucus. The General of the Achaians was a member of the General Assembly, and was accustomed to speak and explain his ideas in that body. He also moved motions. An Achaian Federal law was a motion of the General which had met with the assent of the Assembly. *Council of Ten, Functions of.* *Probable adoption by Caucus.* *Achaian Federal law.*

All matters of State were brought to the notice of the General, who after consultation with his Council of Ten, had power to summon if necessary an extraordinary meeting of the Assembly to consider them. *The General in Council.*

The largest powers of the Executive were vested in the General, larger powers than were subsequently vested by the people of the United States in their President. *Executive powers.*

When matters came before the General Assembly and it was necessary to take the vote the duty of doing so devolved upon the Council of Ten. *Taking the vote.*

In addition to the General, the Federation possessed a Secretary of State, who probably authorised all public despatches. There was also an Under-General and a General of Cavalry. *Secretary of State.*

Taxes for Federal purposes in all probability were raised by requisition upon the cities composing the Federation, each city being assessed at a certain sum, which it could raise as it pleased. *Raising of Taxes.*

The military forces were requisitioned from the cities,

Military forces.   sometimes from particular cities, at other times from the whole League. A standing army of mercenaries was kept which must have been paid for out of the Federal treasury.

Supremacy of Federal power.   In all external matters the League or Federal power was supreme, and the existence of an Achaian nation as distinguished from a cluster of States was recognised. The National power governed on behalf of the whole.

Restraints on cities.   No single city of the Federation could wage war of its own authority, nor could it make peace or entertain embassies or despatch them to foreign States. In its later history it is true that instances occur of individual cities breaking this rule and despatching ambassadors, but these were exceptions to the general rule, and resulted from the fact that with the growth of the League unwilling cities had been coerced into membership.

Independence of cities.   Of the cities which composed the Federation each city in itself was an independent unit, supreme in the management of its domestic affairs. It had its assembly, its magistrates, and governed itself as it chose. It is believed that a citizen of any city of the League was entitled to intermarry with an inhabitant of any other city and possess landed property in any Federated city. Each city had the fullest rights of self-government, and whether large or small its vote was of equal importance in the General Assembly.

Double allegiance.   If the two requisites of Federal Government are as Mr. Freeman considered them, that the members of the Union should be wholly independent in those matters which concern each member only and yet be subject to a common power in those matters which concern the whole body of members collectively, then was the League of Achaia a perfect Federal Constitution.

Its citizens owned two allegiances, one to their city, the other to Achaia. In the same way, as in the United States, a citizen is a citizen of his State and a citizen of the Republic.

The history of the League shows that it did not fall asunder, rent by jealousies, but rather by the increasing power of Rome. It also proves that such a Confederation can be a bulwark of national liberties.

Another fact emerges from its history, that in a Federal Constitution considerable powers may be left in the executive head without involving serious consequences. Fears of the absolute rule of one man, such as led to the limitation of the power of the Doge of Venice and the reduction of absolute to constitutional monarchy in England, are not conceivable ; rather is the struggle between the central power and the units which compose the Federation, which without a strong executive head would end in disrupture. *Power cau be left in Executive.*

The framers of the American Constitution seem also to have had some acquaintance with the Lycian Federation, but it is pertinent to notice that " Lycia had nothing which could be called a history, and its Federal Constitution arose," says Mr. Freeman, " at so late a period that its independence was provincial rather than strictly national." *Lycian Federation.*

In one particular the Lycian Federation, which has been accounted a perfect one, is said by some to show to advantage over that of Achaia. In its general assemblies cities ceased to vote equally, the larger were allowed greater power.[1] In the American House of Representatives, as will be subsequently seen, the representation is adjusted to the population of each State, although in the Senate the States possess an equal representation, whatever the size or population of the State may be.

In the search for precedents, modern history was also examined to discover the working principles of Federal Constitutions. The Germanic Federation from a parade of its Constitutional powers in the representative and head of the Confederacy, suggested that it might form an exception to the general character which belonged to its kind. "Nothing could be further from the reality," says Madison,[2] " the fundamental principle on which it rests, that the Empire is a community of sovereigns, that the Diet is a representation of sovereigns, and that the laws are addressed to sovereigns, renders the Empire a nerveless body, incapable *The Germanic Federation.* *Weakness of.*

---

[1] The view has been maintained that deputies from the several cities met in the Assembly.

[2] " Federalist," No. xix.

of regulating its own members, and insecure against external dangers."

Nature of. The Germanic Federation was composed of a Diet, representing the component members of the Confederacy ; the Emperor, who was the executive magistrate with a negative on the decrees of the Diet ; and an Imperial Chamber and an Aulic Council ; the latter two were judicial tribunals having supreme jurisdiction in controversies concerning the Empire or happenings among its members.

Powers of Diet. The Diet possessed general powers of legislation for the Empire, the right of declaring war or making peace, contracting alliances, assessing quotas of troops and money, constructing fortresses, regulating coin, admitting new members, and subjecting disobedient members to the ban of the Empire, the effect of which was to degrade a party from his sovereign rights and forfeit his possessions.

Power of Emperor. The Emperor had the " exclusive right to make propositions to the Diet, to negative its resolutions, to name ambassadors, to confer dignities and titles, to fill vacant electorates, to found universities, to grant privileges not injurious to the States of the Empire, to receive and apply the public revenues, and generally to watch over the public safety. In certain cases the electors formed a Council to him. In quality of Emperor he possessed no territory within the Empire, nor received any revenue for his support. But his revenues and dominions in other qualities constituted him one of the most powerful princes in Europe." " The members of the Confederacy were expressly restricted from entering into compacts prejudicial to the Empire ; from imposing tolls and duties on their mutual intercourse without the consent of the Emperor and Diet, from altering the value of money, from doing injustice to one another, or from affording assistance or retreat to disturbers of the public peace. And the ban was denounced against such as should violate any of these restrictions. The members of the Diet as such were subject in all cases to be judged by the Emperor and Diet, and in their private capacities by the Aulic Council and Imperial Chamber."

In surveying the defects of the Germanic Constitution, Defects. Madison pointed out that its internal struggles were between States. At one time Germany was desolated for thirty years with the Emperor with one half the Empire on one side, and the King of Sweden on the other. Its continued existence he largely attributed to the power the Emperor derived from his hereditary dominions.

"Switzerland," he considered, "scarcely amounted to Switzerland. a Confederacy : there was no common hearing, no common troops even in war, no common coin, no common judicatory, nor any other common mark of sovereignty."

"The Cantons are kept together," he continues, "by the peculiarity of their topographical position, by their individual weakness and insignificancy, by the fear of powerful neighbours, to one of which they were formerly subject, by the few sources of contention among a people of such simple and homogeneous manners, by their joint interest in their dependent possessions, by the mutual aid expressly stipulated for suppressing insurrections and rebellions; an aid expressly stipulated and often required and afforded, and by the necessity of some regular and permanent provision for accommodating disputes among the Cantons. The provision is that the parties at variance shall each choose four judges out of the neutral cantons, who in case of disagreement choose an umpire. This tribunal under an oath of impartiality pronounces definitive sentences which all the Cantons are bound to enforce. The competency of this regulation may be estimated by a clause in their treaty of 1683 with Victor Amadeus of Savoy, in which he obliges himself to interfere as mediator in disputes between the Cantons and to employ force if necessary against the contumacious party."

"So far as the peculiarity of their case will admit of comparison with that of the United States, it serves to confirm the principles intended to be established. Whatever efficacy the Union may have had in ordinary cases, it appears that the moment a cause of difference sprang up capable of trying its strength it failed. The controversies on the subject of religion which in three instances have kindled violent and bloody consequences, may be said in fact to have severed the League. The Protestant and Catholic Cantons have since had their separate Diets; when all the most important concerns are adjusted and which have left the general Diet, little other business than to take care of the common bailages.

" That separation had another consequence which merits attention. It produced opposite alliances with foreign powers : of Berne as the head of the Protestant Association with the United Provinces, and of Lucerne as the head of the Catholic Association with France."

The Dutch Republic. The last of the confederations referred to by Madison was the Dutch Republic, which was a confederation of the seven united provinces of the Netherlands, a union which arose in the war of independence against Spain, and lasted in a Republican form till the war of the French Revolution (1579–1795).

Seven States. The union was composed of seven co-equal and sovereign states, and each State was a composition of equal and independent cities. In all important cases unanimity was required not only of the provinces but of the cities.

The States-General. The sovereignty of the Union was represented by the States-General, consisting of about fifty deputies appointed by the provinces. The deputies held their seats some for life, others for six years, three, and one year. In two provinces the office was held during pleasure.

Power of. " The States-General had authority to enter into treaties and alliances to make war and peace, to raise armies and equip fleets, to ascertain quotas and demand contributions, but unanimity in the sanction of their constituents in all these cases were required. The States-General also had authority to appoint and receive ambassadors, to provide for the collection of duties on imports and exports, to regulate the mint with a saving of Provincial rights, to govern as sovereigns the dependent territories. No province could, except with the general consent, enter into a foreign treaty,

nor establish imposts injurious to others, nor charge their
neighbours with higher duties than their own subjects."

The federal administration was strengthened by a Council Council of
State.
of State, a chamber of accounts with five colleges of
admiralty.

The executive magistrate was the Stadtholder, who at Stadtholder.
the time when Madison wrote was an hereditary prince.
"His principal weight and influence in the republic,"
Madison considered, "arose from his independent title,
his great patrimonial estates, his family connections with
some of the chief potentates of Europe, and more than all
perhaps from his being stadtholder in the several provinces
as well as for the union." In the former capacity he
appointed town magistrates under certain regulations,
executed provincial decrees, presided when he pleased in
the provincial tribunals and possessed the power of pardon.

As Stadtholder of the union he had considerable preroga- Prerogatives.
Political
tives. In his political capacity he was entitled to settle capacity.
disputes between the provinces when other methods failed,
to assist at the deliberations of the States-General and at
their particular conferences, to give audiences to foreign
ambassadors, and to keep agents for his particular affairs
at foreign courts.

In his military capacity he commanded the Federal troops, Military
capacity.
provided for garrisons and generally regulated military
affairs, disposing of all appointments from colonels to ensigns,
and of the government and posts of fortified towns.

He was also admiral-general, and superintended and Admiral-
General.
directed everything relative to naval forces and other naval
affairs, presided in the admiralties in person or by proxy,
and appointed lieutenant-admirals and other officers, and
established councils of war whose sentences were not
executed till he approved of them.

Madison was emphatic in his condemnation of this Condemnation
of Confederacy
confederacy. It displayed imbecility in government, discord by Maddison.
among the provinces, foreign influence and indignities,
a precarious existence in peace and peculiar calamities in
war. He quotes from Grotius, that nothing but the hatred

of his countrymen to the House of Austria kept them from being ruined by the vices of their Constitution.

Defects of Constitution. The defects of the Constitution as demonstrated by its history showed a jealousy among the provinces which paralysed the union. A refusal of the provinces to raise contributions resulted in some of the provinces, such as Holland, furnishing their quota and subsequently obtaining reimbursement from the others, even by force.

The union, in fact, could never have continued to exist without the strong controlling force of the Stadtholder.

Conclusions of "Federalist." The conclusion that Madison arrived at was, that a sovereignty over sovereignty, a government over governments, a legislation for communities as contradistinguished from one over individuals, as it was a solecism in theory so in practice was subversive of the order and ends of civil polity by substituting violence in place of law and the destructive coercion of the sword in place of the mild and salutary coercion of the magistracy.

From the views expressed in " The Federalist," it seems clear that all existing forms of modern confederacies, including their own, were viewed with profound dissatisfaction by its authors. A Constitution to satisfy the needs of the people must be built on different lines. Its foundations must be laid deep, and its main springs of energy must be drawn from the American people as a whole, and not from the States.

CHAPTER V

THE CONSTITUTION OF THE LEGISLATIVE POWER

THE legislative power of the United States is vested in a Legislative power. Congress of the United States consisting of a Senate and a House of Representatives. It is the first power created under the Constitution.

THE SENATE

The title of Senate was taken from that great body which The Senate. for years directed the destinies of Rome, perhaps the most remarkable assembly that the world has ever seen, a great Sovereign Council which controlled every branch of administration and nearly all matters of legislation also. In foreign affairs the power of the Roman Senate was absolute except in declaring war or concluding treaties of peace, and in matters submitted to the votes of the people. In its Judicial capacity it was a Court of Justice for the trial of extraordinary offences.[1]

The Senate of the United States, which is the Second One-third of Senate retire every two years. Chamber, is composed of two Senators from each State chosen by the State Legislature for a period of six years. In 1910 it was composed of ninety-six members; two Senators for each of the forty-eight States. A Senator is entitled to one vote in the Senate.

The Constitution directed that after the Senators first assembled as a result of the first election, they should be divided as equally as might be into three classes. The seats of those of the first class were to be vacated at the expiration of the second year, those of the second class at the expiration of the fourth year, and those of the third class at the expiration of the sixth year. It was also arranged when the Constitution was established that the two senatorships from the same State should not be vacated at the same time.

[1] Liddell's *History of Rome*, Vol. I, pp. 427-30.

45

When State
Executive
appoints
Senators.
Should a vacancy happen by resignation or otherwise whilst the Legislature of any State was in recess, the State Executive was empowered to make a temporary appointment until the meeting of the Legislature, which was then authorised to fill the vacancy.

Electoral
qualifications
for office.
No person was declared eligible for the office of Senator who had not reached the age of thirty or had been less than nine years a citizen of the United States. When elected he was required to be an inhabitant of the State for which he was chosen.

Why age
of thirty
selected.
" The more advanced age and longer period of citizenship required for the senatorial qualification," said ' The Federalist,' " was justified on the ground of the nature of the senatorial trust, which required greater extent of information and stability of character, and therefore it was provided that the Senator should have reached a period of life which was most likely to supply these advantages, and further since he participated immediately in transactions with foreign nations it was thought that he ought not to be eligible to the office unless he were weaned from the prepossessions and habits incident to foreign birth and education. Therefore the period of nine years was fixed on, which appeared to be a ' prudent mediocrity ' between a total exclusion of adopted citizens and an indiscriminate and hasty admission of them which might create a channel for foreign influence in the National Councils."

Reason for
State
appointment.
The appointment of Senators by State Legislatures was " recommended by the double advantage of favouring a select appointment and of giving to the State Governments such an agency in the formation of the Federal Government as must secure the authority of the former and may form a convenient link between the two systems."[1]

Equality of
representation.
" The equality of representation," further said ' The Federalist,' " which each State possesses in the Senate was the result not of theory, but of a spirit of amity and that mutual deference and concession which the peculiarity of our situation rendered indispensable."[2]

[1] " The Federalist," No. lxii.　　[2] *Ibid.*

In fact, the small States would never have assented in the Convention to the preponderating influence of the larger States if they had had a representation only proportionate to population.

" The equal vote was a constitutional recognition of the portion of sovereignty remaining in the individual States, and an instrument for preserving that residuary sovereignty, and therefore was acceptable to the large States, who would be sedulous to guard against an improper consolidation of the States into one simple republic." *Other considerations.*

Again, it was an additional impediment on improper legislation, since the concurrence of a majority of the States as well as of the people was required. *Impediment on improper legislation.*

" If the complicated check on legislation were considered to prove as injurious, as beneficial, by impeding legislation, the facility and excess of law-making seemed to be the disease to which the Governments of the American people were most liable." [1]

" The necessity of a Senate was not less indicated," Madison argued in " The Federalist," " by the propensity of all single and numerous assemblies to yield to the impulse of sudden and violent passions and to be seduced by factious leaders into intemperate and pernicious resolutions." *Lessons drawn from American history.*

" Examples on this subject," he added, " might be cited without number, and from proceedings within the United States as well as from the history of other nations. But a position that will not be contradicted need not to be proved. All that need be remarked is that a body which is to correct this infirmity ought itself to be free from it, and consequently ought to be less numerous. It ought, moreover, to possess great firmness and consequently ought to hold its authority by a tenure of considerable duration." [2]

The necessity of a strong Second Chamber was also further emphasized on the ground that no small share of the embarrassments of America were to be charged on the blunders of the Government of the United States.

[1] " The Federalist," No. lxii
[2] *Ibid.*

Madison attributed such blunders to the heads rather than the hearts of most of them. " What, indeed," he asks, " are all the repealing, explaining and amending laws which fill and disgrace our voluminous codes but so many monuments of deficient wisdom, so many impeachments exhibited by each succeeding against each preceding session, so many admonitions to the people of the value of those aids which may be expected from a well-constituted Senate ? "[1]

In the existence of this body " The Federalist " expected to find that rock on which the Constitution might rest. " No Government," it concluded, " any more than an individual will long be respected without being truly respectable, nor be truly respectable without possessing a certain portion of order and stability."[2]

Times, place, and manner of holding elections for the Senate. Article 1, section 4, of the Constitution empowered Congress to make or alter the State regulations as to the times, place and manner of holding elections for the Senate except as to the places of choosing Senators.

In 1866 Congress enacted that each House of a State Legislature should first vote separately for the election of a Senator ; then should the two branches of the Legislature not agree a joint meeting of the two Houses was required to be held and a joint vote taken. A majority of all members elected to both Houses was required to be present and vote.

Indirectly sometimes popularly elected. In practice a candidate for the Senate is now frequently chosen indirectly by the popular vote, through the practice adopted of submitting candidate's claims to party Conventions when they meet to choose candidates for the State Legislatures. The candidate for the Senate whose claim receives most support at the Convention obtains his party's influence, when the time comes for his Legislature to choose a Senator, because future members of the State Legislature have beforehand pledged themselves to his support. Although the letter of the Constitution is observed, its spirit is disregarded. The State Legislatures cannot be said to be

[1] Ibid.
[2] Ibid.

untrammelled in their choice as was intended. The best man, it was originally thought, would be chosen, not the best party man—not necessarily interchangeable terms.

This method of indirect popular election has not altered the Senator's representative character. He is still peculiarly the State representative.

The Senate possesses legislative, executive and judicial powers : under its executive powers may be classed its treaty-making functions, its advice and assent being essential to the making of any treaty by the President. Two-thirds of the Senators present in the Senate must concur in order to render a treaty of any validity.

Thus the Treaty of Peace between the Queen Regent of Spain and the President of the United States signed by Commission in Paris 10th Dec., 1898, was ratified by the Senate 6th February, 1899. A two-thirds majority of the Senate is also essential to the ratification of any convention for the acquisition or alienation of territory by the United States.

The advice and consent of the Senate is required to the appointment of ambassadors and other public ministers, and consuls and judges of the Supreme Court and all other officers of the United States whose appointments are not otherwise provided for in the Constitution, and which may be established by law.

In its judicial capacity the Senate possesses the sole power Judicial capacity. of trying impeachments. When sitting for this purpose every Senator is required to take an oath or affirmation.

If a President of the Republic be tried by the Senate Trial of President. the Chief Justice must preside. No person can be convicted on impeachment without the concurrence of two-thirds of its members present.

The Vice-President acts as President of the Senate, but Vice-President is President of Senate. he possesses no vote except the voting be equal. When absent or when exercising the office of President of the United States, the Senate is at liberty to choose a President *pro tempore*.

No judgment on impeachment extends further than Judgment on impeachment. to declare the guilty person's removal from office, but it amounts to a disqualification to hold and enjoy any office of honour, trust, or profit, under the United States.

A party who has been convicted on impeachment is still
Liability of
party
convicted. liable to indictment, trial, judgment, and punishment according to law.

The power of impeachment which was adopted from England has always been highly prized by the States as a weapon to check abuses in the executive, and most of the States' Constitutions contain clauses incorporating it as part of their fundamental law.

The Constitution of New Hampshire, for instance,
Power in
State
Constitutions. empowered its Senate to try impeachments for bribery, corruption, malpractice, or maladministration in offices. Arkansas renders its Governor and all State officers, judges of the Supreme Court and Circuit Courts, chancellors, and prosecuting attorneys liable to process. One president of the United States, Andrew Johnson, has impeached, but was acquitted owing to a failure to attain the requisite two-thirds majority of the Senate.

The last person so convicted was a judge of a Federal Court who abused his office for the acquisition of land on illegal conditions. In January, 1913, he was declared by the Senate to be for ever unfit and incapable of holding any office of honour or profit under the Government of the United States of America.

Impeachment
of Lord
Melville. The last person impeached in England was Lord Melville in 1806. The proceedings in his case terminated in an acquittal on all charges by a majority of the Lords. [1]

In England the Government generally exercises much discretion in explaining its dealings with foreign powers to Parliament. It is often complained that the House of Commons for this reason cannot adequately control foreign policy. There are reasons for and against too much candour. In the United States the Senate, or rather its Committee of
Committee
of Foreign
Relations. Foreign Relations, usually receives the confidence of the executive early in any negotiations, and is consequently in a position to assure the President beforehand of the Senates'

[1] Howells, *State Trials*, Vol. 39.

support. This is especially useful when a treaty is under discussion. The Senate can hold a secret session when necessary. The Senate may amend any treaty that it does not thoroughly endorse, and it occasionally acts by making amendments.

A Senator on taking his seat binds himself by an oath Senator's oath on or affirmation to support the Constitution, but no religious affirmation. test is required. During the period of his membership he cannot be appointed to any civil office under the authority of the United States which has been created or whose emoluments have been increased during such period. A person holding any office under the United States cannot be a Senator.

A Senator receives a salary of $7,500 per annum, besides Salary of. an allowance of 20 cents per mile for travelling expenses for one journey to and from Washington ; $1,500 for clerk hire, and a sum for stationery. The Constitution directed that Senators and Representatives should receive a compensation for their services to be ascertained by law to be paid out of the Treasury. Payment of members has, therefore, existed from the earliest days.

A Senator in all cases, except treason, felony, and breach Privileges of. of the peace, is privileged from arrest during his attendance, and in going to and returning from the Senate. He cannot be questioned elsewhere for any speech or debate in the Senate.

The Senate is a judge of its own election returns and the Judge of its own qualifications of its members. A majority of its members election returns. constitutes a quorum for the purpose of transacting business, although a smaller number is empowered to adjourn from day to day, and may be authorised to compel the attendance of absent members in such manner and under such penalties as the Senate may provide.

The Senate determines its own rules of procedure, and Rules of procedure. may punish its members for disorderly behaviour, and with the concurrence of two-thirds, expel a member.

It keeps a journal of its proceedings, and may from time Journal of proceedings to time publish it, excepting such parts as may in its and records of votes.

judgment require secrecy : the yeas and nays of the members must at the desire of one-fifth of those present be entered in the journal. The names of Senators for this purpose are called alphabetically. No time limit applies to speakers nor is the Closure in force.

When consent of other House for adjournment required.

Whilst Congress is in session the Senate cannot adjourn without the consent of the House of Representatives for more than three days, nor to any other place than that in which the two Houses are sitting.

President's relation to.

When the President of the United States meets the Senate in the Senate Chamber for the consideration of executive business, his seat is on the right of the presiding officer.

Confidential communica- tions.

Confidential communications made by the President to the Senate are kept secret, so are treaties until the injunction of secrecy is removed by resolution.

Value as a second Chamber admitted.

The Senate, as a Second Chamber, has been highly extolled by competent observers. It is admittedly strong ; as representing the States it has been assured of that solid support which neither a nominated or hereditary chamber can possess. Chosen in a manner different from the House of Representatives and elected for a longer term, it has rarely been the subject of such vigorous attack by the popular Assembly as the House of Lords has been in the United Kingdom.

The history of the revolutionary movement during the French Revolution of 1789 is often referred to as a modern instance of the necessity of a Second Chamber. But the framers of the United States' Constitution looked elsewhere. Its necessity was demonstrated by the history of their own States, and based upon philosophic reasons. Where a State is ruled by one of its political parties the best legisla- tion generally results from criticism and argument ; if this be stifled disaster inevitably follows. Public opinion is often wrong in the beginning, but always right in the end. True public opinion takes time to mature. " The Federalist," states this argument thus—

Opinion of " The Federalist."

" As the cool and deliberate sense of the community ought in all governments and actually will in all free governments ultimately prevail over the views of its rulers, so there are particular moments in public affairs when the people, stimulated by some irregular passion, or some illicit advantage, or misled by the artful misrepresentation of some interested men, may call for measures which they themselves will afterwards be the most ready to lament and condemn. In these actual moments how salutary will be the interference of some temperate and respectable body of citizens in order to check the misguided career and to suspend the blow meditated by the people against themselves until reason, justice, and truth can regain their authority over the public mind. What bitter anguish would not the people of Athens have often escaped if their Government had contained so prudent a safeguard against the tyranny of their own passions!

" Popular liberty might then have escaped the indelible reproach of decreeing to the same citizen the hemlock on one day and statues on the next. The people can never wilfully betray their own interests, but they may possibly be betrayed by the representatives of the people, and the danger will be inevitably greater where the whole legislative trust is lodged in the hands of one body of men than where the concurrence of separate and dissimilar bodies is required in every public act."

THE HOUSE OF REPRESENTATIVES

The House of Representatives is the first or popular chamber chosen every second year by the people of the several States. The Constitution declared that the electors in each State should possess the same qualification that was requisite for election of the most numerous branch of the State Legislature. There is consequently no Federal franchise. *House of Representatives.*

Writing of the franchise, Madison said : " The definition of the right of suffrage is very justly regarded as a fundamental article of Republican government. It was incumbent on the Convention, therefore, to define and establish this right in the Constitution. To have left it open for the occasional regulation of the Congress would have been *Suffrage Views of " The Federalist."*

improper, for the reasons just mentioned. To have submitted it to the legislative discretion of the States would have been improper for the same reason, and for the additional reason that it would have rendered too dependent on the State Governments that branch of the Federal Government which ought to be dependent on the people alone. To have reduced the different qualifications in the different States to one uniform rule would probably have been as dissatisfactory to some of the States as it would have been difficult to the Convention. The provision made by the Convention appears, therefore, to be the best that lay within their option. It must be satisfactory to every State because it is conformable to the standard already established or that may be established by the State itself. It will be safe to the United States because being fixed by all the States' Constitutions, it is not alterable by the State Governments, and it cannot be feared that the people of the States will alter this part of their Constitution in such a manner as to abridge the rights secured to them by the Federal Constitution." [1]

The legal qualification for membership of the House of Representatives demanded by the Constitution was that a representative must have attained the age of twenty-five, and for seven years been a citizen of the United States. At the time of his election he was required to be also an inhabitant of the State for which he was chosen.

Biennial elections.

The system of biennial elections was adopted. Frequent elections were declared at the accession of William III as among the fundamental rights of the people of England, and the principle was later on carried into effect by the establishment of triennial parliaments. It was thought, however, that biennial elections would better serve all the purposes of the United States' Constitution. In the States in 1789 varying periods existed for the duration of the Legislatures. In Connecticut and Rhode Island the periods were half-yearly ; in South Carolina biennial, but elsewhere a system of annual elections prevailed.

[1] " The Federalist," No. lii.

The original House of Representatives consisted of sixty- Original
five Representatives. Of these New Hampshire elected House of Representatives.
three, Massachusetts eight, Rhode Island and Providence
Plantation one, Connecticut five, New York six, New Jersey
four, Pennsylvania eight, Delaware one, Maryland six,
Virginia ten, North Carolina five, South Carolina five, and
Georgia three.

The Constitution provided that a census should be taken Provision for census.
of the population of the States within three years after the
first meeting of Congress, and within every subsequent term
of ten years in such manner as Congress should by law direct,
and further provided for the apportionment of Representatives and direct taxes amongst the State according to their
respective numbers, prescribing how this should be effected.

In 1868 representatives were apportioned amongst the The 14th amendment.
States according to their respective numbers, counting the
whole number of persons in each State, excluding Indians
not taxed (14th amendment, 2nd section).

The Constitution provided that the number of Representatives should not exceed one for every thirty thousand,
but each State was to have one Representative at least.
In 1891 the number of Representatives was fixed at 356,
according to the census. This number was determined
without regard to any precise ratio of representatives to
population. In 1909 the number of representatives was
391.

It has been the practice to admit territorial delegates Territorial delegates.
from territories which have not been advanced to the
dignity of States. The delegates have no right to vote
but only to sit and speak.

The State, when Congress has allotted it its proper quota Congressional districts.
of Representatives, fixes the districts for which the
Representatives are to be elected. These districts are called
congressional districts.

· When a vacancy occurs in the representation the Governor
issues a writ for a new election, which must then be held.
A member who wishes to resign effects his resignation by
intimating his intention to the Governor of his State.

Suffrage.

It has already been mentioned that the electoral franchise is the same as that required for electing a member to the more numerous branch of the State Legislature. As the States can fix the franchise for their State Legislatures, they can widen the Federal franchise or limit it by widening or limiting their own. They have gradually adopted the former course. A reason for this may be discovered in the proviso to the 14th Amendment, which declares that when the right to vote at any election for the choice of electors for President and Vice-president of the States, Representatives in Congress, the Executive and Judicial Officers of a State, or the members of the State Legislature is denied to any of the male inhabitants of such State being twenty-one years of age and citizens of the United States, or in any way abridged except for participation in rebellion or other crime, the basis of representation therein shall be reduced in the proportion which the number of such male citizens bears to the whole number of male citizens twenty-one years of age in such States.

Reasons for wide franchise.

Since a State naturally desires to have the fullest voice in the national affairs, it is certainly not inclined to limit its franchise, since any such limitation would operate to limit the Federal franchise.

Times, places, and manner of holding elections.

Article 1, section 4, of the Constitution provided that the times, places, and manner of holding elections should be prescribed by each State, but Congress might at any time by law make or alter such regulations. This Congress did.

After its election the House of Representatives does not meet until the December of the following year. The President, however, can convene it earlier if he chooses for an extraordinary session. In practice the old House sits and acts for some time after the new House has been elected.

The Speaker.

The House of Representatives chooses its Speaker and all its other officers, including the Sergeant-at-Arms, who is the treasurer of the House. The Speaker is considered a great official. He receives a salary of $12,000 a year. In taking

his seat he takes an oath or affirmation of fidelity to the
Constitution.   The Speaker is an official whose title has
been copied from that of the Speaker of the English House
of Commons, but unlike the Speaker of the House of
Commons, he is a party leader, and is expected to use his
power to forward the business of his party.   The committees *Committees of the House.*
of the House are partly chosen by him ; at one time he
chose them all.   Some of the former powers possessed by
Speakers are now exercised by a committee.   At Westminster the conduct of the House of Commons subject to its
standing orders rests with the political leader of the House
who settles it in consultation with the Chief Whip.

The present system of Standing Committees was   first *House of Commons' Committees.*
introduced in the House of Commons in 1883.   The present
practice is for four Standing Committees to be appointed
each session to consider such bills relating to law and courts
of justice and legal procedure, and to trade, shipping,
manufactures, and agriculture as may be committed to
them, and to business referring especially to Scotland.   The
Standing Committees are nominated by a Committee of
Selection, consisting of the Chairman of the Select Committee
or Standing Order Committee, and ten others nominated by
the House at the beginning of each session.

The chairman of each Standing Committee is appointed
from a chairman's panel nominated by a Committee of
Selection.   Select Committees are subject to regulation by
standing orders.   They are variously appointed, sometimes
partly by the member in charge of a bill, sometimes wholly
or partly by the Committee of Selection, but usually by the
whole House.   A Committee of the whole House consists
of the House sitting in a less formal manner.   The Chairman
of Committees then takes the place of the Speaker.[1]   In
the United States the bulk of the work of the House is done
by committees, which are extremely numerous.

Congress, after sitting in the autumn after its election *Sessions of Congress.*
in the previous year, adjourns at Christmas for a recess, and
then continues on in session till the July or August following.

[1] Ilbert's *Legislative Methods and Forms*, p. 214.

In December there is a fresh sitting, which is continued
until the 4th March. The two sittings are respectively
known as the long and short session.

Expiry of
bills.

In the House of Commons bills expire at the end of each
session, but this is not the case in Congress, where bills are
carried over from the long to the short session.

A suggestion has been made that a similar practice should
be introduced in the House of Commons, but the same
pressing reason does not appear as exists in the United
States, where the whole working life of Congress, as a rule,
does not extend longer than twelve months.

Payment of
members.

All members of the House of Representatives receive
payment for their services. The salary and allowances are
the same as those of a Senator. (*Ante*, p. 51.)

Payment of
Members of
the House
of Commons.

Although the principle of payment of members has so
long existed in the United States, it was not until the
summer session of 1911 that it was adopted by the House
of Commons. The principle was then approved by a resolution of the House, and the amount voted in a committee of
supply.

Privileges of
Members.

Members of the House of Representatives, like Senators,
are in all cases except treason, felony, and a breach of the
peace, privileged from arrest during their attendance at
the session of the House, and in going to or returning from
it. They cannot be questioned in any other place for any
speech or debate in the House.

This provision of the Constitution was directly borrowed
from Article V of the Articles of Confederation, and this in
turn was borrowed from the British Constitution. Similar
provisions appear in many of the State Constitutions. The
House of Commons' privilege renders immune the persons
of its members during the continuance of the session, and
for forty days before its commencement and after its
conclusion.

Origin of.

" The object of the privilege was doubtless to secure the
safe arrival and regular attendance of members on the
scene of their parliamentary duties. The privilege itself
may perhaps relate back to the Saxon rule that such persons

as were on their way to the gemot were in the king's peace. It was never held to protect members from the consequences of treason, felony, or breach of the peace."[1] The privilege of immunity does not extend to the writing and publishing of seditious libel,, nor to any indictable offence, nor to contempt of court.

As in the case of Senators no member of the House during the time for which he is elected may be appointed to any civil office under the authority of the United States which shall have been created or the emolument whereof shall have been increased during such time, and no person holding any office under the United States shall be a member of the House during its continuance. (Article I, section 6.) *Disqualifications.*

The House of Representatives is master of its own internal affairs. It has power to determine the rules of its proceedings, punish its members for disorderly behaviour, and with the concurrence of two-thirds of its members to expel a member. A majority of its members constitutes a quorum to do business, but a smaller number may adjourn from day to day, and may be authorised to compel the attendance of absent members who may be required under penalties. *Master of its own procedure.*

The House is bound to keep a journal of its proceedings and publish it except such parts as it may not deem desirable on the grounds of secrecy. In this journal the yeas and nays of the members on any question if a fifth of the members present desire it must be entered. The House cannot adjourn whilst Congress is in session for more than three days without the consent of the Senate, nor to any other place than that in which the two Houses are sitting. *Journal of the House.*

The House possesses the sole power to impeach, as does the House of Commons. Under circumstances that will hereafter be explained, the choice of a President may occasionally devolve upon it. (*Post*, p. 64.). The House judges its own election returns and the qualifications of its members. *Power to impeach.*

In considering this body with its powers of internal management a general likeness is observable to the House of Commons. There are, however, points of difference. Whilst *Likeness to House of Commons.*

---

[1] Anson, *Law and Custom of the Constitution*, 4th Edition, 156 (1911).

a power to expel members exists in both Houses, a two-thirds majority is required in Congress, a bare majority is sufficient in the House of Commons. The keeping of a journal of the proceedings is a feature common to both Houses. The English Commons Journal commenced in 1547.

Commencement of English Commons' Journal.

Whilst the House of Representatives retains its right to judge election returns, the House of Commons has resigned most of its former powers. Under the Parliamentary Electors Act, 31 & 32 Vict., c. 125, and the Amending Act, 42 & 43 Vict., c. 75, the trial of election petitions in the United Kingdom takes place in England before two judges of the High Court in the borough or county where the representation is at issue. The judges, after a trial, certify their decision to the Speaker, and their decision cannot be questioned. Notwithstanding these Acts, the House of Commons is still entitled to examine as to the existence of a legal disqualification. The need to remove the trial of election petitions from the political to the judicial sphere has never been felt to the same extent in the United States as in Great Britain owing to the shorter period for which the House of Representatives sits and the lesser political weight attaching to the position of a representative. Prior to the Parliamentary Electors Act, the trial of election petitions by a committee of the House of Commons led to grave abuses. The scandal of corruption among members of a legislative body has always greatly excited public opinion. A legislator, like Cæsar's wife, should be above suspicion. As early as 1808 Congress passed an Act declaring that no Member of Congress should directly or indirectly, himself or by any other person, undertake or enjoy any contract with any officer of the United States on their behalf, or with any person authorised to make contracts on the part of the United States. The offence named was constituted a misdemeanour punishable by fine.

Judges deal with election petitions.

Corruption.

Government contracts.

In 1853 further legislation was passed, and both Senators and Representatives were declared liable to indictment for misdemeanour if for compensation certain or contingent

Legislation of 1853.

they prosecuted any claim against the United States or assisted in the prosecution of any claim or received any gratuity or share or interest in any claim from any claimant against the United States with intent to assist or in consideration of having assisted in the prosecution of it.

The provision did not apply to the prosecution or defence of any action or suit in any judicial court of the United States.

In the House of Commons the acceptance of office of various kinds disqualifies a member.   The statute, 6th Anne c. 7, section 25, enacts that no one shall be capable of election who has accepted from the Crown any new office created since 1705. Another section, section 26, enacts that the acceptance of any office of profit under the Crown by a member of the House of Commons shall avoid his election, but he shall be eligible for re-election. The Statute, 22 George III, c. 45, renders void the election of any person who directly or indirectly himself, or through the intervention of a trustee holds or undertakes any contract or commission for or on account of the public service and imposes a penalty of £500 a day upon any person who sits and votes whilst thus disqualified. There are many other disqualifications. [1]

These penal provisions originated in the desire of the House of Commons to curb the power of the Crown and its ministers.

At one time Sir Robert Walpole was accused with reason of having carried on government by a regular payment of bribes. Lord North employed the Secret Service money and money that the King had saved from the civil list in influencing members of Parliament. [2]

Hamilton, in " The Federalist," refers to this : " The venality of the British House of Commons has been long a topic of accusation against that body in the country to which

Disqualification in House of Commons.

Bribery.

Hamilton's views.

---

[1] Anson, *Law and Custom of the Constitution.*   Vol. I, Chapter iv, 4th Edition, revised 1911.

[2] *Correspondence of George III with Lord North,* Vol. II, 421-42.

they belong as well as in this, and it cannot be doubted that the charge is to a certain extent well founded."[1]

The provisions of the United States' Constitution and subsequent legislation have been directed not only as a check upon the executive, but for the purpose of putting an end to that form of corruption known as bribery, the acceptance of which debases the member and brings discredit upon the assembly to which he belongs. In estimating the political value of the House of Representatives it is considered to have little or no real power and to possess but an extremely small influence over the people. Occasionally when some extraordinary and sensational measure is introduced in the House by some active Representative it becomes a nine days' wonder only to fall flat after the first period of excitement. Among such measures may be instanced Mr. Jones' Bill for the declaration of the Independence of the Philippine Islands, and a recent proposal to make a marriage between a black and a white American illegal.

The people of the United States do not set their hopes at all in the labours of the House of Representatives. The real power is elsewhere.

[1] " The Federalist," No. lxxvi.

CHAPTER VI

THE EXECUTIVE POWER OF THE UNITED STATES

THE word power is used here as elsewhere in three different Power, the meaning of, in the Constitution. senses in the United States' Constitution. It includes the method of creating the power, the authority conferred by the power when created, and the exercise of the authority when created. Thus the executive power means the method prescribed for the election of a President in whom the executive power with one or two exceptions is vested, the authority with which he is endowed, and the exercise of the authority within the limits of the Constitution.

The President of the United States must be a natural- Persons capable of being Presidents. born citizen, who has attained the age of thirty-five, and he must have been for fourteen years a resident of one of the United States.

The method prescribed for his election is as follows : Method of election. Each State of the Union appoints as its legislature directs a number of electors equal to the whole number of Senators and Representatives which the State is entitled to in Congress; but no Senator or Representative holding an office of trust or profit under the United States is eligible to be an elector. The twelfth article of the amendment to the Constitution requires these electors to meet in their respective States and to vote for ballots for a President and Vice-president, one of whom at least must not be an inhabitant of the same State with themselves. They must name in their ballots the person who is voted for as President, and in distinct ballots the person who is voted for as Vice-president. Distinct lists must be made of all the persons voted for as President, and of all persons voted for as Vice-president and of the number of votes for each. The lists must be signed and certified, and transmitted sealed to the seat of the Government of the United States, directed to the President of the Senate. The President of the Senate then, in the presence of the Senate and the House of Representatives, opens all the certificates and the votes are counted. The person who obtains the greatest number of votes for President is President, provided that he has obtained a majority of the whole number of electors appointed ; if no person has secured the required majority, the House of Representatives chooses immediately by ballot from the persons having the highest numbers of votes not exceeding three on the list of those voted for as President.

When choice by House of Representatives.

In this choice of the President, the votes are taken by States, the Representation from each State having one vote. A quorum of the House for this purpose consists of a member or members from two-thirds of the States and a majority of all the States is necessary to a choice.

Federal principle observed.

Should the House of Representatives not choose a President, whenever the right of choice devolves upon it before the fourth day of March next following, the Vice-president acts as President as in the case of the death or other constitutional disability of the President.

Vice-president acts on failure of House of Representatives.

Before the passing of the twelfth amendment, the person who received the most votes was deemed to have been elected President, and the person who stood second, Vice-president. [1]

Practice prior to twelfth Amendment.

The method of double election was devised to secure a choice of the best man for the Presidency. It was thought the Presidential electors would be chosen for their merits, and would be more likely to agree upon a better person than the people : the method, however, has not worked as its promoters hoped. The Presidential electors have become merely party nominees, who are pledged in advance to vote for some particular candidate. The way this has occurred has been as follows—

The object of the double election.

It was left to each State to provide as their Legislature directed for the election of the electors. Some States originally appointed the electors through their State Legislatures, but others left the matter to popular election. Gradually, however, all the States adopted the more

Diminished importance of electors.

[1] *Post*, p. 146.

democratic course, and at the present time a single popular vote is taken throughout the States. The whole of the electors on one ticket are now generally voted for by one or other of the great parties, each party supporting the ticket of electors pledged to vote for its particular candidate. The electors have, therefore, long ceased to be persons exercising an independent choice; they are mere nominees for the execution of a party trust.

The polling for the Presidential electors takes place on the same day throughout all the States, and is fixed at an early date in the month of November. Polling for Presidential electors.

Amongst the many exciting elections for the Presidency, one curious one that took place in 1876 may be mentioned. The Republican candidate was Mr. Hayes, and Mr. Tilden, the Democratic. The former secured his electoral list in 17 out of a total of 38 States, with an aggregate of 163 electors; the latter secured an electoral list of 17 States, with an aggregate of 184 electors. The returns in 4 States, were disputed; two sets of electors had been chosen, and each claimed to be the qualified electors for the 4 States The electoral votes of these States numbered 22 : since the total number of electors was 369, should any one set of electors out of the four have been properly chosen, the Democratic candidate had obtained a majority of the electoral votes, since he was only one short. If the Republican candidate had secured them all, he would have a majority of one. Elections of Vice-presidents.

The Constitutional deadlock was solved by the passing of an Act of Congress, which constituted an electoral commission of five Senators, five members of the House of Representatives, and five justices to decide the validity of the double returns. The Senate nominated three Republicans and two Democrats, the House of Representatives nominated two Republicans and three Democrats: the Senate at the time was Republican and the House of Representatives Democratic. Of the four judges, two were Republican, two Democratic; but they had power to choose a fifth judge, and they chose a Republican judge. The Electoral Commission.

All the points in dispute were settled by a majority of one in favour of the Republican electorate. Mr. Hayes, it was declared had received 185 votes and his opponent 184.

Legislation of 1887. In 1887 Congress passed an Act that provided that each State should appoint a tribunal to declare what votes were legal where double returns were made. Failing the establishment of such a tribunal, the power was left to the two Houses of Congress.

Vice-president. On the death, resignation, or incapacity or removal of the President, the Vice-president succeeds him. On the death of a Vice-president who has thus succeeded to the Presidency, the Secretary of State succeeds, and, in turn, other officers of the Government, according to their relative rank.

Functions of Vice-president. The Vice-president has few functions. He acts as President of the Senate, but possesses no vote unless the Senate be equally divided.

Model of office. The office of a Vice-president has been described as superfluous. Hamilton found its model in the Lieutenant-Governor who, under the State Constitution of New York, was chosen by the people at large. He presided in the Senate, and was the constitutional substitute for the Governor in casualties similar to those which authorises the Vice-president to exercise the authorities and discharge the duties of the President. [1]

Election of Vice-president. When the Senate chooses. Like the President, the Vice-president is elected by the greatest number of votes, should such number be a majority of the whole number of electors appointed. Should no such majority be obtained, the Senate chooses a Vice-president from the two highest numbers on the list. A quorum of the Senate for this purpose consists of two-thirds of the whole number of Senators, and a majority of the whole number is necessary for a choice.

Disqualifications for office. No person constitutionally ineligible for the office of President is eligible to that of Vice-president of the United States.

Term of office. A President is elected for a term of four years. The

[1] " The Federalist," No. lxviii.

general or chief officer of the Achaian League had been permitted to hold office only in alternate years, the better to prevent his acquiring a permanent position. The framers of the United States' Constitution, saw no reason why the President should hold office for less than four years, and should he be again chosen for a further term : Washington was chosen for a second term, but refused a nomination for a third term ; and this precedent having been established, since his time no President has held office for three terms.

Commenting on the absence of any prohibition in the Constitution against successive terms, Hamilton enquired "if it would promote the peace of the community or the stability of Government to have half-a-dozen men who had credit enough to raise themselves to the seat of the supreme magistracy, wandering among the people like discontented ghosts, and sighing for a place which they were destined never to possess." Hamilton's views.

To ensure the President's loyalty to the Constitution, he is bound to make an oath or affirmation, before entering upon the execution of his office, that he will properly execute the office of President, and to the best of his ability preserve, protect, and defend the Constitution. The Presidential oath.

To render him independent, his salary, not a large one for the office, equivalent to £15,000 a year, can neither be increased nor diminished during his term of office. He is debarred from receiving whilst President any other emolument from the United States. Salary of.

By virtue of his office he becomes Commander-in-Chief of the Army and Navy ; and of the Militia of the several States, when called into the actual service of the United States. Commander-in-Chief of the Army and Navy.

The President possesses the power to reprieve or pardon all offences against the United States, except convictions on impeachment. Power to reprieve or pardon.

The power of the King of England to pardon in cases of impeachment was discussed in England in 1679, in Danby's case, which raised the point as to whether a royal pardon could stop an impeachment. The discontinuance of the proceedings left this important constitutional question Power of pardon in England. Danby's case.

unsolved. The Act of Settlement enacted that a royal pardon could not be pleaded to an impeachment, but the prerogative power to pardon a person found guilty after sentence was left untouched. In 1715 this prerogative was exercised, and three of the lords who had been engaged in the Jacobite rebellion were reprieved and pardoned after impeachment and sentence.

No power to make war.

The President possesses no power to make war ; this power, as well as the power to grant letters of marque, is vested in Congress. He can, however, make treaties, but only with the advice and consent of the Senate.

In practice, the Senate is rarely consulted until after a treaty is completed. It is then laid before them for ratification. (*Ante*, p. 49.)

Madison's views in "The Federalist."

Madison defends this requirement of the Constitution with much ability : he denies that either the declaring of war or the making of treaties properly belong to the Executive Power—"A declaration that there shall be war," he writes, "is not an execution of laws : it does not presuppose pre-existing laws to be executed : it is not in any respect an act merely executive. It is, on the contrary, one of the most deliberative Acts that can be formed ; and, when performed, has the effect of repealing all the laws operating in a state of peace, so far as they are inconsistent with a state of war ; and of enacting, as a rule, for the executive a new code adapted to the relation between the Society and its foreign enemy. In like manner, a conclusion of peace annuls all the laws peculiar to a state of war, and revives the general law incident to a state of peace. . . . Treaties, particularly treaties of peace, have sometimes the effect of changing not only the external laws of the Society, but operate also on the internal code which is purely municipal, and to which the legislative authority of the country is of itself competent and complete." [1]

Hamilton's views.

Hamilton considered that a treaty-making power was "neither wholly executive nor wholly legislative, since it related neither to the execution of the subsisting laws nor

[1] *Letters of Helvidius*, by James Madison, No. 1.

to the enaction of new ones ; and still less to an exertion of common strength. Its objects were contracts with foreign nations which have the force of law, but derive it from the obligations of good faith. . . . The power, therefore, forms a distinct department, and belongs properly neither to the legislative nor to the executive. The executive was the most fit agent in the management of foreign negotiations, whilst the importance of the trust and the operation of treaties as laws pleaded strongly for the participation of the whole or a portion of the legislative body in the making of them."[1]

In the United Kingdom the power to make a treaty of peace is vested in the Crown, but whether this of necessity implies a power residing in the Crown to compel its subjects to obey the provisions of a treaty made by it (which has been arrived at for the purpose of putting an end to a state of war) is a moot question. So is the further question, whether the power equally extends to the provisions of a treaty which has for its object the preservation of peace or an agreement to avert a war which is imminent, since it is akin to a treaty of peace. It is probable that legislative authority is required.[2] *Power in the United Kingdom.*

The independence of the United States was recognised in 1782 by Act of Parliament (22 Geo. III, c. 46). This statute authorised the King to make peace with certain colonies in North America and vested the power in the King to repeal all statutes relating to them by letters patent. *Independence of United States : a legislative Act.*

Treaties and laws in the United States are of equal standing. A treaty is on the same footing and of like obligation with an Act of the Legislature, both are supreme laws of the land, and no superior efficacy is given to the one over the other. When the two have reference to the same subject, the judges will construe them so as to give effect to both, if this can be done ; but where the two are inconsistent, the one later in date will prevail. Where a treaty operates by its own force and relates to a subject within the *Treaties and laws.*

---

[1] " The Federalist," No. lxxv.
[2] *Walker v. Baird*, App. Cas. (1892), 491, 497.

power of Congress, it can be deemed in that particular only the equivalent of a legislative Act to be repealed or modified at the pleasure of Congress. In either case, the last expression of the Sovereign will controls.

President's powers of appointment.

The Constitution assigned to the President the power of nominating and appointing, with the advice and consent of the Senate, ambassadors and other public ministers, consuls, and judges of the Supreme Court, and other officers whose appointment was not otherwise provided for by the Constitution.

Powers of Congress.

It left to Congress, however, the power by law to vest the appointment of such superior officers as it might think proper in the President alone, in the courts of law, or in the heads of departments.

President's Cabinet.

The Senate will not, as a rule, interfere with the appointment of the President's principal officers or executive. Although these officers were not directly mentioned in the Constitution, their existence was inferred from the fact that the President was entitled " to require the opinion in writing of the principal officers in each of the executive departments upon any subject relating to the duties of

Constitutional position.

their respective offices." The constitutional view of the President's position is that he speaks and acts through them

Powers of Congress.

in respect to the business committed to them. Congress, however, is entitled to impose independent duties upon them, provided that the duties imposed are not antagonistic to any rights secured by the Constitution.

Washington's practice.

Washington was in the habit of holding a consultation with heads of departments. Sometimes, however, he obtained their views in conversation, although the strict letter of the Constitution required that they should be given in writing.

Cabinet meetings.

The practice of holding Cabinet meetings was introduced by Jefferson, a practice that has since been followed by successive Presidents.

Departments.

Congress created Federal Executive departments, commencing with those of a Secretary for State, a Secretary of the Treasury, a Secretary of War, and Attorney-General.

Four secretaries have since been added : One for the Navy, one for the Interior, one for Agriculture, and one each for commerce and labour, with a Postmaster-General. At the present time there are ten chief executive officers who compose the President's Cabinet. Each of these officers receives Salaries of officers. a salary of £2,400 a year.

The executives are never spoken of as ministers but as executive or ministry only. A minister is the representative of the United States accredited to a foreign country and ranks below an Ambassador. In England the Ministers or Secretaries of State are persons delegated to exercise so much of the Royal Prerogative as is allotted to them. In the United States the Secretaries are practically the Presidents' staff. The Presidents can remove a Secretary at will ; so can the King of England in theory, but in practice he would only do so on the recommendation of the Prime Minister, the Minister in question would not, however, wait for that but resign of his own accord. The Secretaries in the United States forming collectively the Cabinet have no direct political power ; in the United Kingdom it is the reverse, the Cabinet directs the whole policy of the Government for the time being and under the rigid party system their followers passively follow that dictation.

The Constitution provided that the President should Posts not provided for by the Constitution. obtain the advice and consent of the Senate in making appointments to posts which were not expressly provided for by the Constitution, but which might afterwards be established by law. In respect to such appointments a system originated which now practically compels the President to consult the Senators of his party for the particular State for which the appointment is to be made before he makes the nomination. The system is known Courtesy of the Senate. as the "Courtesy of the Senate."

A further power was given to the President to fill up all Vacancies during the recess of Congress. vacancies occurring during a recess of the Senate by granting commissions to expire at the end of the next session.

It is noticeable that nowhere did the Constitution mention Absence of power for removal of officers. the existence of any power to remove officers except in the case of the Judges, whose tenure of office was declared to be during good behaviour. Unless Congress prescribed in the Act creating the office its duration, or named the person by whom the removal of the officer might be made, it was a question of doubt to whom the power properly belonged.

In the first Congress a construction of the Constitution was adopted that gave the President power to remove all officers.

In 1829, on the appointment of President Jackson, the Spoils System was introduced under which holders of Federal offices were removed on the accession of a new President, to make way for others whose services the new President was desirous of requiting. The evils of the Spoils System, admittedly great, have of late years been considerably diminished by removing appointments to offices from the nomination of the President and by placing candidates under competitive examination.

The Cabinet of the President or the President's Ministry as it would be called in England, do not occupy seats in either House of Congress. Article 1 (sec. 6) of the Constitution provides " that no person holding any office under the United States shall be a member of either House." Hence the Ministry is absolutely unlike a British Ministry. In no sense is there Responsible Government.

In Great Britain the constitutional position of the King makes him unaccountable for his administration. His person is sacred. The Cabinet are solely responsible to Parliament for the advice they give him. Nevertheless, the King, in the exercise of his royal office, is constitutionally absolute master of his conduct, and may observe or disregard any counsel tendered to him at his discretion.

In Great Britain and the Dominions the theory of ministerial responsibility for the acts of the executive has been adopted universally. The theory is essentially of modern creation, and has only been slowly evolved since the Revolution of 1688.

"'Ministerial responsibility'" means, in ordinary parlance, the responsibility of Ministers to Parliament or the liability of Ministers to lose their offices, if they cannot retain the confidence of the House of Commons."[1] "Ministerial responsibility," in both senses, is recognised as part of the convention of the British Constitution. It originated with the growth of the power of the House of Commons; for, after the Revolution, when the business of Government could not be carried on except with the continuous support of the House of Commons, the King's Ministers found it necessary to rely upon that support. Hence by degrees it was considered that the King should choose all his Ministers from one of the two great political parties into which the country had divided itself. The Cabinet thereafter became responsible to Parliament, and Parliament, in turn, to the people; but the innovation introduced into the Constitution in this way was not arrived at without opposition. The elevation of Members of the House of Commons to places under the Crown was regarded at one period with grave suspicion. The Act of Settlement in 1700, by one of its sections, declared that no person who held office or a place of profit under the King should be capable of serving as a Member of the House of Commons. The section, however, was repealed before it actually came into force. If it had remained upon the Statute Book, then a like provision to that which exists in the American Constitution might have resulted in a similar development of the British Constitution.

The Act of Settlement.

The President's Cabinet is not an advisory Council in the constitutional sense.

President's Cabinet not a Constitutional body of advisers.

Hamilton disapproved of a Council to advise and consult with the President. He considered that "the executive power was more easily confined when it was one, that it was safer that there should be a single object for the jealousy and watchfulness of the people; in a word, that all multiplication of the executive was rather dangerous than friendly to liberty. Hence, seeing that a Constitutional Council would have relieved the President of the responsibility that it was desired that he should assume, the framers of the Constitution rejected it.

Hamilton's views.

[1] Dicey, *The Law of the Constitution*, 6th Edition, p. 319.

The limitation of the Presidential term of office, enjoyed in the glare of publicity, rendered it possible to create one chief executive officer—the President—to whom the energy of the Republic could with safety be confided.

Power to recommend legislation. The President has not a right to speak in Congress, but whilst he cannot introduce Bills directly in Congress, since he is not a member of either House of Congress, he is entitled in accordance with the Constitution, to recommend legislation theoretically and invite Congress to act ; as the triple division of powers in the Constitution left him with executive functions only the recommendatory power was important, as an executive is often directly conscious of abuses for which the proper remedy is legislation. The President may call attention to abuses or indicate measures which he considers that the requirements of the people demand. The practice introduced by Jefferson of addressing communications to Congress by written message to which no answer was returned or expected has since been followed by succeeding Presidents.[1] The President can send a delegate to the Senate or to the House of Representatives to make a verbal communication. Neither he nor his executive, as in the United Kingdom prepare legislative measures to be forced through the Chambers by the might of the majority in agreement with the Executive. In the United States of America the Ministers or Secretaries do not figure politically at all. They have no right to sit or vote in Congress. If the position of the American President be compared with that of the King in the United Kingdom, it is at once observable that the King is a member of the legislative body. This appears by the enacting clause of a statute which runs : " It is enacted by the King's Most Excellent Majesty, and by and with the advice and consent of the Lords spiritual and temporal and Commons, and by the authority of the same. . . ."

President not a member of the legislative body. The President of the United States is not a member of the legislative body : he signs a Bill presented to him as

[1] The practice has been departed from by President Woodrow Wilson who has adopted the practice of Washington.

approved ; but a law can be enacted under certain circumstances without his approval. It is one of the duties of the President to inform Congress of the state of the Union, and to take care that the laws are faithfully executed.

On extraordinary occasions, he possesses the power to convene both Houses or either of them ; and in case of disagreement between them with respect to the time of adjournment, he may adjourn them to such time as he may think proper. *Power to convene Congress.*

It is his duty to receive ambassadors and other public ministers. *Duty to receive ambassadors.*

He must commission all the officers of the United States. *Commission officers.*

The power to convene and the power to adjourn Congress are necessarily executive powers. The former because some emergency may arise which will require its assembling ; the latter power because it may be the only way of terminating a controversy, which can lead to no result. *Power to convene and adjourn Congress.*

The President is removable from office on impeachment for, and conviction of, treason, bribery, or other high crimes and misdemeanours. (*Ante*, p. 49.) *President removable from office.*

The President possesses a power to veto legislation. The power, however, is only a qualified negative. When a Bill is presented to him by Congress, he may refuse to sign it ; and, if he refuses, he must return the Bill with his objections to that House in which it originated. The objections will then be entered at large in the journals of the House. If the Bill, at a later period, be reconsidered and proceeded with, it must be approved by a two-thirds majority of the House in which it originated, and then sent to the other House. If it be there approved by a two-thirds majority, it will become law. The votes of both Houses must be determined by " yeas " and " nays," and the names of the persons voting for and against. The Bill must be entered in the journal of each House respectively. If any Bill be not returned by the President within ten days (Sunday excepted) after it is presented to him, it becomes law just as if he had signed it, unless Congress by their adjournment prevent its return. *Veto power.*

Presidential power theoretically inferior, in practice superior.

Although in theory the presidential power of veto is less than that of a British Sovereign, who is entitled to place an absolute negative upon all Acts of Parliament, in practice it is far greater. One reason being that it more often happens than not that the two thirds of each House of Congress cannot be obtained. A British Sovereign has never exercised the power to veto a Bill since 1707, when Queen Anne withheld her consent to the Scotch Militia Bill ; but in the United States the President frequently exercises his power of veto, and this generally with full public approval. It may seem at first sight surprising that legislation which has passed Congress should be vetoed in this way ; but when it is remembered that the President receives a direct mandate from the people, it may not be thought so strange. In the eye of the people the President is the court of power and political wisdom. In legislative practice, which does not always attract the direct attention of the people the Committees constitute the all powerful working medium. The history of England has shown how great has been the people's jealousy of any influence not emanating from themselves. The history of the United States, on the other hand, has demonstrated how the people are willing to surrender to their chief executive officer large power because the power emanates from themselves.

CHAPTER VII

THE JUDICIAL POWER

THE judicial power of the United States was vested by the Constitution in one Supreme Court, and in such inferior courts as Congress might from time to time ordain and establish.

The judges, both of the Supreme and Inferior Courts, hold their offices during good behaviour; they receive payment for their services, which cannot be diminished during their continuance in office.

The Supreme Court was originally composed of six judges; there are now nine. The Chief Justice receives a salary of $13,000, and the eight associate justices $12,500 each. The justices are nominated by the President, and their appointments are confirmed by the Senate.

The Supreme Court sits from October till June in every year at Washington. Six judges must be present to pronounce a decision. Every case is discussed by the court twice over: once to ascertain the view of the majority, which is then directed to be set forth in a written judgment; a second time, when the judgment, which has been prepared, is submitted for adoption as the judgment of the court. A judgment of the Supreme Court is rarely overruled by a subsequent judgment of the same Court: an earlier decision of the House of Lords is never reversed by a later one; should an alteration in the law be desired, it must be effected by legislation.

Thus, for instance, when the House of Lords, in the case of the Bartonshill Coal Co. *v.* Reid,[1] adopted the narrow view that a master was not liable to a workman for the acts of another workman when both were working in a common employment, although one was in superintendence over the other, legislation became necessary to meet the needs of the

[1] 3 *Macq. H. L. Cases,* 266.

77

community, and the Employers' Liability Acts and the Workmen's Compensation Act were passed establishing the liability of the employer, not only in respect of certain specified classes of negligence, but in respect of accidents not based on negligence. Under the United States' Constitution no power exists in many instances to correct a judgment of the Supreme Court by Congressional legislation, and nothing short of an amendment of the Constitution will put matters straight.

The Supreme Court is the Final Court of Appeal both in civil and criminal matters against decisions rendered in the United States ultramarine provinces such as Porto Rico and the Philippine Islands.

Circuit Courts of Appeals. Circuit Courts. District Courts.

Congress, which was given the power under the Constitution to form inferior courts, has established (1) Circuit Courts of Appeals ; (2) Circuit Courts ; and (3) District Courts.

Circuit Court of Appeals.

The Circuit Court of Appeals was established in 1891. To this court, appeals may be brought from Circuit or District Courts, with a further right of appeal in some classes of cases to the Supreme Court.

The Circuit Courts are nine in number, and to each of these is allotted two or three judges called Circuit Judges, and to each court is also assigned one of the nine Supreme Court justices. The judges receive a salary of $7,000 a year. The district courts are now a large class, and in 1910 were eighty-eight in number. They were established originally by the Judiciary Act of 1789. For the purpose of these courts the United States was then divided into thirteen districts. A district court judge receives a salary of $6,000 a year. In England the Lords of Appeal in Ordinary receive a salary of £6,000 a year, the Master of the Rolls £6,000, the Lords Justices of Appeal £5,000, the Lord Chief Justice £8,000 and the judges of the High Court a salary of £5,000 a year. The majority of County Court judges receive salaries of £1,500 a year.

District Courts.

Salaries of judges.

Court of Claims.

The claims of private persons against the Federal Government are dealt with by a Court of Claims, which consists of a Chief Justice and four other justices. The Chief Justice receives a salary of $6,500 and the other justices $6,000.

An appeal lies direct from this court to the Supreme Court.

In 1909 a Court of Customs Appeals was established. Court of Customs The first Chief Judge appointed was James Smith, Ex- Appeals. Governor-General of the Philippine Islands. It consists Judges, how appointed. of five judges. The judges are nominated by the President, and their nomination confirmed by the Senate following the same rule laid down by the Constitution in the case of the justices of the Supreme Court.

The Federal courts, already mentioned, were established Federal jurisdiction. for the purpose of dealing with all Federal cases. To ascertain what is meant by a Federal case, reference must be made to section 2 of Article III of the Constitution, which declares that "the judicial power of the United States shall extend to all cases arising under this Constitution; the laws of the United States and treaties made or which shall be made under their authority; to all cases affecting ambassadors, other public ministers and consuls; to all cases of admiralty and maritime jurisdiction; to controversies to which the United States shall be a party; to controversies between two or more States; between a State and citizens of another State; between citizens of different States; between citizens of the same State claiming lands under grants of different States; and between a State or the citizens thereof and foreign States, citizens, or subjects." In consequence of an early decision of the Supreme Court that a State could be sued by a citizen of another State,[1] the eleventh amendment was passed.[2]

The jurisdiction of the Supreme Court in certain class Original jurisdiction. of cases is termed original. This original jurisdiction extends to all cases affecting ambassadors, other public ministers and consuls, and those to which a State is a party.

[1] Chisholm v. Georgia, 2 Dall. (U.S.) 419.
[2] Infra, p. 146.

Appellate
jurisdiction.

In all other cases the Supreme Court exercises appellate jurisdiction both as to law and facts, according to the words of the Constitution, " with such exceptions and under such regulations as the Congress shall make."

Judiciary
Act, 1789.

One of the first works of Congress was to provide for the establishment of the judiciary ; accordingly, an Act to establish the judicial courts of the United States was passed in 1789.

Section 25.

From a constitutional point of view, its most important section, one that led to the fiercest controversy, was section 25. The power of Congress to pass it was assailed by Calhoun and other supporters of State rights, since it reduced the State courts to a position of inferiority enabling the Supreme Court of the United States to exercise an appellate jurisdiction over them, whenever their decisions were in favour of the States. [1]

The section empowered the Supreme Court to re-examine and reverse or affirm by a writ of error any final judgment or decree in any suit in the highest court of law or equity of a State where the judgment or decree involved the question of a validity of a treaty or statute of the United States, or an authority exercised by them when the decision was against the United States.

It also empowered the Supreme Court, in the same way, to deal with a judgment or decree of the highest State court where the validity of a State statute or authority exercised under any State was questioned on the ground of its being repugnant to the Constitution of the United States, if the decision were in favour of their validity.

It further empowered the Supreme Court to interfere, in like manner, when the construction of any clause of the Constitution, or of a treaty or statute of or commission held under the United States, was involved, or the decision was against the title, right, privilege, or exemption specially set up or claimed by either party.

[1] Calhoun on *The Constitution and Government of the United States,* pp. 322-9.

In 1816 the Supreme Court decided in the great con- Martin *v.* stitutional case of Martin *v.* Hunter's Lessees,[1] where the Hunter's Lessees. authority of Congress to enact this section was in question, that Congress had rightfully enacted it, and that the section was supported by the letter of the Constitution. By a subsequent series of decisions the Supreme Court has from time to time fully explained its meaning and the extent of their jurisdiction. They have held that it is not sufficient that the construction of a statute of the United States should be drawn in question, and that the decision should be against the title of the person relying upon the statute. It must appear that the title that was set up depended upon the statute ;[2] they have further held that the court will not decide a hypothetical question, but only a question which has assumed such a form that the judicial power is capable of acting on it, and that this means that the power is capable of acting only where the subject is submitted to it by a party who asserts his rights in the form prescribed by law,[3] and they have also decided that the court has no jurisdiction unless the judgment or decree of the State court be a final judgment or decree ;[4] but the fact that one party is a State and the other a private citizen of the State is not a ground for objecting to the jurisdiction.[5]

It has been necessary to refer specially to section 25 because the Supreme Court based its claim to decide on the constitutionality of all laws, and in the last resort all questions which involved a conflict between the Constitution of the United States, and laws and treaties made in pursuance thereof on the one side and the Constitution and laws of the several States on the other. It may be argued that upon a question as the supremacy of the judicial department finally to interpret the Constitution, it is unfair

---

[1] 1 Wheat (U.S.), 304.
[2] Williams *v.* Norris, 12 Wheat, 117.
[3] Osborn *v.* Bank of the United States, 6 Wheat, 738.
[4] Honston *v.* Moore, 3 Wheat, 433.
[5] Cohens *v.* The State of Virginia, 6 Wheat, 264.

to rely upon the decisions of the judges upholding their power. Story, in his *Commentaries on the Constitution of the United States*,[1] assumes that such an argument may be raised. He quotes from " The Federalist " in support of the intention of the Framers of the Constitution to constitute a court which was ultimately to decide controversies between two jurisdictions—State and National—and also from the speeches of Mr. Webster in the Senate in 1830, and from the works of eminent writers.

The Constitution declares that the Constitutions and Laws of the United States made in pursuance thereof shall be the supreme law of the land, anything in the constitution or laws of any State to the contrary notwithstanding.

" This," said Mr. Webster, " is the first great step. By this the supremacy of the Constitution and Laws of the United States is declared. The people so will it. No State law is to be valid which comes in conflict with the Constitution or any Law of the United States passed in pursuance of it. But who shall decide this question of interference ? To whom lies the last appeal ? This the Constitution itself decides also by declaring that the judicial power shall extend to all cases arising under the Constitution and Laws of the United States. These two provisions cover the whole ground. They are, in truth, the keystone of the Arch. With these it is a Constitution ; without them it is a Confederacy."[2]

The supremacy of the Supreme Court, as arbiter of the Constitution so declared by its own judgment, supported by the pronouncement of "The Federalist," and by the debates in the Conventions which ratified the Constitution acquiesced in also for over one hundred years, must now be regarded as unquestionable.

McCulloch v. Maryland. Following its declaration of its supremacy as interpreter of the Constitution, it decided in 1819 the great Constitutional case of McCulloch v. Maryland. (*Post*, p. 86.) The

---

[1] Story's *Commentaries on the Constitution of the United States*, 4th edition, p. 293.
[2] Quoted, Story's *Commentaries*, 4th edition, p. 292.

facts stated were .that in 1816 Congress passed an Act to incorporate the subscribers to the Bank of the United States. Under the powers of the Act a branch of the Bank was established at Baltimore, in Maryland. In 1818 the Legislature of the State of Maryland passed an Act imposing a tax on all banks or branches of banks in the State of Maryland which were not chartered by the Legislature of Maryland. The highest Judicial Court of Maryland pronounced in favour of the validity of the State legislation. The Supreme Court reversed the State Court's judgment, deciding the following important constitutional points, (1) Some points decided. that Congress had power to incorporate a bank—notwithstanding that it was a corporation; a power to erect corporations not having been amongst the enumerated powers given to Congress. It was suggested in the Convention that such a power should be conferred on Congress when the discussion took place as to what particular powers should be inserted in the Constitution; but, on debate, the proposed clause had been struck out. A particular power to establish a national bank was also proposed; but on its being stated that the question of a bank had been the great bone of contention between the two parties of the State of Pennsylvania from the establishment of its Constitution, it was rejected, as was every other special power, except that of giving copyrights to authors and patents to inventors, the general power of incorporating being whittled down to a shred.[1]

(2) The power of establishing a corporation such as a bank was not a distinct sovereign power, but only a means of carrying into effect other powers which were sovereign.

(3) There was nothing in the Constitution of the United States to exclude incidental or implied powers.

(4) If the end be legitimate and within the scope of the Constitution, all the means which are appropriate, which are plainly adapted to that end, and which are not

[1] Jefferson's *Memoirs* quoted, Elliot's *Debates on the Federal Constitution*, 1787, p. 611.

prohibited, may constitutionally be employed to carry it into effect.

(5) If a certain means to carry into effect any of the powers expressly given by the Constitution to the Government of the Union be an appropriate measure not prohibited by the Constitution, the degree of its necessity is a question of legislative discretion and not of judicial cognizance.

(6) The Act of 1816 to incorporate the subscribers to the Bank of the United States was a law made in pursuance of the Constitution.

(7) The Bank of the United States had constitutionally a right to establish its branches or offices of discount and deposit within any State.

(8) The State within which such branch may be established could not, without violating its Constitution, tax that branch. The Act of the legislature of Maryland was therefore unconstitutional and void.

(9) The State Government had no right to tax any of the constitutional means employed by the Government of the Union to execute its constitutional powers.

Effect of decision on growth of Federal powers.

On carefully examining the various points decided, it will be at once recognised that the legislative powers of Congress were enormously increased, and the powers of the States proportionally diminished by this decision. The original grant of powers to the United States contained certain powers which were called Sovereign powers, yet the court held that there was nothing to exclude their reading in incidental or implied powers as adjuncts to these sovereign powers : that is, they said, that although Congress had no authority expressly granted to it to establish a national bank as a means for carrying into effect the sovereign powers, since the Constitution had expressly conferred on Congress the great powers to levy and collect taxes ; to borrow money ; to regulate commerce ; to declare and conduct a war ; and to raise and support armies, the grant of such powers implied the ordinary means of executing them. Thus said Chief Justice Marshall by way of illustration : " Raising revenue and applying it to national purposes implied the power of conveying money from place to place, as the exigencies of the nation required or of employing the usual means of conveyance." [1]

The Government, which has a right to do an act, and has imposed on it the duty of performing that act, must, according to the dictates of reason, be allowed to select the means, if they were appropriate and not prohibited. A further point was made clear by the Supreme Court that they would not question the degree of necessity of any measure passed by Congress, since that was a matter for political and not for judicial cognizance. The State power was restricted by the declaration that it could not be exercised on the means employed by the Government of the Union. It was said that "a power to tax involved the power to destroy, and the power to destroy might defeat and render useless the power to create." [2] " If the States may tax one instrument employed by the Government in the execution of its powers, they may tax any and every other instrument. They may tax the mail; they may tax the Mint; they may tax patent rights; they may tax judicial process; they may tax all the means employed by the Government to an excess which would defeat all the ends of Government." [3]

The Supreme Court in a later case decided that the question whether a law was void for reason of its repugnancy to the Constitution, ought seldom, if ever, to be decided in the affirmative, except in a doubtful case. " There should be such an opposition between the Constitution and the law that the judge should feel a clear and strong conviction of their incompatibility." [4] *Fletcher v. Peck.*

In construing the extent of the powers expressly given to the United States, they decided that whenever the terms in which a power was granted by the Constitution to Congress, *Exclusive jurisdiction when necessary.*

[1] McCulloch v. State of Maryland, 4 Wheat, 409.
[2] Ibid., p. 431.
[3] M'Culloch v. Maryland, 4 Wheat, 432.
[4] Fletcher v. Peck, 6 Cranch 87, 131.

or whenever the nature of the power itself required that it should be exercised exclusively by Congress, the subject was as completely taken away from the State Legislatures as if they had been expressly forbidden to act on it ;[1] thereby asserting their rights to imply powers of prohibition on certain State legislation with the consequent result of nullifying State Acts.

Federal
prohibits
State
jurisdiction.

By these decisions and many others of the highest import-ance the Constitution began to assume shape and form. The tendency of the Supreme Court, during the chief justice-ship of Marshall, was to decide almost universally in favour of national as against State contentions, with the result that on his death in 1835 the Constitution was a wonderful working instrument. An American lawyer who lived during the years 1801 to 1835, as each new judgment of the Supreme Court was given, must have felt like a mountaineer, who ascends the heights to see with each fresh step a widening landscape unfolded beneath him. Marshall, by common repute, was the greatest of American judges ; he aimed at making the Constitution an instrument in every way fitted for the purpose of National government, and he succeeded in his aim. He was, by reason of his peculiar position, more than a judge called upon to interpret a written document according to the ordinary canons of construction. He was a law-giver. Many of the powers whose existence he declared belonged to the National Government were implied powers or invented. For example, if the case of the National Bank (McCulloch v. Maryland) is examined critically, it will be seen that there was no apparent reason why the State of Maryland should not have possessed the power to tax a Federal bank. National and State powers of taxation under the Constitution were concurrent. Parliamentary and Local Taxation in England are exercised upon the same subject-matter without proving mutually destructive. A house, for instance, may be rated for local purposes, but it will yet bear the additional burden of the inhabited house duty, which is a Government tax. A power to tax may be a

Chief
Justice
Marshall.

[1] Sturges v. Crowninshield, 4 Wheat, p. 193.

power to destroy ; but common sense suggests that such a power would not be carried to extremes. If it were, it would defeat the very objects it was imposed for—the raising of revenue. Marshall knew, however, that the States probably would destroy the branches of the National Bank by taxation, so great was their hostility towards its establishment. Expediency suggested the invention of an implied power which had not been expressly prohibited by the Constitution. Much of the greatness of Marshall's judgments consisted in the reasoning with which expediency was clothed. In the doctrine of implied powers he was able to draw on the underlying reservation of power in the Constitution to the whole of the people of the United States. If it were not clear whether a power belonged either to the National Government or the States, to whom should it belong ? If its possession were desirable for the National Government, then as the people willed the Constitution, it was obvious that they meant that the Constitution should be made an effective instrument, and the power belonged to the National Government.

The Constitution had declared that if a power were not delegated to the United States nor prohibited by it to the States, the power was reserved to the States respectively or the people. It was fruitless, therefore, for the States to argue that any particular power was not delegated in terms to the United States, and, therefore, was a State power. The words of the Constitution were not expressly delegated, but delegated, therefore, the powers might be powers impliedly delegated. If they were powers impliedly delegated, then the implication of a grant to the United States might be inferred from the existence of other powers, which were expressly granted, and from the supplementary grant of power to the United States to " carry into execution laws which were necessary and proper to any of the powers expressly delegated. It has been said that the Constitution of the United States has largely been invented ; if this is true, it perhaps explains the unique position that Marshall holds in public estimation as the maker of the Constitution.

There is no English judge who has occupied a similar
position. It has been suggested somewhat disparagingly
that had the Judicial Committee of the Privy Council
construed the American Constitution as they have the
Canadian Constitution, that the result would have been
very different. It is impossible to say that this is a just
criticism since the Judicial Committee have construed an
entirely different constitution, and canons applicable to the
one are not applicable to the other.[1]

Chief Justice
Taney.
Chief Justice Taney succeeded Marshall in 1836, and died
in 1874. In his hands there was a tendency to restrict the
national powers : an anti-slavery man, it was his ill-
fortune to give the greatest offence by his decision in the
Dred Scott case.

It would be wearisome if it were possible to even mention,
let alone discuss, all the stately procession of constitutional
cases that have filled innumerable volumes of American
Law Reports, and judgments that have elucidated with
ample detail the principles enunciated by Marshall. Some
of these cases will be found referred to elsewhere. Outside
its own province the Judiciary will not travel, it confines
itself strictly to its sphere, and declines to adjudicate on
political questions. It will not pronounce opinions on
hypothetical cases, but will only decide cases where a
definite issue has been presented to it by parties in litigation.
The State courts follow Federal decisions when a Federal
point arises in a case before them. The Supreme Court
and Federal courts likewise follow by judicial comity State
decisions when a point of State law arises in a Federal case.

[1] Bryce, *The American Commonwealth.* New Edition, Vol. I, p. 387.
See footnote.

CHAPTER VIII

POWERS OF LEGISLATION

THE Constitution only confers upon Congress certain powers *Powers of legislation.* of legislation. All other powers belong to the State Legislatures. Whether a power belongs to the one or other sphere has often proved a difficult question that has led to considerable controversy. On the wide field of legislation claims have met in opposition ; and the story of the development of the American Constitution is, therefore, largely made up of the story of disputes peacefully decided by the Judiciary.

Legislation takes the form of Acts of Congress. These *Acts of Congress.* are first introduced as Bills, but the distinction that exists in the British Parliament of Government Bills and private Members' Bills is unknown. All Bills are private in this sense that they are introduced by private members. A distinction, however, does exist, as in the Parliament of the United Kingdom, between public Acts and private Acts. When a Bill becomes an Act, the enacting power is solely the power of the Legislature. It is thus expressed : " Be *Legislative form.* it enacted by the Senate and House of Representatives of the United States of America in Congress assembled." The assent of the President is denoted by the words "approved," with the date of his approval. A joint resolu- *Form of joint resolution.* tion of the two Houses takes the form : " Resolved by the Senate and House of Representatives of the United States of America in Congress assembled."

To render legislation valid, it must be within the constitutional power of Congress. If its authority is doubtful, it can be questioned in the Supreme Court. The burden of proof, however, rests upon the party challenging its constitutionality. The longer it remains unchallenged, the greater the presumption of its validity.

The express powers of legislation conferred upon *Express powers.*

89

Congress were not numerous. Still, they have, till recent years, on the whole, been sufficient for the purposes of the Union, owing in a large measure to the wide construction that has been placed upon them.

Powers of taxation. With reference to taxation, Congress was declared to have the power " to levy and collect taxes, duties, imports, and excises ; to pay the debts and to provide for the common defence and welfare of the United States " ; but " all duties, imposts, and excises were required to be uniform throughout the United States."

The construction of this power led to considerable discussion. It was asked, Were two powers hereby granted or one ? Did Congress possess a power to levy and collect taxes, duties, imposts, and excises, and also possess the separate power to provide for the common defence and welfare of the United States ; or was the clause to be construed as a power granted to Congress *in order* to provide for the common defence and welfare of the United States. The latter construction was adopted, the principal reason being that if there were two powers granted to Congress, they would be so wide as to render any subsequent enumeration of powers useless or embarrassing.

Limitations of power. The taxing power is, therefore, considered as limited to objects of common defence or general welfare, and is not treated as a general unqualified power that would extend to matters wholly extraneous to the common defence and welfare.

The taxing power is, moreover, not exclusive, that is to say, it does not exclude the State from taxing, since the Constitution contains no clause or sentence which prohibited the State from exercising rights of taxation. But the States are forbidden to lay any imposts or duties on imports or exports without the consent of Congress, except such as are absolutely necessary for executing their inspection laws. The restriction impliedly admits that if it were absent the States would possess the power which is thus excluded. The prohibition contains the further admission that as to other taxes the State power of taxation remains unimpaired. The rule of construction adopted was that a negation of one thing was an affirmance of another : in legal phraseology, it was termed a negative pregnant.

It may be said that if both Congress and the State legislatures could tax the same subject-matter, the respective powers might be used so as to be mutually destructive, since a power to tax is necessarily a power to destroy. The Constitution had not expressly defined the respective limits of national and State taxation. The answer given by the Supreme Court was that the power from its nature must be used judiciously. What object could there be in a taxation of mutual destructiveness. Taxation is primarily levied for the purpose of revenue ; a tax, therefore, which fails in this object is worthless. *Federal and State taxation.*

Nevertheless, with respect to taxation in the form of Custom dues the primary object avowed is subordinate to the political object of protection against foreign competition.

" Without the possession of a great power of taxation," says Dr. Story, " the Constitution would have long since, like the Confederation, have dwindled down to an empty pageant. It would have become an unreal mockery, deluding our hopes and exciting our fear. It would have flitted before us for a moment with a pale, ineffectual light, and then have departed for ever to the land of shadows." *Dr. Story on taxing power.*

The power to levy and collect taxes was qualified by the now repealed portion of Article 1, which directed that representation and direct taxes should be apportioned among the several States according to their respective numbers, and by the fourth Clause of section 9 of the Constitution, which declared that no capitation or other direct tax should be laid, unless in proportion to the Census ; the direction as to apportionment led to what is known as the rule of *apportionment,* which applied to the raising of direct taxation. It might be asked what does the Constitution mean by the expression " direct taxation " ? The imposition of Poll taxes is direct taxation ; so are taxes on lands, houses, and other permanent real estate ;[1] many *Limitation by direction as to apportionment.* *Rule of apportionment.*

[1] Springer v. The United States, 102, U.S., 586.

other taxes might be so ; the test applied is to examine whether the tax is capable of apportionment among the States. The rule adopted was to prevent inequalities and preferences of one State over another by Congress.

Land Taxes. Direct taxes on land have not often been resorted to by Congress, owing to the difficulties and expense attendant upon their collection. Most of the Federal taxation is indirect, and is raised chiefly by duties of customs and excise. At one time it was argued that such duties could be levied legally for the purposes of revenue only, and not for the protection of industries ; the argument, however, was not accepted. It was decided that should any income be **Protective taxes.** derived from the levy, the fact that an incidental protection was given to home industries would not invalidate the tax. All taxes, it was said, may be laid with reference to their effects upon the prosperity of the people and the welfare of the country ; their validity cannot be determined by the insignificance of their money returns. The principle of non-interference with the political motives that imposed taxation has been carried so far that it has been decided that a tax was good when the levy resulted in no returns whatever. It is now not even competent to assail the motives of Congress by showing that the levy was made not for revenue purposes, but to annihilate the subject of the levy by imposing a burden upon it which it could not bear. [1]

The rule of uniformity. All taxes, other than direct taxes, such as duties, imposts, and excises are subject to the *rule of uniformity*. The levy must be uniform throughout the United States ; but no tax or duty may be laid on articles exported from any State, and no preference may be given by any regulation of commerce or revenue to the parts of one State over another, and no vessel bound to or from one State must be obliged to enter clear or pay duties in another. It would seem obvious that a Federal Government could not tax otherwise than uniformly without destroying the Union by the jealousies engendered by discriminating preferences.

[1] National Bank *v.* United States 101, U.S. 1.

The States, it has already been stated (*ante,* p. 90), have State powers.
no power, except with the consent of Congress, to lay any
imposts or duties on imports or exports, except such as are
absolutely necessary for executing inspection laws, nor can
they obtain any advantage by this limited power given
them, since the net produce of all duties and imposts laid
by any State on imports and exports must be for the use
of the United States Treasury. All State laws that contravene this rule are subject to the revision and control of
Congress.

" Inspection laws " are laws passed to improve the quality Inspection laws.
of goods either for domestic use or export ; and like laws
respecting quarantine, health roads, and internal commerce
are purely within the sphere of State legislation.

There is a further implied prohibition directed against the Implied prohibition
States, no State by taxation or otherwise may retard or on State taxation.
impede or in any manner control the operations of Constitutional laws enacted by Congress for the purpose of carrying
into execution the powers of the Federal Government. A
similar power has been implied exempting State agencies
from Federal taxation.

The borrowing power of the Federal Government comes Borrowing powers
within this rule, and funds raised for national purposes are within prohibition.
consequently exempted from State taxation.

Bills for raising revenue must originate in the House of Revenue bills must
Representatives, but the Senate may propose or concur rise in Senate.
with amendments as in other Bills. Powers of Senate.

No money may be drawn from the Treasury, but in con- Money drawn from
sequence of appropriations made by law ; and a regular Treasury under
statement and account of the receipts and expenditures of Appropriation laws.
all public money must be published from time to time.

The practice is for the Secretary of the Treasury to send Budget.
once a year to Congress a report of the national income and
expenditure, with a statement of the condition of the
National Debt and an annual letter enclosing the estimates
for the public services. An Act, dated Sept., 1789, established that the Secretary of the Treasury should make his
report or give information to the two Chambers in person

or by writing. Owing to the inherent fear of the Chambers of the formation of an aristocratic ministerial group within the Chambers, this communication is made not in person but in writing. In brief neither the President nor his Secretaries, nor any representative of the Executive has any representation in the debates of either Chamber. The annual letter is what is known in the United Kingdom as the budget. Each State Department is required to furnish its estimate of expenditure and revenue (if any) for presentation to Congress through the Treasury, but there is no single Budget discussed as in England, this is apparently due to the large local taxing powers of the States.

Reference to Committee. The Secretary's report is referred to a Committee of Ways and Means, which prepares and reports upon the requisite Bills for imposing or continuing duties. The *Presidential powers.* President is entitled to examine the estimates, and he is also entitled to make recommendations.

Practice. The proposed appropriation Bills are brought before the House, and the amounts suggested are often increased. The Bills are next referred to the Senate, which, in its turn, refers them to two committees, one of which deals with appropriations and the other with supplies. They are then brought before the Senate, which is entitled to amend them. Should these amendments be acquiesced in, the Bills pass Congress; but if not, a Conference Committee of both Houses generally arranges a compromise.

Committees. The spending Committees and the appropriation Committees are different bodies; consequently, there is no relation between the amount proposed to be raised and the contemplated expenditure, with the result that a Deficiency Bill is often required to make good the grants to meet the needs of departments appropriations to which have been insufficient.

Commerce power. One of the most interesting powers is the Federal power over commerce. The power was conferred on Congress by the Constitution in the following terms: " To regulate commerce with foreign nations and among the several States and with the Indian tribes." In 1824 this power was

held to be wide enough to cover legislation regulating navigation.   This decision was arrived at by the Supreme Court
because the Constitution had declared that no preference   Reason why
should be given by any regulation of commerce or revenue   implied.
to the ports of one State over those of another, nor should
vessels bound to or from one State be obliged to enter
clear or pay duties in another. Although not in terms
expressed, a power to legislate over navigation was held to be
implied. As there were plain inhibitions to the exercise
of the power in a particular way, it was decided that this
was proof that those who made the exceptions and prescribed these inhibitions understood the power to which
they applied as being granted.[1]

Commerce is more than traffic : it is intercourse. The Nature of
word is apt to describe the commercial intercourse between commerce.
nations and parts of nations in all its branches, and is
regulated by prescribing rules for carrying on that
intercourse.

The power of Congress to legislate on commerce com- Extent of
prehends navigation within the limits of every State in the powers.
Union, so far as that navigation may be in any manner
connected with foreign nations, or among the several States,
or with the Indian tribes.

It was not decided that a State was excluded from the When State
exercise of a similar power, but any right a State might power
possess was held lost when Federal legislation dealt with concurrent.
the same subject-matter. In 1851 the Supreme Court
decided that the commercial power was partly exclusive
and partly concurrent, that is to say, in matters admitting of
uniformity of regulation and requiring national action, the
commercial power was exclusive, but that in many local
matters that admitted of a variety of treatment the
concurrent action of the States was admissible.[2]

In 1872 it was decided that a State tax on freight trans- Tax on freight
ported from State to State was bad, since freight was the transported
reward for the transportation of the subjects of commerce, from State
to State.

[1] Gibbons v. Ogden, 9 Wheat, 1, 189-191. *Ibid.*, 196-197.
[2] Cooley v. Port Wardens, 12 How, 299.

whether by land or water, and was a constituent of commerce ;[1] the power was, therefore, a Federal power.

Growth of commerce power.

The commerce power was not confined to the instrumentalities of commerce, as they were known and used when the Constitution was adopted : " It keeps pace with the progress of the country, and adapts itself to the new developments of times and circumstances. It extended from the horse with its rider to the stage-coach, from the sailing vessel to the steamboat, from the coach and the steamboat to the railroad, and from the railroad to the telegraph, as these new agencies are successfully brought into use to meet the demands of increasing populations and wealth."[2]

Restraint of trade.

Congress under its commerce power may forbid contracts and combinations between private individuals in restraint of trade.[3] Legislation against trusts is an instance. The law, however, can be evaded. (*Post*, p. 105.)

Powers of Congress.

The commerce power entitles Congress to authorise persons to construct railroads across the States and territories of the Union.[4] It is so wide and important that it has been " employed for the purpose of revenue : sometimes for the purpose of prohibition, sometimes for the purpose of retaliation and commercial reciprocity ; sometimes to lay embargoes ; sometimes to encourage domestic navigation, and the shipping and the mercantile interest, by bounties, by discriminating duties and by special preferences and privileges ; and sometimes to regulate intercourse with a view to mere political objects, such as to repel aggressors, increase the pressure of war, or vindicate the rights of neutral sovereignty.[5]

Inter-State Commerce Commission Court.

Under and by virtue of the commerce power, an Inter-State Commerce Commission Court was established in 1887. The Act establishing it has been amended on several

[1] The Reading Railroad Co. *v.* Pennsylvania, 15 Wall (U.S.), 232.
[2] Pensacola Telegraph Co. *v.* Western Union Telegraph Co., 96, U.S. 1 (1877).
[3] Addystone Pipe and Steel Co. *v.* United States, 175, U.S., 211.
[4] California *v.* Central Pacific Railway Co., 127, U.S., 1.
[5] Story's *Commentaries*, p. 1061.

occasions. No power to establish such a court had been given by the Constitution.

This court is an administrative body, to supervise the execution and prevent the violation of laws relating to inter-State and foreign commerce. It can investigate and prosecute, but cannot adjudicate. The court has never exercised its authority to fix passenger or freight rates. It can refuse to allow rates to be advanced, but cannot say what rates shall be.

A power was given to Congress to establish an uniform rule of naturalisation and uniform laws on the subject of bankruptcy. Naturalisation is, by its terms, an exclusive power; but since the rule must be uniform, although the States individually have a concurrent authority, they cannot exercise their jurisdiction to contravene the rules laid down by Congress. A State cannot exclude a citizen who has been adopted by the United States but they can adopt him upon easier terms than those imposed by Congress.[1] The bankruptcy power is not exclusive.[2] The several States have power to legislate on the subjects of bankrupt and insolvent laws, subject, however, to the authority conferred upon Congress to adopt an uniform system of bankruptcy. When Congress exercises such an authority, however, it is paramount, and State legislation in conflict must give way. *Naturalisation and bankruptcy.*

An historical distinction exists between bankruptcy and insolvency laws. The former were passed for the protection of creditors against insolvent and fraudulent traders; the latter for the protection of ordinary private debtors— poor and distressed, but honest. *Distinction between bankruptcy and insolvency.*

Congress has power to coin money, regulate the value thereof and of foreign coin, and fix the standard of weights and measures. It possesses under this power, as well as under the commerce power, authority to legislate for the punishment of persons bringing counterfeit coin into the *Coinage, Tonnage, and Weights and Measures.*

---

[1] Collett v. Collett, 2 Dall., 294.
[2] Tua v. Carriere, 117, U.S. 201. Sturges v. Crowninshields, 4 Wheat, 122.

United States with the intention of passing it, and to punish persons for passing, altering, publishing, or selling such false or counterfeit com.[1]

It also possesses power to legislate for the offence of counterfeiting the securities and current coin of the United States.

Power of Congress over the postal service was conferred in the following terms : " The Congress shall have power to establish post offices and post roads."

Postal service, extent of power.

The power of Congress over the postal service may be classed with, but not under, the power to regulate commerce and Foreign Nations and among the several States because the power extends to postal communications within a single State, as well as among the States. Congress has claimed the power to establish a government monopoly of the postal business over all government postal routes ; and since every route may be declared a government postal route, the monopoly is complete at the option of Congress. Under this power all mail operations are regulated, postmasters appointed and their duties prescribed, mail contracts made, and carriers of mails regulated.[2] Congress can completely regulate the postal service, etc.; but if any matters are excluded Congress cannot forbid their transportation by other means so as to interfere with the freedom of the powers.[3]

The right to carry the mail.

From the postal power has been inferred the right to carry the mail and to punish those who rob it.

Promotion of Science and Art.

Judiciary.

Congress has power " to promote the progress of science and useful arts by securing for a limited time to authors and inventors the exclusive right to their respective writings and discoveries " ; to constitute tribunals inferior to the Supreme Court. The latter power has been exercised in the creation of inferior tribunals. The nature of these was dealt with when the judicial system of the United States was explained. (*Ante*, p. 77.)

[1] The United States *v.* Marigold, 9 How, 560.
[2] Sturtevants *v.* City of Alton 3, M'Lean, 393.
[3] *Ex parte* Jackson, 96, U.S., 727.

A series of important powers follow in the enumeration Piracies and felonies on the high seas. of the powers of Congress in the Constitution. A power was given to define and punish piracies and felonies committed on the high seas and offences against the law of nations. The power seems closely allied to the commerce power : " The ' high seas ' may be taken to mean that part of the Meaning of " high seas." ocean which washes the sea coast, and is without the body of any county according to the common law ; and so far as regards foreign nations, any waters on their sea coasts below land water-mark." [1]

A power was also granted to declare war, grant letters of Power to declare war. marque and reprisal, and make rules concerning captures on land and water. This power has been exercised in authorising general hostilities, as in the war with Great Britain in 1812, when Congress passed an Act that " war be Legislative authority. and hereby is declared to exist between the United Kingdom of Great Britain and Ireland, and the dependencies thereof, and the United States of America and their territories." The power is an exclusively Federal one, since the States were Nature of power. prohibited from engaging in war unless actually invaded, or in such imminent danger as would not brook of delay.

The States are also forbidden from granting letters of marque.

Incidental to the power of declaring war is the comple- Power to raise armies. mentary power to raise and support armies. The power is unlimited, and necessarily so, since it is impossible to foresee what the national requirements would be should war exist. A limitation in practice does occur, since there can be no appropriation of money for the raising and support of armies for a longer term than two years.

In England, Parliament, by the Bill of Rights in 1688, The Bill of Rights. prohibited the keeping of standing armies in the Kingdom without the consent of Parliament ; an annual appropriation has since been requisite instead of the biennial appropriation that Congress has been empowered to make. In practice, however, Congress makes an appropriation only for the current year.

[1] Story, *Constitution of the United States*, 5 Ed., Vol. 2, pp. 89-90.

Conscription.   The question whether the United States Army would be raised by conscription was formerly doubted. Conscription, however, became imperative during the war of secession, and was resorted to by the Southern States as well as by the Northern, and the power may be considered to exist. Under the war power, President Lincoln proclaimed the freedom of the slaves in States held by the Confederacy, and subsequently the proclamation was held to be a valid

Establishment of Provisional Government. executive Act ;[1] so was the appointment of a provisional Government over an insurgent State, and the establishment of courts by military authority within insurrectionary districts occupied by the Army—

Navy.   " The power to provide and maintain a Navy is a most important one," and its necessity might have been imagined to have been readily admitted at the time of the framing of the Constitution. The Southern States, however, were lukewarm, and its advantages were not so apparent as they were to the seaboard States. A Navy promised to be a burden without adequate compensating benefits. Blackstone said : " The Royal Navy of England hath ever been its greatest defence and ornament. It is its ancient and natural strength ; the floating bulwark of the island ; an Army, from which, however, strong and powerful, no danger can be appprehended from liberty." The gallantry of the United States seamen in the naval war with Great Britain justified the Navy in the eyes of many who had protested against this grant of power. At the present moment they are few who would be found to object to its existence.

Army and Navy regulations.]   A power to make rules for the government and regulation of the land and naval forces seems consequential upon the former grants of power to make war, raise armies, and provide and maintain a Navy. The power is an exclusive one; with that jealous regard that the Constitution has of the freedom of the individual it is not one that the people of the United States would have left to the executive.

Insurrections and Invasions.   The duty of common defence which may involve the

[1] Slabach v. Cushman 12 Fla, 272 ; Texas v. White 7 Wall, 200. Mechanics' Bank v. Union Bank, 22, Wall, 276.

putting down of insurrections and repelling invasions was recognised in the grant of an express power " to provide for calling forth the Militia to execute the laws of the Union, suppress insurrections, and repel invasions, also in the grant of a power to provide for organising, arming, disciplining the Militia and for governing such part of them as might be employed in the service of the States ; reserving to the States respectively the appointment of officers and the authority of training the Militia according to the discipline prescribed by Congress." These powers were far in advance of those that had been given to the United States in Congress under the Confederation. The inadequacy of the powers then conferred must have been present to the minds of the leading American statesmen during the meetings of the Convention.

The grant of the power, however, led to strong objections on behalf of the States.

The power of judging whether an exigency exists requiring the calling out of the Militia is vested by statute in the President.[1] Whether it always vested in him was at one time a matter of controversy. Two of the State Governors in 1794 contended that the Governors of States to whom the President issued orders for the calling forth of the Militia had a right to judge for themselves of the necessity. *President judge of exigency.*

A judgment of the Supreme Court settled the matter by deciding that the President was the sole judge of the necessity, and his judgment was binding upon all persons. The nature of the power and its objects requiring action upon emergencies justified the Act of Congress.[2]

The President, it has already been stated, is only commander-in-chief of the Militia when it is in actual service. *President Commander of Militia when in actual service.*

The power of Congress to exercise exclusive jurisdiction over the seat of Government and other ceded places will be found dealt with elsewhere. (*Post*, p. 118.) *Seat of Government.*

The remaining power of Congress enables it to make all laws which shall be necessary and proper for carrying into *Necessary laws for execution of powers.*

---

[1] Act of 1795, Ch. 101.
[2] Luther *v*. Borden, 7 How. 1.

execution the foregoing powers, and all other powers vested by the Constitution in the Government of the United States or in any department or officer thereof.

Dr. Story[1] says of this power: "Few powers of the Government were at the time of the adoption of the Constitution assailed with more severe invective and more declamatory intemperance than this. And it has ever since been made a theme of constant attack and extravagant jealousy. Yet it is difficult to perceive the grounds upon which it can be maintained or the logic by which it can be reasoned out. It is only declaratory of a truth which would have resulted by necessary and unavoidable implication from the very act of establishing a national Government and vesting it with certain powers. What is a power but the ability or faculty of doing a thing? What is the ability to do a thing but the power of employing the means necessary to its execution? What is a legislative power but the power of making laws? What is the power, for instance, of levying and collecting taxes but a legislative power or a power to make laws to levy and collect taxes? What are the proper means of executing such a power but necessary and proper laws? In truth, the constitutional operation of the Government would be precisely the same if the clause were obliterated, as if it were repeated in every article."

The meaning of the words "necessary and proper" have been the subject of much debate, if they do not enlarge, they do not restrain the powers of Congress or impair the right of the Legislature to exercise its best judgment in the selection of measures to carry into execution the constitutional powers of the National Government. "Let the end be legitimate; let it be within the scope of the Constitution; and all means are appropriate which are plainly adapted to that end, and which are not prohibited but are consistent with the letter of the spirit of the instrument, are constitutional."[2]

Dr. Story on nature of power.

Meaning of "necessary and proper."

[1] Story on *The Constitution of the United States*, 5th edition, chapter xxiv, p. 137.
[2] M'Culloch *v.* Maryland, 4 Wheat, 423.

Incidental and necessary powers are powers which must be implied from one or the other of the enumerated powers.

Thus the power to establish a national bank (since a Corporations. bank is a corporation) can only be deduced from a power to create a corporation. No such power was expressly given by the Constitution ; yet such a power was held to be implied ; a power to erect a corporation was not given by the Constitution, but it was said a corporation is but a means to an end, and the power to erect it is or may be an implied and incidental power.

" A corporation is never the end for which other powers are exercised, but a means by which other objects are accomplished. No contributions are made to charity for the sake of an incorporation, but a corporation is created to administer the charity. No seminary of learning is instituted in order to be incorporated, but the corporate character is conferred to subserve the purposes of education. No city was ever built with the sole object of being incorporated ; but it is incorporated as affording the best means of being well governed. So a mercantile company is formed with a certain capital for carrying on a particular branch of business. Here the business to be prosecuted is the end ; the association, in order to form the requisite capital, is the primary means. If an incorporation is added to the association, it only gives a new quality, an artificial capacity which enables it to prosecute the business with more convenience and safety. In truth, the power of creating a corporation is never used for its own sake, but for the purpose of effecting something else. So that there is not a shadow of reason to say that it may not pass as an incident to powers expressly given as a mode of executing them."[1]

The power to establish a national bank was held to be National Bank. deducible from the great powers of collecting taxes, borrowing money, regulating trade between the States, and raising the naval and military forces. Acquisition

Under the implied powers, alleged to be incidental to the of territory, Louisiana.

[1] M'Culloch v. Maryland, 4 Wheat, 316, 411 ; Hamilton on Bank, 1 Hamilton's Works, pp. 152, 153.

National sovereignty, Louisiana was acquired in **1803**, since the action is part of the implied power of every sovereign State of acquiring territory by conquest or by purchase. No specific power was given by the Constitution, for none was needed.

Plenary powers.

To all the express powers of Congress the fullest meanings are given : they are what are known as plenary powers. Once an implied power is recognised as existing, the same rule of construction is adopted.

There are certain prohibitions and limitations on the powers of Congress. These have already been referred to.[1]

Legislation.

The enumeration of the main powers of Congress might lead to the belief that legislation could only be carried out within a narrow sphere, but the contrary has been the case. Each year since the establishment of Congress there has been a steady output of legislation. In fact, the appetite for legislation has been insatiable. Innumerable Bills, however, that have been introduced have never proceeded further than the stage of discussion ; they have been dropped, or if they have passed Congress the President's veto has been exercised to destroy them. The curse of over-legislation has not been felt since the national checks of the Constitution have prevented it.

Criticism on powers.

In weighing the powers of the National Government, some criticism as to their sufficiency is permissible. In recent years further powers have been asked for. Power over Companies, for instance. Every State must give full

Company law.

faith and credit to the laws of another State. Should a company be incorporated in one State, it may carry on business in another where company laws are entirely different. A company in one State may be prohibited from carrying on business unless its capital is fully subscribed, whilst another State may allow a company incorporated under its laws to carry on business with little or no capital. A company in the latter State is permitted to carry on business in the State whose State laws deny a like power to companies incorporated under its laws. It is extremely

[1] *Ante,* p. 83.

difficult for investors under these circumstances to ascertain the solvency or responsibility of a joint-stock company. Again, in some States, shares of a company are taxable, but in others they are not. Some States insist that a local office shall be kept by foreign companies, and also an agent authorised to accept legal process. In other States no such law exists, consequently a person beginning an action against a company is often driven to the expense of suing in the State where the company is incorporated. Similar difficulties, however, have arisen in Canada.

The power to deal with combinations and trusts is another instance in which some may think that the Federal power is insufficient. There is legislation directed against trusts, but it is not completely effective. The Supreme Court have decided that manufacturing is not commerce. Consequently, it has been possible to establish combinations by rival manufacturing companies carrying on business in different States to agree not to sell in other States where their rivals carry on business. A manufacturing firm in Pennsylvania, for instance, may agree not to sell its manufactures in New Jersey, in consideration of a manufacturing company in New Jersey agreeing not to sell like manufactures in Pennsylvania. The State power in both cases is powerless to prevent such a combination. The States in both cases are helpless against a complete monopoly. The States cannot interfere, because the matter is one of inter-State commerce and outside their jurisdiction; the Federal Government is powerless also. The Sherman Act would only be partially effective to meet such a case. *Combinations and Trusts.*

There are many other instances of a minor character where it might be urged that it would be advantageous to increase the national powers or create greater uniformity in State laws.

CHAPTER IX

THE STATES

PRIOR to the Declaration of Independence none of the colonies were strictly sovereign States in the sense in which the
term sovereign is applied to States. It has been already
stated that they were all originally settled under and
subject to the British Crown. Their powers and authorities
were derived from and limited by their charters and by
legislation of the British Parliament, which controlled their
legislation by prohibiting them from making laws repugnant
or contrary to those of England. "They could make no
treaty, declare no war, send no ambassadors, regulate no
intercourse or commerce, nor in other shape act as sovereigns
in the negotiations usual between independent states. In
respect to each other they stood in the common relation of
British subjects; the legislation of neither could be controlled by any other, but there was a common subjection
to the British Crown."[1]

If the Colonies were in any sense sovereign it was because
they exercised within a circumscribed orbit some of the
usual powers of sovereignty.

"The Declaration of Independence was the United Act
of all the Colonies, not done by the States' Governments,
nor by persons chosen by them, but was emphatically the
Act of the whole people of the United Colonies by the
instrumentality of their representatives chosen for that
among other purposes."[2]

Dr. Story considered that the States at no time were
sovereign in the full sense in which sovereignty may be used
as applied to States. Since even prior to the Articles of
Confederation, which were not signed until 1778, and not

[1] Story on *The Constitution of the United States*, 5th edition, Vol. I
pp. 115, 3.
[2] 2 Dall, 476, 471.

ratified so as to bind all the States until 1781, Congress had assumed the exercise of some of the highest functions of sovereignty; they had organised the national defence, raised an army, borrowed money and authorised the captures and condemnation of prizes in prize courts.

The people of each State framed its constitution and, like Constitutions framed by the people. the national Constitution, each State constitution is paramount over its executive, legislative, and judicial power. Nearly all the State constitutions declare " that the people ordain and establish it," and where this language is not used it may be considered as implied.

The Constitution is the fundamental law and basis of Constitution fundamental law. government of the State, and has been defined as " that body of rules and maxims with which the powers of sovereignty are habitually exercised." [1]

When the Constitution of the United States was ratified thirteen separate State constitutions existed. Each State was in the exercise of all its powers of government.

Besides the fundamental law of the Constitution, each The common law. State possessed its common law, which it had transplanted from England.

" It was the peculiar excellence of the common law of Excellence of common law of England. England," says Judge Cooley, " that it recognised the worth, and sought especially to protect the rights and privileges of the individual man. Its maxims were those of a sturdy and independent race accustomed to an unusual degree to freedom of thought and action, and to a share in the administration of public affairs; and arbitrary power and uncontrolled authority were not recognised in its principles. Awe surrounded and majesty clothed the King, but the humblest subject might shut the door of his cottage against him, and defend from intrusion that privacy which was as sacred as the kingly prerogatives." [2]

All the English common law, however, was not adopted. How far adopted. The colonists brought with them only that portion applicable to their condition. It could not be expected that

---

[1] Cooley, *Constitutional Limitations*, 6th edition, p. 4.
[2] *Ibid.*, p. 33.

men, many of whom had fled to escape the hardship of laws which their conscience did not approve should adopt it all. A portion they discarded and instead enacted laws not contrary to the laws affecting the general rights of Englishmen, but suitable to their condition. When the colonists became independent, " the laws which governed them consisted first of the common law of England, so far as they had tacitly adopted it as suited to their condition ; second, of the **The amended common law.** statutes of England or Great Britain, amendatory of the common law which they had in like manner adopted ; and third, of the colonial statutes. The first and second constituted the American common law, and by this in great part are rights adjudged and wrongs redressed in the American States to this day." [1]

Amendment of States' Constitution. The States possess full power to alter their Constitutions. A State Constitution, therefore, can be amended in one of two ways, either by the people since it was originally framed by them, or in the mode prescribed by the States' Constitution itself. Since it is impossible for all the people to meet and make amendments, amendments must be prepared and considered by some body of representatives chosen for the purpose. Unless such a body is specially clothed with the power it cannot take definitive action without submitting the amendment or revisions to the people : " The constitutional convention or conventions elected to make amendments is the representative of sovereignty only in a very qualified sense, and for the specific purpose and with the **Must be enacted by people.** restricted authority to put in proper form the questions of amendment upon which the people are to pass judgment ; the changes from the fundamental laws of the States must be enacted by the people themselves. . . ."

Distinction between Federal and State Governments. The distinction between the Government of the United States and that of the States may be stated as follows : " The Government of the United States is one of enumerated powers ; the national Constitution is the instrument which specifies them and in which authority should be found for the exercise of any power which the National

[1] Cooley, *Constitutional Limitations*, 6th edition, p. 37.

Government assumes to possess. In this respect it differs from the Constitutions of the several States which are not grants of power to the States, but which themselves apportion and impose restriction upon the powers which the States inherently possess.

The Constitutions of the States are of various kinds, but all now contain provisions for their amendment. The power, however, of amendment is limited by the National Constitution in some particulars. No State may abolish the republican form of government. "As long as existing republican forms are continued by the States they are guaranteed by the Federal Constitution. Whenever the States may choose to substitute other republican forms they have a right to do so and claim the Federal guaranty for the latter. The only restriction imposed on them is that they shall not exchange republican for anti-republican constitutions." [1] *Differences in States' Constitutions, restrictions in amendment.*

No State may provide titles of nobility, and there are additional limitations. *Titles of nobility.*

Subject, however, to the foregoing principles and limitations, each State must judge for itself what its constitution is to be and how the powers of government are to be apportioned. *State judge of its own Constitution.*

In the original Constitutions of the thirteen States, although a triple division of the powers of Government was regarded as an axiomatic principle to be followed, the several departments of power were not kept absolutely distinct. *Triple division of powers. Constitution of New Hampshire.*

"New Hampshire," said Madison in "The Federalist," "whose constitution was the last formed, declared that the legislative, executive, and judiciary powers ought to be kept as separate from and independent of each other as the nature of free government will admit." Her constitution mixed these departments in many respects.

To prevent an encroachment on any of the separate branches of her Government, Pennsylvania created a Council of Censors, who first assembled in the years 1783–1784. It *Pennsylvania.*

[1] "The Federalist," No. xliii.

Council of
Censors.
was part of a Censor's duty to enquire whether the Constitution had been preserved inviolate in every part, particularly whether the legislative and executive branches of the Government had performed their duty as guardians of the people or assumed to themselves or exercised other or greater powers than they were entitled to by the Constitution.

Constitution
of Oregon.
Article III of the Constitution of Oregon of 1859 declared that the powers of her Government should be divided into three separate departments : the legislative, the executive (including the administrative), and the judicial, and that no person charged with official duties under one of these departments should exercise any of the functions of another except as in the constitution expressly provided.[1]

Constitution
of Wyoming.
Of a similar nature was the Constitution of Wyoming, 1889.

In all the States it was accepted as axiomatic that every step should be taken to prevent a tyrannical concentration of all the powers in one hand.

A declaration of rights for the protection of individual minorities is also another feature of a State Constitution.

The Bill of
Rights of
Dakota.
The sixth Article of the State of Dakota affords an illustration of this. It is entitled " Bill of Rights." It states that all men are born equally free and independent and have certain inherent rights among which are those of enjoying and defending life and liberty, of acquiring and protecting property, and the pursuit of happiness. To secure these rights governments are instituted among men deriving their just powers from the consent of the governed. In support of this declaration, some provisions are enumerated similar to those contained in the United States' Constitution, with additional provisions such as that "no person shall be imprisoned for debt arising out of or founded upon a contract."

A moral note is sounded in the declaration that the blessings of a free government can only be maintained by a firm adherence to justice, moderation, temperance, frugality, and virtue and by frequent recurrence to fundamental principles.[2]

---

[1] Hill's *Annotated Laws of Oregon*, Vol. I, p. 86.
[2] *Annotated South Dakota Statutes*, Vol. I (1899),

All the States possess the amplest powers of legislation within the limits of their constitutions, and subject only to the prohibition and limitations of the Constitution of the United States. Whether, however, a particular State Act is justified under the States' Constitution is often so moot a question as to be necessarily left to the discretion of the particular branch which executes it, unless however, the Act whether of a legislative or executive character, be subsequently questioned before the State Supreme Court it cannot be controverted.

In construing a State Constitution, the judges have declared that the construction must be uniform. The intention of the people in adopting it must be given effect to, and the whole instrument examined. In carrying out general grants of powers, all implied powers which are necessary to give full effect to the power must be inferred, but the implied powers must be necessary and not conjectural. *Construction of State Constitution.*

Another rule of construction is that the English common law must be kept in view ; although English decisions since the Revolution are sometimes referred to, and some weight attached to them, they are considered as of less importance than decisions prior to the Revolution. These are direct authorities. *Rule as to English law.*

Some few of the States have endeavoured to solve their doubts as to the constitutionality of their Acts, whether of a legislative or executive nature, by obtaining beforehand an opinion from their judges. In Maine, New Hampshire, and Massachusetts, the judges of the Supreme Court were required when called upon by the Governor in Council or either House of the Legislature to give their opinions upon important questions of law and upon solemn occasions. *Opinions of judges on Constitutional points.* *Maine, New Hampshire, Massachusetts.*

In Florida the Governor may require an opinion upon any question affecting his executive powers and duties, but a duty with reference to a bill before it becomes an Act has not been deemed to be such an executive duty. *Florida.*

In Massachusetts the judges decline to express an opinion upon the proper construction of any existing Act which may be amended. *Massachusetts.*

Checks on
powers.
The Constitution provided certain checks or limitations
on a State's inherent power. No State was permitted to
enter into any treaty, alliance, or confederation, or grant
letters of marque and reprisal. The prohibition was rendered necessary, since these powers had been conferred
upon the National Government.

Paper
money.
The States were forbidden to coin money; for the power
had been granted to Congress. It was desired to procure
uniformity of coinage through the States. Coinage was
a sovereign power, and likely to be abused if concurrently
exercised.

The States were forbidden to emit bills of credit. In
referring to this prohibition, " The Federalist " said : " It
must give pleasure to every citizen in proportion to his love
of justice and his knowledge of the true springs of public
prosperity. The loss which America has sustained since
the peace from the pestilent effects of paper money on
the necessary confidence between man and man ; on the
necessary confidence in the public councils ; on the industries and morals of the people, and on the character of
republican government constitutes an enormous debt
against the States chargeable with this unadvised measure which must long remain unsatisfied, or rather an
accumulation of guilt which can be expiated not otherwise
than by a voluntary sacrifice on the altar of justice of the
power which has been the instrument of it." [1]

Crises during
and after
the War.
The United States passed through two crises, one during
the War, and one after the Peace of 1783. During the War
Congress issued an enormous quantity of bills of credit,
proposing to redeem them on receipt of the amounts due
to them from the receipt of the taxes they had requisitioned
on the States. But the States made little or no response,
and ultimately the bills became practically valueless.

Object of
prohibition.
Bills of credit were generally understood to mean paper
redeemable at a future day, which was intended to circulate
through the community for its ordinary purposes as money.
The object of the prohibition was not to prohibit the thing

[1] " The Federalist," No. xliv.

when it bore a particular name, but to prohibit the thing whatever form or name it might assume.

During the Civil War Congress had issued a large quantity of Treasury notes, which Acts of Congress declared to be legal tender for all public and private debts, except duties on imports and interest on the public debt. The validity of these Acts of Congress was questioned; they were at first held to be valid by the Supreme Court by a majority of one as to debts incurred after the passing of the Acts, but not as to debts contracted before their passage. A year later the decision of the Supreme Court on the latter point was overruled by its subsequent judgment by a majority of one. The result, however, was only arrived at by the appointment of two additional judges. The constitutionality of the power to make paper money a legal tender in times of peace as well as during a war was upheld in a later decision. *Paper currency.*

Whilst the National Government can make paper money a legal tender, the States cannot.[1] They are expressly prohibited from making anything but gold and silver coin a valid discharge in payment of debts.[2] *States prohibited from making.*

The prohibition on the State was instituted to create one uniform standard of value. *Reason of prohibition of Bills of attainder and ex post facto laws.*

The States, like the National Government, were prohibited from passing bills of attainder and *ex post facto* laws. They were also forbidden to pass any law impairing the obligation of contracts.

" The Federalist " says, in commending this prohibition, that " the sober people of America were weary of the fluctuating policy which had directed public councils. They had seen with regret and indignation that sudden changes and legislative interferences in cases affecting personal rights became jobs in the hands of enterprising and influential speculators and snares to the more industrious and less informed part of the community. They had seen, too, that one legislative interference is but the first link in a long *Laws impairing the obligation of contracts.*

---

[1] Craig v. The State of Missouri, 4 Peter, Sup. Court. Rep., 410.
[2] Juilliard v. Greenman, 110 U.S. 421.

chain of repetitions every subsequent interference being naturally provoked by the effects of the preceding.[1]

Meaning of contract. Much discussion has taken place as to the meaning to be attached to the expression contract. The Courts have decided that it includes executed and executory contracts, whether express or implied. What is an obligation of a contract but the means provided by law by which the parties can be obliged to perform it ? Hence a law lessening the effectiveness of these means impairs the obligation of the contract.

Instances of. A law, for instance, which deprived a municipal corporation of the power to levy taxes and so pay its debts would impair the obligation of the contract. So also would a law which deprived a mortgagee of a right to possession under a mortgage until after foreclosure, since he would be deprived of his right to the rents and profits, which are a valuable portion of the right secured by the contract and further he would be compelled to incur the additional expense of foreclosure before obtaining possession. Innumerable cases have been decided on this clause of the Constitution, and they have ramified in unexpected directions.

Dartmouth College v. Woodward. The leading case is Dartmouth College *v.* Woodward,[2] which decided that a Government had no power to revoke a grant even of its own funds which it had given to a private person or corporation for special uses, nor could it recall its own endowments granted to a hospital or college or city or town for the use of such corporation.

Effect of prohibition on municipal corporations. Municipal corporations are much affected by this prohibition in the Constitution. Whilst the State creating them can strip them of political rights, since it would be an unsound and even absurd proposition that political power conferred by a legislature should become a vested right in any individual or body of men as against the Government, the Legislature has no power except through the judiciary to ascertain the validity of a grant, enforce its proper uses, suppress frauds, and when the uses are charitable

[1] " The Federalist," No. xliv.
[2] 4 Wheat, 518.

secure their regular administration through the means of
equitable tribunals in cases where there would otherwise
be a failure of justice. Public corporations, therefore, which
exist only for public purposes may be changed by the
Legislature, or they may be enlarged or restrained, but the
property held by them must still be secured for the use of
those for whom and at whose expense it was purchased.

Marriage is not a contract within the meaning of this *Marriag*.
clause,[1] otherwise a State Legislature would have had no
authority to declare a marriage void or to award a divorce.

A further prohibition in the Constitution forbids a State *Further*
laying any duty on commerce, keeping troops, or ships of *prohibitions.*
war in time of peace, entering into any agreement or compact
with another State or with a foreign power, or engaging in
war unless actually invaded or in such imminent danger as
would not admit of delay. The necessity of prohibiting the
States from levying tonnage duties was obvious. The concession of such a power to the States would have led to
diversities of regulations, and induced the States to enter
into a warfare with each other, embittering the harmony
so essential to the Union. How likely the States were to
take umbrage at any discrimination was seen during the
existence of the tariff laws of 1828, when it was said that the
cotton industry was injuriously affected in the South by
the action of Congress. South Carolina was so incensed *The " tariff*
at the " tariff of abominations," as it was called, that *tions."* *of abomina-*
her State Convention passed a nullification ordinance, *Nullification*
threatening to secede. *ordinance.*

In 1833, however, Henry Clay, the great pacifier, introduced *Compromise*
a Compromise Bill which brought about peace. If an *Bill.*
individual State threatened revolt against the National
Government on this issue, what a number of inter-State
quarrels would not have been fomented by a power to lower
or raise tonnage rates with a view to the diversion of
commerce ? *State laws*
have no
By reason of the declaration that the Constitution Laws *operation on*
laws or
and Treaties of the United States are supreme, State laws *treaties of the*
United States.

[1] Maynard *v.* Hill, 125, U.S., 190.

have no operation upon the rights or contracts of the United States.[1]

Declining faith in legislatures. The States' legislatures are bound by the prohibitions of the National Constitution and by their own Constitutions they exercise only that certain portion of the sovereign power delegated to them by the people, the residue remains in the people of the State. Mr. Bryce considers that there is now less inclination on the part of the people to trust their legislatures than there formerly was. In theory the power of a State legislature to legislate is unlimited, subject to the before-mentioned restrictions, and it possesses a general authority to make all laws at discretion. It, however, must not trend upon either the executive or judicial powers which are generally kept separate, following, as previously stated, the well-known triple division contained in the Constitution : " How far the power of giving the law may involve every other power in cases where the Constitution is silent never has been and perhaps never can be definitely stated."[2]

Power of legislation not capable of delegation. The power to legislate cannot be delegated to any other body or authority. Bureaucratic Government, therefore, does not exist.

Locke, the great political thinker, had said : " The Legislature neither must nor can transfer the power of making laws to anybody else or place it anywhere but where the people have."

State Governor. All the States possess governments, consisting of a Governor and legislature. The Governor is universally elected and holds office for varying terms in different States. In some cases the Governor nominates the **Executive.** State's judges. He generally possesses a power to veto legislation. His executive are mostly elected, but in no sense are the executive the Governor's executive, as the President's executive are. Nearly all the States number amongst their executives Secretaries of State and Treasurers.

[1] United States v. Wilson, 8 Wheat, 253.
[2] Fletcher v. Peck, 6 Cranch, 87, 136.

The State Judiciary comprises Supreme Courts or final State Judiciary.
Courts of Appeal, Superior Courts, and Local Courts.

A great variety of names distinguish the local courts, Courts.
such as Orphans' Court, Hustings Court, and County Court.
There is also a Court for the conciliation of domestic
differences.

No appeal lies from a State court to a Federal court Appeals.
except Federal jurisdiction be in some way involved.

Judges, when not appointed by the State Governors,
are elected by the State Legislature, and in the majority of
cases directly by the people. A judge is not elected for life,
but usually for a term. Hence may be seen what would
appear to the Englishman the curious spectacle of ex-judges
practising as advocates in the courts and retaining the
honorary title of judges. A judge's salary is generally
lower than that paid to a County Court judge in England.

The Sheriff is the State, as the Marshall is the Federal Sheriffs.
officer.

CHAPTER X

THE TERRITORIES AND ADMISSION OF NEW STATES

The Seat of Government. THE question of the seat of government is important in a Federal constitution. It led to trouble at the time of the great confederacy of the Achaian League. Aware of the dissensions likely to be engendered by fixing upon a capital at the time of the framing of the Constitution, the framers of the Constitution vested in Congress a power to exercise exclusive legislation over a district not exceeding two square miles obtainable by cession of territory from particular States. Prior to 1789 Congress had no fixed abode. At different periods under the Confederation it Washington. sat at Philadelphia, Princeton, and Annapolis. Washington during his Presidency selected a site for the seat of the National Government situated on the Potomac River, acquired by a cession of territory from Maryland and Virginia. It was named Washington, after its illustrious founder, the Father of the Republic. It is called the Federal District, abbreviated from Washington F.D., because Washington is virtually not in a State at all.

Congress meets at Washington, and there also the Supreme Court sits.

Position of inhabitants. The inhabitants of this territory are citizens of the United States, but not of any particular State. In 1871 a territorial government was provided for them, carrying with it a right to send a delegate to Congress.

Further power to Congress for the erection of forts, arsenals, etc. A further power was given the National Government, with the consent of the State legislatures, to exercise authority over all places purchased in particular States for the erection of forts, magazines, arsenals, dockyards, and other needful buildings.

Subject to reservation of State rights. Innumerable cessions of land by the States have been made for these purposes, subject to a reservation of the State right to serve all State process upon persons found

118

there. The States had no desire to create Alsatias for the benefit of absconding criminals or fugitive debtors.

In other respects, inhabitants of all ceded places are citizens of the United States, and cease to enjoy State rights, and become liable for offences to punishments prescribed by Congress. The power to punish was deduced as incidental to the power to exercise exclusive jurisdiction.

One great question among the many that had threatened in early days to shipwreck the making of a constitution was the dispute as to the unoccupied Crown Lands. The Crown Lands had belonged to the British Crown prior to the rebellion. Were they to be considered as the property of the Federal Government or the property of the States within whose chartered area they were situated ? The disputes ended in a compromise, Congress and States agreeing that they should be disposed of for the general benefit of the Federation and ultimately formed into new States. The proceeds of the sale of the lands were to be used for the payment of State debts, which had been mostly incurred during the war with England. In 1787 Congress passed an ordinance providing for the organisation of territorial governments according to their respective populations. *Crown Lands.*

Sub-section 2 of section iii of Article IV of the Constitution empowered Congress to dispose of and make all needful rules and regulations respecting the territory or other property belonging to the United States ; nothing in the Constitution was to be so construed as to prejudice any claims of the United States or of any particular State. The proviso was inserted to meet the cases of North Carolina and Georgia, which had not ceded at the time their unappropriated lands. *Congress to make rules and regulations for disposal of territories.*

A power to expand the territory of the United States has been always considered to exist, though at the time when Louisiana was acquired by purchase and annexed it was thought doubtful. The validity of the power has since been assumed by all the departments of the Government. It has been construed as authorising the acquisition of territory not fit for admission into the Union when acquired, *Acquisition of territory.*

but susceptible of becoming so as soon as its population and situation warrant. Territory is, therefore, acquired for the purpose of its becoming a State and not with the intention of allowing it permanently to be governed by Congress with absolute authority.

The territories.

No doubt has ever existed as to the National Government's powers to organise territorial governments within the original territory of the United States; but a doubt did exist as to territories which had been acquired by conquest or by treaty such as Florida and Louisiana.

These acquired by conquest.

Congress possesses a power to confer on any territorial government a legislature, executive and judiciary whether in exercise of its power of national sovereignty or under the clause of the Constitution which authorised it to make all needful rules and regulations respecting the territory of the United States.[1]

Formation of new States.

The people of the several territories were entitled to form for themselves State constitutions whenever enabling Acts of Congress were passed for that purpose, but only in the manner allowed by such Acts, and through the action of such persons as such Acts clothed with the elective franchise to that end. The people of the territory have no right of their own motion to meet in convention, frame a constitution, and demand admittance to the Union. Any such action would not entitle them to admission, since the power given to Congress to admit also implies the power to refuse admission, and if admission be refused the territorial status also continues until Congress is satisfied to suffer the territory to become a State.

Rights of admission.

Article IV, section iii, sub-section 5, expressly gave the power to Congress to admit new States to the Union. It also contained a prohibition against the formation or erection of a new State within the jurisdiction of any other State, and forbade the junction of two or more States or parts of States without the consent of the legislatures of the States concerned as well as of Congress.

[1] American Insurance Co. *v.* Canter, 1 Peter's Sup. R., 511, 546.

The Philippine Islands came under the administrative control of the United States by virtue of the Treaty of Peace, concluded between the United States of America and Spain, signed in Paris on 10th December, 1898, and ratified in Washington on 6th February, 1899. [1]

Article 3 of the above Treaty says : " Spain cedes to the United States the archipelago known as the Philippine Islands, and comprehending the islands lying within the following line : [here follows the demarcation]. The United States will pay to Spain the sum of $20,000,000 within three months after the exchange of the ratifications of the present treaty."

It is unnecessary to quote the other provisions of the treaty, as they refer chiefly to a temporary state of affairs now no longer existing.

The treaty was preceded by a Protocol of Peace, signed in Washington on August 12th, 1898, between the French Ambassador, M. Jules Cambon, who had been specially appointed " plenipotentiary to negotiate and sign " by decree of the Queen Regent of Spain, dated 11th August, 1898, and the United States' Secretary of State, Mr. William R. Day.

Article 3 of that Protocol says : " The United States will occupy and hold the city, bay and harbour of Manila, pending the conclusion of a treaty of peace which shall determine the control, disposition, and *government of the Philippines.*"

The United States were in temporary possession of the archipelago from 13th August, 1898, to 6th February, 1899, when, on exchange of the ratifications above mentioned, they established a provisional military government which was, for civil matters, assisted by a Philippine Commission from 4th July, 1901. Finally, by Act of Congress, dated 1st July, 1902, military government was entirely superseded by civil government from 4th July of the same year.

---

[1] The full text of the Treaty of Paris is set out in Senate Document No. 62, Part I of the 55th Congress, 3rd Session. Published by the Government Printing Office, Washington, 1899.

The local government is at present composed (1) of a Philippine Commission with a majority of American and a minority of native commissioners numbering about eight or nine in all, and appointed by Congress ; and (2) a Philippine Assembly (established in 1907), the members of which are elected bi-annually by popular suffrage.   The members of both Houses receive large salaries.   The government of the islands is subject to the Congress of the United States and under the immediate control of the War Department section of Colonial affairs.   The Secretary of State for War is the minister responsible for the conduct of Philippine affairs.   The Philippine Commission acts as an Upper House, and the Assembly as a Lower House.   Theoretically, all bills are proposed in the Lower House and pass to the Upper House for confirmation or rejection, as the case may be.   The Commission, however, has the right to initiate bills which are then passed to the Lower House for the vote and returned to the Commission for acceptance, perhaps with amendments.

In practice, however, the Commission virtually dictates to the Assembly the legislative course to be pursued, thus checking, in advance, the passage through the Lower House of an annual batch of fantastic legislative projects conceived in the fertile Oriental imagination of the native deputies.

The powers of the Assembly are, moreover, limited to the proposal of laws for the government of the civilised population (6,987,686), the control of the wild inhabitants (647,740)[1] being allotted to one of the members of the Commission, on whose report and advice measures for their government are enacted, independently of the Assembly.

The Act providing for the Philippine Assembly stipulates that the elected deputies shall not be less than 50 and not more than 100.   The archipelago is divided into

---

[1] *Vide Population of the Philippines*, Bulletin 1, published by the Department of Commerce and Labour and Bureau of the Census, 1904, Washington.   Census taken in 1903 under the direction of General J. P. Sanger, U.S. Army.

provinces, to each of which a Governor is appointed by the Commission.

" Besides the lower courts established in many provincial Judiciary. centres, sessions are held in circuits, each usually comprising two or three provinces. The provinces are grouped into sixteen judicial districts, in each of which there is a Court of First Instance, and there is, moreover, one additional " Court of First Instance at large." The Chief Justice of the Supreme Court, some of his assistant judges, several provincial judges, the Attorney-General, and many other high legal functionaries are Filipinos. The provincial Justices of the Peace are also natives." [1]

The exact relation of the Philippine Islands to the United States is not easy to define. The archipelago is not a protectorate which would imply the existence of a *de facto* native government. Neither is it a State, a Territory, nor a Colony, for it has been frequently declared officially, and with pride, that the intention of the United States is to set an example unique in the world's history, namely, not to acquire the territory, but to teach the Filipinos to govern themselves with the view of granting them independence when the United States shall consider them able to rule their own affairs. In the insular case of Armstrong *v.* United States, (1900, appeal cases, Supreme Court No. 500), the Solicitor-General stated, with reference to the Philippine Islands : " I believe they are but a possession—territory belonging to the United States—which we can part with whenever it becomes apparent that their interests or our welfare demands a separation."

This confirms the general understanding that the Philippine Islands constitute not an integral part of the Republic, but a *mere possession* in virtue of the cession (made under compulsion, for which statement see the Senate Document No. 62, already referred to in foot-note at p. 121, for the protest made by the Spanish Commissioners against the forced cession).

The Philippine Islands may, therefore, be called a territory

[1] *The Philippine Islands*, by John Foreman, 3rd Edition, page 618.

held *pro tempore*, and until it shall suit the policy of the United States to relinquish it.   The United States being a republic, there can be no such person as a United States subject.   The Filipino is not an American citizen, he cannot call himself an American.   The denomination " Filipino " does not indicate any nationality, because there is not, and never has been, a Philippine nation.

A Filipino travelling abroad can have a passport in which he is described as " a Filipino travelling under the protection of the United States of America," and he can claim and obtain that protection in any American Consulate.   A Filipino is so called because he is a person born on that soil known to the world as the Philippine Islands, in the same sense that a native of Jamaica is styled a Jamaican.

It may be added that with regard to " Imperial expansion," and in particular the retention of the Philippine Islands, the United States public are somewhat lukewarm, and whilst the policy of the Republican party seems to favour the maintenance of the *status quo* in the Far East, the Democratic party leans very plainly towards the abandonment, in the near future, of the United States' new Oriental possession which they regard as a costly and unproductive enterprise.

" The undisputed attitude of the executive and legislative departments of the Government has been and is that the native inhabitants of Porto Rico and the Philippine Islands did not become citizens of the United States by virtue of the cession of the islands by Spain by means of the Treaty of Paris.   It was not the intention of the Commissioners who negotiated the Treaty to give those inhabitants the status of citizens of the United States." [1]

[1] *A Digest of International Law*, by John Bassett Moore, LL.D., Vol. III, page 317.   Washington, Government Printing Office, 1906.

CHAPTER XI

THE NATURE OF THE UNITED STATES CONSTITUTION

THE purpose of the Constitution of the United States was *Purpose of creation expressed.* clearly expressed in its preamble. It was created " in order to form a *more perfect union*, establish justice, insure domestic tranquillity, provide for the common defence, promote the general welfare and secure the blessing of liberty to ourselves and our posterity."

" It was ordained to form a more perfect union." Under *To form more perfect union.* the Articles of Confederation, the Union had been declared to be perpetual. What can be indissoluble if a perpetual union made more perfect is not so ? When a State is once in the Union there is " no place for reconsideration or revocation except through revolution or through the consent of the States." [1]

Without the States in union there could be no such *Indestructible union of indestructible States.* political body as the United States. Not only, therefore, can there be no loss of separate and independent autonomy to the States through their union under the Constitution, but it may not unreasonably be said that the preservation of the States and the maintenance of their governments are as much within the design and care of the Constitution as the preservation of the Union and the maintenance of the National Government. The Constitution in all its provisions looks to an indestructible union composed of indestructible States. [2]

The Constitution is the supreme law; it was declared so *Constitution the supreme law.* to be by the Constitution itself. " This Constitution and the laws of the United States which shall be made in pursuance thereof and all treaties made or which shall be made under the authority of the United States shall be the supreme law of the land and the judges in every State shall be bound

[1] Texas *v.* White, 7 Wall, 700, 726.
[2] Cooley, *Constitutional Law*, 2nd edition, p. 28.

125

thereby, anything in the constitution and laws of any State to the contrary notwithstanding."[1]

How ordained and established.

The Constitution, said Mr. Justice Story, was not ordained and established by the States in their sovereign capacities, but emphatically, as the preamble of the Constitution declares, by the *people of the United States*. It was not necessarily carved out of existing State sovereignties, nor a surrender of powers already existing in State institutions, for the powers of the States depended upon their own constitutions, and the people of every State had the right to modify and restrain them according to their own views of policy or principle.[2]

Nature of State sovereignty.

The sovereignty of a State, said Chief Justice Marshall, extends to everything which exists by its own authority or is introduced by its permission, but does it extend to those means which are employed by Congress to carry out executive powers conferred on that body by the *people of the United States?* We think it demonstrable that it does not. These powers are not given by the

People of the States: people of the United States.

people of a single State. They are given by the *people of the United States*, to a government whose laws made in pursuance of the Constitution are declared to be supreme."[3] Article X of the first amendment declared that " the powers not delegated to the United States by the Constitution nor prohibited by it to the States were reserved to the States respectively or the people."

Meaning of people.

It has been contended by many writers that the " people " meant the " people of the States," and that the ultimate reservation of power remained in the " people of the States separately "[4] and not in the whole people. Had this contention been adopted the Constitution of the United States would hardly have attained that national character that it now has.

[1] Article 6.

[2] See judgments of Mr. Justice Story, Martin *v.* Hunters Series, 1 Wheat, p. 324.

[3] McCulloch *v.* Maryland, 4 Wheat, p. 429.

[4] Calhoun on *The Constitution and Government of the United States.* The constitutional view of the war between the States by A. H. Stephens and many other writers.

It is important to note the difference between, what may be termed, its national and its federal character, as bearing on the War of Secession.

" The Federalist," in applying certain tests, assumed Views of "The Federalist." that the difference between a federal and national government was supposed to consist in this, that in a federal government the powers operated on the political bodies composing the confederacy in their political capacities, in the latter on the individual citizens composing the nation in their individual capacities. Tested by this criterion, the Constitution was of a national and not a federal character. In strictness, however, it must be considered as neither a national nor a federal Constitution, but a composition of both. In its foundation it was federal and not national. In the sources from which the ordinary powers of Government were drawn, it was partly federal and partly national. In the operation of these powers it was national and not federal, and in the extent of these again it was federal and not national, and finally in the authoritative mode of introducing amendments it was neither wholly federal nor national.

The framers of the Constitution feared the Federal Govern- Nature of struggle ment might fail from weakness, and they looked to a struggle between between the Government of the United States and the National separate governments of the several States as furnishing the and State Government. means of resisting the encroachments of the one or the other, but time and experience established that the struggle lay between the Government of the United States, supported by a majority of the States and a minority of the States. As a result the Government of the United States proved to be immeasurably the stronger. The system had, therefore, instead of tending towards dissolution from weakness, tended strongly towards consolidation from exuberance of strength.[1] Whether the Constitution was Calhoun's views. wholly federal, as many have contended, or not is not of such importance now as it was prior to the War of Secession. The existence of its national as well as its federal aspect has since been generally recognised.

[1] Calhoun, *Constitution and Government of the United States.*

Triple
division
of powers.
In the Constitution itself is found a triple division of powers. The legislative, the executive, and the judicial. Locke had declared such a division essential to liberty, and had asserted that legislative and executive functions ought to remain separate.

Effect of
Bill of Rights
in England.
In England the Bill of Rights subjected the executive power to checks, and the Act of Settlement continued the process further by making the judiciary practically independent. The judges then became irremovable, except only after conviction in the law courts or on an address presented by both Houses of Parliament in the same session.

Excellence of
Constitution
in division
of powers.
Montesquieu, who highly praised the English Constitution, declared the triple division of powers which then took place as its characteristic excellence.

He affirmed that there could be no liberty where the legislative and executive powers were united in the same person or body of magistrates, or if the power of judging was not separated from the legislative and executive powers.

"The
Federalist"
views on
Montesquieu's
meaning.
In examining Montesquieu's position, " The Federalist " explained that Montesquieu did not mean that these departments ought to have no partial agency in or control over the acts of each other. His meaning, as his words imported, and still more conclusively as illustrated by the example in his eye, amounted to no more than this, that where the whole power of another department is exercised by the same hands which possessed the whole power of another department the fundamental principles of a free constitution are subverted.

Object of
framers of
Constitution.
The framers of the United States' Constitution aimed at the making of a constitution that should be a sure safeguard for freedom. Hence they followed the triple division of powers which the French jurist had so highly extolled, but the better to secure their ends they contrived a series of checks which has rendered the Constitution so admirably balanced.

State
Constitutions.
It may be asked if the result was wholly due to the teachings of Montesquieu. Great as his influence was, and its greatness cannot be denied, other causes were at work.

The States possessed their own Constitution ; they were familiar with the existence of a legislature consisting of two chambers : a popular assembly checked by an Upper Chamber, and both Chambers subject to the executive veto of the Governor. The States had indeed whilst under British dominion frequently protested against the exercise of this veto, and more particularly against the further power of the King in Council to disallow their legislation. Nevertheless, on the whole, the system of checks seemed so admirable that it was deemed worthy of imitation. Nothing seemed more likely to recommend the Constitution to the people of the States than to commend its likeness to their States Constitutions. The teachings of Montesquieu were in accordance with what the people had already in their minds.

The Constitution of the United States is a written one, Written and in this respect resembles the Canadian, the Australian, Constitution. and South African Constitutions. It is also fundamental Constitution and legislation in disregard of its provisions is of no effect. fundamental.

This was so held in the great case of Marbury v. Madison, Marbury v. decided by the Supreme Court in 1803.[1] In the course of Madison. the judgment it was said " that the people have an original right to establish for their future government such principles as in their opinion shall most conduce to their happiness. The exercise of this original right is a very great exertion, nor can it nor ought it to be frequently repeated. The principles, therefore, so established are deemed fundamental. And as the authority from which they proceed is supreme, and can seldom act, they are designed to be permanent. This original and supreme will organises the Government and assigns to different departments their respective powers. It may either stop here or establish certain limits not to be transcended by those departments.

" The Government of the United States is of the latter description. The powers of the Legislature are defined and limited, and that those limits might not be mistaken or forgotten the Constitution is written. To what purpose are

[1] 1 Cranch, 175, 176.

9—(2125)

powers limited or to what purpose is that limitation committed
to writing if those limits may at any time be passed by those
intended to be restrained ? The distinction between a
Government with limited and unlimited powers is abolished
if these limits do not confine the persons on whom they are
imposed, and if acts prohibited and acts allowed are of equal
obligation. It is a proposition too plain to be contested
that the Constitution controls any legislative Act repugnant
to it, or that the Legislature may alter the Constitution by an
ordinary Act. Between these alternatives there is no
middle ground. The Constitution is either a superior
paramount law unchangeable by ordinary means, or it
is on a level with ordinary legislative Acts, and like other
Acts is alterable when the Legislature shall please to alter
it. If the former part of the alternative be true then a
legislative Act contrary to the Constitution is not law.
If the latter part be true, then written constitutions are
absurd attempts on the part of the people to limit a power
in its own nature illimitable. Certainly all those who have
framed written constitutions contemplate them as forming
the fundamental and paramount law of the nation, and
consequently the theory of every such government must
be that an Act of the Legislature repugnant to the Constitution is void. This theory is essentially attached to a
written constitution, and is consequently to be considered
as one of the fundamental principles of our society.''

Distinction
between
Constitution of
United States
and Great
Britain.   In the existence of a fundamental written constitution
the United States Constitution differs from that of the
United Kingdom. Its permanent unchangeable character
is the antithesis of what is popularly known as the Constitution of the United Kingdom. It is rigidity versus
elasticity. In the United Kingdom the King, the House
of Lords, and the House of Commons acting together
Parliamentary
sovereignty. in legislation form a parliamentary sovereignty so high
that no authority has power to overrule it. " Parliament," it has been said, " hath sovereign and uncon-
Nature of. trollable authority in the making, conferring, enlarging,
restraining, abrogating, repealing, revising and expanding

of laws concerning matters of all possible denomination, ecclesiastical or temporal, and military, maritime, or criminal. This being the place where that absolute despotic power which must in all governments reside somewhere is entrusted by the Constitution of these kingdoms.[1] Therefore there is no fundamental law in Great Britain as there is in the United States, and even the Union with Scotland which is considered to have had something of the nature of a treaty about it could be as readily repealed as any other Act."

Since in Great Britain Parliament is supreme, it cannot act unconstitutionally in the sense that Congress can. To say that an Act of Parliament is unconstitutional in Great Britain means no more than the Act is opposed to the spirit of the Constitution, and in this sense the word unconstitutional in the mouth of a speaker conveys a term of censure, but in the United States, if the term be applied to an Act of Congress, it means that the Act was beyond the power of Congress to enact. *Meaning of unconstitutional.*

The triple division of powers already referred to was pre-eminently designed to preserve the liberty of the individual citizen, which the framers of the Constitution were satisfied was his greatest blessing. Tyranny and injustice might arise in the exercise of the Executive, the Legislative, or the Judicial power. Accordingly each of these powers must be so constituted as to check the other. *Triple division to preserve individual liberty in United States.*

The Constitution was Republican, based upon the people's rights. No title of nobility could be granted, and no person holding any office under the United States could accept of any present, emolument, office, or title of any kind whatever from any king, prince, or foreign State. *Republican character.* It was also Democratic, since the suffrage could be exercised by every American citizen qualified to vote for the most numerous branch of the State Legislature. *Democratic.*

The Constitution further partook of the nature of a compact or treaty, by which the States and the people bound themselves to each other. The Federal Government was, therefore, a Federal compact. " So long as the separate *Federal compact in the nature of a Confederation.*

[1] Coke, 4th Institute, p. 36.

organisation of the members remains and must form the nature of the compact, it must continue to exist both for local and domestic and for Federal purposes. The Union was in fact as well as in theory an association of States or a confederacy."[1]

Social compact.

The Constitution was also to some extent a social compact, as distinguishable from a Federal compact. A Federal compact may be defined as an act of the State or body politic, and not of the individual, whilst a social compact is generally understood to mean the act of individuals about to create and establish a State or body politic among themselves. Thus, where a number of States bind themselves together, and the body politic and not the individual is answerable, the obligation is said to be a Federal obligation. On the other hand, "when by any compact express or implied a number of persons bind themselves to contribute their proportions of the common expenses or to submit to all laws made by the common consent, and in default of compliance with these engagements the society is authorised to levy the contribution or to punish the person of the delinquent, it is understood to be more in the nature of a social than a Federal obligation."[2]

The Constitution, however, may be looked at from another standpoint, more especially when it is considered as a whole with the amendments added from time to time.

Charter of rights.

It is a charter of the rights of the people of the United States, not that it contains a clear and full enunciation of all rights such as are generally considered indefeasible to full liberty, but it asserts important declarations of rights which many of the States at the time of its establishment thought of the utmost importance.

Hamilton's views.

Hamilton considered[3] "all such pronouncements unnecessary." "Bills of Rights," he argued, "were in their origin stipulations between Kings and their subjects, abridgments of prerogative in favour of privilege, reservations

[1] Story, *Constitution of the United States*, 3rd edition, Vol. I, p. 225.
[2] *Ibid.*
[3] "The Federalist," No. lxxxiv.

of rights not surrendered to the Prince." According to their primitive signification, they had no "application to Constitutions professedly founded upon the power of the people and executed by their immediate representatives and servants." Nevertheless the Constitution did contain certain declarations of rights, and whilst Hamilton agreed that declarations might in certain cases prove dangerous, he pointed out that it possessed provisions which were altogether independent of the structure of Government.

In the Constitution it will be found that individual liberty and Republican principles were both established and cherished. Whilst the weapon of impeachment was kept it was safeguarded with a restriction. The privilege of Habeas Corpus was preserved by the provision that the writ should only be suspended in cases of invasion or rebellion when the public safety required it. *Impeachment.* *Habeas corpus.*

Bills of attainder and *ex post facto* laws, probable sources of injustice to persons or property, were prohibited to the legislative power. *Bills of attainder and ex post facto laws.*

Trial by jury, except in the solitary case of impeachment, was recognised as the fundamental right of every citizen charged with a crime. On any criminal trial it was declared that an accused person must be charged in the State where the crime was committed. If not committed in any State Congress had power to provide for the place of trial by legislation. Treason was considered too serious a crime to be left to the judges to define. The treason the Constitution recognised was that which consisted in levying war against the United States or in adhering to their enemies, giving them aid and comfort. No person could be convicted of this crime unless two witnesses testified to the same overt acts, or the person charged confessed in open court. To Congress also was assigned the power to declare the punishment for treason, but even this power of Congress was limited. Attainder for treason could work no corruption of blood or forfeiture except during the life of the person attainted. *Trial by jury.* *Local venue.* *Treason defined.* *Congress to fix punishment.*

But even this enumeration of rights and safeguards of

liberty did not satisfy some of the leading States, who were only induced to ratify the Constitution on the assurance that a Bill of Rights would be added subsequently to the Constitution. The passing of the Ten Articles of the first Amendment which were ratified during the years 1789 to 1791, eight of which dealt with individual liberty, completed the sum of the enumerated fundamental rights

Free exercise of religion. Freedom of speech and the press. Right to assemble and petition. Bearing arms. Quartering of soldiers.

of the American people. By these Congress was prohibited from making any law establishing or prohibiting the free exercise of religion or abridging the freedom of speech or of the Press, or of the right of the people peaceably to assemble and to petition the Government for a redress of grievances. The right of the people to keep and bear arms was not to be infringed; for a well-regulated militia was essential for the security of a free State. In time of peace no soldier was to be quartered in any house without the owner's consent, nor in time of war but in a manner prescribed by law. The people had a right to be secure in their persons, houses, papers, and effects against unreasonable

Searches.

searches and seizures, and this right must not be violated. No search warrant was to be permitted to issue but upon probable cause, supported by oath or affirmation, and particularly describing the place to be searched, and the persons or things to be seized. No person was to be held to answer

Warrant required. Indictment on presentment.

for a capital or otherwise infamous crime unless on presentment or indictment of a grand jury except in cases arising in the land or naval forces or in the militia when in actual service in time of war or public danger. No person could for the same offence be twice put in jeopardy of life or limb,

Criminal charges.

nor could a person be compelled in any criminal case to be a witness against himself, nor be deprived of life, liberty, or process without due process of law. If a man's private

Compensation.

property were taken for public use it was necessary to pay him just compensation. In all criminal prosecutions the accused was to enjoy the right to a speedy and public

Right to speedy trial.

trial by an impartial jury of the State in the District where the crime was committed, which district was to be previously ascertained by law. He was to be informed of the nature

and cause of the accusation, to be confronted with the Trial.
witnesses against him, to have compulsory process for
obtaining witnesses in his favour and to have the assistance
of counsel for his defence. Excessive bail was not to be Excessive
required nor excessive fines imposed, nor cruel and unusual bail.
punishments inflicted. In practice, however, this measure
is not now regarded. Enormous bail is in fact often exacted.

The right of trial by a jury in civil cases at common law Trial by
where the value in controversy exceeded twenty dollars was civil cases.
preserved, and no fact tried by a jury could be otherwise
re-examined in any court of the United States than according
to the common law.

Such were the rights of the American citizen secured by
the Constitution, and the immediate amendments that
followed on its establishment. Truly a noble declaration
of civil and religious liberties.

If it be asked from whence did this charter of rights Origin of
spring, it must be answered: "From the land whence charter.
the American people came." "Man was born free,"
Rousseau had said, "but everywhere he is in chains."
The philosopher's well-known saying with its false premises,
but unbounded popularity, was less true of the people of
England than of the people of the rest of Europe. The
Englishman was free. By slow degrees since the time of
Charles I he had shaken off the shackles of a tyrannical
executive, and had attained to a position of great political
freedom. In the process of emancipation, the right of free
speech, an uncensored press, and an independent Judiciary
assisted. The truth of principles that had been once established created precedents for further advances. The struggle
for civil and political freedom was long and arduous, and not
unstained with blood, but at its close it had left England a
land of freedom then comparable with none other in the
world.

As Æneas took his gods with him as he escaped from
Troy over the seas, so the American people seized the noblest
traditions of liberty from their Mother Country, and
enshrined them in their Constitution.

CHAPTER XII

COMPARISON WITH THE BRITISH CONSTITUTION

Comparison with British Constitution in 1789.

IN regarding the Constitution with its amendments as a charter of the rights of the people of the United States, the civil and religious freedom conferred may be measured with that which existed in England in 1789. The comparison shows a striking similarity. The great precedents of English constitutional history were in the nature of beacon lights to the framers of the Constitution. The people of the United States were familiar with their own State Constitution, the common law and Sir William Blackstone's commentaries on the laws of England. They adopted much of English constitutional law : in some instances improved upon it. Thus in England it was possible to pass

Bills of Attainder.

an Act of Attainder by the provision of which a man could be condemned to punishment without trial. The power to pass an Act still exists, although no Act has been passed for years ; Acts of Attainder found no place in the American

Habeas corpus.

Constitution. The writ of habeas corpus as it existed in England could be employed to stop arbitrary imprisonment ; but in 1789 it had not been applied to meet the case of a person who had been deprived of liberty otherwise than on a criminal charge. The " change," which now gives the writ its present wide application, did not

Ex post facto legislation.

take place until the later years of George III.[1] *Ex post facto* legislation, which was prohibited in the United States, has never been prohibited in England, although it has been said that such legislation is undesirable. In the United States the prohibition against such legislation was early held[2] to extend to criminal matters, to prohibit States legislatures from passing punitive laws after an act done by a subject or citizen which should have relation to such

[1] 56 George III, c. 100.
[2] Calder *v.* Bull, 3 Dall, 386.

act and punish him accordingly. The prohibition against such legislation was intended to secure the person or subject from injury or punishment by reason of such laws.

Ex post facto laws are construed to mean : (1) Laws which Nature of. make an action done before the passing of the law innocent when done, criminal afterwards, and which inflict punishment for such action ; (2) laws which aggravate a crime or make it greater than it was when committed ; (3) laws that change the punishment and inflict a greater punishment than the law annexed to the crime when committed ; (4) laws that alter the legal rules of evidence and receive less or different testimony than the law required at the time of the commission of the offence, in order to convict the offender.

Every *ex post facto* law is necessarily retrospective, but Necessarily retrospective. every retrospective law is not an *ex post facto* law. " Every law,"[1] said Mr. Justice Chase, " that takes away or impairs rights vested agreeably to existing laws is retrospective, and is generally unjust, and may be oppressive, and there is a good general rule that a law should have no retrospect ; but there are cases in which laws may justly, and for the benefit of the community and also of individuals, relate to a time antecedent to their commencement, as statutes of oblivion or pardon." No law is *ex post facto* within the prohibition of the Constitution that mollifies the rigour of the criminal law.

Blackstone was familiar with the expression *ex post facto* Blackstone's views. laws. The expression had acquired an appropriate meaning to legislators, lawyers, and authors long before the Revolution. In writing concerning the necessity of a widespread publication of laws, he refers to " Caligula (who, according to Dio Cassius) wrote his laws in a very small character, and hung them up the more effectually to ensnare the people. There is a still more unreasonable method than this which is called making laws *ex post facto ;* when, after an action (indifferent in itself) is committed, the Legislature then for the first time declares it to be a crime,

[1] 3 Dall, U.S., p. 390, 391.

and inflicts a punishment upon the person who committed it."[1]

Instances of *ex post facto* legislation are found in the history of England : in the cases of the Earl of Strafford (1641), Sir John Fenwick (1696), the banishment of Lord Clarendon (1669), and of Bishop Atterbury (1723), and in the Coventry Act (1670).

Trial by jury had long been established, but religious equality was far from being recognised in England in 1789. Roman Catholics, Nonconformists, and Jews were all at that time under serious disabilities.

Treason in England was held to be sufficiently proved by the evidence of one credible witness up to the passing of the Treason Act of 7 Will. III. After the passing of this Act, no person could be indicted, tried, or attainted of treason but upon the oaths and testimony of two lawful witnesses either both to the same overt act or one to one and the other to another overt act of the same treason ; and, further, it was declared, that if two or more distinct treasons of divers heads or kinds were alleged in one indictment, one witness produced to prove one of these treasons and another another, were not deemed to be two witnesses to the same treason.

Freedom of speech and freedom of meeting both existed in England, but the former was subject to the laws which punished blasphemy, sedition, libel and slander, and incitements to riots and meeting.

Since 1695 the Press had ceased to be licensed, and censorship had been abolished.

The Bill of Rights had established the right of all subjects to petition the King ; all commitments and prosecutions for such petitioning were illegal.

The quartering or billeting of soldiers and mariners, had been felt to be an intolerable grievance since the time of Charles I. In the Petition of Right it was expressly prayed that His Majesty would be pleased to remove the said soldiers and mariners that his people might not

[1] *Blackstone's Commentaries*, 21st edition, p. 45.

be so burdened in time to come. An Act of Charles II declared that no officer should thenceforth presume to billet soldiers on any inhabitant without his consent. Never-theless, the mode of billeting troops continued to be a griev-ance till William III, by proclamation in 1688, prohibited it unless with the consent of the owners in all-houses, except victualling houses and houses of public entertainment. An Act of William III confirmed this prohibition, and an Act of Anne further confined the power of billeting to places where no sufficient barracks were provided and to the marches of soldiers ; in the latter case for six days only at a time. The only persons, therefore, who were liable to receive billeted soldiers in England in the year 1789 were publicans who kept victualling houses.

The law in respect of the issue of a general warrant for General warrants. the arrest of a person, where the warrant specified no par-ticular person, had been settled only a few years previously ; but it may be surmised that the framers of the American Constitution were familiar with the English judicial deci-sions. The practice of issuing a general warrant to arrest Origin of practice. non-specified persons was supposed to have originated with the Star Chamber. It was revived after the Restoration by the Licensing Act of Charles II, and the practice is believed to have continued until after the Revolution. Its legality was, however, doubted, and was tested in the The three test cases. three cases of Wilkes v. Wood (1763), Leach v. Money (1765), and Entinck v. Carrington (1765).

As a result of these cases, it became settled law : (1) That a general warrant signed by the Secretary of State to search for the authors, printers, and publishers of a paper, and to apprehend them with their papers, was bad ; (2) that a trespass was committed in breaking a house and locks under the power of such a warrant, since if such a power as were claimed vested in the Secretary of State, and he could delegate it, it might affect the person and property of every man, and was totally subversive of the liberty of the subject ; (3) that under such a warrant papers could not be seized.

Resolution of
Commons.

In 1766 the House of Commons passed resolutions declaring such warrants not only to be illegal, but if they were executed on the person or paper of a Member of the House, they would constitute a breach of privilege.

The provisions of the United States Constitution relating to the administration of the criminal law show that its framers considered that the system in force in England required improvement, but substantially the two systems remained the same.

Presentment.

The method of prosecution of offenders in England was by presentment or indictment : " A presentment generally taken," says Sir William Blackstone, " is a very comprehensive term ; including not only presentments properly so-called, but also inquisitions of office and indictments by a grand jury. A presentment *properly* speaking, he explains, is the notice taken by a ' grand jury of any offence from their own knowledge and observation, without any bill of indictment laid before them at the suit of the King.' "

Indictment.

An indictment is a written accusation of one or more persons of a crime or misdemeanour preferred to or presented upon oath by a grand jury. If the grand jury on such indictment are satisfied of the truth of the accusation, they endorse upon the indictment the words "a true bill" ; but to find a true bill, twelve of the jury must at least agree, " for so tender is the law of England of the lives of the subjects, that no man can be convicted at the suit of the King of any capital offence unless by the unanimous voice of twenty-four of his equals and neighbours, that is, by twelve at least of the grand jury, and afterwards by the whole *petit* jury of twelve more finding him guilty upon his trial."

Informations,
Two kinds of.

The only proceedings at the suit of the King, without a previous indictment or presentment by a grand jury, known in England were informations for enormous misdemeanours. These were of two kinds : (1) Those which were the King's own prosecutions for offences so high and dangerous in the punishment or prevention of which a moment's delay would be fatal; in respect of which the law had given the Crown the right to an immediate prosecution without waiting for any previous application to any other tribunal ; (2) those brought in the King's name as nominal prosecutor on the relation of some private person or common informer.

Informations still exist at common law in the United *Informations in the* States, but the process is rarely recurred to, and has never *United States.* yet been formally put into operation by any positive authority of Congress under the National Government in mere cases of misdemeanour, though common enough in civil prosecutions for pains and penalties.

Another principle of the English common law recognised *Trial.* in England in 1789 was that no person should be subject for the same offence to be twice put in jeopardy of life and limb, and the clause in the first amendment of the Constitution that no person should be deprived of life, liberty, or property without due process of law was but the affirmation of the English common law privilege ; so was the clause that no person should be compelled to be a witness against himself.

The provision in the Constitution that private property *Private* should not be taken without just compensation was intended *property.* solely as a limitation of the exercise of power by the Government of the United States, and was not applicable to the legislation of the States : [1] " This, again, was but an affirmance of the great doctrine established by the common law of England for the protection of private property founded on natural equity. In a free Government almost all other rights would become utterly worthless if the Government possessed an uncontrollable power over the private fortune of every citizen." [2] The right to a speedy and public trial by an impartial jury was conferred *Speedy* on the Englishman by his common law. His right, if *trial.* accused, to have compulsory process for obtaining witnesses *Witnesses for* in his favour in all cases of treason and felony, was not *defence.* admitted until the time of Queen Anne (1 Anne, St. 2, c. 9), although it had never been denied in cases of mere

---

[1] Barron *v.* Baltimore, 7 Pet., U.S. 250.
[2] Story, 5th Edition, Vol. II, p. 570.

misdemeanour. ✦A right to have counsel for his defence upon his trial in any capital crime did not exist unless some point of law arose during the trial fit for discussion. Nevertheless, the judges allowed counsel to instruct a prisoner as to the questions he should ask, and even ask them as matters of fact. The Statute (7 Will. III, c. 3) allowed prisoners to make their full defence by counsel on indictments for such high treason as worked a corruption in blood or on indictments for misprision of treason, except treason in counterfeiting the King's coins or seals. The counsel in such cases were named by the prisoner and assigned by the
court. The State (20 Geo. II, c. 30) extended this indulgence to parliamentary impeachments for high treason ;
but it was not till the year 1836 that a full defence by counsel was allowed to all prisoners charged with felony.

The provision in the first amendment that excessive bail should not be required, nor excessive fines imposed, nor cruel and unnecessary punishments inflicted, followed the words of a
clause in the Bill of Rights framed at the Revolution of 1688.

"During the time of the Stuarts a demand for excessive bail was often made against persons who were odious to the Court and its favourites; on failing to produce it, they were committed to prison."[1] It was felt necessary in the American Constitution to affirm principles so justly in accord with reason and humanity.

It has been decided that this provision does not apply to punishments inflicted in the State Courts for a crime against the State, and that the prohibition applies only to the National Government.[2]

One important matter, however, remains—the question of slavery. The existence of slavery was distinctly recognised, although the word "slave" does not occur in the Constitution. Slaves were considered as property in the United States. In England, slavery was recognised even up till 1771–72, till the decision in the famous case of the slave Lewis Somerset.[3] Lord Mansfield then declared that

---

[1] *Rawle on Cons.*, ch. x, pp. 130, 131.
[2] Fox *v.* Ohio, 5 How, 432. Smith *v.* Maryland, 18 How, 71.
[3] Howells, *State Trials*, Vol. XX, p. 1.

it could not exist in the free air of England. Nevertheless, up to the time of his judgment, slaves had been freely bought and sold at the Royal Exchange (London) and elsewhere. In 1771 there were 15,000 negro slaves in England. Even later some of the white population of the country were in a state of servitude. The preamble to an Act of Parliament of 1775 recited "that many colliers, coal-heavers, and salters were in a state of slavery or bondage bound to the collieries and salt works, where they worked for life, transferable with the collieries and salt works when their original masters had no use for them." The very object of this Act of 1775 was to remove the reproach of allowing such a state of servitude to exist in a free country. Outside Great Britain, slavery continued to be recognised in most of her Colonies. In many instances England was originally directly responsible for forcing it on them. If the framers of the Constitution of the United States could have followed the judgment of Lord Mansfield and the dictates of humanity and abolished slavery in America, no doubt they would have done so, but it was impossible. Massachusetts had abolished it Massachusetts by a decision of her Supreme Court in 1781, which had declared its existence to be inconsistent with the declaration of the State Bill of Rights, "that all men were born free and equal." The framers of the Constitution provided that after the year 1808 Congress should have power to prohibit the further importation of slaves in the United States. It was as far as they dared go.

If in this one respect the Constitution were unworthy of a free republic, in all others it breathed the loftiest spirit of freedom. Its creation marks an epoch in the history of civilisation : the torch of democratic liberty, which had been kindled at Athens, re-lighted in Rome, but extinguished by the Cæsars, had been rekindled on the fields of Runnymede, thenceforward never ceasing to shine in England ; it was now to shine over the Western hemisphere to illuminate and guide a great branch of the Anglo-Saxon race along the highway of progress.

CHAPTER XIII

THE DEVELOPMENT OF THE CONSTITUTION

Amending power. THE Constitution of the United States has developed in a variety of ways since its establishment. Its framers were confident that it would, and therefore provided for its alteration by amendments. The difficulty, however, of working the amending process has often been pointed out by critics as keeping it too rigid in view of new conditions constantly created by the play of modern forces. The criticism is to a large extent true, and would have been proved much more so, except for the generous interpretation it has received from the judiciary, which has resulted in the placing in the hands of the executive and legislative branches of the National Government great and, perhaps, originally unsuspected resources. Nevertheless, the Constitutional power was once stretched to breaking point during the War of Secession, when the sword was drawn to cut a knot, which in other ways defied unravelment. Natural developments following the rule that bodies entrusted with powers will extend them to their full extent have added powers in many directions. Congress has passed Acts which no one has questioned, and however doubtful their legal force once was as years have elapsed long custom has sanctioned these exercises of the legislative and executive authority.

The method of amendment provided by the Constitution is set out in the fifth Article. Congress may propose amendments whenever two-thirds of both Houses deem such necessary, or Congress may call a Convention for proposing amendments whenever two-thirds of the State legislatures apply; but in neither case will amendments become valid until they are ratified by three-fourths of the State legislatures, or three-fourths of the Conventions, as one or other mode of ratification may be proposed by

144

Congress. A proviso to this Article, however, declares that the State representation in the Senate cannot be altered without the consent of the State. The Second Chamber, therefore, has remained permanent, as fixed by the Constitution, and is likely to be so, for so far, no State has been found willing to reduce its representation. The views that influenced the framers of the Constitution in proposing this system of amendment were well explained in " The Federalist "[1]— Amendment of State representation requires consent of State.

" The plan for the amendment of the Constitution adopted by the Convention was stamped with every mark of propriety. It guarded equally against that extreme facility which would have rendered the Constitution too mutable ; and that extreme difficulty which might have perpetuated its discovered faults. It enabled the general and the State Governments to originate the amendment of errors, as they might be pointed out by the experience on one side or the other. The exception in favour of the equality of suffrage in the Senate was probably meant as a palladium to the residuary sovereignty of the States implied and secured by that principle of representation in one branch of the Legislature, and was probably insisted on by the States particularly attached to such equality." Views of " The Federalist."

The President has no power over amendments, nor is his consent required to the proposals of Congress. President has no power over amendments.

The method of amendment has proved, in practice, slow : few amendments have been made. Over sixty years elapsed between the passing of the 12th and the adoption of the 13th amendment. This and the two subsequent amendments were only carried by the driving force created by the Civil War. Method of amendment proved slow.

The Ten Articles of the first Amendment have already been referred to in detail.[2] Their origin is to be found in the proceedings of the Conventions called to ratify the Constitution. The Convention of Virginia at the close of its deliberations[3] Origin of the Ten Articles of the 1st Amendment.

---

[1] " The Federalist," No. xliii.
[2] *Ante*, Chapter xii.
[3] Elliot's *Debates on the Federal Constitution* (Virginia).

resolved "that to relieve the apprehensions of those solicitous for amendments that necessary amendments be recommended to the consideration of the first Congress." New York ratified the Constitution; but in a circular letter addressed to the Governors of the several States in the Union, urged the necessity of amendment. It was only the invincible reluctance of this great State to separate itself from its sister States that prevailed upon it to ratify the Constitution without stipulating for further amendments.

Adoption of Amendments.

Many amendments were proposed by other States. In fact, so universally were they desired, that Congress took them into its consideration during its first session, and framed twelve Articles, which were subsequently submitted to the States for ratification; ten of these were adopted and form the Ten Articles of the first amendment.

The 2nd Amendment.

Article XI of the second Amendment was the direct outcome of a decision of the Supreme Court in 1794, that a State could be sued by a private citizen of another State. The realisation of this fact led to such an outcry amongst the States, whose dignity was insulted by this decision, that in the second session of the third Congress an amendment was proposed that the judicial power of the United States should not be construed to extend to any suit in law or equity commenced or prosecuted against one of the United States by citizens of another State, or by citizens or subjects of any foreign State. On the adoption of this Amendment, the proceedings against Georgia, which was the State sued, dropped. [2]

The 3rd Amendment.

In 1800, before the Constitution was amended by Article XII, the rule prevailed that the candidate for the Presidency securing the largest number of votes became President, and the candidate standing second Vice-president. Jefferson and Burr, in 1800, each received the same number of votes. Jefferson and Burr were members of the same party, and the supporters of Jefferson voting for

[1] Elliot's *Debates on the Federal Constitution* (New York), p. 414.
[2] Chisholm *v.* Georgia, 2 Dall, 419.

Burr intended Jefferson to be President and Burr Vice- Death of
president. In the result, after a bitter struggle, Jefferson ^Hamilton.
was elected. Resentment against Hamilton led to a duel,
in which this accomplished statesman lost his life. To
prevent the recurrence of a similar deadlock, the twelfth
Article directed that distinct ballots for the Presidency and
Vice-presidency should be taken. Both President and Vice-
president were in future directed to be chosen by a majority
of the whole number of Presidential electors by distinct
ballots. If such a majority were not obtained, the House
of Representatives was at liberty to choose three out of the
persons having the highest number of votes, instead of five,
as originally directed by the Constitution.[1] The vote was
then required to be taken by ballot and by States, the
representatives from each State having one vote. A quorum
for this purpose was declared to consist of a member or
members from two-thirds of the States, and a majority of
all the States was requisite for the choice. On the House of
Representatives failing to choose a President before the 4th
of March next following, the Vice-president was empowered
to act as President in the same way as in the case of the
death or other constitutional disability of the President.

If no candidate for the Vice-presidency had a majority Vice-d
of the whole number of electors appointed, the election fell ^Presi ency.
to the Senate, who were directed to choose from the two
highest numbers on the list. A quorum for the purpose of
this choice was directed to consist of two-thirds of the
whole number of Senators. A majority of the whole
number of the Senate was necessary to ensure a choice;
it was left open for the Senate to adopt the ballot or
not.

To understand the causes that brought about the next The 13th,
three amendments, a brief survey of the anti-slavery move- 14th, and 15th
ment and its connection with State Rights is necessary. Amendments.
Although the word " slavery " was not mentioned in the
Constitution, its existence was expressly recognised.[1] At

[1] Sect. i, Article ii.
[2] Article iv, Sect. 2. *Ante*, p. 142.

the establishment of the Constitution, some States were slave-owning and others not. If the framers of the Constitution had attempted to abolish slavery, the States would never have agreed to union. Therefore, the anomaly of a free Constitution was exhibited, which conferred the greatest freedom on the white man and denied it to the black. One clause of the Constitution enabled States to recover their fugitive slaves who had escaped into free States. Under an Act of 1793[1] a slave who had escaped from one State to another was restored to his owner on *primâ facie* evidence of ownership. In 1850 even more stringent provisions for the recovery of fugitive slaves were provided by Act of Congress. [2]

Anomaly of the Constitution.

Whilst the private ownership of property in slaves was from the first acknowledged by the Constitution, as time passed on it met less and less with the moral assent of the people of the United States. The question of the admission of new States with slave-owning Constitutions into the Union became the battle-ground of parties.

By the Constitution.

In 1803 Louisiana was acquired from the French. Its acquisition met with considerable opposition. A substantial objection was that as a Southern territory its future admission to the Union later on would strengthen the interests of the slave-owning States. In 1819, to use Jefferson's picturesque simile, "like a fire bell in the night," a bitter conflict sprang up on the proposal made to admit Missouri into the Union. Missouri was a new State that had been formed out of Louisiana. The slavery party inserted in its proposed Constitution clauses not only recognising slavery, but proposing to perpetuate it by depriving its legislature of power at any time to abolish it. Its proposed Constitution further forbade the admission of free negroes within its boundaries. After a year's fierce struggle over these clauses, Congress adopted a compromise by which Missouri was admitted, in 1821, upon the understanding that all legislation should be abstained from that interfered with the admission of free negroes into her borders, and that

Acquisition of Louisiana.

Admission of Missouri.

The Missouri compromise.

[1] Act of 1793, ch. 51, s. 7.
[2] Ableman v. Booth, 21 How, 506.

slavery should be prohibited in all of Louisiana lying north of Prohibition of slavery. 36° 30′ North latitude, excepting such parts as were included within the limits of Missouri.

The political compromise proved only temporarily suc- Agitation for emancipation of slaves. cessful. An agitation was started for the emancipation of the slaves. In 1840 and in 1844 anti-slavery candidates for the Presidency sought the popular suffrage.

In 1845 Texas was annexed. Its annexation was followed Annexation of Texas. by the Mexican War, which resulted in the acquisition of further territory by the United States. The larger portion of the new territory acquired was situated south of the Missouri compromise line; should this line be maintained Consequences of. the number of slave-owning States would be considerably increased—a contingency not sufficiently realised when the compromise was effected. Although new States at the time were clamouring to join the Union, such was the prevailing feeling of Congress that their admission became increasingly difficult. It was immaterial whether the proposed Constitution was free or recognised slavery.

The Southern States were prepared to accept an extension of the compromise line to the Pacific, but the opposition to this proved remarkably strong; since the portion of Mexico acquired had hitherto been free from slavery, and the introduction of slavery into it was considered by many to be a disgrace to the national honour and morality.

In the Presidential election of 1848 the anti-slavery party Further compromises developed increasing strength; nevertheless they were not in the ascendant. In 1850 a new compromise was arranged by which California, lying south of the Missouri compromise line, was admitted into the Union as a free State. Slavery was introduced in Columbia, whilst Texas was permitted to be organised on the understanding that new States might be carved out of her territory; a more stringent law was passed dealing with the arrest and return of fugitive slaves. The formation of new territories was permitted, without slavery being [either expressly prohibited or permitted.

Failure of
compromise.

This compromise proved just as ineffective as the earlier one of Missouri.

In truth, the national conscience was gradually awakening to the shame of slavery. In Kansas fierce contests took place between rival parties anxious to obtain control of the local Government, with a view ultimately to shape its future constitution. A raid was made in Virginia by an anti-slavery party for the purpose of freeing the slaves, which, however, proved disastrous, and induced the bitterest feelings. The slave-owning States relied, with every justification of law, upon the Constitution which acknowledged slavery, and bitterly protested against attacks made upon their domestic affairs. On the other hand, the Constitution was denounced. James Russell Lowell, in one of his poems, describes the feelings of the then minority—

Views of
Lowell.

" Though we break our fathers' promise, we have nobler duties first,
The traitor to humanity is the traitor most accursed :
Man is more than Constitutions ; better rot beneath the sod
Than be true to Church and State while we are doubly false to God !
We owe allegiance to the State ; but deeper, truer, more
To the sympathies that God hath set within our spirits' core.
Our country claims our fealty : We grant it so, but, then,
Before Man made us citizens, great Nature made us men."[1]

Repeal of the
Missouri
Compromise
Act.

In 1854 the Missouri Compromise Act of 1820 was repealed, and an Act for the organisation of the two new territories of Kansas and Nebraska, in the region west of Missouri and north of the Missouri compromise line, passed. To the people of these territories was left the choice of saying whether they would be slave-owning States or not. The effect of this Act was to legalise the existence of slavery in a district where hitherto it had not been

The Dred
Scott case.

permitted. In 1856 a most important decision was given by the Supreme Court in what is known as the Dred Scott case.[2]

The Supreme Court decided that a free negro of Africa, whose ancestors had been brought into the country and sold as slaves, was not a citizen, since negroes were not, on the

---

[1] On the capture of certain fugitive slaves near Washington.
[2] Dred Scott v. Sandford, 19 How., 393.

adoption of the Constitution, regarded in any of the States as citizens. A free negro was, therefore, not entitled to sue as a citizen in the Courts of the United States. The Court further decided that a State could not make foreigners or any other description of person citizens of the United States, nor entitle them to the rights and privileges secured to citizens by the Constitution, although it was at liberty to enact laws which put a foreigner or any description of persons on a footing with its own citizens. The Court further decided that an Act of Congress that prohibited a citizen of the United States from taking with him his slaves on his removal to a territory of the United States was an exercise of authority over private property not warranted by the Constitution. A slave was property protected by the Federal Government ; and when à slave's status had been fixed by the laws of the State where he resided, on leaving that State for a State where slavery was not permitted, he did not become free on his return to his original State. Congress had therefore no power to exclude slavery from the territories of the United States.

The judgment led to a great outcry, and the Chief Justice of the Supreme Court, Taney, was especially the object of attack. From a legal point of view, the bulk of the judgment may be considered one great *obiter dictum*. The decision that an African negro could not sue as a citizen in the Courts of the United States disposed of the case, making the rest of the judgment unnecessary. According to English law, all else was of no higher value than the expression of a distinguished opinion.

The judgment was subsequently disregarded by President Lincoln and by Congress. Taney's successor (Chief Justice Chase) admitted coloured persons to practise in Federal Courts, thus passing an implied rebuke upon the judgment of his predecessor. The anti-slavery party were not at this time in the ascendant in the United States, but it became increasingly evident to them that slavery must be destroyed or acknowledged throughout all the States. Lowell wrote— *Disregard of judgment.*

"Once to every man and nation comes the moment to decide,
In the strife of Truth with Falsehood for the good or evil side.
Some great cause God's new Messiah, offering each the bloom
or blight :
Parts the goats upon the left hand and the sheep upon the right ;
And the choice goes by for ever 'twixt that darkness and that
light."

In 1857 a Constitution for Kansas, framed at Lecompton, was presented to Congress, but was opposed with much vehemence on the ground that it had been cunningly drafted for the purpose of introducing slavery into a new State, notwithstanding the opposition of the people of the State ; it, nevertheless, received the sanction of Congress, prior to the outbreak of the War. Subsequently, however, on the withdrawal of the Southern Members, a Constitution framed at Wyandotte in 1859, was adopted, under which Kansas joined the Union.

The Presidential contest of 1860 resulted in the success of the Anti-Slavery party, the movement finding in the new President, Abraham Lincoln, an illustrious, wise, and humane leader of the last great Crusade.

The result of the election acted as a warning signal to the Southern States. South Carolina ordered the election of a Convention to consider the question of secession from the Union. The Convention met and adopted a secession ordinance, which declared that the Union between South Carolina and other States under the name of the United States was dissolved. Before the end of May, 1860, many other States had adopted similar ordinances.

Notwithstanding that the Union was believed to be legally incapable of dissolution, the dissentient States claimed the right to leave it, and furthermore announced their unalterable intention of disputing any attempt to subvert their claims by force.

With reference to the Constitutional questions involved in the subsequent War, it may be said that the anti-slavery party had no legal right to interfere with the internal government of the slave-owning States. On the other hand, it may be urged that these States possessed no legal right to leave the Union unless with the consent of all other States. Constitutional questions, however, become submerged in the greater moral question of slavery or no slavery.

During the War many acts were done for which no warrant could be found in the Constitution. Some acts were justified as exercises of authority under the war power ; others may not have been justifiable at all. The close of the war led to the 13th amendment of the Constitution, which made law those principles for which the struggle had been waged by the anti-slavery party. *Validity of Acts during the War.*

On December 18th, 1865, it was declared that (1) "neither slavery nor involuntary servitude, except as a punishment for crime, whereof the party should have been duly convicted, should exist within the United States or any place subject to its jurisdiction ; (2) Congress should have power to enforce this Article by appropriate legislation." *13th Amendment.*

The passing of the 13th Amendment freed the slaves and, at the same time, the United States from the reproach of slavery. On April 9th, 1866, Congress gave effect to this amendment by passing an Act to protect all persons in the United States in the enjoyment of their civil rights and furnish the means of their vindication. The Dred Scott judgment of the Supreme Court, however, still remained. It still was the law that an African negro could not be a citizen of the United States.

To dispose of this point, the 14th Amendment was passed. The Amendment declared that all persons born or naturalised in the United States, and subject to its jurisdiction, were citizens of the United States and of the State in which they resided. The States were prohibited from making or enforcing laws abridging the privileges or immunities of citizens of the United States. No State should deprive any person of life, liberty, or property without due process of law, nor deny to any person within its jurisdiction the equal protection of laws. *14th Amendment.*

The first portion of this Amendment settled for ever [the question whether a coloured person was a citizen of the *Effect of Amendment.*

United States or not. Its affirmation of his citizenship abrogated the Dred Scott judgment. The amendment extended the right of suffrage to no one, but afforded to all females as well as to all males the protection of the National Government. Two only exceptions were made —the case of Indians preserving their tribal relations and foreigners cherishing their allegiance to the country of their birth. The second portion of the Amendment contained a prohibition on the States, since all persons were in future recognised as citizens of the United States, and their privileges and immunities were protected from State interference.

Meaning of privileges and immunities.
It is difficult to arrive at a satisfactory classification of the meaning of " privileges and immunities." Doubtless they include the right to inherit, purchase, lease, sell, hold, and convey real and personal property ; to make contracts and enforce them by law ; and possess the full benefit of all laws. The franchise itself is not an indispensable right of citizenship, since a wider meaning is attached to citizenship than that of votes ; for instance, a woman may have no vote, though her right to the protection of the law may not be denied.

The privileges and immunities conferred by the Amendment were only such as the National Government could give, and only such as could be given were protected by the prohibition. In all other respects the position of the States was unaffected. It afforded its own citizen the safeguard of its constitution and laws.

Life, liberty, and property.
" Life, liberty, or property were not to be taken away without due process of law." This guarantee necessarily implied the administration of equal laws, according to established rules by competent tribunals, having jurisdiction and proceedings upon notice and hearing.[1] No State, after the amendment, could legally deny to any person within its jurisdiction the equal protection of its laws. The existence of laws in States, where the newly-emancipated negroes resided, which discriminated against them as a

---

[1] The United States v. Billings, 190 *Federal Reporter*, p. 559.

class, with gross injustice and hardship, was the evil meant to be remedied by this clause, and by it all laws specially directed against negroes were forbidden.   If a State declined to conform its laws to the requirements of the Amendment, then by the 5th section of the Article, Congress was authorised to enforce its requirements by suitable legislation.[1]

This Amendment, said the Supreme Court, does not profess to secure to all persons in the United States the benefit of the same law and the same remedies.   Great diversities may and do exist in many respects in different States : one may possess the common law and trial by jury ; another, the civil law and trial by the Court.   But like diversities may also exist in different parts of the same State.   The States frame their laws and organise their courts with some regard to local peculiarities and special needs, and this violates no constitutional requirement.   All that one can demand under the last clause of section 1 of the 14th Amendment is that a person shall not be denied the same protection of the laws which is enjoyed by other persons or other classes in the same place and under like circumstance.[2]

Section 2 of the 14th Amendment declared that representation should be apportioned among the several States, according to their respective numbers, counting the whole number of persons in each State, excluding Indians not taxed.   But when the right to vote at any election for choice of electors of President and Vice-president of the United States Representatives in Congress, the Executive and Judicial officers of a State, or the members of the Legislature thereof, is denied to any of the male inhabitants of such State being twenty-one years of age, and citizens of the United States, or in any way abridged, except for participation in rebellion or other crime, the basis of representation therein shall be reduced in the proportion which

14th Amendment, sect. 2.

---

[1] The Live Stock Dealers and Butchers' Association v. The Crescent City Live Stock Landing and Slaughter-House Company, 16 Wall, 36.
[2] Missouri v. Lewis, 101 U.S., 22 ; Hayes v. Missouri, 120 U.S., 18. Kentucky R.R., Tax cases, 115 U.S., 321.

the number of such male citizens shall bear to the whole number of male citizens twenty-one years of age in such State.

Object of Section.

The object of this section of the Amendment was to preclude States which denied the franchise to its coloured citizens from having the benefit of a numerical basis for the purposes of representation.

14th Amendment, 3rd Section.

The third section to the 14th Amendment declared that " no person should be a Senator or Representative in Congress, or elector of President and Vice-President, or hold any office (civil or military) under the United States, or under any State, who, having previously taken an oath as a member of Congress or as a member of a State Legislature, or as an Executive or Judicial officer of any State to support the Constitution, should have engaged in insurrection or rebellion against the same, or given aid or comfort to the enemies thereof. Congress was empowered by a vote of two-thirds to remove the disability."

4th Section.

A fourth section affirmed the validity of the National debts, including debts incurred for payment of pensions and bounties for services in suppressing insurrection and rebellion. But neither the United States nor any State could assume to pay any debt or obligation incurred in aid of insurrection or rebellion against the United States, nor any claim for the loss or emancipation of any slave. All such debts, obligations, and claims were declared to be illegal and void.

In an early stage of the War, President Lincoln had offered, with the approval of Congress, to provide some compensation to persons deprived of their slaves ; but the offer was not accepted. Possibly it was made too late, possibly it would never have been accepted under any circumstances.

Abolition of slavery in British Colonies, 1833.

In 1833 slavery was abolished throughout the British Colonies by Act of Parliament (3 & 4 Will. IV, c. 73), compensation was then provided for slave-owners.

14th Amendment, Section 5.

The 5th section of the Amendment empowered Congress to enforce its provision by appropriate legislation. Such

legislation was subsequently enacted in a statute entitled :
" An Act to enforce the provisions of the 14th Amendment
to the Constitution of the United States and for other
purposes."

The 15th Article of the Amendment was ratified on Ratification
March 30th, 1870. of 15th Article, 1870.

It provided against discriminations at the polls : " The
right of citizens of the United States to vote," it declared,
" shall not be denied or abridged by reason of race
colour or previous condition of servitude " ; and Congress was
empowered to enforce this Article by appropriate legislation.

Legislation was passed, the naturalisation laws amended
and extended to Africans, and the National Government Legislation of Congress.
assumed the right to preserve order at elections in towns
whose population exceeded 20,000 or more, when
Congressional Representatives were chosen.

Over forty-two years passed before a further amendment
was made. The Constitution when it emerged from the
Civil War was, in some respects, more unified ; and in one
great respect, completer. Human rights were no longer
the victims of laws of compromise. The same constitutional
freedom that was accorded to the white man was accorded
to the black. For good or evil, in prosperity or misfortune,
the two races were left to work out their destiny, side by
side, in the full fruition of constitutional liberty.

The 16th Amendment was submitted to the States in
1909, and is as follows : " Congress shall have the power to
levy and collect taxes on incomes from whatever source
derived, without apportionment among the several States
and without regard to any census or enumeration." On the
3rd February, 1913, the vote of the Delaware and Wyoming legislatures ratifying the proposed amendment secured
for it the necessary majority of three-fourths of the States.
The fact that Delaware's time was three hours earlier than
Cheyenne's, gave Delaware the honour of being the State
to complete the ratification. The history of the attempt
to impose income tax in the United States is an interesting
chapter in the constitutional development of the nation.

During the Civil War when many acts were done, which were not strictly justifiable under the Constitution, Income Taxes were imposed.

Income Tax Act of 1894.

In 1894 an Act to reduce taxation and to provide revenue for the Government and for other purposes was passed by Congress, but was not returned by the President to the House in which it originated within the time prescribed by the Constitution, consequently became law without his approval. The Act imposed a tax of 2 per cent. on the amounts derived from income, over and above four thousand dollars, and laid down rules for its assessment and collection.

The question as to the legality of the sections of the Acts dealing with its imposition was raised in a case of Pollock v. Farmer's Loan and Trust Company [1] on appeal from the Circuit Court of the United States for the Southern District of New York to the Supreme Court.

Decision of the Supreme Court.

The Supreme Court decided that a tax on the rents on income of real estate was a direct tax as used in the Constitution, and that a tax upon income derived from the interest on bonds issued by a municipality was a tax upon the power of the State and its instrumentalities to borrow money: consequently those portions of the Act that provided for the levying of taxes upon rents on incomes derived from real estate or from the interest on bonds were invalid. The Court was equally divided on the point as to whether the invalidity of these provisions rendered void the whole Act, and also whether as to the income from personal property as such the Act was unconstitutional as laying direct taxes and on the further point whether any part of the tax if not considered as a direct tax was invalid for want of uniformity. The result of this decision was considered so unsatisfactory that a petition was filed for its rehearing. The case came on for rehearing before a fully constituted Court, who decided by a majority of one that taxes on personal property or on the income of personal property were direct taxes like taxes on the rents or income of real

[1] 157 U.S., (1894), p. 429.

estate.[1] The Income Tax Act was consequently unconstitutional.

In distributing the power of taxation, the Constitution reserved to the States absolute power of direct taxation, but granted to the Federal Government the power of the same taxation upon condition that in its exercise such taxes should be apportioned among the several States according to numbers ; and this was done, in order to preserve for the States who were surrendering to the Federal Government so many sources of income, the power of direct taxation which was their principal remaining resource.

" The founders of the Constitution " anticipated that the expenditure of the States, their counties, cities, and towns, would chiefly be met by direct taxation on accumulated property, whilst they expected that that of the Federal Government would be for the most part met by indirect taxes. And in order that the power of direct taxation by the general government should not be exercised except on necessity ; and, when the necessity arose, should be so exercised as to leave the States at liberty to discharge their respective obligations, and should not be so exercised unfairly and discriminatingly, as to particular States or otherwise by a mere majority vote, possibly of those whose constituents were intentionally not subjected to any part of the burden the qualified grant was made."[2]

Apportionment of Taxation.

It will be remembered that under the older Confederation, Congress had experienced the greatest difficulty in obtaining requisitions of money that they had asked for from the States. The direct taxation given to Congress took the place of requisitions, but the apportionment was purposely restrained to apportionment according to representation in order that the former system as to ratio might be retained while the mode of collection was changed.

The assent of the States to the imposition of an income tax by the ratification of the 16th Amendment ended a struggle which began in the earliest days of the Republic.

[1] Pollock *v.* Farmers' Loan and Trust Co., 158 U.S. (1894), p. 601.
[2] *Ibid.*, p. 621.

Changes in the Government of the English after American independence. First Colonial Secretary. THE changes that took place as the result of the War of American Independence in the Government of the Empire were of an important character. The increasing tendency of the British Parliament to interfere in Colonial Affairs was seen in the establishment of a third Secretary of State in 1768, whose special province was the care of the Colonies. The Earl of Hillsborough was the first occupant of this office ; he was followed, in 1772, by Lord Dartmouth, who, in turn, in 1775, found a successor in Lord St. Germaine.

Burke's attack on Colonial Secretaryship. During the period from 1768 to 1782 there were two authorities responsible for colonial administration—the Board of Trade and Plantations and the Secretary of State. In 1780 the necessity for the existence of both authorities was attacked by Burke in the debate on the Bill known as the " Establishment Bill." Burke considered that " the office of Colonial Secretary had thrown the Empire into the miseries of the Civil War that had cost us America." In humorous terms he declared that the " third Secretaryship was extinct. It was deposited with the corpse of Lord Suffolk in a superb cemetery ; its funeral obsequies were performed on that occasion ; it was laid aside with that which became it—pomp, ensigns, scutcheons, flambeaux, etc. A successor after a year was, indeed, appointed him ; but if you ask the reason, no other can be given than the Irishman's : ' The other Secretaries were doing nothing, and a third was appointed to help them.' " [1]

The Board of Trade and Plantations. Influence of Parliament on. For at least forty years prior to 1780 the administration of the Board of Trade and Plantations had been inefficient : the British Parliament was largely responsible for this state

[1] Cobbett's *Parliamentary History of England*, Vol. XXI, 1780-1, p. 205.

of things.   Members of Parliament had been placed on the Board for any merit but that of a knowledge of Colonial affairs.

According to Mr. Eden, a member of the Board, and its principal defender in the House of Commons against Burke's attack, the Board of Trade and Plantations' records at that time consisted of upwards of 2,300 volumes in folio, and these volumes contained the names of Locke, Addison, Prior, Lord Molesworth, and Charles Townshend, and many others of the first rank and first-rate abilities who had at different times enjoyed seats on the Board.

The mere mention of these very voluminous records afforded Burke an opportunity for banter. "He was willing," he said, " to bow his head in reverence to the great and shining talents of its several members.   The historian's labours, the wise and salutary result of deep religious searches,[1] the essence of epistolary correspondence,[2] and the great fund of political and legal knowledge displayed most unanswerably the high abilities of four of its members, and entitled them to every mark of respect ; whilst the poetical accomplishments of a fifth (Lord Carlisle), which in an age of poetry would have given him rank among the best of our minor poets, in this age, which was of a more serious form, made him deservedly regarded as a great poet. To the professors themselves he owed all possible deference, and from that it was that he resolved to rescue them ; from the ignominy of being degraded to a Board of Trade.   As an academy of Belles Lettres, he should hallow them ; as a Board of Trade, he wished to abolish them."

" The great writers," he added, " who sat at the Board of Trade were immersed in a skeleton which was death to the freedom of their genius, and the strong ribs of which barred them from all opportunity of taking those soaring flights they were otherwise capable of.   He meant to destroy the skeleton of death and to give them liberty."

Burke on the Board of Trade and Plantations.

---

[1] Gibbon's *Decline and Fall of the Roman Empire.*
[2] Mr. Eden's letters addressed to Lord Carlisle and his observations on the Criminal Law.

Conduct during the War

During the course of the disputes with America, not so much as a single scrap of paper had been laid by the Board before Parliament respecting the state, condition, or temper of the Colonies. Grenville and almost every other member for fifty years had complained, and Townshend (from his experience of the Board) had often held it up as an object of ridicule.

Abolition of offices of Colonial Secretary and Board of Trade; Government of the Colonies, how carried on.

In 1782 the office of the Colonial Secretary and the Board of Trade and Plantations were abolished, and the Government of the Colonies was controlled by the Privy Council, in conjunction with a subordinate branch of the Home Office, then called the Northern Department, managed by an Under-Secretary and three clerks, in what was then styled the Plantations Branch of the Home Office. A Law Officer was appointed to report on Colonial Acts. By an order of September 11th of the same year, circular instructions were issued to the Governors of the Plantations directing them to transmit to the Privy Council those duplicates of returns and accounts which it had hitherto been the practice to furnish to the Committee of Trade and Plantations.

Formation of Committee of Privy Council.

In 1784 a Committee for the consideration of all matters relating to Trade and Plantations was appointed ; and in 1786 a new Committee, which took over all matters that had been referred to the Committee of 1784 by Order in Council. By a subsequent Order of August 25th of the same year, this Committee was placed on a definite footing, and the business which had hitherto been transacted by the Plantations branch of the Home Office, was transferred to it.

Revival of office of Colonial Secretary : cessation of active functions of Committee of Privy Council.

Such state of things continued until 1794, when the office of Secretary for State for the Colonies was revived by Lord Melville, then Secretary of War, who took over the department. The administrative functions of the Committee of the Privy Council appointed in 1786 appear about this time to have ceased.

Appointment of separate office, 1854.

The Departments of War and the Colonies continued to be united until 1854, when a distinct Secretary for the Colonies was appointed.

The Committee of the Privy Council, which dealt with appeals from the Plantations throughout all these changes, exercised its jurisdiction till the Judicial Committee of the Privy Council was constituted in 1833.

Amongst the many appeals brought during the years 1829 to 1831 was one from Canada and one from the Cape of Good Hope, and others of considerable importance from different parts of the Empire.

The Act for the better administration of justice in His Majesty's Privy Council (1833) recited that the right of appeal existed from the Plantations, Colonies, and other dominions of His Majesty abroad, to His Majesty in Council ; and that matters of appeal or petition were usually heard before a committee of the whole of the Privy Council, who made a report to His Majesty in Council, whereupon the final judgment or determination was given by His Majesty. Since 1833, petitions and appeals have been constantly heard by the Judicial Committee. The composition of this body, however, has undergone very many considerable changes.

The administration of the Empire beyond the seas has now long passed away from the Privy Council, and become located in the Colonial Office, over which the Imperial Parliament exercises a direct control.

The history of the relations of the United Kingdom since 1794 with those Colonies which now constitute parts of the three great Dominions may be divided into three periods : The first period of Colonial Office administration ended about 1848 ; the second terminated with the meeting of the first Colonial Conference in 1887 ; and the third period comprises the history of the last twenty-six years.

During the first period may be distinctly observed the slow growth and development of Colonial Governments, gradually emancipating themselves by stages from nominated Councils, with a strict submission to Downing Street edicts, to freer institutions and Representative Governments.

Canada obtained a Representative Government in 1840 ; ten years later, Representative Government was conceded to

New South Wales, Victoria, Tasmania, and South Australia. By 1852 the Cape of Good Hope enjoyed a free Constitution.

It cannot be said during the first of these periods that Colonial affairs were much understood either by the Colonial Office or by Parliament. Rebellions in Upper and Lower Canada, and discontent in many different Colonies were the distinguishing signs of the times. The period covers years when the colonists were busy digging, ploughing, exploring, and opening up new regions ; when skirmishes occurred with Indians and bushmen ; when marvels of fresh fauna revealed themselves like the wonders of Aladdin's cave to enchanted discoverers ; when learned societies in England pored over maps of continents whose coast lines were imperfectly defined, whose rivers were unexplored, and whose vast areas were marked with the title of unknown lands ; when the North-West of Canada was untraversed except by the hardy trapper and hunter ; and South Africa was in fear of the assegais of the Zulus. When Hume crossed over the Murray, and Strzelecki climbed the Austra-lian Alps, naming after his Polish compatriot Koskiusko that beautiful mountain from whose summit he beheld the silvery sources of the river which Hume had first sighted. When Stokes navigated in the *Beagle,* and all the Empire was alive with the voices of the pioneers like the hum of bees. There was little time during this period for men to think of Constitutions. Nevertheless, so great is the love of the Briton for constitutional freedom, that Governments began to assume more popular shapes, forming the rising pillars on which the massive arches of Federation were subsequently to rest.

The second period begins with the administration of Earl Grey, who is often referred to as the founder of modern Colonial policy.

In 1848 he invoked the assistance of the Committee of the Privy Council appointed for the consideration of all matters relating to trade and foreign plantations, an attempt to revive the former political functions of that governing body of the Empire.   ·

The Committee made two reports, which were approved Reports of the Committees of Privy Council. by the Sovereign in Council on May 1st, 1849, and January 30th, 1850. They dealt with projected Constitution for the Australian Colonies and the Cape of Good Hope.

In the Report of May 1st, 1849, the Committee dis- Report of May 1st, 1849. tinguish between the practice in the nineteenth century and the earlier practice respecting the establishment of systems of civil government in the Colonial dependencies of the British Crown.

"There prevailed," the Report says, "until the com- Type of legislature. mencement of the nineteenth century, the almost invariable usage of establishing a local legislature consisting of three estates, that is, of a Governor appointed by the Sovereign of a Council nominated by the Sovereign and of an assembly elected by the people. Although, in some cases, other schemes of Colonial polity had at first been established, yet these schemes had all, with one exception, progressively been brought before the end of the eighteenth century into conformity with this general type or model.

"Further, these Colonial Constitutions were all (except in Created by letters patent. the Canadas) created by letters patent under the Great Seal either of England or of Great Britain ; and these letters patent were used in the exercise of an unquestionable and undisputed prerogative of the Crown. But in Lower and Upper Canada the three estates of Governor, Council, and Parliamentary authority in Upper and Lower Canaaa. Assembly were established not by the Crown, but by the express authority of Parliament. This deviation from the general usage was unavoidable, because it was judged right Reasons for. to impart to the Roman Catholic population of the Canadas, privileges which in the year 1791 the Crown could not have lawfully conferred on them.

"There is also reason to believe that the settlement of the Canadian Constitution, not by a grant from the Crown merely, but in virtue of a positive statute, was regarded by the American loyalists as an important guarantee for the secure enjoyment of their political franchises.

"But during the nineteenth century the British Crown has New Colonies. acquired by conquest and cession from foreign States three transatlantic colonies, one colony in Southern Africa, and four colonies to the eastward of the Cape of Good Hope. During the same period the British Crown has acquired by the occupation of vacant territories two colonies on the western coast of Africa, three in New Holland, one in Van Diemen's Land, one in New Zealand, and one in the Falkland Islands. In no one of these sixteen colonies has the old Colonial polity of a Governor, Council and Assembly been introduced. In no one of them (except New South Wales) has any electoral franchise been granted to the Colonists or any share in the local legislation to their representatives. . . .

System of Government.

"In all the colonies acquired during the nineteenth century by the occupation of vacant territories, the same system of internal legislation by a Governor and a Council appointed by the Crown has been introduced by the authority of Parliament.

Extent of Royal Prerogative.

"In colonies so acquired, the Royal Prerogative was competent only to the establishment of civil governments, of which a legislature—comprised in part at least of the representatives of the people—formed a component part. To dispense even for a while with such a legislature, Parliamentary aid was requisite." [1]

"If we were approaching," continue the Committee, "the present question under circumstances which left to us the unfettered exercise of our own judgment as to the nature of the legislation to be established in New South Wales, Victoria, South Australia, and Van Diemen's Land, we should advise that Parliament should be moved to recur to the ancient constitutional usage by establishing in each a Governor, a Council, and an Assembly. For we think it desirable that the political institutions of the British Colonies should thus be brought into the nearest possible analogy to the Constitution of the United Kingdom. We also think it wise to adhere as closely as possible to our ancient maxims of government on this subject and to the precedents which these maxims have embodied. The

[1] *Report of the Privy Council*, May 1st, 1848, p. 34.

experience of centuries has ascertained the value and the practical efficiency of that system of Colonial polity to which those maxims and precedents afford their sanction.

In the absence of some very clear and urgent reason for breaking up the ancient uniformity of design in the government of the Colonial dependencies of the Crown, it would seem unwise to depart from that uniformity. And, further, the whole body of constitutional law which determines the rights and the duties of the different branches of the ancient Colonial Government, having with the lapse of time been gradually ascertained and firmly established, we must regret any innovation which tends to deprive the Australian Colonies of the great advantage of possessing such a code so well defined and so maturely considered.'

Whilst this was the view expressed by the Committee, they felt constrained, by what they believed to be the wish of the Colonists, to adopt the proposal of one legislature for each of the Australian legislatures, a third of whose members were to be nominated by the Crown, and the remaining two-thirds to be elected by the Colonists. How far they were misled by statements as to the desire of the people for this peculiar form of government it is difficult to say. It is perfectly clear, from what subsequently took place, that such a form of Constitution was not desired by the people of New South Wales or Victoria. *Recommendation of one Legislature.* *Not desired by Colonists.*

The Committee, however, considered that the legislatures should have the power to alter their Constitutions by resolving single Houses of Legislature into two Houses, and should be entrusted generally with the power to amend their Constitutions. *Power to amend Constitution.*

The Committee recommended that a uniform tariff should be established throughout Australia; that one of the Governors of the Australian Colonies should be the Governor-General of Australia, with power to convene a General Assembly of Australia, but that that body should not be convoked until the Governor-General should have received from two or more of the Australian legislatures addresses requesting him to exercise the power. The *Uniform tariff.* *Governor-General.* *General Assembly.*

proposal contained the seed of Federation, and ultimately fructified, fifty-two years afterwards, in the establishment of the Commonwealth of Australia.

The ten powers that the Committee thought should be entrusted to the General Assembly were—

1. The imposition of duties upon imports and exports.

2. The conveyance of letters.

3. The formation of roads, canals, or railways traversing any two or more of such colonies.

4. The erection and maintenance of beacons and light-houses.

5. The imposition of dues or other charges on shipping in every port or harbour.

6. The establishment of a General Supreme Court to be a Court of original jurisdiction and a Court of Appeal for any of the inferior Courts of the separate provinces.

7. The determining of the extent of the jurisdiction and the forms and manner of proceeding of such Supreme Court.

8. The regulation of weights and measures.

9. The enactment of laws affecting all the Colonies represented in the General Assembly on any subject not specifically mentioned in the preceding list, but on which the General Assembly should be desired to legislate by addresses for that purpose presented to them from the legislatures of all these colonies.

10. The appropriation to any of the preceding objects of such sum as may be necessary by an equal percentage from the revenue received in all the Australian Colonies, in virtue of any enactments of the General Assembly of Australia.[1]

This statesmanlike document led to the passing of the Australian Colonies Government Act, which closes the first of the three periods that have been adopted in narrating the constitutional story of the Mother Country and her Colonies.

The grant of Constitutions to Australia and to the Cape of Good Hope introduced a new era. The Constitution of

[1] *Ibid.*, 1848, p. 44.

the Cape of Good Hope was Earl Grey's favourite Constitution. It provided for a legislature consisting of Governor and a Legislative Council of twenty-six, with a House of Assembly of 107 members—both Houses were elected by the same voters, but a property qualification was prescribed for the franchise. The Constitution was established by letters patent of May 23rd, 1850.

The principle of the elected Second Chamber received the approval of Mr. Gladstone. He argued that " if the Government desired to draw out a plan for a Second Chamber, they must base it mainly and entirely upon the elective principle ; and it would be of no use or value in checking the movements of a popular assembly unless the elements of election were included in it." [1] *Mr. Gladstone's approval of elected Second Chamber.*

The story of the Empire subsequently to 1848 and up to the time of the first Colonial Conference is marked by a great event in 1867, when by the British North America Act the great Federal system of Canada was established. [2] The story of the movements in Canada, Australia, and South Africa are referred to elsewhere. *Period from 1848-1887.* *Dominion Act of 1867.*

A question was asked at the Quebec Conference as to the views of the Imperial authorities on Canadian Federation. The Duke of Newcastle's despatch of July 6th, 1862, was referred to in reply : " If a Union, either partial or complete, should hereafter be proposed, with the concurrence of all the Provinces, to be united, I am sure that the matter would be weighed in this country, both by the public, by Parliament, and Her Majesty's Government, with no feelings than an anxiety to discern and promote any course which might be conducive to the prosperity, the strength, and the harmony of all the British Commonwealth in North America."

In introducing the measure in the House of Lords, Lord Carnarvon, the then Colonial Secretary, said : " It is not every nation or every stage of the national existence that admits of a federative Government. Federation is only

[1] *Hansard's Parliamentary Debates*, 1850, Vol. 108.
[2] Post, p. 191.

possible under certain conditions, when the States to be
federated are so far akin that they can be united, and yet
so far dissimilar, that they cannot be fused into a single
body politic."

During the second period may be noticed the growing
independence of feeling amongst the people of the Dominions
and the increasing reluctance of the Imperial Parliament
and the Colonial Office to interfere with their affairs. Lord
John Russell and a large school of thought in the United
Kingdom considered that the widening of the limits of the
Home Rule granted to the Colonies led to separation.
" Let us give them," he said, when speaking in the House of
Commons on the 8th February, 1850, " as far as we can the
capacity of ruling their own affairs. Let them increase in
wealth and population, and whatever may happen we of this
great Empire shall have the consolation of saying that we
have contributed to the happiness of the world.

Final abandonment of idea of interfering with internal affairs of Colonies. In 1873 an Act was passed when, according to Mr. Bernard
Holland, the extreme point of legalised commercial disinte-
gration within the British Empire was, perhaps, reached.
At the instance of the Australian Colonies, the Imperial
Parliament somewhat reluctantly passed an Act quite
opposed to the general commercial principles never more
than then dominant in England, and gave these Colonies
perfect freedom to tax each other's goods, but provided
that no duty should be levied or remitted contrary to or
at variance with any Treaty or Treaties for the time being
subsisting between Her Majesty and a Foreign Power.
This Act repealed the Act of 1850, by which the Australian
Colonies were forbidden to impose differential duties as
between the Colonies and any other countries." [1]

The Act of 1873 also marked the abandonment of the idea
that the Imperial Parliament could assert its theoretical
rights to legislate in the internal government of the
Colonies.

The Imperial legislative functions are now directed to
passing enactments at the request of Colonial legislatures,

[1] 13 and 14 Vict., c. 59, Sect. 27.

and only interfering where the prerogative of the Crown
and the powers and privileges of the Imperial Parliament,
and of the legislatures of other parts of the Empire, are
affected.

In 1887, the year that witnessed the golden Jubilee of 1887.
Queen Victoria, saw the first of the great meetings of Conference.
Colonial statesmen, which have since shown that the Empire
is responsive to the appeal for increased unity.

During the months of April and May Colonial delegates
who had been specially appointed, met in London under
the presidency of the Colonial Secretary. Amongst the
matters then discussed were Colonial defence, Imperial
penny postage, etc.

The assembling of a Conference of the Premiers of the
self-governing Dominions brings the second period to an end.
It marks a further development of the Imperial idea ; one
only of the outward signs of an increased feeling of belief
in the common destiny of its peoples " under the Flag."
On the fields of South Africa, Canadian and Australian
blood was yet to be shed in support of this belief ; nor was
it to be shed in vain, but the first conference in the heart
of the Empire was the material triumph of the idea of
Imperial unity.

CHAPTER XV

THE CONSTITUTIONAL DEVELOPMENT OF CANADA

The year
1759. 1759 was a glorious year in the annals of Great Britain. The time when two old rivals—France and England—met in deadly conflict in two hemispheres and fought for the ascendancy of the seas and the possession of Colonial Empire. The spirits of the British people never ran higher than at this juncture. Secretary Pitt was at the helm of State. Parliament liberally voted whatever money was required for the prosecution of the war by land or sea ; for the nation understood the supreme issue involved in the struggle—an insular destiny or a world-wide empire.

Colonial
Empires. In the Eastern hemisphere victory was already assured by the triumph of Clive at Plassy, but in North America matters were far from satisfactory. The French had extended their power up the river St. Lawrence and thence along the great chain of lakes. It was far from improbable but that further conquests would lead them south to join hands with Louisiana, and so hem in the North American Colonies.

The naval victories of Admiral Hawke and other captains assured the command of the seas. Consequently, it was rendered possible to prepare an expedition for the capture of Quebec, the great gate of Canada.

Pitt entrusted its command to a young general, Wolfe, an officer's son, who had been born at Westerham, in Kent, in 1727.

Founders of
Empire :
Wolfe and
Cook in the
St. Lawrence. Whilst the summer of 1759 was yet young, the channel of the St. Lawrence river, on which Quebec stands, was in course of survey. The ship *Mercury* was employed for the purpose of taking soundings, on board of which was a master named James Cook, who was the son of an agricultural labourer, who had been born near Cleveland, a year after Wolfe. The officer's son and the son of the agricultural

labourer were instrumental in securing for the Empire her
two greatest dominions. The former planting the British
flag on the walls of Quebec gave her Canada ; the latter
rearing the standard on a strange land, which he named
from its fancied resemblance to the coast of Wales lying
to the north of the Bristol Channel—New South Wales—
added Australia.

Wolfe was a man of heroic mould, but of a delicate Wolfe and Cook
physical frame, nurtured in the contemplation of great compared.
deeds ; his death crowned his victory on the heights of
Abraham. Cook was a daring mariner, whose end also
came violently when his life's greatest work was accomplished. Whilst a tablet is inscribed to the memory of the
soldier by a grateful nation in Westminster Abbey, a place
in the national Pantheon has yet to be found for the
discoverer.

Pitt, Wolfe, and Cook—statesman, soldier, and sailor— Pitt, Wolfe, Cook.
a noble triumvirate of Empire builders.

The capture of Quebec in September of 1759 was cele- Capture of Quebec.
brated by the people of Great Britain with universal
rejoicings, sobered only by the loss of the nation's hero.
The Fleet brought Wolfe's body to England. From London
it was carried to its last resting-place amidst the sorrow
of thousands.

Thirty-five years after, when another Pitt guided the
national affairs in another great crisis, *The Victory* brought
home the body of another national hero from Trafalgar,
stricken like Wolfe in the hour of triumph, but conscious
like him that he had done something for his country.

On October 7th, 1760, the French forces in Canada Treaty of Paris.
capitulated, and on February 10th, 1763, by the Treaty of
Paris, Quebec passed completely under British domination.

In the same year a Royal Proclamation was published, New Government established by proclamation.
which provided for the government of the Colony. It
established four new governments—Quebec, East Florida,
West Florida, and Grenada ; it added Labrador from St.
John's river to Hudson's Bay and Anticosti and the Mag-
dalen Islands to Newfoundland ; and placed Prince Edward

Island and Cape Breton under the government of Nova Scotia.

Prerogative form of government. The Governors of the new Governments thus established were empowered by Royal Authority to summon general Assemblies and make laws for the peace, welfare, and good government of these Colonies, with the advice and consent of the Councils and Assemblies.

Establishment of courts. Courts for the hearing of civil and criminal causes were directed to be established as near as might be agreeable to the laws of England, with a right of appeal in all civil cases to the Privy Council.

The General Assembly of Quebec never met, although convoked, as the French population declined to take a test oath, the work of administration, in consequence, was carried on by the Governor, with the assistance of an Executive Council.

Uncertainty of laws. Affairs for years after the Royal Proclamation of 1763 remained in an unsettled condition, largely owing to the uncertainty as to whether French or English law should prevail. The English population contended that French law had been abrogated by the Conquest; the French population, on the contrary, asserted the continued existence of their ancient customs and usages. The Treaty of Paris had been silent on the subject of legal rights. According to English law,[1] the French contention was right, as Quebec was a conquered country ; and, as such, she retained her right to laws originally possessed until altered by her conqueror !

Introduction of English Criminal Law. The only alteration that had hitherto been applied had been the introduction of English criminal law in 1763.[2] The prevailing dissatisfaction created by this unsatisfactory state of things led to the passing of the Act of **First British Act of Parliament.** 1774,[3] the first British Act of Parliament which dealt with Quebec. Its purpose was to make more effectual provision for the government of the Province ; and an Act was chosen

---

[1] Campbell v. Hall, 20 *State Trials* at 323.
[2] Reg. v. Coote, L.R. 4, P.C., 599.
[3] 14 George III, c. 83.

in preference to an exercise of the royal authority, in Constitution of 1774. order to give a legislative, instead of a royal sanction to the benefits which were then introduced on behalf of the French-Canadian population.

By this Act the Government of the country was placed under the control of a Council, which was not to exceed twenty-three in number nor to be less than seventeen. The Council was empowered to make ordinances with the consent of the Governor, but ordinances were required to be transmitted to England for allowance. The French-Canadians, who had been left undisturbed in the exercise of their religion since the Treaty of Paris, were now confirmed in its free exercise, and the clergy were empowered to receive their accustomed dues from persons professing the Roman Catholic faith.

The test which had hitherto prevented the meeting of Abolition of test. Assemblies was abolished, and an oath of allegiance substituted.

The Governing Council constituted had no power to levy Minor powers of taxation. taxes or duties, except to a minor extent, for local purposes. The revenue for administrative purposes was provided from a duty which was imposed on spirits and molasses, and the deficiency made up from the Imperial Treasury.[1]

It was declared that in all matters of controversy where Paramount laws. civil rights and property were concerned, the French-Canadian law should prevail, but the criminal law of England was to continue to the exclusion of every other criminal code that had been in force prior to 1764. Power was given to the Legislature to amend both the civil and criminal law.

Labrador and the islands annexed to Newfoundland were now made part of the Province.

In 1776 a Privy Council was established, consisting of Establishment of Privy Council. five members : the Lieutenant-Governor and four members of the Legislative Council. Its functions were purely advisory.

During the war between Great Britain and her American

[1] 14, George III, c. 88, 1774.

Colonies, many attempts were made to 'sap the loyalty of the people of Canada and induce them to join the Confederation. Washington, in 1775, and Baron D'Estaing, the Commander of the French Fleet, in 1778, addressed proclamations to the French-Canadians for this purpose, but in vain ; nor did attempts at invasion by the Americans meet with better success. Canada remained firm in her adhesion to the British connection, and her spirit of loyalty was neither shaken by bribes or threats. During the war and afterwards, her population was increased by the influx of a large body—some 40,000 in number—of American
Colonists, who followed the British flag and quitted the United States to settle in Canada, where they were known by the proud title of "United Empire Loyalists." The
majority found a home in Nova Scotia, founding the province of New Brunswick ; others located themselves in Upper Canada.

The cession of Canada to Great Britain caused a similar movement of the French population, many of whom, after 1760, returned to France, with the result that the balance of population was altered, with a proportionate increase in the British element.

The changed condition of affairs led to the passing of the Constitutional Act of 1791. Some of the features of the original Bill found no place in the Act. The Bill professedly attempted to establish a Constitution in Canada as near as possible to that of Great Britain. It divided the province into two distinct Governments, under the names of Lower Canada and Upper Canada. It established in each a Legislative Council and Assembly, with power to make laws. The Legislative Councils—nominee Councils—were to be appointed by the King for life. In Lower Canada the Council was to consist of not less than fifteen ; in Upper Canada of not less than seven.

Hereditary titles of honour might be created, conferring the right of summons to the Councils. In the Representative Assembly the numbers were not less than fifty for Lower Canada nor less than sixteen for Upper Canada.

The limits of districts, which were to receive representatives, and the number of representatives for each was fixed by the Governor-General.

County members were elected by owners of lands in free- County members. hold or in fief, or roture to the value of forty shillings sterling a year over and above all rents and charges payable out of the same.

Town and township members were elected by persons Town members. who had a dwelling-house and lot of ground therein of the annual value of five pounds or upwards ; the voting quali- fication was also extended to any person who had resided in the town twelve months previous to the election and paid one year's rent for his residence at the rate of £10 sterling or upwards.

The Governor's authority extended to convene, pro- Legislature's term. rogue, and dissolve the Legislature ; but it was required to be summoned once a year and continue for four years, unless sooner dissolved by the Governor. The Governor had power to give or withhold his assent to Bills, or he could reserve them for the pleasure of the Crown.

The British Parliament reserved the right to make regu- Power of British lations in respect of imposing, levying and collecting duties Parliament to regulate for the regulation of navigation and commerce to be carried inter- on between the two provinces, or between either of them, and provincial any other part of the British Dominions or foreign country. duties, etc.

It also reserved the power of appointing or directing the payment of duties, but all moneys levied were left to the Legislatures to exclusively apportion to such public uses as they thought most expedient.

The free exercise of the Roman Catholic religion was Guarantee of the free guaranteed, but power was given to set apart a seventh exercise of the Roman part of all unclaimed Crown Lands for the use of the Catholic religion. Protestant clergy.

The right to bequeath real and personal property was Unrestrained power to will declared to be unrestricted. The public officers were property. appointed by the Crown to hold their several offices during the Royal pleasure. The Speaker of the Council was Speaker, Appointment appointed by the Governor-General. of.

Septennial
Assemblies.
Proposed
right of appeal
from the
Privy Council
to House of
Lords.
The Bill had proposed septennial Assemblies, but in the Act a duration for four years was provided. The Bill had also conferred a right of appeal from the Privy Council to the House of Lords, but such a right did not appear in the Act.

During the passage of the Bill through the House of Commons there occurred those memorable scenes between Fox and Burke which broke up a lifelong friendship.

Fox, under the glamour of the French Constitution and the philosophical doctrines of the rights of man, as his opponents stated, advocated an assembly for Lower Canada of not less than one hundred with an elective Legislative Council; but he strongly objected to the introduction of the principle of an hereditary legislature: " Are those red and blue ribbons," he declaimed, " which have lost their lustre in the Old World, again to shine forth in the New ? "

" It is, perhaps, indiscretion at any period," said Burke, " but especially at my advanced years to provoke enemies or give friends an occasion for desertion ; but if a firm and steady adherence to the British Constitution should place me in such a dilemma, I will risk all, and with my last words exclaim : ' Fly from the French Constitution ! ' "

The question whether the Canadian Constitution was to be framed " according to the old light of the English Constitution or by the glare of the new lanterns of the clubs at Paris and London," was decided by the passing of the Act, which by its terms expressly stated that " it was to assimilate the Constitution of Canada to that of Great Britain as nearly as the differences arising from the manners of the people and the situation of the Province admitted."

The Act of 1791, though at first successful in restoring harmony to the Colony, ultimately failed to work happily. Conflicts took place between the Governors and the Assemblies and between the Upper and Lower Houses. The official classes generally ranged themselves with the Legislative Councils against the popular majority in the Assemblies to thwart them. In Lower Canada " the dispute became at last so aggravated as to prevent the harmonious

operation of the Constitution.   The Assembly was constantly
fighting for the independence of Parliament and the exclusive
control of the supplies and the Civil List." [1]   The Government dissolved the Quebec Legislature with a frequency
unparalleled in political history, and the Governor was
personally drawn into the conflict.

The trouble began at the close of the American War of Origin of
troubles.
1813.   The Royal revenues, which were raised under
Imperial statute 14 Geo. III, c. 31 (1775) and required to
be applied towards defraying the expenses of the administration of justice and the support of the Civil Government
of the province proved insufficient (with the addition of the
territorial revenues) to meet the Government expenditure.
Up to the period of the war with the United States, money
was drawn from the military funds, but during the war further
drawings became impossible.   The Provincial Assembly
had jurisdiction only in respect of duties raised by them
under their own legislation.   The Government continued
to draw from the Provincial funds till a debt of well over
£100,000 was incurred, without any Legislative sanction.
The conduct of the Government was unconstitutional,
justifiable only on the ground of the exigencies of the
situation.

In 1818 the Government was induced by its necessities
to accept the Assembly's offer to raise additional revenue
by fresh taxes.

As in the political history of England, so in that of Canada Power of
appropriation
the power to vote appropriations of money led to an led to demand
for redress of
accompanying demand for the redress of grievances, the grievances.
Assembly insisting on closely scrutinising the expenditure
for the Civil List and the administration of the Governor.
The Council, as a rule, stood by the Governor in resisting
these claims, some of which may be termed extravagant.
Nevertheless, step by step, the Assembly made good its
assertions, as the House of Commons had formerly done in
England.   In 1831, by an Imperial Act, a concession was
made that it should be lawful for the Legislature to

---

[1] Bourinot, *Parliamentary Practice and Procedure* (Canada), p. 20.

appropriate the duties which had been raised by the Imperial Act of 1775, to meet the administrative charges of Civil Government.

Joseph Papineau.

During the bitter controversies that ensued, Louis Joseph Papineau, a French-Canadian, assumed a leading part amongst his colleagues as a reformer; on several occasions he was chosen as Speaker of the Assembly. In 1827 the Governor refused to.confirm his election, principally on account of his violent conduct. The Assembly claimed the right to elect their Speaker without the Governor's confirmation, and in the next Session, Papineau was again elected as Speaker, a change of Governors having in the meantime taken place. Papineau's great popularity amongst his compatriots at last led him to think that he could found a French-Canadian nation, and he began to plot to that end.

Plot to found a French-Canadian nation.

In 1834 ninety-two resolutions were passed, principally at his instigation, by the Assembly, and submitted to the Imperial Government, who peremptorily rejected them. The position, however, now became serious. Supply was refused and again refused in 1835. The Imperial Government despatched three Commissioners to Canada, one of whom was Lord Gosford, the new Governor-General, to enquire into all grievances. Lord Gosford failed to please either of the contending parties—French or English.

Demand for elected Council and Responsible Government.

One of the Assembly's demands was for elected Councils : this the Imperial Government declined to concede. The most important demand was for Responsible Government. The passing of hostile resolutions in the House of Commons and the subsequent Canadian Trade Acts, which provided a means by which Upper Canada could obtain a fairer share of the import duties, led to the outbreak of a rebellion, in which Papineau played an undignified part.

Troubles in Upper Canada.

In Upper Canada similar troubles also existed, but not to the same extent as in the Lower Province. As in Lower Canada, there were quarrels between the two Houses, constant irritation over the disposal of Government patronage, and complaints of an official ring. Dissatisfaction existed also in the other Provinces.

In New Brunswick there were financial difficulties ; in Nova Scotia disputes between the Assembly and the executive and legislative Councils ; and in Prince Edward Island the unsettled question of the land monopoly created by the unfortunate disposal of the island by lottery many years before. Troubles in New Brunswick, Nova Scotia, and Prince Edward Island.

Responsible Government had not yet come with its sovereign solution ; so far, neither Parliament nor the Colonial Office had shown any disposition to introduce it. It may seem strange, when looking into this maelstrom of politics, that whilst the principles of Responsible Government had been so carefully recognised and appreciated in the United Kingdom, that they had hitherto never been applied to the Colonies. Responsible Government not recognised.

One difficulty, no doubt, was felt as to how far it was possible to reconcile Imperial supremacy with Colonial aspirations. If the Governor were to be the servant of the Crown, how could he, at the same time, be the servant of the Colonial Legislature? Responsible Government created a conflict of duties in the Colonies. This was the dilemma that even the Reform Ministry of 1832 lacked the courage to face. Reasons for.

In Lower Canada the position was aggravated by a conflict of races and religions. The French population were enormously in the ascendant, and generally during the constitutional struggle the two peoples arrayed themselves against each other in the bitterest antagonism. " I expected to find a contest between a Government and a people," reported Lord Durham, " I found two nations warring in the bosom of a single State ; I found a struggle not of principles, but of races." Conflict of races and religions in Lower Canada.

In 1838 the Imperial Government suspended the Constitution of Lower Canada, and made provision for its Government by a special Council. Suspension of the Constitution of Lower Canada.

Whilst the affairs of Canada were in this disastrous condition, Lord Durham was appointed Governor-General, Lord Durham's administration.

succeeding Lord Gosford. The new Governor-General accepted " his onerous charge with inexpressible reluctance." He said that " he felt he could only accomplish it by the cordial and energetic support of his noble friends, the Members of Her Majesty's Cabinet, and the generous forbearance of the noble lords opposite, to whom he had always been politically opposed."

On his arrival at Quebec on May 29th, 1838, he found 161 prisoners in custody : of these, seventy-two were charged as being principal promoters of the rebellion, in which Papineau had taken a leading part. The difficult problem confronted him as to their trial. Owing to the sympathy of French juries, it was deemed impossible to secure the unanimity of a jury of twelve men, should any of the prisoners be put upon their trial through the political character of the offences charged. A trial and conviction by a specially-created tribunal would have led to an accusation of condemnation by an *ex post facto* law. A party of rebels at the time had actually been acquitted after they had been proved guilty of murder by the clearest possible evidence, and jury and prisoners had been applauded as the finest and noblest of patriots. A further alternative remained, to pack the juries ; but this seemed to Lord Durham a perversion of the forms of justice. In the end he adopted another course, which in the result proved most unfortunate, he accepted the offer of the prisoners to place themselves at his disposal. An ordinance was passed by the Government on the 28th of June, which declared that certain persons who were named therein had acknowledged their participation in high treason, and submitted themselves to Her Majesty's pleasure ; it enacted that they should be transported to Bermuda during pleasure, there to be subject to such restraints as should be deemed fit. This ordinance was illegal, since no jurisdiction existed to order deportation out of the Colony. The ordinance might, however, have been confirmed by the Imperial Parliament had Lord Melbourne possessed a majority independent of the Irish vote. Another course was adopted by the Imperial

Government ; the ordinance was assailed in the bitterest terms by Lord Brougham. It was repealed ; but an act indemnifying its authors passed. Lord Durham, in consequence of the attacks made upon him, resigned.

During his short tenure of office he collected an amount Lord Durham's of valuable information on the state of provincial affairs, report. which he embodied in a most masterly report. One of its most important recommendations was that " no time should be lost in proposing to Parliament a Bill for restoring the Union of the Canadas under one legislature, and reconstructing them as one province." On the question of the relationship of the executive to the Assembly, he reported that he did not know how it was possible to secure harmony in any other way than by administering the Government on these principles which had been perfectly efficacious in Great Britain. " The Crown," he wrote, " must submit to the necessary consequences of representative institutions ; and if it has to carry on the Government in union with a representative body, it must consent to carry it on by means of those in whom that representative body has confidence."

In 1840, Lord John Russell acted upon this report, and The United introduced a Bill for re-uniting Upper and Lower Canada. Canadas. The Bill received the Royal Assent on July 23rd of that year, although it did not come into force until February 10th of the following year. The first Parliament of the United Canadas met at Kingston on June 14th, 1841.

The Union Act provided for the constitution of a Legis- Legislative Council. lative Council of not less than twenty members, and for Legislative a Legislative Assembly of eighty-four members. Each Assembly. division of the Province was to receive equal representation. The appointment of Speaker in the Legislative Council was vested in the Crown. A majority of the votes of the members was required to decide a question, but in the case of equality the Speaker was given a casting vote. Ten members, including the Speaker, constituted a quorum. With regard to the popular Chamber, its composition, so far as the division of equal representation in the Provinces was concerned, was arranged so that it could not be altered without the concurrence of two-thirds of the Members of each House. The Speaker was elected by a majority of the House, and possessed, as in the Legislative Council, a casting-vote only in case of the votes being equal on any question. A quorum consisted of twenty, including the Speaker.

Property qualification.

A property qualification for membership was fixed. No person was eligible for election unless he possessed lands and tenements to the value of £500 sterling over and above all debts and mortgages. A session of the Legislature was to be held once at least every year and each House was to continue for four years, unless sooner dissolved. It was prescribed that the English language should be solely used in the legislative records.

Consolidated fund.

Provision was made for the establishment of a consolidated revenue fund, on which was first to be charged the expenses of collection, management, and receipt of revenues, interest of public debt, payment of the clergy, and the Civil List. Such portion of the fund as was available after these payments the Legislature was at liberty to appropriate to the public service.

Money bills and resolutions.

Money bills, votes, and resolutions involving the expenditure of money were required to be first recommended by the Governor-General.

Dawn of Responsible Government.

The passing of this Act marks the beginning of the era of Responsible Government in Canada. Its advent in Australia was not seen till some years later.

Mr. Poulett Thomson, afterwards Lord Sydenham, now became Governor-General; he communicated the Royal intentions that thereafter certain heads of departments would be called upon to retire from the public service whenever sufficient motives of public policy might suggest its expediency.

The Assembly during its first session agreed to certain resolutions which laid down the principle that, "in order to preserve between the different branches of the Provincial Parliament that harmony which was essential to good government, the chief advisers of the Representative of the

Sovereign constituting a Provincial administration under him ought to be men possessed of the confidence of the representatives of the people, thus affording a guarantee that the well understood wishes and interests of the people which our Gracious Sovereign has declared shall be the rule of the Provincial Government, will on all occasions be faithfully represented and advocated."

Prior to this, Lord Durham, whose genius had largely solved the problem which had perplexed the minds of political thinkers, by indicating the changes necessary to restore happiness and prosperity to Canada, died of a broken heart, the victim of attacks by his own party, on whom he had conferred the most essential services. He left Canada in a snowstorm, landing at Plymouth on December 1st, being received without any honours by the special orders of Government, who sent down a special messenger to prohibit them.[1] His two mistakes were the passing of the Ordinance deporting the prisoners and a proclamation to the people of Canada justifying his acts. His success has been justified by time.

During the period from 1841 to 1867 much important Legislation legislation was passed, and the independence of Parliament up till 1867. assured by the prohibition on judges and officials sitting in either House.

Reforms were also instituted in the Civil Service, securing Civil Service. to whatever Government might be in power the services of a highly-trained body of permanent officials.

To name the various reforms that took place after the Canadian Union Act of 1840 is to demonstrate the advances made progress. by Canada on the road to complete self-government ; 1846 saw her Legislature, with the consent of the Imperial Government, in possession of the complete control of the Civil List and the Post Office, and the Colony free from interference in all matters affecting trade and commerce.

The Imperial Statute, 9 & 10 Vict. c. 94, empowered the Effect of British Colonies in America to reduce or repeal by their own free trade. legislation all duties imposed by Imperial Acts on foreign

[1] Martineau.

goods imported from foreign countries into the Colony in question.

The Act was the direct outcome of the Free Trade policy of Great Britain, and in response the Canadian Legislature passed an Act to meet the altered state of their Colonial relations with the Mother Country. It was further urged by the Government of Canada that since it was no longer the policy of the Empire to give preference to Colonial products in the markets of the United Kingdom, no reason could possibly exist for monopolies and restrictions in favour of British shipping. Following on a memorandum, sent to the Imperial Government, the 12 & 13 Vict. c. 29 was passed which repealed the navigation laws and opened the river St. Lawrence to the ships of all nations.

In 1856 an elective Upper House was established, under powers conferred by Imperial legislation.

One of the principal features of the Act of 1840 had been the equality of representation that was given to each portion of Canada in the Union in the Assembly. Insufficient representation was at one time a grievance on the part of Lower Canada ; but afterwards the greater influx of population to the Upper Province made that Province a complainant.

A principle was at last adopted by the political parties that no measure should be passed which affected either of the Provinces unless the majority of members in the particular Province affected by the legislation assented.

From 1862 to 1864 legislation practically stopped. The faulty working of the Constitution was fully recognised by the leaders of both parties. A coalition Government was, in consequence, formed on the platform of a Federal union of all the British-American Provinces, or of the two Canadas, in case of failure of the larger scheme.

So far, attention has been directed to the history of the two Canadas. It is now necessary to turn to the history of the three provinces of Nova Scotia, New Brunswick, and Prince Edward Island, two of which were parties in 1867 to Federation.

Nova Scotia was settled by the French, and in its early Nova Scotia.
days was known as Acadia. The first French settlement
took place on an islet off the mouth of the St. Croix river,
which is the present boundary between the State of Maine
and New Brunswick. The most important French settlement was at Port Royal, named by Champlain, who subsequently founded Quebec in 1608. The growth of the French
settlements was slow: a hundred years later the whole
population of the Acadian Peninsula did not exceed 1,500
persons, 1,000 of whom were settled in the pleasant country
of Grand Pré and Minas. Forty years later, however, the
population of Acadia had increased to 12,000.

By the Treaty of Utrecht (1713) France surrendered this The Treaty of Utrecht.
country to the British ; and in 1749 Halifax was founded by
Governor Cornwallis, who introduced between 2,000 to
3,000 emigrants ; the Governor's first Council was sworn on
board of one of the transports. The French population
declined to acquiesce in the British rule, refusing to take
the oath of allegiance, and calling themselves neutral.

In 1755, after the capture of two forts from the French,
to which many of the Acadians had resorted (partly stimulated by promises and partly by threats), the Governments
determined to remove the Acadians, and pronounced
sentence of banishment upon them. Their subsequent
removal was justified on the grounds of policy, and took
place whilst Lawrence was Governor of Halifax.

In 1760 the Province received a great number of Ulster immigration.
settlers from the New England Colonies ; at a later day,
immigrants arrived from the North of Ireland, who, in
the name of " Londonderry," perpetuated a memorable
triumph in the Old World by a fresh foundation in the
New.

Later on, in 1772, a considerable immigration from Scotch immigration.
Scotland began, and continued for many years.

In 1758 Governor Lawrence opened the first Legislative
Assembly in Nova Scotia.

At this period only the settled portion of the Province of
what is now known as New Brunswick sent representatives

to the Nova Scotia Assembly. Cape Breton was also a part of the Province.

In 1763 the island of St. John was added to Nova Scotia.

Prince Edward Island. In 1798 St. John was re-named Prince Edward Island, after Edward, Duke of Kent, the Father of Queen Victoria. Prior to that date, in 1769, it had been separated from Nova Scotia and given a distinct government.

In 1773 its first Assembly met. The population at that time was exceedingly sparse, and four years before it had not exceeded 150 families.

Settlement by lottery. The island was populated after the Treaty of Paris in 1763 by means of a lottery held on one day, the whole land, with some few reservations, was then given away to officers of the Army and Navy who had served in the preceding war, and to others who sought land. subject only to the payment of quit-rents. This unwise proceeding led to trouble, which lasted till 1873.

Originally the Island had a combined Executive and legislative Council and eventually a Legislative Assembly of eighteen members. In 1850-51 Responsible Government was fully recognised.

New Brunswick. In 1784 New Brunswick was created. Its Government consisted of a Council of twelve members, possessing executive and legislative functions, and an Assembly of twenty-

Introduction of Responsible Government. six members; in 1848, as in Nova Scotia, Responsible Government was instituted.

First idea of Federation. The idea of a Union of all the provinces of British North America was first suggested by Chief Justice Smith, of Quebec, in that memorable year 1789, which witnessed the outbreak of the French Revolution and the meeting of the first Congress of the United States. In 1790 he wrote to Lord Dorchester that Mr. Grenville's plan will most assuredly lay a foundation for two spacious and flourishing Provinces and for more to grow out of them, and compose at no remote period a mass of Power very worthy of immediate attention.

I miss in it, however, the expected establishment to put what remains to Great Britain of her Ancient Dominions in North America under one general direction for the United interests and safety of every branch of the Empire. [1]

About a quarter of a century later, Chief Justice Sewell, of Quebec, in a letter which he addressed to the Duke of Kent, followed up the idea.

In 1839 it received the further endorsement of Lord Durham in his memorable report.

Ten years later, the British American-League took up the matter, and in 1854 it was submitted to the Legislature of Nova Scotia. British-American League.

In 1858 the Cartier-Macdonald Government, a coalition Government of both parties in Canada, made Federation part of their ministerial policy. The growth of the country had by this time made the question of Union one of necessity. There had been a large increase in numbers in the Western Province and there was a clamour for a greater share in the representation. Ministerial policy in the Canadas.

In 1859 a Convention was held at Toronto, which sug- gested that " the best practical remedy for the existing state of affairs was the formation of two or more local Govern- ments, to which should be committed the control of all matters of a local and sectional character, and some general authority charged with such matters as were necessarily common to both sections of the Provinces." Convention at Toronto.

It has already been stated that between 1862 to 1864 legislation had been practically stopped. In consequence of this the Cartier-Macdonald Ministry was pledged to introduce a new constitution embracing the Federal principle.

During the progress of the Federal movement, Mr. Howe, the Liberal leader in Nova Scotia in 1861, had carried in the Assembly a resolution in favour of Federation. This was subsequently adopted in 1864 by the Government, during the premiership of Sir Charles Tupper, who pressed the matter forward. Position in Nova Scotia.

The three Provinces of Nova Scotia, New Brunswick, and Prince Edward Island agreed to send delegates to a Conference. Charlotte Town Conference.

[1] *Canadian Constitutional Development*, Egerton & Grant, p. 104.

conference at Charlotte Town. Canada also resolved to attend, and the general idea of Federation met with so much favour, that it was agreed that a further Conference should be held at Quebec in the following October.

Quickening of Federal impulse.

It will be observed in reviewing the Federal movement that the growth of the Federal idea was slow, and only quickened into life by the practical requirements of the Provinces. The history of Federation shows that it has always emerged from the realm of academic dreams, either by the force of outside pressure such as the existence of a common danger or by the internal necessities of governments.

The first American Federation sprung hurriedly into life under the stress of common defence, whilst the second Federation was brought about by domestic difficulties. The Grecian Federations were all primarily shields to preserve the liberties of communities that, remaining isolated, would have fallen, divided and impotent, one by one, a prey to the intrigues or attacks of more powerful enemies. No outside danger threatened Canada when she federated, but she had witnessed without her borders a war in which thousands had sacrificed themselves for the principle of Federal Unity. The continuance of her own internal dissensions might have led to serious disasters. The ambition of creating a Canadian Federation inspired the thoughts of her statesmen and was based upon solid reason. Whatever the future had in store for her, she was determined to face it as one Great Dominion—stretching from the Atlantic to the Pacific, a united people, a mighty nation.

CHAPTER XVI

THE FORMATION OF THE DOMINION

WHEN the Convention met at Quebec in 1864 it comprised Quebec Convention. thirty-three delegates, amongst whom was Sir John The delegates. Macdonald, afterwards to be the first Premier of Canada ; Sir George Etienne Cartier, one of the ablest of the French-Canadians, a namesake of that Jacques Cartier who, sailing from St. Malo in Brittany, voyaged up the St. Lawrence, giving France the right to claim Quebec by discovery ; Sir Alexander Galt ; D'Arcy McGee, a brilliant Irishman identified with the Young Ireland Movement, who, fleeing from Ireland in 1848 to the United States and thence to Canada, became a loyal Canadian in 1857 ; the advocate of a Union in Canada which he had opposed in Ireland, he was subsequently murdered by the order of a secret society ; Sir Oliver Mowat, afterwards Prime Minister of Ontario ; Sir Hector Langevin, and others, including Sir Etienne Paschal Taché, Chairman of the Convention, who gave utterance to that supreme saying of French-Canadian loyalty, " that the last gun to be fired for British supremacy in America would be fired by a French-Canadian."

From Nova Scotia came Sir Charles Tupper, Mr. Archibald, Mr. Henry, and two others. New Brunswick sent seven delegates, who were drawn from both political sides of the House ; Prince Edward Island, seven also ; whilst Newfoundland was represented by the Speaker of the House, and by Mr. Ambrose Shea, who afterwards became Governor of the Bahamas.

Statesmanship, literature, and law were all represented, for Canada sent of her wisest and best.

The Convention sat in sessions for eighteen days, with Proceedings at Convention. closed doors. It left no official record of its deliberations. A number of documents, however, edited by Mr. Joseph Pope, were published in 1895. Mr. Pope was the biographer of Sir John Macdonald, as the literary executor of this great statesman he obtained possession of a large collection of papers relating to the Confederation negotiations of 1864-67.

It had been the intention of the Conference to have preserved a complete record of its proceedings. The record of discussions which now would have been invaluable only consists of deficient and fragmentary notes ; and Mr. Pope had to rely on those taken by Lieutenant-Colonel Bernard, the Secretary of the Conference.

The first resolution which was put and unanimously carried was that " the best interests and present and future prosperity of British North America will be promoted by a Federal Union under the Crown of Great Britain, provided that such Union can be effected on principles just to the several Provinces."

The second resolution, which was also unanimously carried, was " that in the Federation of the British-North American Provinces the system of government best adapted under existing circumstances to protect the diversified interests of the several Provinces and secure efficiency, harmony, and permanency in the working of the Union, would be a General Government charged with matters of common interest to the whole country ; and a Local Government for each of the Canadas and the Maritime Provinces charged with the control of local matters in their respective sections, provision being made for the admission into the Union, on equitable terms, of the North-West Territory, British Columbia, and Vancouver."

In voting on the resolutions, the delegates voted by Provinces ; however many the number of delegates present from a Province the Province registered but one vote— Canada, with its Upper and Lower Province, counted as two.

The resolution as to the model on which the Constitution should be built was not unanimously carried.

An amendment, which became a substantive resolution, received the support of four votes to two. Its terms were, " that in framing a Constitution for the General Government, the Conference, with a view to the perpetuation of our connection with the Mother Country and to the promotion of the best interests of the people of these Provinces, desires to follow the model of the British Constitution so far as our circumstances will permit." *perpetuation of connection with Mother Country.*

Nova Scotia and Prince Edward Island were dissentients. Their dissent, however, was not expressed against the perpetuation of the Canadian connection with the Mother Country, but because the delegates from these Provinces thought it not judicious to fetter their actions by the passage of a resolution of a simple declaratory character, which might embarrass their action in the selection of the best means for providing for the general and local government of the country.

All the delegates were animated with a desire to found a Federal Constitution that should embody the principles of the Constitution of the United Kingdom, with a view to the perpetuation of the connection with the Mother Country.

They rejected the idea of reserving the residuum of power to the Provinces ; they equally rejected the idea of a mere legislative Union. In the opening remarks of Sir John Macdonald, of which a fragment only is recorded, he said— *Relection of idea of leaving the residuary powers to the Provinces.*

"The various States of the adjoining Republic had always acted as separate Sovereignties. The New England States, New York State, and the Southern States had no sympathies in common. They were thirteen individual sovereignties, quite distinct the one from the other. The primary error at the formation of these constitutions was that each State reserved to itself all Sovereign rights, save the small portions delegated. We must reverse the process by strengthening the General Government and conferring on the Provincial bodies only such powers as may be required for local purposes. All sectional prejudices and interests can be legislated for by local legislatures. Thus we shall have a strong and lasting Government under which we can work out constitutional liberty as opposed to democracy, and be able to protect the minority by having a powerful central Government. Great caution, however, is necessary. The people of every section must feel that they *Sir John Macdonald's speech.*

are protected, and by no overstraining of central authority should such guarantees be over-ridden. Our Constitution must be based on an Act of the Imperial Parliament, and any question as to over-riding sectional matters determined by : ' Is it legal or not ? ' The judicial tribunals of Great Britain would settle any such difficulties should they occur.

" As regards the constitution of our Legislatures, in order to have no local jealousies and all things conciliatory, there should be a different system in the two Chambers. With the Queen as our Sovereign, we should have an Upper and a Lower House. In the former, the principle of equality should obtain. In the Lower House the basis of representation should be population not by universal suffrage, but according to the principles of the British Constitution. In the Upper House there should be equality in numbers.

" With respect to the mode of appointments to the Upper House, some of us are in favour of the elective principle. More are in favour of appointment by the Crown. I will keep my own mind open on that point, as if it were a new question to me altogether. While I do not admit that the elective principle has been a failure in Canada I think we had better return to the original principle, and in the words of Governor Simeon, endeavour to make ours an image and transcript of the British Constitution."

Quebec resolutions.

The Convention passed seventy-two resolutions that became famous as the Quebec Resolutions. On the basis of these resolutions the Constitution of the Dominion of Canada was subsequently established.

The resolutions were subsequently submitted to the Canadian Legislature in January, 1865, and passed by large majorities in both Houses.

After the session was finished, Messrs. Macdonald, Cartier, Galt, and Brown visited England and conferred with the British Ministers. Their report was laid before Parliament about August and September of that year.

Whilst the Quebec resolutions met with support in the Canadian Legislature, difficulties grew in other quarters, which threatened disaster to the Federation proposals.

The three Maritime Provinces originally contemplated only a maritime Union, and considered that their delegates had exceeded their authority by pledging themselves to a measure for a larger Union. The difficulty was of a like nature to that which at one time threatened to shipwreck the work of the framers of the United States' Constitution, then delegates chosen to improve an existing Constitution had agreed to a wholly new one. In New Brunswick the Government's proposals for Federation were defeated at the polls; but later, on a dissolution occurring, the Federation party recovered ground owing to the then Fenian threats of invasion. In Nova Scotia, Federation was never submitted to the approval of the people, for fear of an adverse result. Prince Edward Island and Newfoundland both positively declined to join the Union.

In 1866 a conference of delegates from the Provinces of Canada, New Brunswick, and Nova Scotia met at the Westminster Palace Hotel in London. The meeting was convened to remove certain difficulties in the financial arrangements as to Federation that pressed hardly upon the Provinces. A Bill was then drafted and introduced by Earl Carnarvon in the House of Lords on February 17th, 1867. In the original draft of the Bill it is stated that the Provinces were called the "Kingdom of Canada !!"; but a change was made, and the term "Dominion" substituted. Sir J. C. Bourinot states that he was informed by Sir John Macdonald that the amendment did not emanate from the Colonial delegates, but from the Imperial Ministry, one of whose members was afraid of wounding the susceptibilities of United States statesmen.[1] On March 29th of the same year, the Royal Assent was given to the Act, which bears the title of the British North America Act.

Subsequently, in the same year, the Imperial Parliament passed an Act that guaranteed a loan of £3,000,000 for the construction of an inter-Colonial railway between Quebec and the coasts of the Maritime Provinces. The Queen's Proclamation of the new Constitution was issued

Westminster Palace Hotel Conference.

Loan by Imperial Government.

[1] *Canada*, 1760-1901, p. 215.

on May 22nd, 1867, and the first Dominion Parliament met on November 7th following, at Ottawa.

Section 145 of the Constitution Act recited that the Provinces of Canada, Nova Scotia, and New Brunswick had joined in a declaration that the construction of the inter-Colonial Railway was essential to the consolidation of the Union of British North America, and to the assent thereto of Nova Scotia and New Brunswick ; and had agreed that its construction should be immediately commenced. It was therefore declared to be the duty of the Government and Parliament of Canada to provide for the commencement, within six months after the Union, of a railway connecting the river St. Lawrence with the City of Halifax in Nova Scotia, and for its construction without intermission and its completion with all practicable speed. This great railway was ultimately completed on July 1st, 1876.

Agitation for repeal by Nova Scotia.

Meantime, whilst the Union was yet young, an agitation for its repeal had sprung up in Nova Scotia. Mr. Howe, originally one of the ablest supporters of the Federal movement, proceeded to England with an address from the Assembly to urge its repeal. He found the Imperial Government so opposed to the idea, that he abandoned the movement. The agitation, however, was not barren of fruits : one result was to obtain better financial terms for the Province by the addition of further allowances, estimated on increased amounts of debts, compared with the maximum fixed in the Union Act.

Accession of Prince Edward Island.

In 1873 Prince Edward Island joined the Federation. In doing so, she obtained excellent financial terms, enabling her to extinguish the land monopoly, which had been a source of trouble ever since the country had been divided up by lottery.

British Columbia.

The Constitution Act provided for the subsequent admission of British Columbia on the receipt of addresses to the Crown from both Houses of the Dominion Parliament and from her Legislature. It also provided for the admission of Rupert's Land and the North-Western Territory, or either of them, on such terms and conditions as should be expressed in the addresses to the Crown, subject to the Royal approval and the terms of the Act. British Columbia became a member of the Union in 1871 ; she had had but a short existence as a province. Her history was as follows : The Island of Vancouver was erected as a Crown Colony in 1849. In 1856 her first Assembly met. In 1858 New Caledonia was constituted a Crown Colony, uniting with Vancouver Island in 1866, under the designation of British Columbia. At the time of her accession to the Union, the Province .was governed by a legislature, comprising heads of departments and elected members. Her Lieutenant-Governor was appointed by the Crown. On admission to the Union, she obtained Responsible Government. One of the strongest inducements that led her to join the Federation was the promise of the construction of a railway to connect her seaboard with the Canadian railway system.

In 1869 the rights over the huge territory occupied by the Hudson's Bay Company were acquired and an Act was passed dealing with the Government of Rupert's Land and the North-West Territory. This great acquisition of territory led to the Red River War, in which Louis Riel played a prominent part. The half-breed population who inhabited the territory believed that the Act meant the confiscation of their lands. *Rupert's Land and the North-West Territory.*

In 1870, after suppression of Riel's rebellion, Manitoba was formed by an Act of the Canadian Parliament, its inhabitants thereby obtaining representation in the Parliament of the Dominion and in a local legislature. Manitoba was admitted under the authority of a statute of 1870 ; but a doubt having arisen as to its validity, the Imperial Parliament, in 1871, passed an Act to make the Canadian Act valid and effectual. The North-West Territories Representation Act (49 Vict. c. 24), which was assented to in June, 1886, gave two members to Assiniboia, one member to Alberta, and one to Saskatchewan. *Manitoba.*

The territories now constituting the provinces of Alberta and Saskatchewan were, in 1905, erected into the provinces *Alberta and Saskatchewan.*

of Alberta and Saskatchewan ; the unorganised territories are still without representation.

The work of Federation, which began with the four provinces, is now virtually concluded, and the Canada of to-day is one great Dominion, reaching from the Pacific to the Atlantic, Newfoundland alone stands aloof.

CHAPTER XVII

FEATURES COMMON TO BRITISH FEDERAL CONSTITUTIONS

IN the three British Federal Constitutions there are certain Command of naval and military forces. distinctive features which are more or less common to all. Thus there is the recognition of one Sovereign in whom the supreme executive power vests. In Canada he is Commander-in-chief of the land and naval Militia, and of all naval and military forces.[1] In Australia, though in terms, the command of the naval and military forces of the Commonwealth vests in the Governor-General, it only so vests as the Sovereign's representative;[2] whilst in the Union of South Africa the command-in-chief vests either in the King or in the Governor-General as his representative.[3]

In the United Kingdom the King's personal command The Army. In the United Kingdom. of the Forces was given up in 1793, when the first commander-in-chief was created; " but by prerogative at common law, and by statute, the supreme government of all forces by sea and land, and of all ports and places of strength, belongs to the Crown."[4]

The last time that a British Sovereign took the field was at Dettingen, in 1743, when George II rode in the firing line encouraging his troops.

At the present time the command of the Army is vested in a Council in purely administrative matters, and in executive matters in an Inspector-General, and President of the Selection Board, who are assisted by a staff officer and five inspectors. The Army Council and Inspector-General, with their various departments form the headquarters' staff of the Army.[5]

---

[1] British North America Act, (1867), 30 and 31, Vict. c. 3.
[2] Commonwealth of Australia Constitution Act, (1890), 63 and 64, Vict. c. 12, s. 68.
[3] South Africa Act (1909), 9 Edw. VII, c. 9, s. 17.
[4] *Laws of England* (title) *Constitutional Law*, Vol. VI, p. 418.
[5] *Ibid.*

In all military matters the Crown now acts upon the advice of the Secretary of State for War who is a member of the Cabinet and of the Army Council, and is responsible to Parliament for the advice given to the Crown and to the Crown and Parliament for all the business of the Army Council.

The Navy.　In naval matters the Crown acts upon the advice of the First Lord of the Admiralty, who is a Member of the Cabinet responsible to Parliament for the advice he gives. The supreme command of the Navy is delegated to the Commissioners for executing the office of Lord High Admiral of the United Kingdom of Great Britain and Ireland, known as the Admiralty ; the First Lord is one of the Commissioners. The Commissioners exercise the jurisdiction and powers enjoyed by the Crown at common law or conferred upon it by statute. When the Fleet is on active service its command is entrusted to its various admirals, vice-admirals, rear-admirals, and other officers holding their commissions from the Admiralty.[1]

The Governor-General represents the King.　In the three Federal Constitutions, the Governor-General represents the King and is the chief executive officer. He is appointed by His Majesty's Commission, which confers upon him his powers, and in conjunction with his instruc-
How appointed.　tions defines his duties. Three instruments are required to constitute the office : Letters patent under the Great Seal of the United Kingdom ; instructions under the Sign Manual or Signet ; and the Commission which appoints him to act according to the two previous instruments.[2] The Governor-General also receives certain instructions from the Secretary of State on behalf of the Crown. Great though his powers are, a Governor-General is not a Viceroy, nor can it be assumed that he possesses a general Sovereign power[3] ; his authority is derived from his commission, and is confined to the powers that are expressly or impliedly

---

[1] *Laws of England* (title), *Constitutional Law*, Vol. VI, p. 419.
[2] *Laws of England* (title), *Dependencies*, Vol. X, p. 526.
[3] Cameron *v.* Kyte (1835), 3 Knapp, 332, 343.

entrusted to him.[1] The issue of letters patent is not an exercise of the Crown's legislative power.

The powers assigned to the Governor-General cover all the executive authority of the Crown.

In the three Federations he generally acts on the advice Acts on advice of his Council. of his Council created by Statute, but he also exercises certain prerogative rights, which lawfully belong to the Functions of. Sovereign, in regard to the summoning, proroguing, or dissolving of Parliament; thus, either in person or by deputy he opens Parliament. It should be noticed that these rights have been conferred upon him by law.

A function which calls for the exercise of his greatest care is the grant of a dissolution of Parliament. This is recognised as an executive act, the ministerial responsibility for which can be established.

By the theory of Responsible Government, the Governor, Theory as to dissolution of Parliament. as the King's representative, is generally supposed to act upon the advice of his executive Council created by Statute; but he is not bound to accept their advice in a case of dissolution. To refuse a dissolution recommended by the Government is not an executive act, but a refusal to carry out an executive act. Burke considered the power " of all trusts the most critical and delicate." Its too frequent exercise proved a cause of trouble, particularly during the early portion of the nineteenth century in Canada.

The Governor-General is personally responsible to the Responsibility to Crown. Crown for the lawful exercise of this prerogative; but he is likewise bound to take into account the welfare of the people, being unable to divest himself of a grave moral responsibility towards the Colony he is commissioned to govern. The constitutional discretion of the Governor should be invoked in respect to every case where a dissolution may be advised or requested by his ministers, and his judgment ought not to be fettered or his discretion disputed by inferences drawn from previous precedents, when he decides that a proposed dissolution is unnecessary and undesirable.

[1] Musgrave v. Pulido, L.R. (1879), 5 App. Cases, 102, 111.

Considerations probably justifying a dissolution.

Some of the leading considerations that may justify a dissolution are when a vote of no confidence is carried against a Government that has not already appealed to the country ; or a reasonable belief that an adverse vote against the Government was not in accordance with the opinion of the country, and would be reversed on a dissolution ; or when an existing Parliament has been elected under the auspices of the opponents of the Government, and where the majority against the Government is so small as to justify the belief that a strong Government could not be formed by the Opposition.

A dissolution where the term of Parliament's duration is short should, save in special circumstances, be granted only when it is clear that in no other way can the Government be carried on.

Powers, authorities, and functions at establishment of Constitution.

In the three British Constitutions, all powers, authorities, and functions which were vested in or exerciseable by the Governors of Provinces, States, or Colonies, so far as they continued to exist at the time when the Constitutions came into force, are vested in the Governor-Generals ; but there is considerable diversity in the language used in each Constitution. The various instruments under which they are appointed have reference to this. Foremost among a Governor-General's powers and functions is the execution and maintenance of the Constitution and the laws passed under it, which are guaranteed by the oath that the Governor-General is required to take.[1]

The Governor-General stands in each of these Constitutions as the representative of the Imperial element. He is a real link of Empire : the sign of the Union with the Mother Country.

In the Union of South Africa.

The position of the Governor as an Imperial officer is seen in the Constitution of the Union of South Africa, where he has special functions with reference to the care of the native races ; where no Imperial interests are involved, as a rule, a Governor should follow the advice of his ministers except where he is entitled to exercise a legitimate discretion.

---

[1] As to the oath taken by the President of the United States, *ante*, p. 67.

As the Crown is the source of all executive honour, so the Governor-General is partially its representative.

He is only partially the representative, because he cannot "grant titles of honour, and his discretion in granting precedence is followed by authoritative instructions which he is bound to obey. *Report from a representative of the Sovereign.*

Honours.

"It is not, therefore, within the power of a Governor-General to approve of the issue of decorations, even for services rendered within his Government, if it purports in any way to be an award from the Crown."

The Governor cannot exercise the prerogative power of the Crown in respect of coinage ; nor can he pardon, unless the power has been delegated to him, or unless statutory authority has been conferred. This view was expressed by the Chief Justice of the Supreme Court of Canada. "By the law of the Constitution, or, in other words, by the common law of England, the prerogative of mercy is vested in the Crown, not merely as regards the territorial limits of the United Kingdom, but throughout the whole of His Majesty's Dominions. The authority to exercise this prerogative may be delegated to Viceroys and Colonial Governors representing the Crown. Such delegation, whatever may be the conventional usage established, on grounds of political expediency—a matter which has nothing to do with the legal question—cannot, however, in any way exclude the power and authority of the Crown to exercise the prerogative directly by pardoning an offence committed anywhere within the King's Dominions. I take it to be the invariable practice in the case of Colonial Governors, to delegate to them the authority to pardon, in express terms, either by the Commission under the Great Seal or in the instructions communicated to them by the Crown. This being so, and this practice having prevailed, as far as I can discover, universally and for a long series of years, I should have thought that it at least implied that, in the opinion of the Law Officers of the Crown, an authority on such a point second only to that of a Judicial decision, the prerogative of pardoning offences was not incidental *Coinage.*

Power to pardon.

to the office of a Colonial Governor ; and could only be executed by such an officer in the absence of legislative authority under powers expressly conferred by the Crown." [1]

The question whether such a power has been conferred by the Constitution is a matter of fact. In Australia, the executive power extends to the execution and maintenance of the Constitution and of the laws of the Commonwealth. [2] " It would seem that under this section " (says Mr. Harrison Moore [3]) that the Governor-General " has statutory authority to pardon offenders. The Imperial Government, however, appears to hold a different view, for the power is expressly given, with certain limitations, by section 8 of the Instructions."

In the three Constitutions the Governor-General acts on the advice of his executive council in capital. cases except when the interests of the Empire or of any country or place beyond the jurisdiction of his Government are affected.

In theory, the Crown conducts all the affairs of State. A Governor-General holds office during the pleasure of the Crown, although the period of service is generally confined to six years.

Existence of Responsible Government.
In the three Constitutions, Responsible Government exists. The nature of this has been already explained as a later development of the British Constitution not coming into force until after the Revolution of 1688. Its introduction into the British Colonies occurred many years later, approximately about the middle of the nineteenth century.

Not recognised in the United States.
It has also been previously shown that this principle of government is not recognised in the United States, where the Legislature cannot control the executive, but remains independent and the executive is not subordinate to the legislative power as in the three Imperial Constitutions.

Written Constitutions. Method of creation.
The three Imperial Constitutions are all written Constitutions, enacted by the Imperial Parliament at the

---

[1] The Attorney-General for Canada *v.* The Attorney-General of the Province of Ontario, 23 S.C.R., pp. 468, 469.

[2] Sect. 61.

[3] Harrison Moore, *The Commonwealth of Australia*, p. 219.

request of the peoples of the several States concerned. It would have been impossible to have created them in any other way. Federal Constitutions only exist because at some time or other either independent or dependent States, Provinces, or Colonies desire to form an alliance or treaty and to surrender or delegate some of their powers to a central authority. . Such delegation or surrender can only take place by consent ; and such consent can only be given by the States, Provinces, and Colonies in question, or by their people. Therefore, all Federal Constitutions, in a sense, partake of the nature of a pact.

In Republics the power to enact is vested in the People who, in the case of the Constitution of the United States, gave their consent directly through their Conventions elected specially for that purpose. Where Representative Government is in force, representative assemblies of the States may be empowered by the people to pass Acts, vesting some of the powers they possessed in a central authority, but where there is any doubt as to the authority, the people should be directly consulted as they were in some of the Provinces of Canada and Natal. *Enacting power in a Republic.*

In the case of the Imperial Constitutions, the only legislative force capable of translating the desires of the people of various portions of the Empire for Federation into effect was the Imperial Parliament, which possess supreme authority, since the Imperial Parliament has the power to confer all constitutions, and can alter or amend, or suspend or take them away, as it pleases. As soon as the Provinces of Canada, and South Africa, and the States of Australia signified their desire to unite, the Imperial Parliament was able to give effect to their wishes, by enacting the Dominion, the Commonwealth of Australia Constitution and the Union of South Africa Acts.

The preamble of each of the Acts clearly expresses this. *Preambles.* The North British-America Act states : " That the Provinces of Canada, Nova Scotia, and New Brunswick have expressed their desire to be federally united into one Dominion under the Crown of the United Kingdom of Great Britain and

Ireland, with a Constitution similar in principle to that of the United Kingdom ; and that such a Union would conduce to the welfare of the Provinces and promote the interests of the British Empire."

The Australian Constitution Act states : " That the people of New South Wales, Victoria, South Australia, Queensland and Tasmania, humbly relying on the blessings of Almighty God, have agreed to unite in one indissoluble Federal Commonwealth under the Crown of the United Kingdom of Great Britain and Ireland, and under the Constitution hereby established." [1]

The South African Constitution states : " That it is desirable for the welfare and future progress of South Africa that the several British Colonies therein should be united under one Government, in a legislative Union, under the Crown of Great Britain and Ireland ; and that it is expedient to make provision for the Union of the Colonies of the Cape of Good Hope, Natal, the Transvaal, and the Orange River Colony on terms and conditions to which they have agreed to by resolution of their respective Parliaments ; and to define the executive, legislative and judicial powers to be exercised in the Government of the Union." [2]

Admission of new territories.

All the three Constitutions make provision for the admission of new States, provinces, or territories to the Federation.

In all the Constitutions the .practice of the Imperial Parliament is closely followed as seen in the Governor's choice of his executive Council, and generally in the practice of the Imperial Parliament, such as in the recommendation

Nature of Constitutions.

of money bills, etc., subject to the special provisions of each Constitution. All three Constitutions provide for a bicameral legislature, the closure or gag does not exist in any House of the legislature.

None of the Federal Legislatures created under the

[1] The Commonwealth of Australia Act, 63 and 64, Vict., c. 12.
[2] South Africa Act of Edw. VII, Ch. 9.

Constitution Acts are delegates, or agents acting under a mandate from the Imperial Parliament. Within the limits which circumscribe their powers, they have, and were intended to have, plenary powers of legislation as large and of the same nature as those of the Imperial Parliament itself.

The three Constitutions, however, are all legislative enactments, and must be construed by the same methods of construction and exposition applied to other statutes of a similar character, such as, say, Constitutional Charters. *Legislative enactments.*

" Remembering," said a Canadian judge, " that a constitution of Government does not and cannot, from its nature, depend in any great degree upon mere verbal criticism, or upon the import of single words, and that while we may well resort to the meaning of single words to assist our enquiries, we should never forget that it is an instrument of government we are to construe ; and, as has been already stated, that must be the truest exposition which best harmonises with its design, its objects, and its general structure." [1] *How interpreted.*

" If the text of a Constitution is explicit," said Lord Loreburn, " the text is conclusive alike in what it directs and what it forbids. When the text is ambiguous, as, for example, when the words establishing two mutually exclusive jurisdictions are wide enough to bring a particular power within either, recourse must be had to the context and scheme of the Act. Again, if the text says nothing expressly, then it is not to be presumed that the Constitution withholds the power altogether. On the contrary, it is to be taken for granted that the power is bestowed in some quarter, unless it be extraneous to the statute itself (as, for example, a power to make laws for some part of His Majesty's Dominions outside of Canada), or otherwise clearly repugnant to its sense. For whatever belongs

---

[1] Henry, J., in City of Fredericton v. Queen citing. Vattel, Book II, c. 17, sects. 285, 286, quoted Lefroy, *Legislative Power in Canada*, p. 29.

to self-government in Canada belongs either to the Dominion or to the Provinces within the limits of the British North America Act."[1]

Charters of rights. None of the three Constitutions contain charters of individual rights, securing guarantees of personal liberty, such as are found in the Constitution of the United States with its Amendments. Hamilton, in his time, had thought them unnecessary.[2] In the three Federal Constitutions such charters would be unnecessary, since the citizen of each portion of the State comprised in the Federation retains the rights, privileges, and immunities that he formerly possessed as a citizen of his State at the time of Federation, except in so far as they may have been altered by any subsequent Imperial or Colonial legislation. His rights, in the main, are those of a British citizen ; for when a British subject settles in an unoccupied country he carries with him the laws, privileges, and immunities of his native land, suitable to his own situation and the condition of the colony in which he settles.[3] But where territories are acquired by conquest ; and where existing laws are found, he accepts them, and such laws remain unaltered until he alters them.[4] Thus the French laws in Canada,[5] and the Roman-Dutch[6] laws in South Africa, continue,[7] except so far as they have been subsequently modified.

Laws contrary to fundamental principles. To this statement there is only one exception : Laws which are contrary to the fundamental principles of the British Constitution cease at the moment of conquest. No law in existence can justify torture ? or perpetuate slavery ? What President Lincoln effected during the War of Secession by proclamation as the armies of the Union advanced through the slave-owning States, is at once accomplished by British occupation. Where the Union

[1] Attorney-General for Ontario v. Attorney-General for Canada, 1912, A.C. 571, 583, 584.
[2] *Ante*, p. 132.
[3] *The Lauderdale Peerage*, L.R. 10, App. Cas., p. 744.
[4] Campbell v. Hall, 20 *State Trials*, col. 323.
[5] Nye v. Macdonald, L.R. 3, P.C., 331.
[6] Denyssen v. Mostert, L.R. 4, P.C., 236.
[7] Fabrigas v. Mostyn, 1 Cowp., 161, 20 *State Trials*, col. 181.

Jack flies, the weapons of torture rust, and the slave stands a free man in the light of day.

Each of the three Constitutions contains the well-known triple division of powers, which is the characterising distinction of a Federal system ; but in no case is the distinction so sharply marked as in the case of the United States, because in all the theory of Responsible Government, adopted from Great Britain, renders the Executive power dependent upon the legislative. Consequently, the administration must either work in harmony with it or be changed.

Triple division of powers.

A right which all the Constitutions confer is that of an appeal to the Judicial Committee of the Privy Council. The extent of the right in federal matters differs in the three Constitutions. Whilst Canada has largely sought an interpretation of her constitution from the Motherland, Australia has claimed to be her own interpreter ; in Australia no appeal lies to the King in Council from a decision of the High Court upon any question howsoever arising as to the limits of the constitutional powers of the Commonwealth and those of any State or States or as to the limits *inter se* of the constitutional powers of any two or more States, unless a certificate of leave to appeal is granted by the High Court of Australia.

Appeal to the Judicial Committee.

The South African Constitution does not expressly exclude the prerogative right of appeal by the grant of special leave, by the King in Council, but allows legislation to l mit the right ; but any Bill limiting the royal prerogative must be reserved.

All the Constitutions are subject to the Colonial Laws Validity Act. The origin of this Act is interesting. When the Plantations were established in America by the grant of governing powers given them, they were not empowered to pass laws expressly repugnant to the laws of England. In the time of William III (1696), when the British Parliament began to legislate for them, it enacted that all laws, bye-laws, usages, and customs in practice in any of the American Plantations which were repugnant to any law, made or to be made in the Kingdom so far as such law

Colonial Laws Validity Act.

should relate to and mention the Plantations, should be null and void. This statute ultimately led the State Courts of the United States to exercise a jurisdiction to control, and declare void State statutes—a jurisdiction which was subsequently exercised by the Supreme Court under the constitution of 1789. An attempt on the part of a judge in South Australia to examine into the validity of South Australian legislation led to the passing of this Act (1865), which declares that any Colonial law repugnant to an Act of the Imperial Parliament extending to the Colony to which such law may relate or repugnant to any order or regulation made under such Act, or having in the Colony the force and effect of such Act, shall be read subject to such Act, order, or regulation, and shall, to the extent of such repugnancy, and not otherwise, be void ; but no Colonial law was void solely because it was repugnant to the law of England, unless also repugnant to some such Act of Parliament, order, or regulation.

Powers as to treaties.

A power which has been slowly conceded by the Imperial Government is the power to make commercial treaties, although the Parliament and Government of Canada, had all powers necessary or proper for performing the obligations of Canada or of any of its provinces as part of the British Empire towards foreign countries arising under treaties between the Empire and such foreign countries. But no express power was conferred by the Dominion Act to make commercial treaties with foreign powers.

The old rule.

The old rule of the Imperial Government was that all negotiations of treaties with foreign powers must be conducted by ambassadors accredited by the Crown and responsible to the British Parliament. The Canadian Government, as well as the Australian Government, pressed, in the early seventies, for the right to active participation in the conduct of negotiations which related to commercial matters in which they were, perhaps, vitally concerned.

In 1871 Sir John Macdonald, the Premier of Canada, was successful in his demand, and he was appointed one of the plenipotentiaries to watch and represent the interests of Canada in negotiations with the United States, in reference to trade, commerce, and fisheries.

In 1874 Senator George Brown, of Canada, was permitted to be associated with the British Minister at Washington in his negotiations for a treaty to promote reciprocal trade between the United States and Canada ; but subject to the understanding that he must not act independently, and that propositions made by the Government of Canada should be previously submitted to the Secretary of State for the Colonies.

In 1879 Sir A. Galt, representing the Canadian Government, shared in the negotiations for improved commercial intercourse between Canada, France, and Spain.

In 1888 Sir Charles Tupper, as High Commissioner, was allowed to act as co-plenipotentiary with the British Ambassador in Spain and the United States. [1]

In 1893 Sir Charles Tupper negotiated a treaty with France, and signed it along with the King's representatives.

In 1907 Mr. Fielding and Mr. Brodeur negotiated a treaty with France on behalf of Canada, which received the approval of the Imperial Government.

The modern rule may be now stated that the King's Minister in the foreign Court concerned should be a plenipotentiary for the purpose of signing the treaty, and that the whole negotiation should be carried on under the supervision and with the approval of His Majesty's Government. [2]

The reason is that any foreign State would apply to the Imperial Government in case of any questions arising under the agreement.   To give the Colonies power of negotiating treaties for themselves without reference to the Imperial Government would be to give them an international status as separate and sovereign States ; and would be equivalent to breaking up the Empire into a number of independent States, a result injurious equally to the Colonies

---

[1] Quick and Garran, *Annotated Constitutions of the Australian Commonwealth*, pp. 634-635.

[2] Keith's *Responsible Government in the Dominions*, Vol. III, 1116.

and the Mother Country, and one that would be desired by neither party.

If an agreement for a treaty is arrived at, it would require the approval by the Imperial Government and also of the Colonial Government and Legislature, if it involved legislative action before the ratification could take place.[1]

It is settled law that the provisions of an Imperial treaty will not over-ride an Imperial Act; "but," says Mr. Lefroy, writing of the treaties of Canada, "it is difficult to understand how an act of the Dominion Parliament or of a provincial legislature can be void and unconstitutional merely because in conflict with an Imperial treaty, unless, of course, such treaty has been confirmed by Imperial statute. Such an Act would no doubt call for the exercise of the veto power; but if within their spheres these legislatures are as sovereign as the Imperial Parliament itself, it may well be asked how can such a conflict render their Act void."[3]

Professor Dicey states the old rule that Imperial treaties legally bind the Colonies; he also observes that the legislature of a self-governing Colony is free to determine whether or not to pass laws necessary for giving effect to a treaty entered into between the Imperial Government and a foreign power. The modern rule is that the Colonies are not bound unless expressly stated.

Peace and war. None of the Imperial Federations possess the power to declare peace or war, although entitled at any time to take steps to repel invasion.

Future consultation of Dominions on instructions to Hague Conference. At the Imperial Conference of 1911 it was resolved that the Dominions should be afforded an opportunity of consultation when framing the instructions to be given to British delegates at future meetings of the Hague Conference; and that Conventions affecting the Dominions, provisionally assented to at that Conference, should be circulated among the Dominion Governments for their

[1] *Ibid.*, 1117, quoting Lord Ripon's Despatch, 1894.
[3] Lefroy's *Legislative Power in Canada*, p. 255.

consideration ; and that a similar procedure, when time and opportunity, and the subject-matter passed, should, as far as possible, be used when preparing instructions for the negotiation of other international agreements affecting the Dominions.

CHAPTER XVIII

THE DOMINION EXECUTIVE

The Governor-
General. THE general position of the Governor-General of an Imperial Federation, as the representative of the Crown, is dealt with elsewhere,[1] and only those matters peculiar to his office in Canada are referred to.

Absence of. In the absence of the Governor-General of Canada, or in case of his death, incapacity, or removal, his powers vest in a Lieutenant-Governor or administrator appointed by the King under his royal sign manual. If no such appointment be made, the Lieutenant-Governorship will devolve upon the senior officer in command of the Imperial troops in the Dominion.

The Governor-General receives a salary of £10,000 a year.

Privy Council. In most matters, in accordance with the theory of Responsible Government, the Governor-General must act with the aid and advice of his Council, which is styled the King's Privy Council for Canada. The Council is composed of persons chosen and summoned by the Governor-General and sworn in as Privy Councillors. Its members are from time to time removable by the Governor-General.

Distinction between the Privy Council in England. Though the name of Privy Council was adopted from that body of the same title in England, its functions are different, since the latter has long ceased to have the direction of public affairs in the United Kingdom ; though it has still an existence as an honorary body, limited in numbers, only liable to be convened on special occasions, and only in theory an assembly of State advisers.

Cabinet Council. Since the Revolution of 1688, the practical discharge of the functions of the British Government has been entrusted to a Cabinet Council, which technically is nothing more than a committee of the Privy Council. The term " Ministry " in England includes all the Ministers of the

Crown. Of these, a smaller number constitute the inner Council, known as the Cabinet.[1]

In Canada the term "Ministry," or "Cabinet," is indifferently applied to all the Ministers and members of the Privy Council, who are called upon by the Governor-General to advise him in the Government of the country. *Ministry or Cabinet indifferently used in Canada.*

The Ministry, in accordance with the practice in the Imperial Parliament, must possess seats in Parliament, and the majority must be members of the House of Commons. *Ministry must possess seats in Parliament.*

The use of the title " Privy Council " seems to have been peculiar to the North American Continent. Canada possessed a Privy Council in 1776.[2] About the same time, Virginia and South Carolina, by their Constitutions, after the declaration of American. Independence, established Privy Councils. *Title peculiar to North America.*

In Virginia the Privy Council was chosen by a ballot of both Houses, either from their own members or from the people at large, to assist in the administration of justice.

Notwithstanding the severance of the ties that bound them to the Mother Country, it is strange to find how closely many of the United States still clung to the old names and institutions of England, many of which had been subjects of strongest animadversion prior to the rebellion, so powerful are ties of national sentiment, one of the strongest and most enduring of all ties. Seventy years after the War of Independence, Lowell mentions people who still talked of England as " home," in the same way as Canadians and Australians will in the present day.

On the establishment of the Dominion. Government in 1867, the claims of the different provinces to representation in the first Cabinet then formed were carefully considered. Ontario was awarded five ministers ; Quebec, four, one a representative of the English section of the community ; Nova Scotia, two ; and New Brunswick, two. *Provincial Claims to representation in Cabinet.*

The Cabinet at that time consisted of the following Ministers : A Minister of Justice and Attorney-General, *Cabinet in 1867.*

---

[1] Cf. Executive in the United States, *ante,* p. 71.
[2] *Ante,* p. 1.5.

Minister of Militia, Minister of Customs, Minister of Finance, Minister of Public Works, Minister of Inland Revenue, Minister of Marine and Fisheries, Postmaster-General, Minister of Agriculture, Secretary of State for Canada, Receiver-General, Secretary of State for the Provinces, President of the Privy Council.

Increase in 1873.

In 1873 the number of the Ministry was increased to fourteen, two of whom were without portfolios ; subsequently the Cabinet was reduced to thirteen. The office of Secretary of State for the Provinces was abolished and replaced by a department of the Interior.

In 1879 the office of Receiver-General was done away with, and the departmental duties taken over by the Minister of Finance. Changes have been made from time to time to suit the requirements of the Dominion. Recently a Minister for External Affairs has been appointed.

Powers of Governor-General.

The British North America Act vested in the Governor-General all the powers, authorities, and functions that had been vested in or exercised by the Governors or Lieutenant-Governors of Upper Canada, Lower Canada, Nova Scotia, and New Brunswick, whether conferred by Imperial legislation or by the legislatures of any of the four provinces, so far as they were not inconsistent with the Act, subject, however, to the right of the Dominion Parliament to repeal any of them, except such as had been constituted by Imperial legislation.

Powers to prorogue and dissolve Parliament. Assent to Bills.

The Governor-General's power to summon, prorogue, and dissolve Parliament are dealt with elsewhere.[1]

The Governor-General assents to all Bills at the end of a session, when he attends to prorogue Parliament ; but in cases of emergency a Bill may receive the Royal Assent at once. The Dominion Act provided that the Governor-General should declare according to his discretion ; but subject to the provisions of the Act and to the Royal instructions either that he assented thereto in the King's name, or that he withheld the King's assent, or that he reserved the Bill for the signification of the King's pleasure.

[1] *Ante*, p. 201.

On assent being given to a Bill in the King's name, a Procedure on assent. Disallowance. copy is sent to one of the King's principal Secretaries of State ; if the Act be disallowed within two years of the receipt of the copy by the King in Council, on the Governor-General signifying its disallowance by speech or message to each House of Parliament, or by Proclamation, it is annulled from and after the day of such signification.

A Bill reserved for the signification of the King's pleasure Reservation of Bills. possesses no force unless and until within two years from the day of its presentation to the Governor-General for the King's assent the Governor-General signifies, by speech or message to each House of Parliament, that it has received the assent of the King in Council.

Since 1878 no Bills have been reserved for the Royal Alteration in practice since 1878. instructions, and the Royal instructions have been amended in material particulars. It is now generally understood that the reserved power of disallowance which the King in Council possesses is sufficient for all possible purposes.

The change in the Royal instructions coincided with the appointment of the Marquis of Lorne as Governor-General, and marks the time when the Imperial authorities recognised that a great Dominion like Canada could not be bound by instructions which were suitable to a small colony.

The appointment and removal of the Lieutenant- Appointment of Lieutenant-Governors. Governors of the Provinces is made by the Governor-General by instrument under the Great Seal of Canada, at the instance of the Executive Government of the Dominion. The act of the Governor-General is, however, the act of the Crown, since the Executive Government of the Provinces is vested in the King. Consequently, a Lieutenant-Governor, when appointed, is as much the representative of His Majesty for all purposes of provincial legislation as the Governor-General is for all purposes of Dominion Government.

The letters patent appointing the Governor-General entitle him to appoint all such Judges, Commissioners and Justices of the Peace as might be lawfully appointed by the Crown.

Veto power, how exercised.   The Governor-General in Council possesses the power to veto provincial Acts of Parliament ; but in doing so he is executing an executive act which is one of political control, set in motion in the interests of the nation, and not a mere power to restrain illegal stretches of jurisdiction, a function which belongs not to a Government but to a court of law. [1]

"As it was considered of importance," says Sir J. C. Bourinot, "that the course of local legislation should be interfered with as little as possible, and the power of disallowance exercised with great caution, and only in cases where the law and general interests of the Dominion imperatively demanded it, the Minister of Justice, in 1868, laid down certain principles of procedure which have been generally followed up to the present time. On the receipt of Acts passed in any province, they are immediately referred to the Minister of Justice. He thereupon reports those Acts which he considers free from objection of any kind, and if his report is approved by the Governor in Council, such approval is forthwith communicated to the Provincial Government. He also makes separate reports on those Acts which he may consider—

" (1) as being altogether illegal or unconstitutional ;

" (2) as illegal or unconstitutional in part ;

" (3) as cases of concurrent jurisdiction clashing with the legislation of the general Parliament ;

" (4) as affecting the interests of the Dominion generally.

" It has also been the practice, in the case of measures only partially defective, not to disallow the Act in the first instance ; but if the general interest permit such a course, to give the Local Government an opportunity of considering the objections to such legislation and of remedying its defects."

Nature of disallowance.   When a Provincial Act is disallowed, it must be totally disallowed. If it is clearly within the competency of a legislature passing it, and is not in conflict with Imperial

[1] Lefroy's *Legislative Power in Canada*, p. 197.

or Dominion policy or interests, it is left to its operations, although open to objection as unjust or otherwise contrary to sound principles of legislation.[1] If it is of doubtful constitutional validity, it is left to be tested by those interested in doing so through the medium of the law courts.

One out of many instances of an exercise of the veto power may be noticed. The Legislature of British Columbia passed an Act to prevent Chinese immigration. The Act was disallowed not on broad Imperial grounds, but because it interfered with the Dominion's power to regulate trade and commerce. The case was found to be of such a nature that the ordinary tribunals were unable to afford an adequate remedy.[2]

Instance of exercise.

" The powers of the legislatures and governments of Canada have been partitioned by a supreme authority, which has given to the Dominion organisation not only all unassigned powers not purely of a private or local nature, but also specially the power to control absolutely by disallowance the legislation of the Province. In the United States, the Central Government holds its authority from the States, and has no power over the States' legislation, other than it may acquire through the Supreme Court."[3]

During the debates in the Parliament of Canada, prior to Federation, the importance of the veto power was generally dwelt on.

Importance attached to veto during Federation Debates.

Sir John Rose said : " The other point which commends itself so strongly to my mind is this, that there is a veto power on the part of the general Government over all the legislation of the local Parliaments ; that was a fundamental element which the wisest statesmen engaged in framing the Constitution saw ; that if it was not engrafted in it, must necessarily lead to the destruction of the Constitution. I believe this power of negative, this power of veto, is the best protection and safeguard of the system ;

---

[1] Lefroy, *Legislative Power in Canada.*   Bourinot, *Parliamentary Practice and Procedure,* pp. 81-82.
[2] *British Columbia Sess. Papers,* 1885, p. 464.
[3] Angier *v.* The Queen Insurance Co., 22 L.C.J., pp. 309-310.

and if it had not been provided, I would have felt it very difficult to reconcile it to my sense of duty to vote for the resolutions."[1]

Object of.

The object of the veto power was to support Federal unity by preserving the minorities in different parts of the confederated provinces from oppression at the hands of majorities.

Writing of the veto power, such a careful and accurate observer as Sir J. C. Bourinot states[2] that " perhaps no power conferred upon the general Government is regarded with greater jealousy and restlessness than this power of dis-

Jealousy of exercise.

allowing provincial enactments ; so far, this power has been exercised in very few cases. Out of the large number of Acts passed since Confederation by the legislatures of the Provinces, over 6,000 Acts have been passed from 1867 to 1882 inclusive ; but only thirty-one altogether have been disallowed. The fact goes to show that the power has been exercised, on the whole, with caution and deliberation. A review, however, of the very voluminous papers relating to this question proves that, whilst but few Acts have been disallowed, the legislation has been considered partially objectionable in many cases by the law officers of the Dominion ; but in such cases, generally every opportunity has been given to the Local Government to remove the objections pointed out by the Minister of Justice."

Since 1884 there have been some changes of policy from time to time on the part of the Dominion Government with reference to the exercise of the veto power. During Sir John Macdonald's ministry there was an active interference with Provincial Laws. In 1887 an Inter-provincial confer-ence demanded the abolition of the Dominion Veto Power. It may be observed that no consent or acquiescence in the Law by non-exercise of the veto power or otherwise can render valid an act otherwise *ultra vires* and unconstitutional under the British North America Act, and such an act could be challenged in the Courts. The veto power, however, is

---

[1] *Debates on Federation*, p. 404.
[2] Bourinot, pp. 77-78.

not so extensive as that possessed by the Federal Courts of the United States since there is nothing to prevent the Provinces passing laws impairing the obligation of contracts as there is in the United States.

The veto power was no doubt adopted from the practice of the Privy Council in the United Kingdom of disallowing acts of Colonial Legislatures on the advice of the Colonial Secretary. It may be interesting to notice some of the attempts that have been made in the past to restrain legislation considered on various grounds as objectionable. Origin of.

The attempt was sometimes made by requiring subordinate Parliaments to submit their legislative proposals to the Royal Authority. Poyning's Act of 1494 in this way regulated Irish legislation from the reign of Henry VII till 1783. Historical examples of Poyning's Act.

Under this Act, all proposed Irish Bills were required to be submitted to the Privy Council for their consent and approval to be certified under the Great Seal of England, the Privy Council occupying a somewhat similar position to the Irish Parliament that the Scottish Lords of Articles did to the Scottish Parliament.

The famous fundamental Constitution of Carolina, drawn up by the celebrated philosopher, John Locke, in 1669, in conjunction with Lord Ashley (afterwards Earl Shaftesbury), contained almost identical provisions, and was no doubt copied from the Irish precedent. The fundamental Constitution of Carolina.

During the reign of Richard II, when the Royal prerogative assumed absolutism, the King sought to override Parliamentary legislation in another way by using his powers in Council, by passing or overriding ordinances. Overriding legislation by ordinances.

" What is the use," asks a contemporary, " of statutes made in Parliament ? They have no effect. The King and his Privy Council habitually alter and efface what has been previously established in Parliament, not merely by the community, but even by the nobility." [1]

In later times, some of the States of America, after the Checks in the United States.

---

[1] Walsingham II, 48. Stubb's *Constitutional History*, Vol. II, 292, cited Maitland's *Constitutional History of England*, 187-188.

Declaration of Independence, devised Constitutions to
check legislation contrary to the spirit of the Constitution.
New York provided a Council to prevent laws being passed
inconsistent with the spirit of her Constitution. The
veto power of the Council was like that possessed by the
President of the United States—no more than a qualified
veto. The Governor, Chancellor, and Judges of the State
Supreme Court constituted a Council to revise all Bills
when they had passed the Senate and Assembly, but before
they became law. Should any bill appear improper to a
majority of the Council, it was returned with the objections
of the Council, in writing, to the House in which it originated.
If both Houses, after considering the objections separately
again, passed them by a two-thirds majority, the bill
became law, the Council's objections notwithstanding.

Value as an Imperial force.

In a Federal system.

Examples of exercise: in Australia and New Zealand.

In estimating the value of a political veto, it may be
regarded from two points of view, first, in its application
to a country possessing Colonies with subordinate legislatures, such as is the case with the United Kingdom and her
Colonies ; secondly, in a Federal system. The veto over
laws of such legislatures can only be sparingly exercised,
as the following instances show : Between 1875 and 1877
four Bills only were not assented to which had been passed
by the legislature of New South Wales, and in every case
the principle embodied in the Bills has since become law.
In Queensland, between 1860 and 1881, six Bills only were
not assented to, and in four cases the principle contended for is now law. In South Australia, between 1860
and 1891, six Bills were not assented to and three were
disallowed ; in six cases the principle contended for has
since been allowed. In Tasmania, from 1859 to 1890,
seven Bills were not assented to, one of which was at the
request of the Colonial Government, and one disallowed,
in six cases out of eight the principle of the Bill has since
become accepted. In New Zealand, between 1856 and 1883,
eight Bills were not assented to, and two disallowed ; in
four cases the principle has since been admitted.[1]

[1] Returns presented to the House of Lords, Aug. 2nd, 1894.

From these instances it seems clear that the veto power is of no great value.   Its exercise is watched with jealousy, and subordinate legislatures justly quarrel with the exercise of an over-riding mastership.

In a Federal Constitution, however, where the political veto power is exercised only in the name of the Federal Government, as it is presumably exercised for the benefit of the majority of the component units, it is therefore necessarily stronger.   The reason is that the unit whose Act is .vetoed is a part of the body exercising the power—thus the veto power in Canada is capable of exercise with more safety, but even then it is regarded with suspicion. [1] *Stronger force in the Federal system.*

The framers of the United States' Constitution considered that the limitations of States' powers were best secured by prohibitions in the Constitution, and the establishment of a judicial tribunal to say what these were ; they left to the executive the task of enforcing judicial decisions. The same system was followed by the framers of the Australian Constitution. *Prohibitions in the United States' Constitution.*

In the old Germanic Federation, force had often to be resorted to to coerce a recalcitrant member of the Federation.   To avoid the inherent weakness of the political veto, the provincial powers in the South African Constitution have been reduced to such an extent, that the Constitution is almost unitary. [2] *Force as a weapon in Germanic Confederation.*

The result of leaving the interpretation of questions to the Judiciary is to create uncertainty as to the validity of legislation, and this has led to the passing of Acts enabling the Executive to put hypothetical questions to the judges as to the constitutional soundness of proposed laws.· *Judicial answers on constitutional questions.*

Although the Executive in the United States possesses no power to obtain answers from the Supreme Court at Washington as to the constitutionality of proposed legislation, some of the States possess a limited power.   The

[1] *Post,* p. 274.
[2] *Post,* p. 423.

Dominion Government is entitled to obtain, by direct request, answers from the Supreme Court of Canada on questions both of law and fact. The original Supreme Court Act imposing this duty on the Supreme Court was passed in 1875 (38 Vict., c. 11). It was re-enacted in substance in 1886, by R.S.C., 1886, c, 135, amended in 1891 by 54 & 55 Vict., c. 25, and again by 6 Edw. VII, c. 50, and finally re-enacted by R.S.C., 1906, c. 139. Most of the Provincial Governments have passed Acts, in similar terms, requiring their own Courts to answer questions put by them. The validity of the provisions contained in the Supreme Court Act was questioned in 1912; the Judicial Committee of the Privy Council then decided it was within the powers of the respective legislatures to impose the above duty on the Courts.[1] The same difficulty that was felt in Canada has also been experienced in Australia, where Commonwealth Acts have been declared *ultra vires* by the High Court. Australia has recently passed an Act on the lines of the Dominion Act.[2]

Privy Councillors' duties. The Privy Council in England are bound, as Privy Councillors, to advise the Crown when called upon, and so is the Judicial Committee, although the procedure is used from time to time, though rarely, and with a careful regard to the nature of the reference.

Summoning judges. The House of Lords has a right, when exercising its judicial functions as the highest Court of Appeal from the Courts of the United Kingdom, to summon the judges and to ask of them such questions as it may think necessary for the determination of a particular case. There is also authority for saying that the House of Lords possesses, in its legislative capacity, a right to ask the judges what the law is, in order to better inform itself how, if at all, the law should be altered. The claim rests upon the unwritten law of the Constitution.

Disuse of practice. The last instance of the Crown's request to the judges to inform them as to the state of law occurred in 1760,

---

[1] The Attorney-General for the Province of Ontario and another, and the Attorney-General for the Dominion of Canada and another, 1912, A.C.
[2] *Post*, p. 334.

when Lord Mansfield, on behalf of His Majesty's judges, did furnish an answer, though with infinite reluctance, as to the Crown's right to summon Lord George Sackville before a court-martial. Whether the judges could be now compelled to do so, or whether the practice has not fallen into desuetude are moot points.[1]

[1] *Ibid.*

CHAPTER XIX

CONSTITUTION OF THE LEGISLATIVE POWER

Powers and
privileges of
Parliament. THE legislative power of Canada was conferred by the
British North America Act of 1867 in the following terms :
" There shall be one Parliament for Canada, consisting of
the Queen, the Upper House (styled the Senate), and the
House of Commons."

The duration of the Parliament was fixed at five years,
unless a sooner dissolution took place. Its privileges,
immunities, and powers to be held, enjoyed, and exercised
by both Houses, and by their members, were to be such as
it might declare from time to time ; but they were never
to exceed those which, in 1867, were held, enjoyed, and
exercised by the Imperial Parliament and its members.

In 1875, in consequence of doubts as to the legality of
an Act of the Dominion which had conferred powers upon
Committees of the Senate to examine witnesses on oath and
a subsequent Act which had given similar powers to both
Houses, an Imperial Act was passed[1] which defined the
privileges, immunities and powers of both of the Canadian
Houses to be such as might be defined by the Parliament
of Canada, but they were not to exceed those possessed
by the House of Commons in England, at the time when any
Canadian Act might be passed.

Speaker
claims
privileges.
Personal
privileges of
members. The Speaker claims these privileges at the commencement of every new Parliament. The personal privileges of
members include their protection during attendance and
freedom from intimidation, freedom from arrest and
imprisonment on civil process for forty days before and
after the meeting of Parliament, and freedom of speech.
By the privilege of Parliament its members are assured
from assault, menace, or insult on their way to and from
the House, on account of their behaviour in Parliament.

[1] 38 and 39 Vict., c. 38.

226

Parliament enforces its privileges by punishing by com- Contempts. mitment for contempts of the privileges of the House, according to their character, in extreme cases, by imprisonment.

The powers and privileges of Colonial Assemblies in General respect of the punishment of contempts have frequently powers of Colonial been discussed by the Judicial Committee of the Privy with regard to. Council. The rule to be deduced from the decisions seems to be that where a Colony has been permitted to carry over to the Colony the privileges, immunities, and powers of the House of Commons, and has, in terms, carried over all the privileges and powers exercised by the House of Commons at the date of the statute, the Colonial Assembly possesses all privileges and powers of the House of Commons connected with contempts, amongst others, the privilege and power of committing for contempt ; of judging itself of what is contempt ; and of committing for contempt by warrant, stating generally that a contempt has taken place.[1]

In the case of Harnett *v.* Crick,[2] under the New South The case of Harnett *v.* Wales Constitution Act of 1902, where the Legislative Council Crick. and Legislative Assembly possessed the power to make standing orders and to regulate the orderly conduct of their meetings, the plaintiff Harnett was found guilty, by a Royal Commission, of misconduct in his office, and a resolution in the Legislative Assembly was thereupon moved to consider the report of the Commission. The Speaker declined to proceed with the resolution as tending to prejudice the plaintiff. The House passed a standing order that whenever it should have been ruled or decided whether before or after the approval of the standing order, that the House cannot proceed on a matter which has been initiated in the House affecting the alleged misconduct of a member, by reason that he might be prejudiced in a pending criminal trial founded on such misconduct, the House may suspend such member till after the verdict of the jury

---

[1] Speaker of the Legislative Assembly *v.* Glass, L.R., 3 P.C., 560. See also in *re* Dill, 1864 1 Moo., P.C., N.S. 487.
[2] Harnett *v.* Crick (1908) A.C., 470.

or till after further order. On the standing order being approved by the Governor, the plaintiff was suspended by the House. The Judicial Committee decided that the passing of the standing order was within the competence of the House.

Instances of breaches of privilege. The following offences may be given as instances of breaches of privilege : Wilful obstruction of the business of the House ; wilful disobedience to particular orders of the House made in the exercise of its constitutional functions ; wilful disobedience to the standing rules and orders of the House, passed in exercise of its constitutional functions ; insults and libels on the character, conduct, and proceedings of the House and its members ; interference with officers of the House when discharging their duties.

Meetings of. The Parliament of Canada meets once a year in session. Twelve months must not intervene between its last sitting in one session and its first sitting in the next session. Parliament consists of two Houses—the Senate and the House of Commons.

Two Chambers. The acceptance of the principle of a two-Chamber Government by the framers of the first British Federal Constitution was noteworthy, apart from the philosophical and practical arguments which support a bicameral system under a unified Constitution.

Necessity in a Federal Constitution. Its applicability seemed even more necessary in a Federal Constitution where the States or Provinces acquiescing in its formation required some share in the Legislature. The arguments in favour of two-Chamber Government in a Federal Constitution received support from the precedent of the United States' Constitution ; there was also the additional historical example of the evils of a single legislative body, witnessed during the French Revolution, which had since been added to the precedents which condemned one - Chambered legislatures. Single - Chamber Governments, it may be asserted, have always failed to preserve the true balance of power between the legislative and executive departments. Where there has been one Chamber only there have been exhibited two effects : The Legislature has either subjected the executive to its will, and thereby introduced anarchy into the administration, which has only proved curable by a military executive that has ultimately ended in a subjection of the Legislature ; or the executive by obtaining control of the Legislature and moulding it to its wishes has established a new species of executive tyranny speciously disguised under legislative forms. Both processes have been observed. The framers of the American Constitution had studied the former in the constitutional struggles of England, and the framers of the Canadian Constitution in the constitutional struggles of France during the French Revolution.

Turning now to the composition of the two Chambers of the Canadian House, it is observable that the title of Senate was chosen for the Upper and that of the House of Commons for the First Chamber. ^{Upper Chamber styled Senate. First Chamber, House of Commons.}

THE SENATE

In 1867, when Parliament first met, the Senate consisted of 72 members, made up of 24 Senators for Ontario, 24 for Quebec, and 24 for the maritime provinces of Nova Scotia and New Brunswick. ^{Senate, composition of.}

The three divisions were made up after the American model, to ensure equality of representation for the Provinces in the Senate. The two Maritime Provinces, for purposes of this equality, were treated as one. The principle of State equality of representation originally established has not been adhered to. ^{Federal principle.}

The Imperial Act of 1871 authorised the Canadian Parliament to establish new provinces in any territories forming for the time being part of the Dominion of Canada, but not included in any existing province and to provide representation in the Senate for provinces subsequently admitted to the Federation. On the admission of Prince Edward Island, a representation of four Senators was allotted to her. This increase, however, did not affect the number of Senators, since the Constitution Act had provided that after the admission of Prince Edward Island the representation ^{Increase of Senate a departure from Federal principle.}

of Nova Scotia and New Brunswick should be reduced on the occurrence of vacancies. The representation of New Brunswick cannot, however, at any time be increased beyond ten, unless the Governor-General recommends a change, and the Crown directs that three or six Senators should be added to the Senate. On the happening of this event, the Maritime Provinces are entitled to one or two additional Senators, as the case may be. The admission of British Columbia in 1871 added three Senators.

Number of Senators.

The Constitution provided that the total number of Senators at no time should exceed seventy-eight, unless Newfoundland were admitted to the Confederation, when the number might be increased to eighty-two.

Total number. Newfoundland has never been admitted; nevertheless, the total number of Senators is eighty-seven.

The increase has been due to the admission of Manitoba, Alberta, and Saskatchewan, which have each received a representation of four Senators.

Limitation of Members.

The limitation as to numbers (imposed by the Constitution Act) is of some importance, since a power to indefinitely increase the number of Senators, on the demand of either party, might tend to diminish its importance as a Second Chamber. In 1877 the Queen was requested to appoint additional Senators; the request was refused. The reason stated by the then Colonial Secretary (the Earl of

Lord Kimberley's views.

Kimberley) was that Her Majesty could not be advised to take the responsibility of interfering with the Constitution of the Senate, except upon an occasion when it had been made apparent that a difference had arisen between two Houses of so serious and permanent a character that the Government could not be carried on without Her intervention, and when it could be shown that the limited creation of Senators allowed by the Act would apply an adequate remedy.[1]

No method of changing composition of Senate.

It is to be observed that, whilst the Royal power is circumscribed by these provisions of the Canadian Constitution,

[1] Quoted in Bourinot's *Parliamentary Practice and Procedure*, foot-note, p. 107.

which admit of only a certain limited increase in the
number of Senators, no real method exists of changing the
political complexion of the Chamber by increasing the
number of Senators. In the Second Chamber of the
Parliament of the United Kingdom such a limitation as
this is unknown. The King can, and does, on the advice
of His ministers, constantly add to the numbers of the
Upper House: more often than not to suit political
necessities.

The Senate is nominated by the Crown; and the How
nominated.
qualifications of a Senator are that he must be a natural- Qualifications
of Senator.
born or naturalised subject, of the full age of thirty years;
resident in the province for which he is appointed; and
possessing real and personal property, worth $4,000 over
and above all debts and liabilities.

Thirty was the age fixed by the United States Con- ge
Qualification.
stitution[1] as the suitable period for the exercise of the
Senator's trust.

In Quebec, the Senator's real property qualification must Quebec
property
be in the electoral division for which he is appointed, or qualification.
he must be a resident in the division.

"The reason is," said Mr. George Brown in the debates
on Confederation in the Provincial Parliament of Canada
prior to Federation, "our Lower Canada friends felt they had
French Canadian and British interests to be protected,
and they conceived that the existing system of electoral
divisions would give protection to these separate interests.
We in Upper Canada, on the other hand, were quite content
that they should settle that amongst themselves and
maintain their existing division if they chose. But so far
as we in the West were concerned we had no such separate
interests to protect, we had no diversities of language or
origin to reconcile, and we felt that the true interest of
Upper Canada was that her very best men should be sent
to the Legislative Council wherever they might happen to
reside or wherever their property was located."

A Canadian Senator is required to take an oath of

[1] *Ante,* p. 46.

allegiance, and he must also make a declaration of the existence of his property qualification prior to taking his seat in the Senate. The declaration is required to be made within the first twenty days of each Parliament. The declaration follows the form in the 5th Schedule to the British North America Act of 1867. If a sufficiently good reason, such as illness, prevents a Senator from making this declaration, which by resolution of the House should be made before the Clerk of the House, he may make it elsewhere before a Justice of the Peace.

Life appointment. Resignation or disqualification.

A Senator holds his seat for life, but may resign it by placing his resignation, in writing, with the Governor-General. He is not eligible to sit in the House of Commons. His seat will also become vacant on his failing to attend the Senate during two consecutive Sessions of Parliament ; or on his taking an oath or making a declaration or acknowledgment of allegiance, obedience, or adherence to a foreign Power ; or on his doing an act by which he becomes a subject or citizen, or becomes entitled to the rights and privileges of a subject or citizen of a foreign Power ; on his being adjudged bankrupt, or insolvent, or on his applying for the benefit of any law relating to insolvent debtors or becoming a public defaulter. It will also become vacant on attainder for treason, or conviction of felony, or of an infamous crime ; or on his ceasing to possess the property qualification or that of residence. In the case, however, of residence, the disqualification will not disqualify him if he be residing at the seat of Government, holding an office under the Government, which requires his presence there.

Vacancy in Senate.

In the case of a vacancy in the Senate, the Governor-General fills it up. A Senator receives payment for his services.[1] The first body of Senators, who assembled in 1867, were summoned by warrant under the Royal Sign Manual. Their names were inserted in the Proclamation of the Union. Since then they have been appointed by Governor-Generals on the nomination of the Government

[1] See *post*, 239.

for the time being. The Senate hears and determines questions respecting the qualification of a Senator or a vacancy in the Senate. The presiding officer of the House is called the Speaker of the Senate, and the appointment is Speaker of the Senate. made by the Governor-General by instrument under the Great Seal of Canada. He is removable by the Governor, who may appoint another in his stead. The speaker receives a salary of four thousand dollars per annum.

A majority vote determines any question before the House, but there must be a quorum of at least fifteen Quorums. Senators, including in that number the Speaker.

The Speaker possesses a vote in all cases ; but when the Speaker no casting vote. voices are equal (content or non-content) the decision is deemed to be in the negative.

A considerable likeness to the House of Lords is trace- Comparison with House of Lords. able in the composition and practice of the Senate—although the hereditary element is absent. The Governor-General, as the King's representative, summons a Senator like the King summons a peer to the House of Lords. In Canada, the summons is by instrument under the Great Seal of Canada. In the United Kingdom, by writ of summons : the issue of the writ, however, in the United Kingdom has a distinguishing feature due to the hereditary character of the Lords of Parliament. The Crown is not entitled to withhold the writ from a man whose ancestor has been summoned by writ and has taken his seat, nor can it summon a man in pursuance of a patent limiting his peerage, and therewith the right to the summons to the term of his life.[1] It may be remembered that the Constitution Act of Canada, in 1791, had provided for the creation of hereditary titles and honours conferring a right of summons to the Legislative Council or Upper House. No title was, however, created ; and the red and blue ribbons, whose appearance in the New World Fox so feelingly deplored, have never shone in the Upper House in Canada.

" The Speaker of the House of Lords is, by prescription, the Lord Chancellor or Lord Keeper of the Great Seal ;

[1] Anson's *Law and Customs of the Constitution*, p. 206.

but, in his absence, his place may be taken by deputy-Speakers, of whom there are several appointed by Commission under the Great Seal ; and, if these should all be absent, the Lords may elect a Speaker for the time being. Neither the Lord Chancellor nor the Lord Keeper for the time being have power either to maintain order or to act in any way as the representative or mouthpiece of the House, unless the House should confer such an authority upon them. The Lord Chancellor may vote ; but if the same number of votes are recorded on each side on division, the question is decided in the negative, for neither the Lord Chancellor nor the Chairman of Committees possess casting votes.[1] The Lord Chancellor collects the voices, and announces the preponderance of the ' contents ' or ' not contents.' In the Canadian House a division is taken by Senators rising in their places. In the House of Lords the Peers pass through the Division Lobbies.''

The House of Commons

House of Commons. In 1867 the House of Commons consisted of 181 members. The four provinces received the following representation : Ontario, 82 members ; Quebec, 65 members ; Nova Scotia, 19 members ; and New Brunswick, 15 members. The Constitution Act provided for additional representation for the Provinces. Quebec, however, was to possess the fixed number of 65.

The adjustment of representation. The completion of each decennial Census compels Parliament to readjust the representation, subject, however, to Quebec retaining her fixed number. The power of Parliament to legislate over representation is limited by the following rules. The number of members assigned to each of the other provinces must be such number as will bear the same proportion to the number of its population (ascertained at such Census), as the number sixty-five bears to the number of the population of Canada (so ascertained). In the computation of the number of members for a Province, a fractional part not exceeding one-half of the whole number

[1] *Laws of England,* Vol. XXI, Title Parliament, 633.

requisite for entitling the Province to a member must be disregarded ; but a fractional part exceeding one-half of that number must be treated as equivalent to the whole number.

When a readjustment takes place, the number of members for a Province cannot be reduced, unless the proportion which the number of the population bears to the number of the aggregate population at the last preceding readjustment of the number of members for the Province is ascertained at the then latest Census to be diminished by one-twentieth part or upward. "Aggregate population of Canada" relates to the whole of Canada as constituted by the Act, and therefore not only includes the four original provinces, but Provinces subsequently admitted into the Union.[1] Such readjustment must not take effect until the termination of the then existing Parliament.

The number of Members of the House of Commons may be from time to time increased by the Parliament of Canada, but the proportionate representation of the Provinces prescribed by the Act must not be thereby disturbed.

This somewhat curious and complicated way of arriving at a redistribution of seats originated in the Quebec Conference, when the best mode of preventing the difficulty in the future of too large a body of members was discussed. "Unless some definite principle had been adopted to keep the representation within a certain limit, the House of Commons might eventually have become a too cumbrous, unwieldy body. It was decided to accept the representation of Lower Canada as a fixed standard—as a pivot on which the whole would turn—since that province was the best suited for the purpose on account of the comparatively permanent character of its population, and from its having neither the largest nor the least number of inhabitants."[2]

In 1882, after the taking of the decennial Census of 1881,

Origin of redistribution plan.

[1] Attorney-General for the Province of Prince Edward Island *v.* Attorney General for the Dominion of Canada, 1905, AC., 37.

[2] Bourinot's *Parliamentary Practice and Procedure*, p. 60, quoting Sir J. A. Macdonald, *Confed. Deb.*, 1865, p. 38.

Ontario received 6, Nova Scotia 2, and New Brunswick 1
additional member. On the admission of Manitoba she
received 4 members, British Columbia 6, and Prince Edward
Island 6 members respectively.

Up till 1882, the total number of members was 206.
A fresh readjustment then took place ; Ontario received
4 additional members and Manitoba 1, making the total
211. At present the membership of the Commons House
is thus made up : Alberta, 7 ; British Columbia, 7 ;
Manitoba, 10 ; New Brunswick, 13 ; Nova Scotia, 18 ;
Ontario, 86 ; Prince Edward Island, 4 ; Quebec, 65 ;
Saskatchewan, 10 ; Yukon, 1. The House of Commons is
thus composed of 221 members.

Provincial laws applicable to elections.   A provision somewhat similar to one in the United
States' Constitution fixed the electoral franchise in Canada.
The laws in force in the provinces at the time of Federation for the qualification of electors, and the qualifications
or disqualifications of the persons to be elected, and the
whole machinery of election, the vacation of seats, and the
execution of new writs were, by the Constitution, directed
to apply to the elections for the Dominion House till
Parliament otherwise provided.

In 1885 a general franchise law for the Dominion was
passed, bringing about uniformity of suffrage on a small
property qualification ; but the preparation of the
electoral lists caused so much expense, that the Franchise
Act was repealed, and the electoral lists of the Provinces
again taken.

In 1874 Parliament made more complete provision for
the election of Members to the House of Commons, establishing simultaneous polling and dispensing with open
nominations, which had been abolished in the United
Kingdom in 1872. No real property qualification is
required of a candidate ; but he must be a natural subject
of the King, naturalised either under Imperial, Canadian,
or Provincial legislation.

All persons qualified to vote for members of the
Provincial Legislative Assemblies can vote for members of

the House of Commons for the several electoral districts
that are comprised within such provinces respectively.
The voters' list applying to the one applies to the other.
Voting takes place by ballot.

In 1878 an Act provided for a recount of votes by a Recounts.
judge, following the precedent that had already been
established in the United Kingdom.

The Canadian statutes closely follow the English statutes Election petitions.
in reference to the trial and determination of election petitions. As in England, so in Canada the House of Commons formerly dealt with the trial of disputed election
petitions.

In 1851 the Canadian House, formed under the Constitution of 1840, transferred its authority in these matters to a
General Committee of Elections; and ultimately, by a
somewhat complicated process, to a committee to try election
petitions specially formed.

In 1874 the duty of trying disputed elections was imposed
on the Judges of the Supreme Courts of the Provinces
by the Controverted Elections Act. The power of Parliament to pass the statute was questioned, but its exercise
was decided by the Supreme Court of Canada and by the
Judicial Committee of the Privy Council to be good.

An appeal under this statute can be brought by any Appeal.
party who is dissatisfied with the decision of the two judges
who have tried the case on any question of law or fact,
or from a judgment rule, order or decision on any preliminary
objection the allowance of which objection is fatal or will
prove fatal if allowed.

The judges who have tried an election petition must Certificate of determination to be sent to House.
certify their determination to the Speaker of the House of
Commons, with a special report of any matters occurring
during the trial which they think should be submitted to
the House of Commons. The House will not again open
the question after it has been decided by a judicial tribunal,
although it retains its right to judge of any legal disabilities
affecting its members in the same way as the Imperial
House does.

Amending and Consolidating Acts dealing with the same subject were passed in 1886 and 1887.

No prerogative right of appeal.

There is no prerogative right of appeal from a decision of the Supreme Court on any point.   It was said by the Judicial Committee of the Privy Council on an application for leave to appeal : " Suppose we recommend Her Majesty to reverse the judgment, how would that decree be carried into execution.   The Speaker could not act on his own authority, and could only act by order of the House.   Suppose the House to say Her Majesty has no prerogative to do this, and we refuse to carry it out, then there would be an immediate conflict between the House of Commons of the Dominion and Her Majesty.   It would not be a very prudent thing for us to advise Her Majesty to reverse a judgment, unless we can see our way to having it carried into execution when Her Majesty ordered it.   Suppose the House of Commons, on the report of the Supreme Court that both parties had been guilty of bribery, ordered a new writ, but Her Majesty orders that writ to be recalled or upset the election which had taken place under it.   It appears to me there is no mode of carrying out the decree ; and we could not advise Her Majesty to reverse a decree unless we saw a mode of carrying it into execution." [1]

Members of Provincial Assemblies are not eligible to sit or vote in the House of Commons, and the acceptance of a seat in a provincial legislature vacates the seat in the Dominion House. [2]

Disqualification by taking office.

Another ground of disqualification is the acceptance or holding of any office, commission, or employment (permanent or temporary) in the service of the Government of Canada, at the nomination of the Crown or at the nomination of any of the officers of the Government, where any salary, fee, wages, allowance, or emolument is attached.

Disqualifications of holders of offices.

The holders of the offices of sheriff, registrar of deeds, clerk of the peace, or county Crown attorney in any of the

[1] Kennedy v. Powell, 59 L.T. 279, P.C.
[2] 35 Vict., c. 15 ; 36 Vict., c. 2 (Dom. Stat.).

provinces of Canada are also disqualified from sitting in Parliament.

Stringent provisions have been inserted in Acts to guard Government contracts. against Members of the House being interested in Government contracts, and provision has also been made for the insertion of special conditions in such contracts, which must recite that no Member of the House is admitted to any share or benefit in them. Members of Parliament who obtain office under the Crown must, as in the Imperial Parliament, seek re-election ; but a minister need not vacate his seat if he resigns his office and accepts another in the same Ministry, in the same month, unless the administration of which he was a member has resigned and a new administration has been formed and occupies the same offices. Many of these important provisions are to be found in the Act respecting the Senate and House of Commons.[1]

A Member is entitled to resign his seat by giving notice Vacating seat. from his seat in the House. The intimation of his intention is then entered by the Clerk on the journals of the House ; or the member may, if he chooses, resign by addressing and delivering to the Speaker a declaration of his intention so to do, made under his hand and seal before two witnesses, either during the session or in the interval between two sessions. This declaration must be duly entered in the journals of the House.[2]

A Member receives payment for his services.[3] The sessional indemnity, as it is termed, is similar to that received by a Senator. The Speaker receives a salary of 4,000 dollars.

For every Session of Parliament which extends beyond Sessional allowances. thirty days a member of either House is entitled to a sessional allowance of 2,500 dollars, but a member is not entitled to this allowance for less than thirty-one days' attendance. His allowance for any less number of days is 20 dollars for each day's attendance.

[1] Revised Statutes, Vol. I, 1906 (Canada).
[2] House of Commons Act, Revised Statutes Canada, 1906, c. II ss. 5 & 6.
[3] Sect. 44, British North America Act, 1867.

The allowance may be paid on the last day of the month to the extent of 10 dollars for each day's attendance, but the remainder must be retained by the Clerk or Accountant of the proper House until the close of the Session when the final payment is made.

Deductions. A deduction of 15 dollars a day is made from such sessional allowance for every day beyond fifteen, on which the member does not attend a sitting. In the case of a member elected or appointed after the commencement of the session, no day of the session previous to such election or appointment is reckoned one of such fifteen days.

Absences through illness or through the member being on duty with his corps in a regularly organised Militia Camp, or engaged in travelling between his Camp and Ottawa do not count.

There are other provisions regulating deduction and Moving or transportation payments. In addition to the sessional allowances members expenses. receive their actual moving or transportation expenses and reasonable living expenses while on the journey between their place of residence and Ottawa, going and coming once each way. The travelling expenses may be commuted. Members give signed statements of their attendances to the Clerk of the House, and non-attendances also, when due to unavoidable illness. Statements as to travelling allowances are also handed to the Clerk of the House. Members are requested to swear as to the truth of their statements.

Leader of the Opposition. The member who occupies the recognised position of leader of the Opposition receives an additional sessional allowance of 7,000 dollars.

Expulsion of Members. Members of the House may be expelled by the House. To quote one historic example, Louis Riel was expelled in 1874 as a fugitive from justice, on evidence that he had fled after being accused of the murder of Thomas Scott. During the recess he was again returned as a member of Parliament. When Parliament re-assembled in 1875, on the exemplification of the judgment of outlawry being laid upon the table of the House, the Premier moved for the issue of a new writ in the room of Louis Riel, adjudged an outlaw. The motion was passed by a large majority. The expulsion of O'Donovan Rossa, which had taken place in the Imperial House of Commons in 1870, was relied on as a precedent. In addition to the power of expulsion the House possesses the power to suspend a member of the House for misconduct.

Choice and duties of Speaker.

Under the North British America Act, the House was directed to choose a Speaker on its first meeting after a General Election ;[1] and a Speaker has since been chosen on the meeting of each new Parliament. When there is a vacancy by death, resignation, or otherwise of the Speaker, the House must, with all practicable speed, elect another Speaker in his stead.[2] The Speaker presides over all meetings of the House ;[3] and the Act, till Parliament otherwise provided, made provision for his absence, if for any reason, from the Chair for forty-eight hours, by empowering the House to elect one of its members to take his place, who was thereupon clothed with all the authority of the Speaker.[4] When the Speaker leaves the chair during any part of the Sittings of the House on any day he may call upon the Chairman of Committees, or, in his absence, on any member of the House to take the chair and act as Deputy Speaker. The Chairman of Committees takes the place of the Speaker on the Clerk of the House informing the House of the Speaker's unavoidable absence.

Quorum.

Twenty Members constitute a quorum of the House, and for this purpose the Speaker is reckoned one.[5]

Speaker possesses casting-vote.

Questions are decided by a majority of votes, other than the Speaker ; but in cases of equality the Speaker possesses the casting-vote[6]—otherwise he cannot vote.

Bills appropriating revenue or imposing taxation.

Bills for appropriating any part of the Public Revenue, or for imposing any tax or impost, must arise in the House

[1] Sect. 44, *Ibid.*
[2] Sect. 45, *Ibid.*
[3] Sect. 46, *Ibid.*
[4] Sect. 47, *Ibid.*, R.S.C. 1906, c. 13, by which provision is made for the Chairman of Committees to take the chair.
[5] Sect. 48, *Ibid.*
[6] Sect. 49, *Ibid.*

of Commons ; but the House of Commons cannot adopt or pass any vote, resolution, address, or Bill for the appropriation of any part of the public revenue, or of any tax or impost, to any purpose that has not been first recommended to the House by message of the Governor-General in the session in which such vote, resolution, address, or Bill is proposed.

Consolidated Revenue of Great Britain. In 1787 the numerous Crown revenues of Great Britain were brought together into a consolidated fund, into which now flows every stream of the public revenue, and whence issues the supply of every public service.

Consolidated Revenue Fund of Canada. The North British America Act (Sec. 103) declared that the Consolidated Revenue Fund of Canada should be permanently charged with the costs, charges, and expenses incident to its collection, management, and receipt ; the sums thus permanently charged form the first charge on the fund, subject to review and audit in such manner as the Governor-General in Council should order till Parliament otherwise provided. The consolidated Revenue and Audit Act provides for the Auditing of the Public Accounts.

Recommendation of Crown for appropriation. The recommendation of the Crown for appropriation must first precede every grant of money in the United Kingdom, and is always necessary in matters which invoke the rights of the Crown, its patronage, its property, or its prerogatives. Consent may be given by special message or by an intimation from a Minister. " This intimation of the consent does not mean that the Crown gives its approbation to the substance of the measure ; but merely that the Sovereign consents to remove an obstacle to the progress of the Bill, so that it may be considered by both Houses and ultimately submitted to the Royal Assent." [1]

Difference in practice. There is some little difference in the practice in Canada as to the time when the consent of the Governor-General, as representative of the Crown, is given. In the United Kingdom it is not, as a rule, given before the third reading of a bill. In Canada it is usually signified on the second.

---

[1] Bourinot's *Parliamentary Practice and Procedure*, p. 472, citing 191, E. Hansard, 1445 ; 192 *ibid.* 732, Established Church (Ireland) Bill.

The requirement that Money Bills should first be recommended to the House by the Governor-General is utterly unlike the practice of Congress, where no obstacle is required to be removed ; but it accords with the practice which exists under British Constitutions.

The privileges which the British House of Commons has claimed with regard to the control of the public money may be stated shortly as follows— Privileges of House of Commons over public money.

1. As the Commons grants the demands of the Crown, Bills, therefore, for granting supplies must originate in the House of Commons.

2. The Lords ought not to amend or alter any grant made by the Commons. The power of the Lords over Money Bills is now subject to the provisions of the Parliament Act of 1911.

3. No public Bill whose provisions would involve the imposition of a charge upon the people by way of taxes may be introduced into the House of Lords.

4. The House of Lords ought not to amend or alter any legislative proposal contained in any Money Bill sent up for their concurrence by the Commons in such a way as to alter the amount of any charge upon the people, or the mode of levying it, or its duration, distribution, management, and collection. [1]

The Parliament Act of 1911 now provides that if a Money Bill, passed by the House of Commons and sent up to the House of Lords at least one month before the end of the Sessions, is not passed without amendment by that House within one month after it has received it, the Bill, unless the House of Commons otherwise directs, must be presented to the Sovereign for the Royal Assent, and become law as soon as such consent has been signified, notwithstanding the fact that it has not been agreed to by the House of Lords. Every Money Bill when sent to the House of Lords, and also when presented for the Royal Assent, must be endorsed with a certificate which must be signed by the Speaker, stating that the measure is, in his opinion, a Parliament Act.

[1] *Laws of England*, Vol. XXI, Parliament 792, 794.

Money Bill. Before giving a certificate, the Speaker must, if practicable, consult two Members of the House of Commons, who are nominated for the purpose from the Chairman's panel by the Committee of Selection at the beginning of each Session.

The Canadian House of Commons have placed the following resolution among their standing orders, that " all aid and supplies granted to the Crown by the Parliament of Canada are the sole gift of the House of Commons." [1]

The Senate never attempts to amend a supply. Money Bills carried back from the Senate bear the endorsement common to other Bills, " Passed by the Senate without amendment." The propriety of such an endorsement has even been questioned in the Commons; but it is now considered a matter of form, and is not noticed in the Commons' Journal." [2]

Though the Senate may not amend a Supply Bill, " yet all the authorities go to show that, theoretically, it has the Constitutional right to reject it in its entirety ; such a right, however, would never be exercised by a legislative body not immediately responsible to the people, except under circumstances of grave public necessity."

Senate never amends supply.

[1] Bourinot's *Parliamentary Practice and Procedure*, p. 502.
[2] *Ibid.*

CHAPTER XX

THE JUDICIAL POWER

THE Dominion Act did not create a great Federal Court of Appeal by the Constitution, such as was established by the Constitution of the United States. It left Parliament to constitute a general Court of Appeal for Canada, and the creation of such other Courts as were required for the administration of justice. The Provinces possess the sole power to provide and maintain courts for Provincial purposes, subject to the power of the Dominion Legislature to cast upon these courts special rules in such matters as bankruptcy and insolvency. *Federal Court not expressly created. Provincial Courts.*

The appointment of the judges of the Supreme, District and County Courts is an executive Act exercised by the Governor-General of Canada. *Appointment of judges.*

In 1875 the Parliament of Canada established a Supreme Court and an Exchequer Court. The Supreme Court consists of a Chief Justice and five puisne judges. It exercises an appellate, civil, and criminal jurisdiction within and throughout the Dominion. *Establishment of Supreme Court. Jurisdiction.*

The Governor-General does not appoint the judges of the Courts of Probate in Nova Scotia and New Brunswick. Until the laws relative to property and civil rights in Ontario, Nova Scotia, and New Brunswick, and the procedure of the Courts in those Provinces are made uniform, the judges must be selected from the local Bars, and the judges of the Courts of Quebec from the Quebec Bar. This rule has been applied to Prince Edward Island. *Judges of Courts of Probate. Selection of judges from local Bars.*

The judges of the Superior Courts hold office during good behaviour, but are removable by the Governor-General on addresses from the Senate and House of Commons. Their salaries are provided by Parliament.[1] *Duration of office.*

[1] The original Supreme Court Act was re-enacted in 1886 by R.S.C., 1886, c. 135, amended in 1891 by 54 and 55 Vict., c. 25 and again by 6th Edw. VII, c. 5, and finally re-enacted by R.S.C., 1906, c. 139.

Special jurisdiction. The Supreme Court possesses, in addition to its appellate jurisdiction, certain special jurisdiction, which gives it a distinction as a Federal Court. It will decide important questions of law or fact, touching—

" (a) the interpretation of the British North America Acts, 1867 to 1886 ;

" (b) the constitutionality or interpretation of any Dominion or Provincial legislation ;

" (c) the appellate jurisdiction as to educational matters by the British North America Act, 1867, or by other Act or law vested in the Governor in Council ; or

" (d) the powers of the Parliament of Canada, or of the legislatures of the provinces, or of the respective governments thereof, whether or not the particular power in question has been or is proposed to be executed.

" (e) Any other matter, whether or not in the opinion of the court *ejusdem generis* with the foregoing enumerations, with reference to which the Governor in Council sees fit to submit any such question."

Power of Governor-General to refer questions. The Governor-General in Council is empowered to refer any question coming within the above category to the Court to hear and consider it. Any question so submitted by the Governor is an important question.

Court certifies to Governor-General. The Court also certifies to the Governor-General in Council for his information its opinion on each question, with the reasons for each answer. A dissentient judge is required to state the reasons for his dissent.

Provinces how represented. The Provinces are entitled to notice through their Attorney-General in certain cases where their interests may be affected by any opinion ; the Attorney-General of the Province in such cases may be heard. Notice must be similarly given to interested persons, or classes of interested persons, who are entitled to be heard.

Treated as final for purposes of appeal. The opinion of the Court, although simply advisory, is treated as final for purposes of an appeal to the Judicial Committee.

Special jurisdiction to report on private bills. Another form of special jurisdiction exercised by the Court is the reporting upon private Bills or petitions for a private Bill presented to the Senate or House of Commons, and referred to the Court under any rules or orders made by the Senate or House of Commons.

The Court also exercises a jurisdiction to determine disputes—

(a) where the parties have raised the question of the validity of an Act of the Parliament of Canada, when in the opinion of the judge of the Court in which the proceeding is pending the question is material ; *Where validity of Canadian Act in question.*

(b) where the parties have raised the question of the validity of an Act of the legislature of the Province, where in the opinion of the judge of the Court in which the proceeding is pending such question is material. *Where validity of Provincial Act in question.*

In such cases, the proceeding is removed to the Supreme Court for decision, whatever be the value of the matter in dispute. *Removal to Supreme Court.*

These particular provisions only apply to civil cases, and only exist where a Province has passed an Act giving the jurisdiction to the Supreme Court to hear it, thus submitting themselves to the jurisdiction. The Supreme Court will in all such cases decide the validity of a Provincial as well as of a Dominion or Federal Statute. *Jurisdiction by legislative consent.*

The process of the Supreme Court runs through Canada, and is directed to the sheriff of any county or other judicial division into which any Province is divided. *Process of Supreme Court runs through Canada.*

The other great Court of Canada is the Court of Exchequer, which is also the Court of Admiralty. *The Court of Exchequer.*

It possesses exclusive original jurisdiction in all cases in which relief is sought which might in England be a subject of a suit or action against the Crown. It is a Court possessing exclusive jurisdiction in claims against the Crown. *Jurisdiction.*

It exercises jurisdiction in revenue cases, claims as to lands for which no patent has been issued, copyrights and trade marks, interpleader, at the instance of the Attorney-General, where relief is sought against any officer of the Crown for anything done or omitted to be done in the performance of his duty, in all civil actions where the

Crown is plaintiff or petitioner. An appeal lies from the Exchequer Court to the Supreme Court in certain cases.

It also exercises jurisdiction to determine controversies between the Dominions and a Province, or between provinces, when a Provincial Legislature has passed an Act agreeing to the exercise of the jurisdiction.[1]

Process runs through Canada. The process of the Exchequer Court, like that of the Supreme Court, runs through Canada.

Provincial Courts. The Provinces possess Supreme Courts which are Courts of Appeal when there are no separate Courts of Appeal.

Divorce Courts. A jurisdiction in Divorce only exists in the Courts of such of the Provinces as possessed jurisdiction to exercise it before the Union. No jurisdiction exists in Ontario, Quebec, Manitoba, Saskatchewan, and Alberta, but it does in the Maritime Provinces and British Columbia. Since the Dominion Parliament has never legislated on the subject of Divorce, the Senate assumes the position of a Court. The Provincial powers extend to the solemnisation of marriage, and the Provincial Power enables Provincial **Solemnisation of marriage.** legislatures to enact conditions as to the solemnisation of marriage which may affect the validity of the contract.

The Dominion Parliament has no power to enact that every ceremony or form of marriage which is performed by any person who is authorised to perform any ceremony of marriage by the laws of the place where it is performed and duly performed shall be deemed, everywhere in Canada, a valid marriage, notwithstanding any differences in the religious faith of the persons married, and without regard to the religion of the person performing the ceremony. Any legislation that declares that the rights and duties as married people of the respective persons married, and their children, shall be absolute and complete, and that no law or canonical decree or custom shall have any force or effect to invalidate or qualify any such marriage or any of

[1] As to the full extent of the Jurisdiction of this Court see R.S. Canada, 1906, c. 140, ss. 19-32.

the rights of the said persons or their children in any matter whatsoever would be *ultra vires*.[1]

Appeals from Canada are of right or by special leave. Orders in Councils were issued in **1910–1** in respect of most of the Provinces.

[1] In the matter of a reference by the Governor-General of Canada in Council to the Supreme Court of Canada on certain questions concerning Marriage, 28 T.L.R., 580.

CHAPTER XXI

POWERS OF LEGISLATION

Powers of
Dominion
Parliament.

THE powers of Parliament over legislation were granted by section 91 of the Act. They were enumerated. Power was given to make laws for the peace, order and good Government of Canada in relation to all matters not expressly coming under the classes of subjects assigned to the Provincial legislatures and for greater certainty, but not so as to restrict the generality of the foregoing terms of this section it was also declared that notwithstanding anything in the Act the exclusive legislative authority extended to all matters coming within the classes of subjects which the section 91 then proceeded to enumerate. Section 92 of the Act then proceeded to enumerate the exclusive powers of legislation with which the Provincial legislatures were invested.

" The scheme of this legislation as expressed in the first branch of section 91, is to give to the Dominion Parliament authority to make laws for the good government of Canada in all matters not coming within the class of subjects assigned exclusively to the provincial legislature. If the 91st section had stopped here, and if the classes of subjects enumerated in section 92 had been altogether distinct and different from those in section 91, no conflict of legislative authority could have arisen. The provincial legislatures would have had exclusive legislative power over the sixteen classes of subjects assigned to them and the Dominion Parliament, exclusive power over all other matters relating to the good government of Canada. But it must have been foreseen that this sharp and definite distinction had not been and could not be attained, and that some of the classes of subjects assigned to the provincial legislatures, unavoidably ran into and were embraced by some of the enumerated classes of subjects in section 91. Hence an endeavour appears to have been made to provide for cases of apparent conflict ; and it would seem that with this object it was declared in the second branch of the 91st section ' for greater certainty but not so as to restrict the generality of the foregoing terms of this section ' that (notwithstanding anything in the Act) the exclusive legislative authority of the Parliament of Canada should extend to all matters coming within the classes of subjects enumerated in that section.   With the same object, apparently, the paragraph at the end of section 91 was introduced, though it may be observed that this paragraph applies in its grammatical construction only to No. 16 of section 92." [1]

It may be convenient before referring to the powers in more detail to now state them—

EXCLUSIVE POWERS OF THE DOMINION PARLIAMENT   Exclusive powers.

1. The Public Debt and Property.

2. The Regulation of Trade and Commerce.

3. The Raising of Money by any Mode or System of Taxation.

4. The Borrowing of Money on the Public Credit.

5. Postal Service.

6. The Census and Statistics.

7. Militia, Military and Naval Service and Defence.

8. The fixing of and providing for the Salaries and Allowances of Civil and other Officers of the Government of Canada.

9. Beacons, Buoys, Lighthouses and Sable Island.

10. Navigation and Shipping.

11. Quarantine and the Establishment and Maintenance of Marine Hospitals.

12. See Coast and Inland Fisheries.

13. Ferries between a Province and any British or Foreign Country or between two Provinces.

14. Currency and Coinage.

15. Banking, Incorporation of Banks and the issue of Paper Money.

[1] Citizens v. Parsons 7 App. Cas. 96 at p. 107, *et seq.*

16. Savings Banks.

17. Weights and Measures.

18. Bills of Exchange and Promissory Notes.

19. Interest.

20. Legal Tender.

21. Bankruptcy and Insolvency.

22. Patents of Invention and Discovery.

23. Copyrights.

24. Indians and lands reserved for the Indians.

25. Naturalisation and Aliens.

26. Marriage and Divorce.

27. The Criminal Law, except the constitution of the Courts of Criminal Jurisdiction, but including the procedure in Criminal matters.

28. The Establishment, Maintenance and Management of Penitentiaries.

29. Such classes of subjects as are expressly excepted in the enumeration of the classes of subjects by this Act assigned exclusively to the Legislatures of the Provinces.

It was further declared that any matter coming within any of the Classes of Subjects enumerated in this section should not be deemed to come within the class of matters of a local or private nature comprised in the enumeration of the classes of subjects assigned exclusively to the Legislatures of the Provinces.

Exclusive Powers of Provincial Legislatures

Exclusive powers of Provincial Legislatures.

In each Province the Legislature may exclusively make laws in relation to matters coming within the classes of subjects next hereinafter enumerated, that is to say—

1. The Amendment from time to time notwithstanding anything in the Act of the Constitution of the Provinces except as regards the office of Lieutenant-Governor.

2. Direct Taxation within the Province in order to the raising of a Revenue for Provincial purposes.

3. The borrowing of money on the sole credit of the Province.

4. The establishment and tenure of Provincial Offices and the appointment and payment of Provincial Officers.

5. The Management and Sale of the Public Lands belonging to the Province and of the Timber and the Wood thereof.

6. The Establishment, Maintenance and Management of Public and Reformatory Prisons in and for the Province.

7. The Establishment, Maintenance and Management of Hospitals, Asylums, Charities and Eleemosynary Institutions in and for the Province other than Marine Hospitals.

8. Municipal Institutions in the Province.

9. Shop, Saloon, Tavern, Auctioneer and other Licences in order to the raising of a Revenue for Provincial, Local and Municipal purposes.

10. Local works and undertakings, other than such as are of the following classes—

(*a*) Lines of Steam or other Ships, Railways, Canals, Telegraphs and other works and undertakings connecting the Province with any other or others of the Provinces or extending beyond the limits of the Province.

(*b*) Lines of Steamships between the Province and any British or Foreign Country.

(*c*) Such works as although wholly situate within the Province are before or after their Execution declared by the Parliament of Canada to be for the general advantage of Canada or for the advantage of two or more of the Provinces.

11. The Incorporation of Companies with Provincial objects.

12. The Solemnisation of Marriage in the Province.

13. Property and Civil Rights in the Province.

14. The Administration of Justice in the Province, including the Constitution, Maintenance and Organisation of Provincial Courts, both of Civil and of Criminal Jurisdiction and including Procedure in Civil matters in those Courts.

15. The Imposition of Punishment by Fine, Penalty or Imprisonment for enforcing any law of the Province, made in relation to any matter coming within any of the classes of subjects enumerated in this section.

16. Generally all matters of a merely local or private nature in the Province.

To the Legislatures of the Provinces also, was assigned the exclusive power to make laws in relation to Education, but the power was given subject and according to the following provisions—

(1) Nothing in any such law shall prejudicially affect any Right or Privilege with respect to Denominational Schools which any class of persons have by law in the Province at the Union.

(2) All the Powers, Privileges and Duties at the Union by Law conferred and imposed in Upper Canada on the separate Schools and School Trustees of the Queen's Roman Catholic subjects shall be and the same are hereby extended to the Dissentient Schools of the Queen's Protestant and Roman Catholic subjects in Quebec.

(3) Where in any Province a system of separate or Dissentient Schools exists by law at the Union, or is thereafter established by the Legislature of the Province, an appeal shall lie to the Governor in Council from any Act or decision of any Provincial Authority affecting any Right or Privilege of the Protestant or Roman Catholic minority of the Queen's subjects in relation to Education.

(4) In case any such Provincial Law as from time to time seems to the Governor-General in Council requisite for the due execution of the provisions of this Section is not made, or in case any decision of the Governor-General in Council on any appeal under this Section is not duly executed by the proper Provincial Authority in that behalf then, and in every such case and as far only as the circumstances of each case require the Parliament of Canada may make remedial laws for the due execution of the provisions of this section and of any decision of the Governor-General in Council under this section.

To effect uniformity of laws in Ontario, Nova Scotia, and New Brunswick, notwithstanding anything in the Act, power was given to the Dominion Parliament to make provision for the uniformity of all or any of the laws relative to property and civil rights in Ontario, Nova Scotia, and New Brunswick, and of the Procedure of all or any of the Courts in those three Provinces, and from and after the passing of any Act on that behalf, the power of the Dominion Parliament to make laws in relation to any matter comprised in any such Act shall, notwithstanding anything in this Act, be unrestricted, but any Act making provision for Uniformity shall have no effect in any Province until it is adopted and enacted as law by the legislature of the Province. *Provincial Act required.*

To the Provinces also was assigned the power of making laws relative to Agriculture in the Province and Immigration into it.[1] The Dominion Parliament, however, had also assigned to them the power of making laws relative both to Agriculture and Immigration[2] into all or any of the Provinces. *Agriculture and Immigration.*

Provincial Laws were only to be effective so long as they were not repugnant to any Act of the Parliament of Canada. *How far effective.*

It will be seen from a perusal of the respective Powers of the Dominion and Provincial Parliaments that they exhibit a fourfold classification ; firstly, over those subjects, which are assigned to the exclusive plenary power of the Dominion Parliament ; secondly, over those assigned exclusively to the Provincial legislatures ; thirdly, over subjects assigned concurrently to the Dominion Parliament and the Provincial legislatures ; and fourthly, over a particular subject, namely, education, which for special reasons was dealt with exceptionally and made the subject of special legislation."[3] *Fourfold classification.*

Passing now to a more detailed examination of the powers, it must be borne in mind, in the first place, that the whole were conferred subject to the Sovereign authority of the Imperial Parliament, and that the powers cannot be added to, altered or restrained except by an Act of the *Nature of powers. Parliament no power to amend powers.*

---

[1] *Post,* p. 263.
[2] *Post,* p. 263.
[3] Lefroy's *Legislative Power in Canada,* p. 305.

Imperial Parliament. Thus "the Federal Parliament cannot amend the British North America Act so as to expressly or impliedly take away from or give to the Provincial legislatures powers which the Imperial Act does or does not give them ; and the same is the case *mutatis mutandis* with the Provincial legislatures."[1]

The powers of the Dominion Parliament are general. They extend to all matters coming within the classes of subjects upon which they can legislate exclusively. From these classes certain matters are excepted and assigned to the Provincial legislatures, and, therefore, the British North America Act, when dealing with the powers of provincial legislatures, uses different language. It might have assigned to Provincial legislation all matters of a purely local or private nature. If it had done so it would have led to confusion. In each case the question would have been : Was the legislation merely local or private within the Province ? To guard against this difficulty the framers of the Act first enumerated certain subjects of a provincial, municipal or domestic character, the items one to fifteen inclusive, and then lest this enumeration should be considered as excluding all other than the subjects enumerated, they conferred a general power on the Provincial legislatures to legislate generally over "all matters of a merely local or private nature in the Province."[2]

The power of the Dominion Parliament to make laws for the peace, order and good government of Canada, except in matters which are exclusively assigned to the Provincial legislatures is, of course, the most extensive of all powers. Any subsequent enumeration of particular powers could not but, in accordance with the well-known rule of construction, have weakened this great grant of power but for the fact that the enumeration was stated to be for the purpose of greater certainty, but was not

[1] Lefroy's *Legislative Power in Canada*, p. 242.
[2] British North America Act, 30 and 31, Vict., c. 3, s. 92, City of Fredericton v. The Queen, 3 S.C.R., p. 562, 2 Cart, p. 55.

intended to restrict the generality of the foregoing terms
that the exclusive power extended to all matters within the
class of cases which were enumerated.

So, to make the matter perfectly clear, it was further
declared that "any matter coming within any of the
enumerated Classes of Subjects (for Dominion legislation)
shall not be deemed to come within the class of matters
of a local or private nature which were comprised in the
enumeration of the classes of subjects which were assigned
exclusively to the legislatures of the Provinces."

It might have been thought from the care thus taken Judicial
to distribute the respective powers of the Dominion and disputes.
the Provinces that there would have been little room for
conflict.   The contrary, however, has been the case whatever
apparent precautions are taken to avoid disputes as to
extent of competing claims to jurisdiction, disputes seem
the invariable concomitants of a Federal Constitution.[1]

Early in the history of the Dominion it was contended
that the Dominion Government, in an Act[2] which provided
for the administration of justice in the North-West Province,
had acted beyond their powers in altering the rights under
English Statute of a man put upon his trial for treason.
Treason, it was said, was peculiarly an action levelled
against the State.   The dispute came before the Judicial Committee, who pointed out that the power had been expressly
given to the Dominion Parliament[3] to pass laws for the
peace, order and good government of such Provinces and the
words of the Statute were apt to authorise the utmost
discretion of enactment for the attainment of the objects.
They were words under which the widest departure from
criminal procedure as it was known and practised in England
had been authorised in India.   Forms of procedure unknown
to the English Common Law had there been established
and acted upon.[4]

[1] *Ante*, p. 89.
[2] 43 Vict., c. 25.
[3] 34 and 35 Vict., c. 28, s. 4.
[4] Riel *v*. The Queen, 10 App. Cas. 675.

A power to legislate for the peace, order and good government of a country is a very wide one, and notwithstanding that specified powers as to the administration of justice, property and civil rights are given in express terms to the Provincial Governments, it has been found that Dominion legislation impinges upon these.

Conflict of powers. Bankruptcy legislation.

This may be illustrated by the interpretation of the power in respect of bankruptcy and insolvent legislation which is granted to the Dominion, whilst the power over property and civil rights in the Province is granted to the Provincial legislature : yet it would be impossible to advance a step in the construction of a scheme for the administration of insolvent estates without interfering with and modifying some of the ordinary rights of property and other civil rights, nor without providing some mode of special procedure for the vesting, realisation and distribution of the estate and the settlement of the liabilities of the insolvent. Procedure must necessarily form an essential part of any law dealing with insolvency. "It is therefore to be presumed," it was said, "indeed it is a *necessary implication* that the Imperial Statute in assigning to the Dominion Parliament the subjects of bankruptcy and insolvency intended to confer on it legislative power to interfere with property, civil rights and procedure within the Provinces so far as a general law relating to these subjects might affect them."[1] Legislation by the Dominion Parliament would be practically impossible in many matters such as Patents of Invention, Discovery and Copyrights, and Paper Money, unless the powers assigned to the Provincial legislatures were encroached upon. In fact, any of the sixteen classes of powers allotted to the Provincial legislatures may be dealt with by the Dominion Parliament when the encroachment may be justified as necessarily incidental to the exercise of any of the powers expressly and exclusively conferred upon it.[2]

Extent of Provincial powers.

Does the contrary hold good ; can the Provincial legislatures by necessary implication impinge upon the field of

[1] Cushing v. Dupuy, 5 App. Cas. 415.
[2] The Liquor Prohibition Appeal, 1896, A.C. 348, p. 393.

legislation secured to the Dominion Legislature ? It has been said that where a power falls within the legitimate meaning of any class of subjects reserved to the Provincial legislatures, their control is as exclusive, full and absolute as is that of the Dominion Parliament over matters within its jurisdiction. [1] " What judicial authority there is," says Mr. Lefroy, " does not seem to carry the matter further than this, that whatever powers the Provincial legislatures have as included *ex vi termini* within the enumerated classes in section 92 when properly understood, those powers they may exercise, although, in doing so, they may incidentally touch or affect something which might otherwise be held to come within the exclusive jurisdiction of the Dominion Parliament under some of the enumerated classes in section 91." [2]

Thus, the power to levy taxes for purposes of Provincial revenue is granted to the Provincial legislatures, but a law which imposes penalties for a violation of the laws relating to licences, is a revenue law which may interfere with the Dominion power over trade and commerce ; yet, in the Courts of Canada, such a law has been held to be within the legitimate scope of Provincial legislation. [3] *Illustration of the principle.*

The Commerce power, again, is a power to regulate trade and commerce in the Dominions. In the United States it has been already shown how this power stopped short at the State which it did not control. In the United States the commerce power of the State is supreme and cannot be interfered with by the Federal Commerce power. In Canada the power belongs to the Dominion Government, and it extends over and within the limits of the Provinces. Still the Dominion Authority is a limited one, because the Provinces have powers of (1) direct taxation to raise revenue for provincial purposes ; (2) they control Municipal Institutions ; (3) their power extends over shop, saloon and auctioneers and other licences for the purpose of raising *Commerce Power.*

---

[1] Bank of Toronto *v*. Lambe, 12 App. Cas., p. 586.
[2] *Legislative Power in Canada*, p. 455.
[3] Exparte Laveille 2 Cart, p. 350.

revenue for provincial and local municipal purposes ; (4) they exercise authority over property and civil rights, and (5) over matters of a merely local, private or provincial nature. The exercise of any of these among other powers may at once bring them into direct conflict with Dominion legislation.

For instance, is the business of carrying on an Insurance Company to insure buildings against fire a " trade " ? if so, was it competent for the legislature of Ontario to pass an Act insisting upon uniform conditions in policies of Fire Insurance ? If the Insurance Company carried on a " trade," was not " trade " a subject for Dominion legislation ? The Judicial Committee decided that the Ontario Act was good, and they did not even rest their view on the ground that the business of insurance was not a trade, although they said that " contracts of indemnity made by Insurers can scarcely be considered trading contracts," but expressed their opinion that the term " trade " included political arrangements in regard to trade requiring the sanction of Parliament and the regulation of trade in matters of inter-provincial concern, and probably the general regulation of trade affecting the whole Dominion.

Licensing cases. The licensing cases further illustrate the nature of the conflicts that arise between Dominion and Provincial jurisdiction. The Dominion Parliament passed a general Act dealing with temperance, the Canada Temperance Act of 1878. Their power to pass such an Act was not questioned, but their authority to pass an Act authorising the inhabitants of each town or parish to regulate or prohibit the sale of liquor within its limits was questioned since this was alleged to be an invasion of Provincial rights. The Judicial Committee upheld the validity of all the provisions of the Act, and said that Parliament did not treat the promotion of temperance as desirable in one province more than another, but as desirable everywhere throughout the Dominion. The objects and scope of the legislation were still general, namely, the promotion of temperance by means of a uniform law throughout the Dominion. The manner of bringing the prohibition and penalties of the Act into force which Parliament had thought fit to adopt, did not alter its general and uniform character."[1]

In 1883-1884 the Dominion Parliament passed amending liquor licence Acts which they intended to supplement and enforce the Canada Temperance Act. Under these Acts the Government of Canada was empowered to issue licences, and a person who did not hold a licence was denied permission to deal in intoxicating liquors. The Acts provided for the issue of wholesale, saloon, hotel licences and licences for vessels. Provision was made tò limit the issue of licences in the various licensing districts. In those parts of Canada where the Temperance Act had not been adopted by local option, the intention was to regulate the traffic by reducing the number of houses. *Licensing legislation.*

The constitutionality of this legislation was questioned in 1885. The Judicial Committee decided that the amending Liquor Licences Acts were not within the competence of the Dominion Parliament.[2]

Another important case dealing with the same subject matter came before the Judicial Committee in 1896, where the question was whether the legislature of Ontario had power to pass an Act giving the council of every city, town and village, authority to prohibit the sale by retail of intoxicating liquors provided that any bye-laws intended to prohibit the sale should be first submitted and approved by the electors of the Municipality. The Judicial Committee decided that the liquor law prohibitions authorised by the legislature of Ontario were within their legislative power, but the prohibition would be inoperative in any locality which had adopted or might adopt the Canada Temperance Act.

To further illustrate the point, the Dominion Parliament passed a law prohibiting railway companies from contracting out of their liability to pay damages for personal injury to their servants. It was argued that the law was beyond

---

[1] Russell v. The Queen, 7 App. Cas. 841-842.
[2] The Governor-General of the Dominions v. The Four Provinces (Wheeler C.C. 144). P.C.

the competence of Parliament since the exclusive power to enact laws in respect to property and civil rights belonged to the Provinces. The making of through Railways was a Dominion power. Was the legislation truly railway legislation, or legislation as to civil rights under the guise of railway legislation ?

Overlapping domain.

It was said "that there can be a domain in which Provincial and Dominion legislation may overlap, in which neither legislation will be *ultra vires*, if the field is clear, and secondly, that if the field is not clear and in such a domain the two legislations meet, then the Dominion legislation must prevail."[1]

In deciding the case the Judicial Committee considered that the law in question was ancillary to through Railway legislation, and was, therefore, a competent exercise of power by the Dominion Parliament.[2]

Naturalisation.

The innumerable cases in which a Dominion power trenches upon one of the enumerated Provincial powers may be seen on referring to the many important decisions of the Judicial Committee. Thus the Dominion Parliament can exclusively legislate with regard to naturalisation and aliens, and the Provincial Parliament in respect of property and civil rights. The legislature of Ontario passed a Coal Mines Regulation Act forbidding the employment of boys under twelve, and girls, women and Chinamen in coal mines. "The subject of naturalisation *primâ facie* would include the power to enact what should be the consequences of naturalisation or, in other words, what should be the rights and privileges pertaining to residents in Canada after they had been naturalised."[3] Therefore, it was decided that the sphere of Dominion legislation was intruded upon, and the Provincial legislation was beyond the powers of the Provincial legislature. Some of the fiercest conflicts of jurisdiction have arisen over questions of education. On this subject the Provincial legislatures possess exclusive

[1] La Compagne Hydraulique de St. François *v.* Continental Heat and Light Company, 1909, A.C., 194.
[2] Grand Trunk Railway *v.* Attorney-General of Canada, 1907, A.C. 66.
[3] As to these, *ante*, p. 252.

powers subject to certain restrictions protective of Roman Catholic minorities in Protestant Provinces.   The Dominion Government, by the use of its political veto, could veto legislation which exceeded the Provincial powers of the Provinces.

The Manitoba School case twice came before the Privy Council and ultimately ended in a compromise in 1896.   Education.

It has been previously stated that there are certain powers which can be exercised concurrently by the Dominion and Provincial Parliaments.   They extend over three separate subjects :   emigration, agriculture and public works. Public works fall into two classes :   first, those which are purely local, such as roads or bridges and municipal buildings, and these belong not only as a matter of right but also as a matter of duty to the local authorities.   Secondly, there are public works which, though possibly situated in a single province, such as telegraphs and canals and railways, are yet of common import and value to the entire confederation and over these it is clearly right that the Central Government should have a controlling interest. [1]   Public works are not specifically mentioned as subjects of concurrent legislation, but on reference to No. 10 of the Provincial Powers [2] it will be seen that works though local, fall under the Dominion power, although they are wholly situate within the Province, when they are before or after their execution declared by the Dominion Parliament to be for the general advantage of Canada or for the advantage of two or more Provinces.

In respect of agriculture and immigration where concurrent jurisdiction exists, the law of the legislature only has effect in and for the Province as long and as far only as it is not repugnant to any Act of the Parliament of Canada.

It will be seen by comparison with the legislative powers of the United States that the legislative powers under the Canadian Constitution Act are dissimilar.   The powers of Congress are not expressed nor interpreted as exclusive

[1] (1895) 24 S.C.R., p. 226, In re Prohibiting Liquor Laws, per Gwynne, J·
[2] Ante, p. 253.

unless such a construction is so repugnant to them as to lead to the conclusion that by necessary implication they were intended to be exclusive. In Canada the Powers of the Dominion and Provincial Legislatures are mutually exclusive, except in the few instances where they are expressed to be concurrent.

As in the case of the Constitution of the United States, so under the Constitution of Canada, there have been numerous decisions as to the meaning and extent of the powers of the Central and Local authorities, and it is likely that there will be many more. As a learned Canadian Judge once said of the Constitution: it has bones and sinew but like the dry bones of the valley, it has yet to be clothed with many a judicial decision from all parts of the Dominion.[1]

[1] Peters J. Kelly v. Sullivan, 2 P.E.I., pp. 90-91.

CHAPTER XXII

THE PROVINCES OF CANADA

THE Provinces of Canada all possess a Lieutenant-Gov- _{The Executive}
ernor as their Chief Executive Officer. He is appointed Government.
by the Governor-General in Council by instrument under _{The Lieutenant-Governor.}
the Great Seal of Canada. He holds office during the
pleasure of the Governor-General and is not removable
within five years from his appointment except for cause
assigned communicated to him in writing within one month
after the order of his removal is made. The reasons for
removal must be communicated to the Senate and House
of Commons by message within one month after the order
for removal is made.

In considering the removal of a Lieutenant-Governor,
the Governor-General acts on the advice of his ministry.
Thus when the Lieutenant-Governor of Quebec, Mr.
Lettellier St. Just, had dismissed his ministry and granted _{Lettellier St. Just case.}
a dissolution under which the Opposition were returned to
power, the Governor-General dismissed him, after referring
the matter to the Colonial Secretary. Prior to the exercise
of the Governor-General of his authority, resolutions had
been passed in both Houses of the Dominion Parliament,
that Mr. Lettellier St. Just's dismissal of his ministry had
been unwise and subversive of the powers of ministers under
Responsible Government.

As chief Executive Officer of the Province, the Lieutenant- _{Oath of allegiance and office.}
Governor takes an oath of allegiance and office on his
assumption of office. This he subscribes before the Governor-
General or some person authorised by him. The oath is
similar to that which the Governor-General takes on his
assumption of office.

The general provisions of the British North America Act _{General provisions of Dominion Act applicable to Governor-General apply.}
relative to the powers and duties of the Lieutenant-Governor
are applicable to the Lieutenant-Governor for the time being

of each Province or the Chief Executive Officer or administrator carrying on the Government. Since Responsible Government is in existence the Lieutenant-Governor acts upon the advice of his ministry in the same way as the Governor-General acts upon the advice of his ministry.

Responsible Government.

In the exercise of his functions the Lieutenant-Governor of a Province should, of course, maintain that impartiality towards political parties which is essential to the proper performance of the duties of his office, and for any action he may take he is under the 59th section of the Act directly responsible to the Governor-General. The only safe principle that he can adopt for his general guidance is that pointed out to him by the experience of the working of parliamentary institutions; to give his confidence to his constitutional advisers while they enjoy the support of the majority of the Legislature. [1]

Instructions from Secretary of Canada.

Lieutenant-Governors receive instructions as to their duties from the Secretary of State for Canada. There have not been apparently any instructions issued as to powers of reservation of Bills, although the practice is to reserve such, as to the constitutionality of which there is any doubt. [2]

Legislative functions.

Most legislation of the Provinces is made in the King's name, who is a part of the Legislature. There are exceptions in Nova Scotia, New Brunswick and Prince Edward Island.

Thus in New Brunswick the enacting power is expressed: " Be it enacted by the Lieutenant-Governor and Legislative Assembly " as follows. In British Columbia the enacting power runs: " His Majesty by and with the advice and consent of the Legislative Assembly of the Province of British Columbia." The exceptions to the usual form are " merely old survivals of no constitutional significance." [3]

Prerogative of mercy.

Although the Governor-General exercises the Royal prerogative of mercy for the whole Dominion, the Provinces have provided for its exercise by Lieutenant-Governors in the Provinces: The Lieutenant-Governor is not a mere

---

[1] Bourinot's *Parliamentary Institutions of Canada*, p. 63.
[2] Keith's *Responsible Government in the Dominions*, p. 183.
[3] *Ibid.*

official, but is a representative of the Crown, and as much the
representative of His Majesty for all purposes of Provincial
government, as the Governor-General himself is for all
purposes of Dominion government.

The provisions as to the disallowance of Acts and the *Assent, reservation and disallowance of Acts.*
signification of the pleasure of the Crown on Bills reserved
which are in force with reference to the Dominion Government, are by the British North America Act declared
to be in force in the four provinces of Canada, with the
exception that a Lieutenant-Governor is substituted for
the Governor-General of the Governor-General for the
Queen and for a Secretary of State, of one year, for two
years and of the Province for Canada.

All powers, authorities and functions exercisable by the *Powers of Lieutenant-Governor of Quebec.*
Governors or Lieutenant-Governors of Upper Canada or
Lower Canada or which were vested in them, either before
or at the time of the Union, as far as they are capable of
exercise in relation to the Governments of Ontario and
Quebec, vest and become exercisable by the Lieutenant-
Governors of these Provinces. Power, however, is given
to abolish or alter any of these except those established
by the Imperial Parliament. The Dominion Parliament
fixes the salaries of Lieutenant-Governors. The Lieutenant-
Governors of Ontario, Quebec and Manitoba receive salaries
of 10,000 dollars. Those of Nova Scotia, New Brunswick,
British Columbia and Saskatchewan and Alberta 9,000
dollars, the Lieutenant-Governor of Prince Edward Island
7,000 dollars.

A Lieutenant-Governor is advised by a Council, which is *Executive Council.*
called the Executive Council. In the two Provinces of
Ontario and Quebec the Councils are composed of such *How composed in Ontario and Quebec.*
persons as the Lieutenant-Governor thinks fit to choose
in his discretion. These Councils originally comprised
the following officers: the Attorney-Generals; the
Secretaries and Registrars of the Provinces, the Treasurer,
Commissioners of Agriculture and Public Works. Quebec,
in addition, included the Speaker of her Legislative Council
and the Solicitor-General.

The Constitution Act impliedly empowered a Lieutenant-Governor to prescribe the duties of his officers and the departments over which they were to preside. He was also empowered to appoint other and additional officers to hold office during his pleasure, to prescribe the duties of these officers and the Departments over which they were to preside or to which they should belong and the clerks and offices.

The Provincial legislatures are not of one uniform pattern. In Ontario the legislative power is vested in the Lieutenant-Governor and one House only, styled the Legislative Assembly. At the time of the Union this chamber consisted of eighty-two elected members.

Quebec, on the other hand, possesses two Houses, the Upper or Legislative Council and the Lower or Legislative Assembly. These with the Lieutenant-Governor constitute the legislative power of Quebec. The Legislative Council at the time of the Union consisted of twenty-four members holding office for life, appointed by the Lieutenant-Governor, but power was given to the Legislature to alter this.

The Lieutenant-Governor appoints the members of the Legislative Council. Ten members constituted a quorum of the Legislative Council in 1867, including in this number the Speaker.

Questions are decided by a majority of votes. The Speaker is given a vote, but not a casting vote. If the numbers on a division prove equal the decision is held to be in the negative, in the same way as it was so directed to be held in the Dominion Senate.

In 1867 the Legislative Assembly of Quebec consisted of sixty-five elected members, but power was given to the Legislature to effect certain changes. The power, however, was restricted by a provision that no Bill altering the limits of electoral divisions should be presented to the Lieutenant-Governor for his assent until the second and third readings of such Bill had been passed in the Legislative Assembly with the concurrence of the majority of members representing all the electoral divisions or districts which were specified in the British North America Act. An address stating that these requirements had been complied with was required to be presented to the Lieutenant-Governor prior to asking his assent to any such Bill.

Disabilities were imposed on persons holding office under the Crown and on persons in receipt of pay or commission from the Governments of both Ontario and Quebec. These disabilities, however, did not attach to members of the Executive Council nor to the holders of the offices of Attorney-General, Secretary and Registrar of the Province, Treasurer, Commissioner for Crown Lands and Commissioner for Agriculture and Public Works, and in addition in Quebec, to the Solicitor-General. Following Imperial precedents a minister on taking office, unless he already held office, was required to submit himself for popular re-election. *Disabilities of office-holders.*

The Legislative Assemblies of Ontario and Quebec are elected for a period of four years. Like the Dominion Parliament, each Assembly must hold one session in the course of every year so that twelve months shall not intervene between the last sitting of the Legislature in each Province in one session and its sitting in the next session. *Duration of Assemblies.*

The provisions applicable to the election, vacancies, duties and absence of the Speaker, and the quorum and method of voting in the Dominion House of Commons are applicable to both Provincial Assemblies. The Constitution of Nova Scotia was left unaltered at the Union. *Provisions applicable to Dominion House of Commons.*

The Legislative Power in the Constitution of Manitoba in 1870 was vested in two Chambers, but in 1876, in one. New Brunswick abolished her Legislative Council in 1891, and Prince Edward Island hers in 1893. Nova Scotia, however, still possesses two Chambers. Alberta in 1905, under the Dominion Act of the same year, which granted her a Constitution, received a Single Chamber Government, as did Saskatchewan. The provisions relating to Appropriation and Taxation Bills and the recommendation of money votes which apply to the Dominion Government apply to all Provincial governments.[1] *Single Chambers.*

[1] *Ante,* p. 242.

Writs for elections. Writs for elections are issued by the Lieutenant-Governor.

Reasons for single Chamber. Whilst the system of One-Chamber Government has been generally adopted in the Provinces regard must necessarily be paid to the limited powers of Government that the Provinces possess and the existence of the political Veto of the Dominion Government. The nominated Chamber has never been popular in Canada, and both in 1906 and 1908 debates took place in the Dominion House as to the possibility of making the Second Chamber elective. [1]

Financial provisions: how arranged. On the establishment of the Dominion Government in 1867, it was necessary both to make provisions for the Government of the Provinces and to adjust their relations towards the central authority. The Dominion Government assumed liability for their debts and liabilities, and all duties and revenues over which the four Provinces who formed the Union possessed powers of appropriation, were formed into one consolidated Revenue Fund becoming subject to appropriation by the Dominion Government for the public service of Canada, with the exception of certain portions of the revenue which were reserved to the Provinces and certain other portions of revenue which the Provinces in future became entitled to raise under the special powers given them by the Dominion Act.

Dominion Government assumes liability.

Primary charges on Consolidated Fund. The Consolidated Fund of Canada, which was created in this way, was directed to be primarily charged: (1) with all the costs of its collection and management; (2) with the annual interest on the debts of the four Provinces; (3) with the Governor-General's salary: but, subject to these charges, the Consolidated Revenue was held subject to appropriation by the Parliament of Canada for the public service.

Redemption of provincial debts. For the purpose of redeeming their debts, the Provinces surrendered all their stocks, cash, bankers' balances and money securities with some specified exceptions and also other certain specified public works and property.

Public works. The public works and property surrendered consisted

[1] *Canada House of Commons Debates*, 1906, pp. 2276-1908.

of canals with land and water-power connections, public harbours, lighthouses and piers, and Sable Island, steamboats, dredges, and public vessels, rivers and lake improvements, railways and railway stocks, mortgages and other debts due by railway companies, military roads, Custom Houses, Post Offices, and all other public buildings except such as the Government of Canada chose to appropriate for the use of the Provincial legislatures and Governments.   Property which had been transferred by the Imperial Government, known as ordnance property, armouries, drill-sheds, military clothing, and munitions of war and lands set apart for general purposes.

Certain other assets, which belonged at the time of the Union to the Province of Canada, after Federation became conjointly the property of the Provinces of Ontario and Quebec.   These comprised schools, court-houses, municipal funds, etc. :—All lands, mines, minerals, and royalties, which had hitherto belonged to the individual Provinces, continued their separate property, as did all assets connected with such portions of the public debt as were assumed by that Province. Conjoint property of Ontario and Quebec.

For the purpose of endowing the Provinces with funds, the Dominion Government was directed to make yearly grants to the Provincial Governments based upon census returns for the support of their governments and legislatures.   The amount, though varying, being fixed, the Provincial Governments were in no way financially at the mercy of the Dominion Government. Dominion grants.

Free trade was established throughout the Provinces in respect of home-made or home-grown articles.   Nevertheless special rights were reserved to New Brunswick in reference to her timber dues. Establishment of Free Trade.

Following the precedents of the Supreme Court of the United States established in the great constitutional cause of McCulloch v. Maryland[1] it was declared that neither land nor property belonging to Canada or to any of the Provinces should be liable to taxation by the one or the other. Land or property belonging to the Dominion or to the Provinces free from taxation of the other.

[1] *Ante*, p. 82.

other authority. The Imperial Act of 1871, which enabled the Parliament of Canada to establish new Provinces entitled it to make provision for the Constitution and administration of each Province.

Annual subsidies to compensation payable to Alberta and Saskatchewan.

The Acts of the Dominion Government of 1905, which established Alberta and Saskatchewan, provided for the payments of annual subsidies by half-yearly instalments in advance in proportion to the population, and compensation was also given for public lands which remained vested in the Crown, administered by the Government of Canada for the purposes of Canada.

In 1907, the Canadian Government determined to make fresh arrangements with the Provinces and recourse was had to the Imperial Parliament. Fixed grants are now made yearly to the provinces for their local purposes and the support of their Government and Legislatures, and certain additional grants in certain cases (7 Edw. VII, ch. 11). The alteration was carried out by the wishes of the Dominion and Provincial Governments.

Each of the Provinces of Canada possess the fullest powers to alter their Constitutions although they are not entitled to interfere with the Office of Lieutenant-Governor.[1]

See *ante*, p. 268, as to the limitation in the case of Quebec.

CHAPTER XXIII

THE NATURE OF THE CANADIAN CONSTITUTION

THE Constitution of Canada adopts the well-known triple *The nature of the Canadian Constitution.* division of powers, so characteristic of Federal Constitutions, following the precedent set by the United States' Constitution. Like the latter Constitution, also, it is written, but unlike in that it contains but small powers in itself of amendment.

Whilst in the making of the United States' Constitution, *Difference between the Canadian and United States' Constitution.* the separate States surrendered some of their powers to the United States and reserved all not surrendered, in Canada the separate Provinces surrendered the whole of their powers to the Federal Government, receiving back under the Constitution grants of power establishing their rights. The Constitution, therefore, created a central Government and simultaneously provincial governments by the same instrument.

As a written Constitution it operates over a far larger *Wider area of Government.* area of Government than does the Constitution of the United States.

Lord Loreburn, ex-Lord Chancellor, in delivering the *A sole charter for British North America.* opinion of the Judicial Committee in a recent case,[1] explained the position thus: "The desire of Canada for a definite Constitution embracing the entire Dominion was embodied in the British North America Act." "Under this organic instrument the powers distributed between the Dominion on the one hand and the provinces on the other hand, cover the whole area of self-government within the whole area of Canada. It would be subversive of the entire scheme and policy of the Act to assume that any point of internal self-government was withheld from Canada."

The British North America Act may be regarded as

[1] Attorney-General for Ontario *v.* Attorney-General for Canada, 1912, A.C. 571, 581.

the sole charter by which the rights claimed by the Dominion and the Provinces respectively can be determined.

Although it was founded upon the Quebec resolutions, and was, therefore, a treaty of Union between the Provinces as soon as it became law, it constituted a wholly new point of departure.

Notwithstanding this, the state of legislation and other circumstances existing in the various provinces of Canada prior to Confederation, sometimes require to be considered in construing the sections of the Act relative to the distribution of the powers, as may also the character of legislation in England itself.

Political
veto power
a fundamental
difference
betwee 1 the
two
Constitutions.
Another distinguishing feature of the Canadian Constitution (which, however, is shared with South Africa), is the existence of a veto power over Provincial legislation, exercisable by the Governor-General in Council. The existence of this power is one of the fundamental differences between it and the Constitution of the United States.

There is nothing similar to this veto power in the United States' Constitution. It is true that the Supreme Court of the United States can supersede State legislation, when the same matter is the subject of legislation by both Federal and State Legislatures. For instance, where a Federal and State Statute operate upon the same subject-matter and prescribe different rules concerning it, provided that the Federal statute is within the powers of the Federal Parliament, the State Statute must give way.[1]

The power to
make laws
for the peace,
order, and
good govern-
n°er't of
Canada.
The great power to make laws for the peace, order and good government of Canada, a power so familiar in Imperial-made Constitutions, is utterly unlike any power granted to the Federal Government of the United States, and far greater, since it extends over a wider sphere of Government. In the United States none of the Federal powers have a greater operation than over the fields of Federal domain. A Canadian realises the existence of his Federal Government in the ordinary business of life far more than an American

---

[1] Davis v. Beason, 133, U.S. 33. Gulf of Colorado and Santa Fé Railway Co. v. Hefley, 158, U.S. 98.

the existence of his Federal Government. The former Government controls agencies and makes laws, which the latter leaves to the States. The restriction on legislation by the United States further hampers Congress. Thus the fundamental law that the obligation of contracts must not be impaired, applying as it does both to the Federal and the State Government, narrows the field of both Federal and State legislation. Whatever the law is that bears on the subject-matter of a contract at the time the contract is made, cannot be changed so as to affect even indirectly the rights accruing by the contract or the legal position of the parties in respect to its enforcement,[1] but Dominion legislation is wholly unfettered. *Fundamental laws in the United States.*

Although the triple division of powers exists separating the Executive, Legislative, and Judiciary, it is not nearly so marked as in the United States. In a great degree the division of powers in the Dominion resembles the division of powers which Montesquieu commended as so admirable in the British Constitution. *Nature of the triple division of powers.*

Another fundamental difference between the two Constitutions will be found in the recognition in the United States of the sovereignty of the people, and in Canada of the Legislature. Again, whilst many checks are directed against legislatures and legislation in the former, hardly any exist in the latter. *The Sovereignty of the people.*

"Trust not legislation nor legislators" has always been the political maxim of the United States. Trust good men has been the guiding policy of the British, on which the Canadian Constitution has been fashioned. *"Trust not legislators."*

The system of Responsible Government, if it stood by itself, would differentiate the Constitution of Canada from that of the United States as surely as the Mediterranean divides Europe from Africa. *Existence of Responsible Government.*

The ideas that actuated the framers of the United States' Constitution have been cherished by the people. They have no great respect for State legislators, with the result that State legislation is viewed with suspicion.

[1] *Ante,* p. 113.

Distrust of
Legislatures
in the
United States. " We see," says an American writer, " communities as the efficient principals binding public agents by their own fundamental rules, cutting down credentials as though deference to statesmanship were at an end. Instead of looking up to the Legislature as the arcanum of fundamental liberties we see the people inclining rather to Governors and the Courts as a needful corrective upon legislatures tempted to go astray."

Constant
alteration
of State
Constitutions. State Constitutions, in consequence, are altered and matters introduced into them which in other Constitutions are left to the discretion of the legislatures. The United States citizen by placing them out of the reach of the legislators evinces his determination not to allow any interference with those principles which he considers fundamental.

Contrast of
the nature
of the powers. In Canada the legislative powers of the Dominion Government are almost wholly exclusive of the Provinces. In the United States the Federal powers are concurrent with those of the State, and will not be construed as exclusive unless from the nature of the power or from the obvious result of its operations a repugnancy exists leading to the necessary conclusion that the power was intended to be exclusive. Therefore, Canadian judges find very little aid from a study of American precedents. Only, therefore, to a very small extent is there the need of considering the question of implied powers. It may be that a Dominion power must intrude on the Provincial domain to make it effective. Is it a natural implication that it should ? The answer may be yes or no.

Federal
principle
everywhere
present in the
United States'
Constitution. Again, the Federal principle is everywhere markedly in evidence in the United States' Constitution : in the election of the Executive officers, the President and Vice-president, in the Constitution of the Legislature and the provision of a Federal Court to interpret the Constitution, in the checks on legislation and in the methods provided for the amendment of the Constitution.

Faintly
visible in
Canadian. In the Canadian Constitution, at the most, it is but faintly visible. In Canada it may be observed in the

existence of a Federal Union and the division of the Senate, but no voting takes place by Provinces on any occasion in any branch of the legislature of Canada. The British North America Act unites the Provinces, and having formed the Union leaves the legislature of the Dominion Parliament to legislate for the whole of Canada : in the same way that the Imperial Parliament legislates for the United Kingdom but with this difference, the Parliament of Canada may not intrude on the provincial sphere.

No Supreme Court in Canada is constituted by implication guardian of the Constitution in the same way as the Supreme Court of the United States is. The natural Supreme Court of Canada is the Judicial Committee, the Court of the Empire. *Judicial power.*

The powers of legislation of the Dominion Parliament are unlike the powers possessed by Congress. The Dominion powers and the Provincial powers are enumerated in such a way that you can place one set of powers on one side, and the other set on the other, and in a general way ascertain the sphere of each. Sometimes they overlap and difficulty arises, which requires a Judicial construction. You cannot do the same thing with the Federal State powers in the United States. To ascertain the respective sphere of the one or the other, it is necessary to explore a mass of Federal law, then will it be understood how judicial decisions have been the cement which has bonded the constitutional brickwork and rendered possible the Stately edifice. *Enumerated powers in Canadian Constitution.*

In the existence of a nominated Senate whose members are entitled to sit for life, again a great difference appears between the two Federal Constitutions.

The framers of the United States' Constitution would have rejected any idea of a nominated body. A nominated Senate would have been considered without strength to check the impulse of a popular Assembly, so as to give the people an opportunity for second thoughts. *Nominated life Senate.*

Again, a substantial distinction between the two Constitutions is clearly indicated in the term, fixed for the duration of the popular Assemblies. The difficulty caused *Duration of popular Assemblies.*

by a constant changing of the executive militating against short Parliaments where Responsible Government is in existence, is not a matter of great importance in the United States since the Executive is not dependent upon Parliamentary support. No doubt it is advantageous, but not indispensable. In Canada it is indispensable since the Government cannot be carried on without it.

The Speaker.   In the United States the Speaker is a great party leader, in Canada he is not. He is only the eyes and ears of Parliament as the Speaker is at Westminster.

Many other points of dissimilarity may be traced. Some of which have been already dealt with.

The divergencies of the two Constitutions spring mainly from historical causes, which have been fully explained.

CHAPTER XXIV

THE CONSTITUTIONAL DEVELOPMENT OF AUSTRALIA

THE name Australia appears to have been originally sug- Australia.
gested by its circumnavigator, Matthew Flinders, somewhere between the years 1813 or 1814. It was not, however, until six or seven years later that it came into use
as descriptive of the Island Continent. Prior to this
period it was known indifferently by the names of Terra
Australis, Austral Asia, or New Holland, according to the
whim of the explorer or the historian. The first statutory
recognition by the Imperial Parliament of the name
Australia occurs in the Act 10 Geo. IV, c. 22, which refers
to Western Australia on the western coast of New Holland.

To understand the principle of the Australian Federation,
it is necessary briefly to trace the creation and growth of
the various States which comprise the Commonwealth and
their constitutional development.

The first step in the annexation of Australia was taken Captain Cook.
on the 23rd of August, 1770, by Captain Cook, the daring
navigator, who had sailed up the river St. Lawrence just
prior to Wolfe's triumphant enterprise. On that day
Captain Cook took formal possession of the eastern portion
of the Continent from latitude 38° to latitude 10½° S, in the
name of His Majesty King George III.

In 1784, by an Act of the Imperial Parliament (24 Geo. III, Captain
c. 56), power was given to appoint places in New South Phillip's commission.
Wales to which felons should be transported; and in 1787
a commission was issued to Captain Phillip appointing him
Captain-General and Governor-in-Chief over New South
Wales extending from Cape York south to the southern
extremity of New South Wales, and westward to the 135°
of east longitude, together with the adjacent islands in the
Pacific between the latitudes of 10·37° and 43·39° south.
By the terms of the commission, Captain Phillip was given

jurisdiction over a larger portion of New South Wales eastwards and over Van Diemen's Land, now the State of Tasmania.

Boundary of New South Wales moved westward.

In 1827 the boundary of New South Wales was moved westward to the 129° of east longitude.

possession of Western Australia.

It was not, however, till the year 1829, when the part of Australia west of the 129° of longitude was taken possession of, that the whole of Australia passed under the jurisdiction of the British Crown.

Council to assist Governor.

Prior to 1823, the Governor had almost despotic control over the Colony under his charge. The first germ of Representative Government appears in that year, when a nominee Legislative Council to assist the Governor was appointed.

A subsequent amendment of the Council's powers was made in 1828, but it was not until the year 1842 that even a partially representative body was created in Australia.

1842. New Legislative Council.

By an Act passed in the latter year, provision was made within the Colony of New South Wales for a new Legislative Council to consist of 36 members, of whom 12 were to be nominated by the Crown and 24 elected by the inhabitants. The new system, however, could not be called in any sense Responsible Government, as the whole executive authority and the appointments under the Crown still remained in the Governor under the direction of the Home Government.

Australian Colonies Constitutional Act.

The passing by the Imperial Parliament of the Australian Colonies Constitution Act, 1850, was a recognition by British Ministers that the time had arrived in the history of Australia when provision should be made for legislatures in the Colonies modelled and capable of development on the lines of the Imperial Parliament, subject to such differences as their altered conditions needed. This important Act made provision for the erection of two Houses of Parliament in each of the Colonies of New South Wales, Van Diemen's Land, and in the Province of South Australia.

Creation of Victoria.

Provision was made for the southern or Port Philip District of New South Wales, which was by the Act separated from the Mother Colony and erected into a separate Colony under the name of Victoria.

After providing the necessary machinery for effecting the above purposes, the Act empowered the new Legislatures to make laws for the peace and good government of the respective Colonies, to impose customs and other taxation, and appropriate the proceeds towards the public service. The Legislatures, however, were forbidden to enact laws repugnant to the Law of England, to impose differential Customs duties, or to interfere with the sale and appropriation of Crown Lands, or to pass appropriation Bills without a previous message of request from the Crown. Under this Act, provision was also made that one-third of the Upper Chamber should be nominated by the Crown. The Imperial ¦Government, whilst thus showing its willingness to concede a considerable measure of self-government, were of the opinion that some official representation in the Legislature was still necessary, and that the control of the public lands and the appointment of Civil Servants should, for the time being, remain under the direct control of the Home Government. *Features of the Act.*

Before the Bill became law, an agitation sprang up in New South Wales protesting against the retention of these safeguards. *Agitation against the Bill.*

The Act of 1850 meanwhile having passed into force, the Secretary for the Colonies, in response to the protests of the Colonists, requested the Legislative Council of New South Wales to draft a Constitution similar to the Canadian one on bicameral lines.

This Constitution, when drafted, subject to some amendments, was finally passed by the Imperial Parliament, and received the Royal Assent on July 16th, 1855, under the name of the New South Wales Constitution Act, 1855. By this measure a full measure of Representative Government was given New South Wales. The control of the Crown Lands and appointments to Civil Servants was vested in the Government of the Colony, but the provision for disallowance of Bills remained intact. *Amended Constitution, 1855.*

Similar Act
for Victoria.
On the same day an Act giving the new Colony of Victoria full Representative Government also received the Royal Assent.

And
Tasmania.
Tasmania (which was known till 1853 as Van Diemen's Land) about the same time by an Act which received the Royal Assent, on October 24th, 1856, received somewhat similar legislative powers.

South
Australia.
Of the other Colonies now forming the Australian Commonwealth, South Australia, in 1856, by an Act modelled on the Tasmanian Constitution Bill, received a considerable extension of the powers of self-government which had been already granted her under the Australian Colonies Government Act, 1850. These powers, although not so extensive as those granted to the other Colonies, were subsequently added to from time to time by numerous amendments of her Constitution.

Queensland.
The Colony of Queensland (formerly known as the Northern or Moreton Bay District of New South Wales) had, since the passing of the Act of 1842, returned eight members to the Parliament of New South Wales.

In 1859, by Letters Patent issued pursuant to the provisions of the New South Wales Constitution Act, 1855, the district was erected into a separate Colony under the name of Queensland, with a Legislative Council and Assembly with substantially similar powers to those of her Mother Colony.

Western
Australia.
The Colony of Western Australia was the last to receive a full measure of Parliamentary Government on July 18th, 1893.

Numerous Acts amending the Constitutions of the various Colonies have from time to time been passed by the respective local legislatures, and in addition further powers have been granted by special Acts of the Imperial Parliament resulting in a general likeness in the Constitutions and powers of the various Colonies at the present time.

What were originally the Colonies of New South Wales, Victoria, Queensland, Tasmania, Western Australia, and the Province of South Australia now form the respective

States of those names in the Commonwealth of Australia. The outline given above of their origin and constitutional development enables a better appreciation to be formed of their position at the time of Federation, and how, although differing in minor details, they possessed substantially similar constitutional powers. They were, each in their sphere, quasi-Sovereign States, and immediately prior to the establishment of Federation, were, all of them, as capable of entering into a Federal compact on equal terms, subject to the approval of the Imperial Parliament, as were the thirteen States of America after their Declaration of Independence or the four Provinces of Canada in 1867.

CHAPTER XXV

THE FEDERAL MOVEMENT IN AUSTRALIA

Motive force of Federation. THE principal motive power that brought about Federation in Australia is considered to have been trade considerations. As early as 1846, whilst as yet Port Phillip was a portion of New South Wales, and before it had acquired the status of a separate colony, Sir Charles Fitzroy, Governor of New South Wales, made the suggestion that there should be a Governor-General for New South Wales. [1] His proposal was approved by the Committee of the Privy Council in 1849.

Proposals for a General Assembly. Other suggestions which were made by this Committee for the establishment of a general executive and legislative authority to " superintend the initiation and foster the completion of such measures as those communities may deem calculated to promote their common welfare and prosperity was not approved, and those portions of the Bill which proposed a General Assembly were abandoned subsequently."

First Governor-General. Notwithstanding this abandonment, it was still possible to carry out those proposals which depended not upon legislation, but on an exercise of the executive power. Earl Grey, Colonial Secretary in 1851, framed fresh instruc-Sir Charles Fitzroy.tions for Governors, and appointed Sir Charles Fitzroy Governor-General for Australia, the remaining Governors in Australia receiving titles as Lieutenant-Governors.

In 1855, however, the Lieutenant-Governors once more became Governors, and in 1861 the Commission to the Governor of New South Wales ceased to be accompanied by the Governor-General's Commission.

Pioneers of Federation. The three pioneers of Federation with whom the Federal movement in Australia will always be identified were Wentworth, Gavan Duffy, and Deas Thomson. The forest of difficulties they had to traverse might have daunted any but the boldest.

[1] Despatch, Sept. 29th, 1846.

In 1857 a suggestion for a Bill for the establishment of a General Assembly was laid before the Home Government with no success. Meantime, difficulties militating against the idea were rather increased than diminished, owing to the imposition of inter-colonial tariffs and the impossibility of arriving at any uniformity.

It was not until 1873 that the Australian Colonies received power to enter into reciprocal arrangements. The power, however, was never used.

Other matters, however, now began to loom large and attract increased attention to the necessity of Federation. Amongst these may be mentioned the opening up by France of a penal settlement in New Caledonia in 1864, and the activity of the United States and Germany in the Pacific.

In 1867, Mr. (after Sir) Henry Parkes became a prominent advocate of Federation. In addressing an inter-colonial Conference called to discuss the question of postal communication with Europe, he said : " I think the time has arrived when these Colonies should be united by some Federal bond of connection. I think it must be manifest to all thoughtful men that there are questions projecting themselves upon our attention which cannot be satisfactorily dealt with by any one of the individual Governments. I regard this occasion, therefore, with great interest, because I believe it will inevitably lead to a more permanent understanding. I do not mean to say that when you leave this room to-night, you will see a new constellation of six stars in the heavens. I do not startle your imagination by asking you to look for the footprints of six young giants in the morning dew when the night rolls away ; but this I feel certain of, that the Mother Country will regard this Congress of the Colonies just in the same light as a father and mother may view the conduct of their children when they first observe those children beginning to look out for homes and connections for themselves." [1]

Notwithstanding the note of optimism sounded by Sir

---

[1] Quick & Garran, *Constitution of the Australian Commonwealth*, p. 104, quoting *Melbourne Argus* of 18th March, 1867.

Henry Parkes, the Federal movement gained but little strength. A memorandum which he laid before a Conference of the seven colonies, held at Sydney in 1881, expressed his views as positions hardly open to debate.

(1) That the time is not come for the construction of a Federal Constitution with an Australian Federal Parliament.

(2) That the time is come when a number of matters of much concern to all the Colonies might be dealt with more effectually by some Federal Authority than by the Colonies separately.

(3) That an organisation which would lead men to think in the direction of Federation and accustom the mind to Federal ideas would be the best preparation for the foundation of Federal Government.

Conference at Sydney, 1883

In November, 1883, after some progress had been made in forming public opinion mainly through the energy of Mr. Service, the Premier of Victoria, a Conference took place at Sydney, which included representatives from New Zealand and Fiji, and from the six colonies.

Resolution for a Federal Australian Council.

The then Prime Minister of Queensland, Mr. (now Sir) Samuel Griffith, at this Conference moved the following resolution : " That it is desirable that a Federal Australian Council should be created for dealing with the following matters—

" 1. The marine defences of Australasia beyond territorial limits.

" 2. Matters affecting the relations of Australasia with the islands of the Pacific.

" 3. The prevention of the influx of criminals.

" 4. The regulation of quarantine.

" 5. Such other matters of general Australasian interest as may be referred to it by His Majesty or by any of the Australasian legislatures."

The resolution was adopted, and on December 3rd, 1883, a committee was appointed which reported on December 4th to the Conference, and the draft of a proposed Bill was also brought forward to establish a Federal Council of Australasia.

By 1884 all the Colonies, except New South Wales and New Zealand, had agreed to accept the Bill, and adopted addresses asking for its enactment by an Act of the Imperial Parliament.

This Bill subsequently became law as the Federal Council of Australasia Act.[1]

This Act constituted neither an executive nor judicial authority, and its membership by any colony was optional. Its legislature consisted of representatives nominated by the legislatures of the Colonies. *Federal Council of Australian Act,*

Up till the year 1895, when the representation of each Colony was increased, the representatives were either ministers or ministerial supporters. With some exceptions, the legislative powers of the Council required to be set in motion on the initiation of the legislatures of the Colonies. It could neither raise nor appropriate revenue. *Alteration of Representatives.*

In 1895, it, however, passed resolutions in favour of uniform company and banking legislation.

During and prior to the existence of this body, which was clothed with far less authority than the Confederation of the United States many important matters were constantly under discussion at inter-Colonial Conferences, including military and naval defence.

In 1889, Sir Henry Parkes, the Premier of New South Wales, on behalf of New South Wales, invited each of the Colonies to appoint through their legislatures six persons chosen from the two political parties in the Colony, for the purpose of a Conference.

The Conference, which met at Melbourne on February 6th, 1890, unanimously resolved that the best interests and future prosperity of the Australasian Colonies would be provided by an early Union under the Crown, and that the time was come for the Union of these Colonies under one legislative and Executive Government on principles just to the several Colonies. *The Melbourne Conference of 1890. Resolutions.*

The members present pledged themselves to endeavour to induce their legislatures to appoint delegates to a *Proposal for a Convention.*

[1] 48 and 49 Vict., c. 6.

National Australasian Convention, with power to consider and report upon a proposal for a Federal Constitution.

Meeting of Convention. Delegates subsequently chosen by the Australian legislatures met at Sydney in 1891. The methods of their appointments were by resolutions of both Houses of the Australian legislatures.

Amongst the many well-known and distinguished men who there assembled were Sir Henry Parkes, the Premier of New South Wales; Mr. (afterwards Sir) J. P. Abbot, the Speaker; Mr. G. R. Dibbs, the Leader of the Opposition; and Mr. Edmund Barton, now a Judge of the High Court of Australia; Mr. James Munro, the Premier of Victoria; Mr. Alfred Deakin, afterwards Premier of the Commonwealth; and Mr. Duncan Gillies; Sir Samuel Walker Griffith, the Premier of Queensland (now Chief Justice of the High Court of Australia); Sir Thomas McIlwraith; Mr. Thomas Playford, Premier of South Australia; Dr. John Cockburn, afterwards Sir John Cockburn, ex-Premier of the Colony.

The representatives of Tasmania included Mr. A. Inglis Clark (Attorney-General); Mr. W. H. Burgess; Mr. Nicholas Brown, the Speaker; and Mr. Philip O. Fysh, the Premier.

Amongst the Western Australian representatives were Sir John Forrest (the Premier) and Mr. J. W. Hackett.

New Zealand sent her Premier (Sir H. A. Atkinson) and Sir George Grey.

Sir Henry Parkes, as the originator of the movement, was appointed President; Sir Samuel Griffith, Vice-president; and Mr. F. W. Webb, Secretary to the Convention.

The meetings of the Convention were not like those held in Quebec, when the Quebec resolutions were passed with closed doors.

The Press and public were both admitted, unless otherwise ordered by the Convention. The first meeting took place on March 2nd, 1891, and the Convention sat until April 9th, 1891.

Principle of reservation of State Rights. The following principle was accepted: that the powers, privileges, and territorial rights of the existing Colonies should remain untouched, except in respect to such surrenders of authority as might be mutually agreed upon as necessary and incidental to the establishment of a National Government.

The Convention thereby signified their adherence to the United States' form of Constitution in preference to that of Canada. The Convention further affirmed the desirability of the establishment of inter-colonial Free Trade within Australia ; the commission of naval and military defence and customs to a Federal authority ; the establishment of a Federal Constitution with a perpetual Senate, which provided for the periodical retirement of a third of its members ; a Federal Supreme Court constituting a High Court of Appeal for Australia ; and an executive consisting of a Governor-General and such persons as might be from time to time appointed his advisers.

The Convention appointed three Committees to work out the details of the Bill : the three Committees dealt with Constitutional functions, finance, and the Judiciary. *Committees of the Convention.*

A change of Government in New South Wales soon after the Convention had finished its labours, followed by years of financial crises in Australia, unfortunately blocked for a time any further advance towards a Federal Constitution. *Causes of further delay.*

Prior to 1893, however, the Australian Natives' Association had taken up the Federal movement with enthusiasm, and began to form Federation leagues. A conference of delegates met at Corowa and adopted, on the motion of Sir John Quick, a scheme for the popular election of a Convention to frame a Federal Constitution, which, subject to the approval of the electors, should be forwarded to the Home Government for enactment. *Action of the Australian Natives' Association.*

In 1895 a conference of Premiers took place at Hobart, where, amongst other resolutions, the following important one was agreed upon ; that a Convention should be chosen, to consist of ten representatives from each Colony, who were to be directly chosen by the electors and charged with the duty of framing a Federal Constitution, and for the submission of the Constitution so framed to the electors for *Conference of Premiers at Hobart.*

acceptance or rejection by a direct vote. A further resolution declared that if such Constitution were accepted by the electors of three or more Colonies, it should be transmitted to the Queen by an address from the Parliaments of those Colonies, praying for necessary legislation, and that a Bill should be submitted to the Parliament of each Colony for the purpose of carrying out these resolutions.

Federal Enabling Acts.

Federal enabling Acts following upon these resolutions were drafted and passed by all the Colonies but Queensland between the years 1895 and 1897.

Adelaide Convention.

The Convention elected under the provisions of Enabling Acts met at Adelaide on 22nd March, 1897. Mr. Kingston, Premier of South Australia, was chosen as its President, and Mr. Barton undertook the leadership of the Convention.

Work of Convention.

The draft Bill of 1891 was adopted as the foundation of the work of the Convention, and three Committees to deal with the Constitution, Finance, and the Judiciary of the proposed Constitution were appointed : their work was subsequently submitted to a drafting Committee, which prepared a Bill which in its turn was submitted to the Convention on 12th April.

The Bill was reported to the Convention on 22nd April, and adopted next day. On 2nd September the Convention met at Sydney to reconsider the draft constitution and amendments which had in the meantime been suggested by the legislatures. The Sydney session, however, adjourned before it had completed its task for a final session at Melbourne. In all the Convention held three Sessions, finally concluding its labours on the 17th March, 1898.

Referendum.

On June 3rd and June 4th a Referendum, in accordance with the terms of the enabling Bills, took place in New South Wales, Victoria, Tasmania, and South Australia, when the necessary majorities in favour of the Constitution Bill were obtained, except in New South Wales, where the Bill was not carried by a requisite majority.

Conference of Premiers in 1899.

In 1899 a conference of Premiers took place, at the request of Mr. (now Sir) George Reid, High Commissioner for Australia. Six Colonies were represented and some amendments made. The Bill was then submitted to the people of the Colonies again. On this occasion the proposals were adopted by all except Western Australia, which did not ultimately join Federation until after the Constitution Bill had become law.

Delegates from Australia visited England, at the request of Mr. Chamberlain, Colonial Secretary. A difficulty then arose mainly because of the wording of the appeal clause of section 74, strong objection to which had been taken by the Home Authorities. The natural difficulty felt by the delegates in yielding to objections was their feeling that the whole Constitution was a Federal pact, which could not be altered without a fresh consent of all parties. *Visit of delegates to England.*

A Conference of Premiers during this crisis met at Melbourne, and agreed that the acceptance of the Bill with an amendment would be preferable to a postponement ; they did not think, however, that they had authority to agree to amendments, although they did not dispute this constitutional power of the Imperial Parliament to make them. *Melbourne Conference.*

In considering the progress of the Federal movement in Australia, one great fact must not be lost sight of. It was not killed by sectional jealousies but merely delayed. Once its importance was fully brought home to the people it was recognised as the transcendent issue. " The tariff was the lion in the path which Federalists had to slay or be slain, but even the tariff question had to subordinate itself. The ideal of an United Australia fired the imagination of Australians in the same way as the ideals of an United States and an United Canada had stirred the souls of the people of North America. In each case Federation was the incarnation of a national life, and a forward step along the road of progress and civilisation.

CHAPTER XXVI

THE COMMONWEALTH EXECUTIVE POWER

Executive power.

In all of the British Constitutions there are many powers which are expressly conferred upon the Executive by the Imperial Act creating the Constitution. Many of these are common to all three, and have been dealt with elsewhere. In Australia the Executive power is vested in the King, but is exerciseable by the Governor-General. The power extends to the execution and maintenance of the Constitution, and the laws of the Commonwealth. The Ministry is, therefore, the King's Ministry. The executive power of the Commonwealth cannot trench on the executive power

Executive power of States.

of the States, for the executive power of the King's Representative, acting in the name of the States, is of the same nature and quality as that possessed by the King's representative acting in the name of the Commonwealth.

Federal Executive Council.

The Governor-General is advised by a Federal Executive Council in the government of the Commonwealth, chosen and summoned by the Governor-General, and sworn as the Executive Councillors to hold office during pleasure. With the Governor-General rests the power to appoint officers to administer the Federal departmental offices. These officers must be members of the Federal Executive Council, and when appointed they form the King's Ministers and constitute the Commonwealth Ministry. They hold office, as stated, during pleasure, but it is provided that no Minister shall hold office for a longer period than three months, unless he is or becomes a Senator or Member of the House of Representatives. These provisions establish a Parliamentary Executive.

Numbers of Ministers.

The Ministry must not exceed seven in number unless Parliament otherwise provide ; they hold, by the Constitution, such offices as Parliament prescribes or, in the absence of provision, as the Governor-General directs.

An annual sum of £12,000 is payable to the King out Salaries.
of the Consolidated Revenues Fund of the Commonwealth
in respect of their salaries until Parliament otherwise
provides.

The appointment and removal of all Federal officers other Civil Servants.
than the Ministry is vested by the Constitution in the
Governor-General in Council, until Parliament otherwise
provides, or unless the Governor-General in Council delegates the appointment to some other authority, or it is
so delegated by some law of the Commonwealth.

The Governor-General in Council also appoints all the Judges.
justices of the Commonwealth Courts.   It will be observed,
therefore, that, whilst the Ministry is appointed by the
Governor-General on his own discretion, the appointment of
all judges and Civil Servants is made on Ministerial
responsibility by the Governor in Council.

There is no express recognition of the Cabinet, or of the
collective responsibility of the Ministry in the Constitution.

The term " Ministry," however, like the term " Ministry " Ministry and Cabinet.
in Canada, is synonymous with the Cabinet.   In England
the Ministry and Cabinet are not interchangeable terms.

Most State Ministries, according to the practice in Austra- Honorary Members.
lia, contain honorary Ministers or Ministers without a
portfolio.   The practice has not been adopted in the
Imperial Parliament ; the first Commonwealth Ministry,
following State precedents, contained two honorary Members.

The following departments of State have been formed : Departments of Affairs.
The Department of External Affairs, the Attorney-
General's Department, the Department of Home Affairs,
the Department of the Treasury, the Department of Trade
and Customs, and the Postmaster-General's Department.

The Minister for External Affairs deals with immigration The Minister for External Affairs.
and emigration, the influx of criminals, relations with the
Mother Country, communications with the Governor-
General and the Home Government, communications with
the various States of the Union, the Executive Council,
the officers of the Parliaments and the railways of the
Commonwealth.

Home
Affairs.
The Department for Home Affairs deals, amongst other matters, with the question of the Federal capital, the inter-State Commission, Federal elections, public service regulations, and old-age pensions.

Customs and
Excise.
The State Departments of Customs and Excise were transferred on the establishment of the Commonwealth to the Federation Department bearing that name.

A State
Executive
with consent
may be used as
instrument of
Federal
Government.
Although a State executive cannot be controlled by the Federal authority, it may, subject to the consent of the State Government, be used as an instrument of the Federal Government. In one matter, it is enacted that the State must assist the Federal authority, for the States must provide for the detention in prisons of persons accused or convicted of offences against the Commonwealth, and for the punishment of persons so convicted. Commonwealth laws may give effect to this provision.

General
vesting
power.
A like power to the general vesting power, which has already been referred to in Canada, under which the powers, authorities, and functions of Governors existing prior to Federation in Canada were transferred to the Governor-General of Canada, appears in the Australian Constitution. It was declared that in respect of all matters which under the Constitution pass to the Executive Government of the Commonwealth, all powers and functions which at the establishment of the Constitution were vested in the Governor of a Colony, or in the Governor of a Colony with the advice of his executive Council, or in any authority of a Colony, shall vest in the Governor-General, or in the Governor-General in Council, or in the authority exercising similar powers under the Commonwealth, as the case requires.

Governor
General's
power of
assent..
The general power that Governor-Generals possess to assent, withhold assent, or reserve proposed laws has been discussed already.[1] In Australia, the Governor-General possesses a special power to return to the House in which it originated any proposed law, with such amendments as he may recommend, leaving the House to deal with his

[1] *Ante*, p. 201.

recommendations. This power was adopted from precedents of similar powers that existed in the Constitutions of Victoria and South Australia.

The Governor-General receives as salary £10,000 a year until Parliament otherwise provides. It cannot be altered during his continuance in office. The provisions of the Constitution applicable to the Governor-General apply to the Governor-General for the time being, or to such person as the King may appoint to administer the Government of the Commonwealth ; but no such person is enabled to receive any salary in respect of any other office during his administration of the Commonwealth.

If authorised by the King, the Governor-General may appoint any person, or any persons jointly or severally, to be his deputy or deputies ; and in that capacity to exercise during the Governor-General's pleasure such of his powers and functions as he thinks fit to assign them, subject to any limitations expressed or directions given by the King. The appointment, however, will not affect the exercise by the Governor-General himself of any power or function. *Power to appoint Lieutenant-Governors, etc.*

CHAPTER XXVII

THE LEGISLATIVE POWER

Legal title of Parliament, Senate, and House of Representatives. THE legislative power of the Commonwealth is vested in a Federal Parliament consisting of the King, the Senate, and the House of Representatives. Its legal title is the " Parliament " or " the Parliament of the Commonwealth."

Both Chambers, the Upper, which is called the Senate, and the Lower, the House of Representatives, are elected bodies directly chosen by the people.

The electoral qualification for both Houses was that prescribed by the State law as the qualification of electors for the more numerous House of Parliament of the State, till Parliament otherwise determined.

This was a provision similar to one in the Constitution of Canada, which fixed the State Franchise, as the Dominion Franchise, but empowered the Dominion Parliament to create a Federal Franchise.[1]

Franchise in the United States. In the United States, it has been shown that the States were originally left unfettered to fix their own franchise,[2] and that the State Franchise was the Federal Franchise. After the War of Secession, however, the passing of the fourteenth and fifteenth Amendments prevented the States from discriminating in legislation affecting the Franchise, and now, although the State right to fix the franchise still exists, it has been impaired by these Amendments, which recognise the existence of a national citizenship.[3]

Commonwealth Franchise. In 1902 Parliament passed the Commonwealth Franchise Act, which provided for a uniform Franchise subject to certain disqualifications applying to persons attainted of treason, persons of unsound mind, and persons under sentence or subject to be sentenced for any offence punishable

[1] *Ante*, p. 236.
[2] *Ante*, p. 53.
[3] *Ante*, p. 153.

under the law of any part of the King's Dominions for a year or longer. All persons, male and female, married or unmarried, who are not under twenty-one years of age, are now entitled to vote, provided that they have lived in Australia six months continuously, are natural born or naturalised subjects, if their names are on the electoral roll for any electoral division. No person can vote more than once.[1] Elections are fixed to be held on one day, Saturday.

The only limitations imposed on the exercise of the Franchise by the Constitution are the provisions that one vote only can be given at any Federal election, and no adult person who has or acquires a right to vote at elections for the more numerous House of the Parliament of a State shall, while the right continues, be prevented by any Commonwealth law from voting at elections for either House of the Parliament of the Commonwealth.

The Commonwealth Electoral Act of 1902 has been amended by the Electoral Divisions Act of 1903, the Commonwealth Electoral Acts of 1905 and 1906, the Disputed Electoral Act of 1909, and the Commonwealth Electoral Act of 1911. The system introduced by these Acts provides for the establishment of a chief Electoral Officer for the Commonwealth, Commonwealth Electoral Officers for the States, Divisional and Assistant Returning Officers and Electoral Registrars. It also provides for the distribution of each State into Electoral Divisions, the appointment of Commissioners for their distribution who, when exercising their power in cases of distribution, must have due consideration to community or diversity of interest, means of communication, physical features, existing boundaries, divisions and boundaries of State electorates : subject to due consideration of these points, the quota of electors[2] is fixed as the basis of distribution. The Commissioner may adopt a margin of allowance, but the quota must not be departed from to a greater extent than one-fifth more or one-fifth less.

If Parliament approve of a distribution the Governor-General will proclaim it. A redistribution may be made

Amendment of the Act of 1902.

System.

Distribution of seats.

When proclaimed by Governor-General.

---

[1] Commonwealth Franchise Act, No. 8, 1902. [2] *Post*, p. 310.

(1) when an alteration in the number of representatives is required ; (2) whenever in one-fourth of the divisions in the State the number of electors differs from a quota (the provisions for the ascertainment of which are regulated by the Act) to a greater extent than one-fifth more or one-fifth less ; (3) when the Governor-General thinks fit.

Electoral rolls.

Under the provisions of the Electoral Acts, electoral rolls are made for each division.

Absent voting. Limitation of expenses.

Absent voting is allowed, and provision made for scrutinies and the limitation of election expenses. In elections for the Senate the electoral expenses are fixed' at £250, and for the House of Representatives at £100. All trade unions and organisations which have expended money on behalf of the interests of any candidate or political party are required to make a return.

Returns of expenses by outside organisations and newspapers.

Newspaper proprietors are also under the necessity of making a return setting out the amount of electoral matter inserted in the paper, the space occupied, and the amount of money paid and owing, and the names of the trade unions or other bodies or persons authorising the insertion.

Canvassing on polling days.

On polling days and on all days to which the polling is adjourned, the following acts are prohibited at the entrance to or within the polling booth. Canvassing for votes or soliciting the vote of any elector, or inducing any elector not to vote for any particular candidate or inducing any elector not to vote at the election.

Court for Disputed Returns.

The High Court of Justice is made a Court for trying disputed returns, and can either on petition or on its own initiative, refer the dispute to the Supreme Court of the State in which the election was held or the return made.

Reference by Parliament.

Parliament is empowered to refer any question respecting the qualification of a Senator or of a member of the House of Representatives, or respecting a vacancy to the Court of Disputed Returns.

Powers of Court.

The Court has authority to declare that any person was not qualified or not capable of being chosen or of sitting, or that a vacancy exists in the Senate or in the House of Representatives.

There are in addition a great number of provisions of an Other provisions. interesting character in the Electoral Acts, intended to insure absolute purity of election in the democracy.

The native population of Australia cannot vote, nor can Coloured races. the natives of Asia, Africa, or the Pacific Islands (with the exception of New Zealand), unless they possess a right to vote at elections for the Lower House of a State Parliament. At present this class of population is excluded from the State Franchise in Western Australia and Queensland.

The Governor-General appoints the times for holding Governor-General Parliamentary Sessions. He is also empowered from time appoints times of to time by proclamation or otherwise to prorogue Parliament Parliamentary Sessions. and dissolve the House of Representatives.[1]

After a General Election the Parliament must meet not Meeting after General later than thirty days after the day appointed for the return Election. of the writs.[2] Every Senator and Member of the House of Representatives before taking his seat must make and subscribe before the Governor-General or some person authorised by him, an oath or affirmation of allegiance to be Oath or Affirmation. faithful, and to bear allegiance to the Sovereign, his heirs and successors according to law.

A member of either House is incapable of being chosen or of sitting as a member of the other House.

The right to declare the powers, privileges, and immunities Privileges of Parliament. of the Senate and House of Representatives, and of its members and committees rests with the Parliament. The Constitution declared that until such declaration was made the powers, privileges, and immunities of the Commons House of Parliament of the United Kingdom, and of its members and committees, obtaining at the establishment of the Commonwealth should prevail.[3]

The power thus conferred on the Commonwealth Parliament exceeds that originally given to the Parliament of Canada, which was bound by the Parliamentary practice of the Imperial House as existing in 1867. The powers of

---

[1] Commonwealth of Australia Constitution Act, sect. 5.
[2] *Ibid.*
[3] *Ibid.*, sect, 49.

the Dominion Parliament, however, were extended by an Act of 1873.

Power to regulate procedure. Each House of the Commonwealth is entitled to make rules and orders with respect to (1) the mode in which its powers, privileges and immunities may be exercised and upheld ; (2) the order and conduct of its business and proceedings either separately or jointly with the other House. [1]

A clear distinction is apparent between the powers, privileges, and immunities which the Parliament can declare to exist, and the rules and orders by which the conduct of the business of each House and its powers, privileges, and immunities are enforceable.

Rules and orders in Imperial Parliament. In the Imperial Parliament rules and orders are capable of classification as (a) standing rules and orders, (b) sessional rules and orders, (c) orders and resolutions whose duration is undefined.

Sir Erskine May describes standing orders as " permanent rules for the guidance and government of the House which endure from Parliament to Parliament." " They relate," he says, " to such matters as the days on which the sittings of the House are held, the hour for the commencement of business, the sequence of business on each day, the distribution of business, the preservation of order, the closure of debate, the taking of divisions, etc. In the House of Lords a standing order cannot be suspended except in pursuance of a notice of motion. In the Commons the rule is not so stringent, and in cases of emergency a standing order may be suspended without notice, but the unanimous concurrence of the House is generally necessary.

Sessional rules and orders are orders and resolutions which are intended and expressed to last for a session only, and which expire at the end of the session. With reference to orders and resolutions whose duration is undefined, Sir Erskine May declares the practice to be that they will determine at the end of each session, "but many of them are a part of the settled practice of Parliament observed

[1] Sect. 50.

in succeeding sessions, and by different Parliaments without any formal renewal or repetition."

The Parliament of the Commonwealth must sit once a year ; twelve months shall not intervene between the last sitting of Parliament in one session, and its fresh sitting in the next session. [1] This is identical with a provision in the Canadian Constitution. In the Imperial Parliament an annual session is only rendered imperative by the necessity of raising money for the annual estimates, since by law, the King is only bound by Statute [2] to issue writs within three years after the expiration of Parliament. *Meeting of Parliament.*

The system of two-chamber Government adopted by the framers of the Constitution, was in accordance with the precedents set by the United Kingdom, with the necessary modifications from the Constitutions of the United States and Canada. It likewise followed the example of the two Federal Constitutions referred to in naming the Upper or Second House the Senate. *Bicameral system.*

The Senate is composed of six Senators for each State, who are directly chosen by the people of the State voting, until Parliament otherwise provides as one electorate. [3] *Senate elected by State electorate.*

The Queensland Parliament was, however, given a special power to make laws for dividing Queensland into divisions, and for determining the number of Senators to be chosen for each division, but in the absence of any such provision the State was to be one electorate. *Exception in case of Queensland.*

This exception was due to the fact that Queensland was not represented at the Conventions that considered the details of the Commonwealth Constitution Bill. Her absence was due to the fact that in 1895, at the conference of Premiers which met at Hobart, one of the resolutions carried determined that a Convention consisting of ten representatives from each Colony directly chosen by the electors, should be charged with the duty of framing a Federal Constitution. Whilst other resolutions provided that *Reasons for the exception in the case of Queensland.*

---

[1] Commonwealth of Australia Constitution Act, sect. 6.
[2] 6 and 7, Will. and Mary, c. 2.
[3] Commonwealth of Australia Constitution Act, sect. 7.

the Constitution so framed should be submitted to the electors for acceptance or rejection by a direct vote, and that a Bill should be submitted to the Parliament of each Colony for the purpose of giving effect to these resolutions amongst others.

A draft Bill was specially prepared at the instance of the Conference for giving effect to these resolutions. The Prime Minister of Queensland felt himself unable to accept it. The Colony, which was tripartite in interest, desired to have separate representations for those interests at the Convention. The people of the North and Central portions had different interests to the people of the South. The Queensland Government, moreover, favoured Parliamentary choice, and not direct election of representatives for the Convention. The Prime Minister, Sir Hugh Nelson, introduced a Bill in the Queensland Parliament providing that the representatives of Queensland to the Convention should be elected by the members of the Legislative Assembly, grouped according to the three divisions. This Bill did not prove acceptable to the Legislative Council, which considered that the representatives of the Convention should be chosen by Parliament, and that the Council, as part of the Parliament, should participate in the election. The claim of the Council as a nominee body was denied, with the result that the Bill was laid aside, and Queensland took no part in the subsequent Conventions. At the conference of Premiers, which met at Melbourne in January, 1899, the Premier of Queensland was present, and he asked for an amendment in the Constitution that would enable the Parliament of Queensland on becoming an original State, to sub-divide itself into divisions for the election of Senators, with the power to allot the number of Senators for each division. This concession was granted, and the case of Queensland was thus specially met.

A power is given to the Commonwealth Parliament to increase or diminish the number of Senators for a State, but the equality of the representation of the original States must be maintained, and no original State can possess less than six Senators. An original State is a State which Original States. formed part of the Commonwealth at its establishment.

The Federal Parliament is also empowered to admit New States. to the Commonwealth or establish new States, but it can then impose conditions on admission or establishment including in such conditions the extent of representation to be allotted in either House of Parliament. No logical principle can, therefore, be said to distinguish State representation in the Senate as in the Senate of the United States. State representation is there unalterable without the Compared with consent of the State, no matter how small the State may United States. be. But in Australia the immobility of representation in the original States is preserved by the provision which declares that no alteration which diminishes the proportionate representation of any State in either House of Parliament, shall become law unless the majority of the electors voting in the State approve the proposed law.[1]

The names of the six Senators who are chosen for each How electors State are certified by the Governor of the State to the certified. Governor-General. This is a recognition of the Federal principle.

In order to provide continuity of the Senate, the Original Division Constitution Act provided for its division into two classes. of Senate into two On the first meeting of the Senate it was accordingly classes. divided into two classes, as nearly equal as possible. The places of the first class were vacated at the expiration of three years, and those of the second class at the expiration of six years from the beginning of their term of service. The places of all Senators now become vacant at the expiration of six years from the beginning of their term of service, that is, from the 1st July following the day of their election, except when the Senate is dissolved, when the term begins to run from the 1st of July preceding the day of election.

The election to fill vacant places takes place within one Election for vacant places. year before the places become vacant.[2]

The Constitution provides for a dissolution of the Senate, Dissolution of Senate.

[1] Commonwealth of Australia Constitution Act, sect. 128.
[2] See Senate Elections, No. 29, 1903, and No. 1, 1907.

but the power to dissolve is only exercisable in a case of a disagreement between the Houses.[1]

Difference between Australian and United States' Senate. The election of Senate by popular vote and voters voting by States are democratic innovations on the United States' Constitution, where Senators are chosen by the State legislatures. The Australian Senate, again, differs from the United States' Senate in the fact that one-half of the Senate retires at the end of the third year, whilst a third of the American Senate retire at the end of the second year. It is further distinguishable by the fact that under certain circumstances it may be dissolved ; but no power exists to dissolve the Senate of the United States.

The Senate, also, like its American prototype, is a distinct recognition of the Federal principle of the equality of States. Since an equal State representation is accorded all the original States in the Senate, the smaller States necessarily possess the same weight in its deliberations as the larger. This was, as it had been in the United States, part of the pact on which the Constitution was founded. It was agreed that each colony represented in the Convention should, on becoming a State, maintain its original relative equality and individuality unimpaired ; without it, probably, the Commonwealth could not have been formed.

Character of. The Senate represents the only conservatism possible in a democracy. The conservatism of maturity of judgment, of distinction of service, of length of experience and weight of character which, said Sir Henry Parkes, " are the only qualities we can expect to collect and bring into one body in a community young and inexperienced as Australia."

Criticism of Senate. It may be doubted, however, whether the system of election by the people of the States as a whole has proved the best system of securing a Second Chamber, qualified to fulfil the proper functions of a Second Chamber as a revising body, and bring into existence that very conservatism which Sir Henry Parkes applauded. The State areas are enormous, and the expense of covering them by individual effort prohibitive. The party ticket candidate has, therefore, become

[1] *Post,* p. 320.

necessary. Weight is consequently not primarily attached either to maturity of judgment, distinction of service, length of experience and force of character. To be on the party ticket is necessarily a candidate's first aim. This, in turn, entails a subordination of judgment to the party managers. In the result the Senators largely become dependent either upon an irresponsible caucus or the influence of powerful sectional newspapers.

The States, since they do not elect Senators through their legislatures, do not possess an influence at all corresponding to the influence exercised by the States under the Constitution of the United States.

Apart, however, from the general desire which influenced Political the Conventions to secure a democratic basis for the Senate, reasons. it is only fair to say that there were practical difficulties in the way of the adoption of the American system. Two out of the six colonies, New South Wales and Queensland, possessed Upper Chambers, nominated by the Crown, and it was thought essentially improper that the election for the Federal Senate should be participated in by non-elective bodies.

At the Sydney Convention three electorates for each State Proposal of were proposed by Sir John Forrest, and six by Mr. Simon Sir John Forrest. Fraser. These amendments were rejected, but the Federal Parliament still possesses power to provide for an election of Senators otherwise than by one State electorate.[1]

The Federal Parliament has power to make laws prescribing the method of choosing Senators, but the method is required to be uniform throughout the States. Subject to the passing of any law, the power of prescribing the method was left with the State Parliament.[2]

To the State Parliaments was assigned the power to make laws for determining the times and places of elections of Senators for the State. Until the Federal Parliament legislated subject to the Constitution, the State laws which were in force relating to elections for the more numerous

[1] *Post*, p. 339.
[2] Laws have been made, *vide* Commonwealth Electorate Acts, 1902-11.

House of Parliament of the State, were as nearly as practicable to apply to elections of State Senators.   Federal legislation has, however, now been passed. [1]

On State failure to provide representation.

The Senate may proceed to the despatch of business notwithstanding the failure of any State to provide for its representation in the Senate.   There is a limitation, however, on such a procedure, for the Senate cannot transact business unless one-third of the whole number is at least present; an absolute majority only is necessary to constitute a quorum in the American Senate, and fifteen in Canada.

The State Governor causes the writs to be issued for the election of Senators for his State; in case of dissolution the writs must be issued within ten days from the proclamation of such dissolution.

Death, disqualification, or retirement of Senator.

The death, disqualification or retirement of a Senator does not exhaust his term, since his successor is chosen for its unexpired residue.

Power to increase Senators.

It has already been stated that there is power for the Federal Parliament to increase or diminish the number of Senators, subject to the condition that the principle of the equality of State representation is continued in the original States, and that no original State has less than six Senators.   In case such increase or diminution takes place, the Federal Parliament may make provision for the vacating of the places of Senators for the State as it may deem necessary to maintain regularity in the rotation.

Filling casual vacancies.

The method of filling casual vacancies so that a State may possess a practically uninterrupted representation is as follows :—the State Houses of Parliament sitting and voting together choose a person to hold the place until the expiration of the term, or until the election of a successor, whichever first happens.

When choice falls on Governor.

If the Houses of Parliament are not in session when the vacancy is notified, the choice devolves upon the Governor of the State, acting with the advice of his Executive Council, but the person appointed to hold the place under such circumstances can sit only until the expiration of fourteen

[1] All the States have passed such laws.

days after the beginning of the next session of the State Parliament, or until the election of a successor, whichever first happens.

At the next General Election of members of the House of Representatives, or at the next election of Senators for the State, whichever first happens, a successor, if the term has not meanwhile expired, must be chosen to hold the place from the date of his election until the expiration of the term.

The State Governor, as in the case of all senatorial elections, certifies the name of the Senator so chosen or appointed to the Governor-General. In the United States casual vacancies occurring during a recess of the State Legislature are temporarily filled by the State Executive.[1] *Certifying choice of Senator.*

A Senator must be of the full age of twenty-one years. He must be an elector entitled to vote at an election for the House of Representatives, or qualified to become an elector. He must have been for three years at least a resident within the limits of the Commonwealth when chosen, a subject of the King, or a subject naturalised under the naturalisation laws of the United Kingdom or the Commonwealth of a colony or of a State. The required qualifications are similar to those required for election to the House of Representatives. No person is qualified who fourteen days prior to his nomination was a member of Parliament of a State. It will be observed that the reasonings on which the senatorial qualification was fixed at the age of thirty in the United States' Constitution were rejected by the members of the Australian Conventions.[2] The age of thirty was adopted, it will be remembered, in the Canadian Constitution. *Age qualification.*

Additional disqualifications for election are stated in section 44 of the Constitution Act, where it is declared that a person is incapable of being chosen or of sitting as a Senator who is under any acknowledgment of allegiance, obedience, or adherence to a foreign power, or is a subject

[1] *Ante,* p. 46.
[2] Commonwealth Electoral Acts, 1902-11, Sects. 95 and 96.

or alien, or entitled to the rights or privileges of a subject or citizen of a foreign power, or is attainted of treason, or who has been convicted and is under sentence or subject to be sentenced for any offence punishable under the law of the Commonwealth or of a State by imprisonment for one year or longer, or is an undischarged bankrupt or insolvent, or holds any office of profit under the Crown, or any pension payable during the pleasure of the Crown out of any of the Commonwealth revenues, or has any direct or indirect pecuniary interest in any agreement with the Public Service of the Commonwealth otherwise than as a member and in common with other members of an incorporated company, consisting of more than twenty-five persons.

The prohibition relating to offices of profit does not apply to the King's Ministers of State for the Commonwealth, nor to any of the King's Ministers for a State, nor to the receipt of pay, half-pay, or a pension by any person as an officer or member of the King's Army and Navy, nor to the receipt of pay as an officer or member of the naval or military forces of the Commonwealth by any person whose services are not wholly employed by the Commonwealth.

If a Senator becomes subject to any disabilities, or takes the benefit, whether by assignment, composition or otherwise, of any law relating to bankrupt or insolvent debtors, or directly or indirectly takes or agrees to take any fee or honorarium for services rendered to the Commonwealth, or for services rendered in the Parliament to any person or State, his seat becomes vacant.   Till Parliament otherwise provides, any person who is declared by the Constitution to be incapable of sitting as a Senator renders himself liable for every day on which he sits, to pay £100 to any person who sues for it in any Court of competent jurisdiction. A member of the Senate is incapable of being chosen or of sitting as a member of the House of Representatives.

The Senate had power to determine the qualifications of its members, vacancies, and disputed elections, but

Parliament had power to legislate for their determination otherwise.[1] Parliament has legislated, and a court has been established for dealing with disputed election returns.[2]

In the United States no attempt has been made to divest Congress of its powers to judge the election returns and qualifications of its members;[3] but in Canada it has been otherwise,[4] Canada has followed the precedent of the Imperial Parliament.[5]

In the Australian Senate each Senator receives an allowance of £600 per annum, reckoned from the day on which he takes his seat. The original sum mentioned in the Constitution was £400, but as power was given to Parliament to make an alteration, the amount has been increased. Certain officers, however, receive £400 as Senators when they are in receipt of other emoluments.

The Presiding Officer of the Senate is termed the President. It is the first duty of the Senate before proceeding to any other business to choose a Senator as President as often as the office becomes vacant. The Senate must choose his successor. The President's office terminates with his ceasing to be a Senator. He is also removable by a vote of the Senate. He can resign either his office or his seat by notice in writing addressed to the Governor-General. The Presiding officer of the Senate of the United States is the Vice-president, who is an executive officer.[6] The Speaker of the Canadian Senate is not appointed by the Senate, but by the Governor-General.[7] Neither the House of Lords, nor the United States' and the Canadian Senates, appoint their own presiding officer.

The President of the Senate.

The President of the Commonwealth Senate is not elected for any fixed term. Before or during his absence the Senate may choose a Senator to perform his duties. He receives a salary of £400 a year as member of the Senate, in addition to his emoluments as President.

The Senate of the United States possesses the power

[1] Sect. 47.   [2] *Ante*, p. 298.   [3] *Ante*, p. 60.   [4] *Ante*, p. 237.
[5] *Ante*, p. 60.   [6] *Ante*, p. 66.   [7] *Ante*, p. 231.

to choose its own officials, but this power was not given to the Commonwealth Parliament.

Resignation of Senator.

A Senator may resign by writing addressed to the President, or to the Governor-General if there be no President, or if he be absent from the Commonwealth. On resignation, his seat becomes vacant. His seat will also become vacant if for two consecutive months of any session of the Parliament without the leave of the Senate, he fail to attend the Senate.

Vacancy.

The President notifies a vacancy to the Governor of the State immediately on its occurrence, but if there be no President or he be absent from the Commonwealth, the duty devolves upon the Governor-General.

Questions decided by majority.

Questions are decided by a majority in the Senate, each Senator possesses one vote. The President is entitled to vote, but when votes are equal the question passes in the negative.

Casting-votes.

In the United States the President of the Senate possesses a casting-vote only. The Australian Constitution follows the British precedents of the House of Lords and the Canadian Constitution, which give it neither to the Lord Chancellor nor the Speaker of the Senate. There seems a substantial reason why a President should possess a vote in a Federal Senate, since if he be deprived of his vote, his State will lose the benefit of equality of representation, whilst if he possesses an additional casting-vote it will receive too much representation. In the United States, where the Vice-president is not a Senator, there seems less reason why he should not have a casting-vote.

THE HOUSE OF REPRESENTATIVES

House of Representatives.

In imitation of the American title the popular chamber of the Commonwealth Parliament is termed the House of Representatives. Its numbers were ordained by the Constitution to be as nearly as practicable double that of the number of Senators.

The numbers of Representatives chosen by the several States were directed to be in proportion to the respective numbers of their people, and until Parliament made other provisions, were determinable whenever necessary in the following manner—

(1) A quota was ascertained by dividing the number of Quota. the people of the Commonwealth, as shown by the latest statistics of the Commonwealth, by twice the number of the Senators.

(2) The number of members to be chosen in each State was determined by dividing the number of the people of the State, as shown by the latest statistics of the Commonwealth, by the quota, and if on such division there was a remainder greater than one-half of the quota, the State could have one more member, but five members, at least, must be chosen in each original State.

The method of taking the quota has been explained and illustrated by Quick and Garran in their exhaustive work, *The Annotated Constitution of the Australian Commonwealth.*

" The quota," state the learned authors, " is that number Method of computation. of the aggregate population of the Commonwealth which considered as a unit is entitled to one member in the House of Representatives. It is obtained by dividing the population of the Commonwealth by twice the number of Senators. The population is that shown in the latest statistics then available. The number resulting from the division of the quotient is called the quota. This is the ratio of representation, there being one representative for every quota of the population of the Commonwealth. The method of obtaining the quota may be shown as follows—

Twice the number of Senators.	Population of the Commonwealth.	Quota.
72.	3,717,700.	51,635.

" It seems clear that strict accuracy requires that the quota should be calculated out to an exact decimal fraction. To neglect the fractions might, in occasional instances, just make the difference of a Representative more or less."

In computing the number of people of the State or Commonwealth, if by any State law all persons of any race are disqualified from voting at elections for the more numerous House of the State Parliament, then in reckoning the number of the people of the State or of the Commonwealth persons of that race resident in that State are not counted.

The method of determining the quota can be altered by Parliament, but not so the distribution of representation or the two-to-one ratio.

An amendment of the Constitution would be required to effect any alteration of these.

Representa-
tion Act.

In 1905[1] the Representation Act was passed for ascertaining the number of the people of the Commonwealth by the chief Electoral Officer of the Commonwealth. For the purpose of this census an enumeration day was fixed, and subsequent enumerations were directed to be taken each five years. The following provisions now regulate the ascertainment of the number of the people : (a) The number of the people of each State as shown by the census are taken. (b) In the case of an enumeration day not being a census day, allowances shall then be made as prescribed by Schedule A of the Act or by the regulations by adding the increases and deducting the decreases in these numbers arising from births, deaths, arrivals and departures during the period from the last census day. (c) There shall be excluded from the reckoning the number of persons who by section 25 or section 127 of the Constitution are required not to be counted. These are aboriginal natives and others not entitled to vote.

The following procedure determines the number of members of the House of Representatives to be chosen by each State.

A quota is ascertained by dividing the number of people of the Commonwealth as shown by the certificate (for the time being in force) of the chief electoral officer by twice the number of Senators. The number of members to be chosen in each State, subject to the Constitution, is determined by dividing the number of the people of the State as

[1] No. 11 of 1905. *See also* Commonwealth Electoral Acts, 1902-09.

shown by the certificate (for the time being in force), of the chief electoral officer, by the quota ; and if, on such division there is a remainder greater than one-half of the quota, one more member must be chosen in the State.

In 1909 the House of Representatives contained seventy-five members, twenty-seven of whom were chosen by New South Wales, twenty-two by Victoria, nine by Queensland, seven by South Australia, and five each by Western Australia and Tasmania.

Members of the House of Representatives, like Senators, are directly chosen by the people. They are elected for a period of three years. Their period of office is one year longer than the period prescribed for the duration of office of an American Representative, but two years shorter than the term of membership in the Canadian House of Commons. *Representatives chosen by the people.*

The three-years' period counts from the first meeting of the House, but the House may be dissolved before its term has expired by the Governor-General. The period of three years finds its precedent in the Triennial Parliament of William and Mary (1694). The Triennial Act then imposed for the first time a limit of duration on Parliaments which might have otherwise continued indefinitely, since by the common law Parliaments are only capable of termination by dissolution or by the demise of the sovereign. Triennial Parliaments only continued in existence in England for twenty-one years. A further change being then effected by the Septennial Act of 1715, which provided for the legal duration of Parliament for seven years. The present period of five years has been established by the Parliament Act, and assimilates the duration of the Imperial House of Commons to that of the Canadian House of Commons. *Three years' term.* *Triennial Parliament of William and Mary.* *Septennial Act of 1715.*

The duration of the Commonwealth Parliament is not affected by the demise of the Crown ; and this rule seems to apply to all legislative Assemblies created by the Imperial Parliament. *Not affected by demise of the Crown.*

The State Parliaments were empowered by the Constitution to make laws for determining the divisions in each State for which members are chosen, and the number of members for each division, subject to a provision that a division should not be formed out of parts of different States. In the absence of other provisions each State had one electorate. The power of the State Parliaments, however, could be abrogated, for their authority only continued until the Parliament of the Commonwealth otherwise provided. The

Common-wealth Legislation. Commonwealth Parliament has now legislated on this subject.[1]

Considerable resemblance may be traced in these provisions to the other two Federal Constitutions.

United States and Canada. Although the people's House in the United States and Canada is elected by the people as a whole and not by States or Provinces, the times, places, and manner of holding elections were originally left to the States and Provinces, but with power for Congress or Parliament to alter the States or Provincial regulations. The Canadian Constitution expressly gave directions as to the formation of electoral districts, but left the Dominion Parliament authority to alter them. The privilege conferred on the State or Province was a recognition of the Federal principle.[2]

Until it was otherwise provided by Commonwealth legislation, but subject to the Constitution, the State laws in force for the time being in relation to elections for the more numerous House of the State Parliament were as nearly as practicable to apply to the elections for Commonwealth Representatives. The Parliament of the Commonwealth has now legislated on this subject.

Governor-General causes issue of writs. The Governor-General in Council causes writs to issue for a General Election. These are issued within ten days from the expiry of a House of Representatives, or from the proclamation of its dissolution.

Speaker issues writ to fill vacancy. The Speaker issues his writ for the election of a member to fill a vacancy in the House; if there be no Speaker, or if he be absent from the Commonwealth, the duty devolves upon the Governor-General in Council.

A Representative must possess the same qualifications

[1] Commonwealth Electoral Acts, 1902-09.
[2] *Ante*, pp. 236, 55.

for election as a Senator, [1] and until the Federal Parliament Qualification of Representative. otherwise provides, must be of the full age of twenty-one, and an elector entitled to vote at an election for a member of the House of Representatives, or a person qualified to become such an elector, not being a person who at the date of nomination, or at any time within fourteen days prior to the date of nomination, was a member of a State Parliament. [2] He must also have been at least three years a resident within the limits of the Commonwealth, as existing at the time he was chosen.   He must, in addition, be either a natural-born subject of the King, or have been at least for five years naturalised under a law of the United Kingdom, or of a Colony which has become or becomes a State of the Commonwealth, or of a State.   Any person convicted of bribery or undue influence, or attempted bribery or undue influence at an election, or who is found by the Court of Disputed Returns to have committed or attempted to commit bribery or used undue influence, when a candidate, is for two years from the date of his conviction disqualified. [3]

The age limit for a member of the House of Representatives Age limits in United States and Canada. is lower than that of the United States, which fixes the age of a representative at twenty-five.   It is similar to that in the Imperial House of Commons.   The age limit fixed by the Provinces of Canada regulates the qualification of a Representative for the Dominion House of Commons.   In the United States a Representative is required to be resident in the State for which he is elected, but no such qualifying residential rule exists in Australia.   At one period in the history of England a member of Parliament was required to be a resident in the County or Borough for which he was elected, but by the time of Elizabeth no such requirement was insisted on.   It would, at the present day, be extremely awkward if a Minister lost his seat and found himself unable to find another seat by reason of such a restriction as exists in the United States.   No inconvenience, however, has been

[1] *Ante*, p. 296.
[2] Commonwealth Electoral Acts, 1902-11, sect. 96.
[3] *Ibid.*, sect. 206 A.

occasioned in the American House of Representatives, since Ministers are excluded from its membership.

The first function of the House of Representatives on its assembly after a General Election, is to choose its Speaker, and whenever the office becomes vacant a fresh Speaker must be chosen. The office is vacated by the Speaker losing his seat or by his resignation. His resignation is effected by intimating the fact in writing to the Governor-General.

Before or during the Speaker's absence the House may choose a member to perform his functions.

A member resigns by intimating in writing his resignation to the Speaker, or if there be no Speaker, or the Speaker be absent from the Commonwealth, to the Governor-General. A failure to attend the House for two consecutive months in any session, without the leave of the House, likewise creates a vacancy.

In the Imperial House of Commons, although no vacancy is occasioned by a member's absence from that body, a member who is elected is bound to serve, and the House has the right by a call of the House to compel the attendance of all its members, but no member of the House of Commons is entitled to resign unless by accepting a nominal office of profit under the Crown.

A third of the Australian House of Representatives constitutes a quorum. In the United States a majority of the House of Representatives is necessary except for the purpose of adjournment. The United States' House has power to enforce the attendance of its members. The North British America Act fixes a quorum in the Canadian House of Commons at twenty at least, including the Speaker.

Questions are determined by the majority in the Australian House, and the Speaker only possesses a casting-vote in cases of equality. This provision is in accordance with the practice of the Canadian House of Commons.

A Representative receives an allowance of £600 a year, but Representatives who are holders of certain offices receive £400, and, in addition, the emoluments of office. The allowance is reckoned from the day that a member takes his seat.

All disqualifications attaching to Senators equally apply to members of the House of Representatives.[1] Questions respecting the qualifications of a member or a vacancy, were determined by the House in the same way that the Senate inquired into and determined similar questions affecting a Senator.[2] But under the Commonwealth Electoral Acts, 1902–1911,[3] the Court of Disputed Returns will determine the questions of an aggrieved party on petitions, or the House by resolution may refer the matter to the Court. A Senator is incapable of being chosen or of sitting as a member of the House.

RELATIONS OF THE TWO HOUSES
Taxation and Appropriation

Proposed laws appropriating revenue or money, or imposing taxation, must not originate in the Senate, but a proposed law, however, does not fall within this prohibition by reason only that it contains provisions for the imposition or appropriation of fines or other pecuniary penalties, or for the demand or payment or appropriation of fees for licences or for fees for services under the proposed law.

The rule here laid down is in substance the same as that which obtains in all the Imperial Constitutions, and follows the practice of the Imperial House of Commons.[4] A fine distinction, however, is drawn in the Australian Constitution between a Bill and a proposed law. A proposed law is said to be a bill or measure which is in course of progress through the Legislature.

Since the Senate is an elected body, there is no reason why it should not have the power to amend or reject most laws, and it possesses this power, but with the exception

Marginal notes:
Disqualification.
Proposed laws appropriating revenue.
Distinction between a Bill and proposed law.
Taxation or appropriation for Government purposes.

---

[1] *Ante*, p. 307.
[2] *Ante*, p. 292.
[3] Sects. 192–206 F.
[4] As to exclusion of fees and penalties, see Standing order, House of Commons, July 24th, 1849.

that proposed laws, imposing taxation or appropriating revenue or moneys for the ordinary annual services of the Government, may not be amended. For it is assumed that the Government is the best judge of their necessity. The Senate, in respect of these matters, is accordingly deprived of a power of amendment. It is also prohibited from amending any proposed law so as thereby to increase any proposed charge or burden on the people.

Senate's power of suggestion. The Senate, however, possesses a suggesting power. It may at any stage return to the House of Representatives any proposed law, including finance, which it is entitled not to amend, and request by message, the omission or amendment of any item or provision therein. The House of Representatives may then, if it think fit, make any such omissions or amendments with or without modifications.

Origin of suggestion. The power of making suggestions to the House of Representatives, adopts a practice which had originated in South Australia. The Assembly of South Australia in 1856, had passed a Bill to repeal a tax on the tonnage of shipping, substituting a wharfage rate. The Legislative Council amended the Bill, a proceeding which the Assembly denounced as a breach of privilege. The Council then passed several resolutions, three of which were accepted by the Compromises. Assembly. (1) That all Bills where the object was to raise money, whether by way of loan or otherwise, or to warrant the expenditure of any portion of the same, should be held to be Money Bills; (2) that it was competent for the Council to suggest any alteration in any such Bill (except that portion of the Appropriation Bill providing for the ordinary annual expenses of the Government), and in case such suggestion was not agreed to by the House of Assembly, such Bills might be returned by the House of Assembly to the Council for reconsideration when the Bill must either be assented to or rejected by the Council as originally passed by the House of Assembly; (3) that the Council, whilst claiming the full right to deal with the monetary affairs of the Province, did not consider it desirable to enforce its right to deal with the details of the ordinary annual expenses of the Government. " That on the Appropriation Bill in the usual form being submitted to the Council, the Council should, if any clause therein appeared objectionable, demand a conference with the House of Assembly, to state the objections of the Council and receive information."

In 1857, the House of Assembly resolved that in order to facilitate the course of public business that the House, whilst asserting its sole right to direct, limit, and appoint in all Money Bills the ends, purposes, considerations, conditions, limitations, and qualifications of the tax or appropriation by such Bill imposed, altered, rejected, or directed free from all changes or alteration on the part of any other House, would nevertheless for the present adopt the resolutions as agreed to and forwarded to this House by message. The practice initiated in this way was subsequently introduced into the West Australian Parliament.

It was said during the debates on Federation, that the Governor was entitled on legislation other than Money Bills in some of the Australian Constitutions, to suggest an amendment on Bills which had passed both Houses. *Governor's powers of suggestion.*

The relations of the two Houses of the Australian Parliament are further regulated by the provision that a proposed law which appropriates revenue or moneys for the ordinary annual service of the Government, must deal only with such appropriation, and laws imposing taxation must deal only with the imposition of taxation, and any provision dealing with any other matter is of no effect. Laws, except laws imposing duties of customs or excise, must also deal with one subject of taxation ; laws imposing Customs duties must deal with Customs only, and laws imposing Excise duties with Excise duties only. *Rules as to appropriation and revenue.*

The object of these provisions was to prevent a resort to the practice of tacking, a favourite weapon with popular Houses in conflict with Second Chambers. Writing of these provisions, more especially money bills, Professor Harrison Moore says, " That in the balance of power in the Commonwealth, it is a factor not to be neglected, that while the *To stop tacking.*

Senate has a recognised power over Money Bills beyond that of any other Second Chamber in the British Dominions, it can hardly exercise the extreme power of rejecting the Bill for the ordinary annual service of the Government upon any other ground than that the Ministry owes responsibility to the Upper not less than to the Lower House. That is a position which in the future the Senate, as the House of States, as well as the Second Chamber, may take up ; but it is a position from which even in the history of Parliamentary Government in the Colonies the strongest supporters of the Upper House have generally shrunk." [1]

Votes, etc., for appropriation must be recommended by Governor-General.

Votes, resolutions, and proposed laws for the appropriation of revenue or moneys may not be passed unless the purpose of appropriation has, in the same session, been recommended, by message, of the Governor-General to the House in which the proposal originated.

Deadlocks.

The provisions of the Constitution to reconcile disagreements between the two Houses known as " deadlocks " are of great importance. They are as follows : " If the House of Representatives passes any proposed law and the Senate rejects or fails to pass it, or passes it with amendments to which the House of Representatives will not

Provisions to avoid.

agree, and if after an interval of three months the House of Representatives in the same or next session again passes the proposed law with or without any amendments which have been made, suggested or agreed to by the Senate, and

Failure to agree after three months.

the Senate rejects or fails to pass it, or passes it with amendments to which the House of Representatives will not agree,

Dissolution of both Houses.

the Governor-General may dissolve the Senate and the House of Representatives simultaneously. But such dissolution shall not take place within six months before the date of the expiry of the House of Representatives by effluxion of time.

After dissolution.

" If after such dissolution the House of Representatives again passes the proposed law, with or without any amendments, which have been made, suggested, or agreed to by the Senate, and the Senate rejects or fails to pass it, or passes

[1] *The Commonwealth of Australia*, p. 122.

it with amendments to which the House of Representatives will not agree, the Governor-General may convene a joint sitting of the members of the Senate and of the House of Representatives. Joint sitting.

" The members present at the joint sitting may deliberate, and shall vote together upon the proposed law as last proposed by the House of Representatives, and upon amendments, if any, which have been made therein by one House and not agreed to by the other, and any such amendments which are affirmed by an absolute majority of the total number of the members of the Senate and House of Representatives shall be taken to have been carried, and if the proposed law, with the amendments, if any, so carried is affirmed by an absolute majority of the total number of the members of the Senate and House of Representatives, it shall be taken to have been duly passed by both Houses of the Parliament, and shall be presented to the Governor-General for the King's assent." [1] Voting together. Treated as one House for purpose of obtaining majority.

It will be observed that the deadlock provisions apply only to legislation which originates in the Lower House. The provisions permit an interval of three months to elapse for reflection when, on a continued rejection, a dissolution of both Houses may take place. After a dissolution it is quite possible that a deadlock may still continue between the two elected Houses, since each House may return from the polls backed by the support of its constituents. To meet such a case members of both Houses may then deliberate in joint session, but they must vote together. On the vote being taken an absolute majority is sufficient to pass the proposed law. Since the membership of the Senate is as near as possible half that of the House of Representatives, this factor will be generally sufficient to enable the views of the House of Representatives to prevail. Applicable only to legislation originating in House of Representatives.

In the South African Constitution some of these provisions have been adopted, but there are differences. [2] Deadlock provisions in South African Constitution.

---

[1] For deadlock provisions in Union of South Africa, *post*, p. 411.
[2] *Post*, p. 411.

CHAPTER XXVIII

POWERS OF LEGISLATION

Powers of
legislation.

THE Commonwealth Parliament can legislate only under
the Federal powers which have been conferred upon it by
the Constitution.

Nature of.

In the enumeration of these, some will be found to be
new and original powers, never before exercised by the
Colonial Legislatures of Australia ; others will be found to
be old powers which these legislatures had exercised long
prior to Federation. Where a federal power has been
granted, the rule is that it is full and ample, sufficient for all
purposes for which it was granted, except where its exercise
has been restricted or hedged by some reservation, as, for
example, the power of taxation, which is only exercisable,
subject to the rule, that taxation must not discriminate
between States.

System of
distribution.

In distributing the legislative powers, a different system
to that which was employed in the Canadian Constitution
was adopted. The Canadian system, as previously pointed
out, was only rendered possible because the Provinces

Compared
with
Canadian.

surrendered their powers, and received a fresh set of powers
under the Constitution, the Canadian Constitution therefore
being a division or distribution of all the powers of
Government in the Dominion by one instrument.

Similarity
to United
States.

In Australia the existence of Colonial legislatures, possessing full powers of quasi sovereign legislation within their
limits, powers which they were unwilling to surrender in
exchange for a new set of powers, rendered the task of
Constitution-making analogous to that of the framers of the
American Constitution. The Australian Colonies were not
unprepared to surrender those powers which they thought
better exercisable by one central authority ; others they
desired to retain unimpaired. Therefore, in dealing with
the legislative powers of the Commonwealth, the framers of

the Constitution proceeded to enumerate them only, and left the States, subject to the Constitution, in full possession of all others not enumerated ; and that this should be clear beyond all doubt, the Constitution declared "that every *Protection of State powers.* power of the Parliament of a Colony which has become or becomes a State shall, unless it is by this Constitution exclusively vested in the Parliament of the Commonwealth, or withdrawn from the Parliament of the State, continue as at the establishment of the Commonwealth, or as at the admission or establishment of the State as the case may be.

In the Canadian Constitution, it has already been shown that the powers of legislation were enumerated but, with few exceptions, they were exclusively assigned either to the Dominion Parliament or to the Provincial legislatures. There were few concurrent powers conferred. The object of this arrangement was to avoid the constant overlapping claims of contending authorities, the story of which had filled innumerable volumes of the United States' Law Reports with judicial learning and wisdom.

In Australia the main legislative powers of the Common- *Not expressly described as exclusive or concurrent.* wealth Parliament are set out in the thirty-nine sub- sections of section 51 of the Constitution Act. They are not expressly described as exclusive of or concurrent to the Commonwealth with the States ; therefore, such powers require separate examination to discover whether they be the one or the other.

Parliament is empowered, subject to the Constitution, to legislate for the peace, order, and good government of the Commonwealth in respect of each of the enumerated powers. The first great power mentioned is the trade and commerce power. The authority is granted to legislate for trade and *Trade and commerce.* commerce with other countries and among the States. In the United States this was a Federal power, conferred in *Federal power in United States and Canada.* somewhat similar terms. Thus Congress was authorised to "regulate commerce with foreign nations, and among the several States, and with the Indian tribes."

It has been previously pointed out that judicial decisions *Interpretation of Canadian power.* have immensely widened the scope of this power in the

United States, since the object aimed at by the power was said to be to secure uniformity whenever practicable against conflicting State legislation. In Canada the power is conferred to regulate trade and commerce. "The words 'trade and commerce,' in their unlimited sense, include every regulation of trade ranging from political arrangements in regard to trade with foreign Governments down to minute rules for regulating particular trades."

The Judicial Committee of the Privy Council, however, declined to give the word " trade " such a wide interpretation. They considered that the authority given to legislate did not comprehend the power to regulate by legislation the contracts of a particular business or trade.

Little help can be obtained from Canadian decisions in interpreting the commerce power in Australia, little more than was found by the Canadian Courts in the decisions of the Courts of the United States. The Commonwealth commerce power is closely akin to that of the United States : whilst the Dominion power, as previously stated, extends over all the Provinces. On the other hand the United States' power stops at commerce in the State and only regulates inter-State commerce.

Legislation. The trade and commerce power in Australia extends to empower the Parliament of the Commonwealth to make laws with respect to trade and commerce, with reference to navigation and shipping, and to railways the property of the State, but in Canada a separate power was given to the Dominion Parliament to enable legislation to be passed over navigation and shipping. The Commonwealth power is both external and inter-State. Under it legislation has been passed dealing with the Sea Carriage of Goods, Seamen's Compensation, Australian Industries Preservation, Commerce Trades Descriptions, Secret Commissions, and Customs. The commerce power is hedged with certain restrictions, for the Commonwealth Parliament cannot by any law or regulation of trade, commerce, or revenue, give preference to one State, or any part thereof over another State, or any part thereof, nor can it abridge the right of a

State, or the residents therein, to the reasonable use of the waters of rivers for conservation or irrigation.

It has been shown how, under the authority of the commerce power, an Inter-State Commission was formed in the United States in 1887. The Australian Constitution did not leave a court to be deduced from a power, but provided for the establishment of an Inter-State Commission, with such powers of adjudication and administration as Parliament should deem necessary for the execution and maintenance within the Commonwealth of the provision of the Constitution relating to trade and commerce, and of all laws made thereunder. The appointment of its members is vested in the Governor-General in Council. Their term of office is fixed at seven years. A member, however, may be removed by the Governor-General in Council, on addresses from both Houses of Parliament in the same session, praying for his removal on the ground of proved misbehaviour or incapacity. The remuneration of members of the Commission rests with Parliament, but is not capable of diminution during their continuance in office.

Within two years from the establishment of the Commonwealth, trade, commerce, and intercourse among the States, whether by means of internal or ocean navigation, became absolutely free.

Parliament, in its legislation with respect to trade or commerce, may forbid as to railways any preference or discrimination by any State, or by any authority constituted under a State, when such preference or discrimination is undue and unreasonable, or unjust to any State ; due regard being had to the financial responsibilities incurred by any State in connection with the construction and maintenance of its railways. But no preference or discrimination, however, must be taken to be either undue and unreasonable, or unjust to any State, unless it is so adjudged by the Inter-State Commission. A rate for the carriage of goods upon a railway, the property of a State, is not unlawful if the rate be deemed by the Inter-State Commission to be necessary for the development of the territory of the State, or when the rate applies equally to goods within the State and to goods passing into the State from other States.

Taxation power. The second great power conferred upon the Commonwealth Parliament is that of taxation ; but taxation must be such as not to discriminate between the States. The power is very wide, for the methods of taxation are left unqualified, and cover every conceivable exaction which it is possible for a Government to make, whether under the name of a tax or under such names as rates, assessments, duties, imposts, excises, licences, fees, and tolls.[1] The Parliament, however, may not impose any tax which bears heavier on one State than another, for this would be discrimination. This is in accordance with the taxing power of Congress : " All duties, imposts, and excises must be uniform in the United States," that is, levied at the same rate on the same article wherever found.[2]

Prohibitions on taxing power. The Commonwealth taxing power is further limited by two provisions : one forbidding the taxation of State property, the other prohibiting the taxation of trade and commerce passing from one State to the other.

Not exclusive unless so declared. Like the taxing power in the United States, the Commonwealth taxing power is not exclusive, except so far as the Customs and Excise exclusive. Constitution directs that it shall be ; the only powers of exclusive taxation are those of Customs and Excise. In all other respects the States possess concurrent powers of taxation, although they cannot tax public property of any kind belonging to the Commonwealth.

Prohibition on State taxation. Whether they could tax the instrumentalities of the Commonwealth, or the salaries of Federal ministers led to conflicting decisions given by the Judicial Committee of the Privy Council and the High Court of Australia. The High Court of Australia declared that the salaries of Federal officers were not taxable, whilst the Judicial Committee of the Privy Council decided the contrary.   As the last case on this subject was taken before the High Court of Australia, and no special leave to appeal from their decision

[1] Hylton v. United States, 3 Dall, 171.
[2] *Ante*, p. 90.

was granted by the Judicial Committee on the ground that the Commonwealth Parliament had, since the decision of the High Court, passed legislation authorising the taxation to be levied on the salaries of Federal officers. The question has been removed at present from the judicial sphere, but there are still these conflicting decisions in existence.

There is no rule requiring the apportionment of direct taxes among the States such as exists in the United States. The apportionment rule in the United States has till recently prevented the imposition of an income tax.[1] *No rule of apportionment.*

The imposition of a Federal income tax is clearly within the power of the Commonwealth Parliament. *Income tax.*

The Commonwealth Parliament has power to legislate for giving bounties on the production or export of goods ; but the power required to be exercised so that bounties are uniform throughout the Commonwealth. *Bounties. Rule of uniformity.*

The control and regulation of the payments of bounties is now vested in the Executive Government of the Commonwealth. *Control vests in the Executive. State powers.*

Nothing, however, prohibits a State from granting any aid to or bounty on mining for gold and silver or other metals ; nor from granting, with the consent of both Houses of the Federal Parliament, expressed by resolution any aid to or bounty on the production or export of goods.

The Parliament is empowered to borrow money on the public credit ; a similar power exists in the United States. *Borrowing power.*

Parliament controls the postal, telegraphic, telephonic, and other like services ; the establishment of post offices and post roads is a Federal power both in the United States and also in Canada. *Postal and telegraph Service in United States and Canada.*

The naval and military defence of the Commonwealth and of the several States, and the control of the forces to execute and maintain the laws of the Commonwealth, is necessarily a Federal power. It is, however, more limited than the power in the United States, since its purpose is defined as being for the naval and military defence of the Commonwealth and of the States. Therefore, it is, probably, *Naval and military defence.*

[1] *Ante*, p. 158.

not such a power as would authorise the Commonwealth
to equip and send a military expedition outside its borders
for the purpose of an aggressive war. On the other hand,
it would be sufficiently wide to provide for all naval emergencies, wherever the defence of the Commonwealth might
be said to be even indirectly affected. The war power in the
United States includes the power to enable Congress to
declare war, but this is not the case with the war power of
Canada or Australia, for the power is with the Mother Country.

The power in Canada includes a power to legislate for the
militia, military, and naval service and defence. A rule
now accepted by the Dominions is for local legislation to
provide that when its troops are voluntarily serving with
Imperial troops outside the Colony the Army Act of 1881
shall apply. The rule is not applicable where the troops
would be acting in the Dominion with Imperial troops.[1]

Lighthouses, beacons, etc.   The power of the Commonwealth Parliament extends over
lighthouses, lightships, beacons, and buoys. It, therefore,
by necessary implication, includes the power to provide
for their construction, equipment, and management. The
Canadian power is expressed to extend to beacons, buoys,
and lighthouses.

Federal Observatory.   In taking astronomical and meteorological observations,
the importance of uniformity throughout Australia was
strongly pressed at the Adelaide Convention ;[2] consequently this was made a Federal Power. The control of the
meteorological observations would seem necessary to pass,
since the principal means of information, namely, the
Post Office and Telegraph, were transferred at the same
time. This power is not, in specific terms, granted to the
Dominion Parliament of Canada."

Quarantine.   The power over " quarantine " is conferred on the Commonwealth Parliament. In Canada the power is specified
as " quarantine and maintenance of marine hospitals.'
In the United States the power to deal with quarantine was
not expressly conferred by the Constitution on Congress.

[1] See Australian Defence Act, No. 59, 1909.
[2] *Proceedings at Adelaide Convention*, 1897, p. 776.

In the United States the States pass quarantine laws, but _{Power in United States.} Congress can interfere with them, either by forbidding State laws or enacting independent legislation, since quarantine laws may operate as a regulation of trade and commerce. The Commonwealth power is very wide, and is in no way limited. How far the Canadian power extends has been a subject of discussion. The preservation of public health in a Province would appear to be a matter of local concern, a power exclusively assigned to the Provinces. In 1869 a Vaccination Bill was introduced in the Dominion Parliament, and for this reason was not proceeded with on account of its doubtful constitutional validity. The Parliament of the Commonwealth passed a Quarantine Act in 1908.

The Commonwealth Parliament has power over all _{Fisheries beyond territorial limits.} fisheries in Australian waters beyond territorial limits, but has no power over the control of fisheries within State territorial limits. The Commonwealth power, therefore, only commences three miles beyond the land.

The Canadian power, on the other hand, extends over sea- _{Canadian power.} coast and inland fisheries, but it does not authorise dealing with the ownership of the beds of the rivers, or of the fisheries, or the rights of individuals thereto.[1]

· The grant of power over fisheries outside territorial limits, _{Operation of Commonwealth power.} may be said to be legally operative to a certain extent only, as according to the law of nations, the Imperial Parliament itself has no jurisdiction over the ocean's highway. Such a jurisdiction might be conferred by treaty.

The taking of the Census and Statistics in the _{Census and Statistics. Currency.} Commonwealth is essentially a Federal power. A Census Act was passed in 1905. The British North America Act particularises Census and Statistics as a Dominion power.

In the same category are Currency, Coinage, and Legal _{Coinage, and Legal Tender.} Tender. The Commonwealth Parliament has passed a Coinage and Australian Notes Acts. The prolonged struggle in the United States over making Treasury notes a legal tender has already been related.[2]

[1] *Re* Provincial Fisheries, 26 S.C.R. (Can.) 444.
[2] *Ante*, pp. 112-3.

The Australian States are forbidden to coin any money or to make anything but gold and silver coins a legal tender in respect of debts. A similar prohibition was also applied to the American States. In all three Constitutions these powers were expressly reserved to the Federal Government: for the Parliament of Canada exercises exclusive legislative authority in relation to currency and coinage.

Prohibitions on States.

The banking power was conferred upon the Commonwealth Parliament in the following terms : " Banking, other than State banking, also State banking extending beyond the limits of the State concerned, the incorporation of banks, and the issue of paper money."

Banking power.

The power in Canada includes banking, incorporation of banks, and the issue of paper money.

Canadian power.

In the United States a banking power was not expressly mentioned in the Constitution. The power, however, was ultimately deduced from the power given to make all laws necessary and proper for carrying into execution other powers ; the banking power being deduced from the existence of these other powers. [1] In 1911 the Parliament of the Commonwealth established a Commonwealth Bank under its express power.

United States.

The Federal banking power in Australia does not include a power to deal with State Banks whose operations are confined to the States ; but should a State Bank establish branches in other States, it becomes amenable to Federal laws. The question of the issue of paper money in the United States has already been discussed. [2] Not only was this power not expressly conferred by the United States' Constitution, but the framers of the Constitution were determined not to entrust Congress with any such power ; nevertheless, the Supreme Court decided that the power could be implied.

Banking power in Australia.

The Commonwealth Parliament has power to legislate in respect of insurance other than State insurance, extending beyond the limits of the State concerned. Under this

Insurance other than State insurance.

[1] *Ante*, p. 83.
[2] *Ante*, p. 112.

power it has passed a Life Assurance Companies Act, in 1905, and a Marine Insurance Act, in 1909.

Congress has no power to deal with Insurance. For insurance is not commerce among the States. It has also been decided that Insurance business is neither trade nor commerce under the Canadian Constitution. Congress without power. Not trade or commerce in Canada.

The Federal power to legislate in respect of insurance in Australia is somewhat similar to the banking power in Australia; for the power cannot affect any Insurance which comes within the meaning of State Insurance, that is, Insurance confined to the States. Nature of Commonwealth power.

There is no special grant of an Insurance power in Canada, Federal jurisdiction there springs from the residuary power; but in Australia the Commonwealth Parliament possesses a special power, whilst on the other hand the State jurisdiction springs from its residuary power. Residuary Dominion power. Residuary State power in Australia.

Weights and measures, bills of exchange, and promissory notes are all matters over which a power to legislate has been entrusted to the Commonwealth Parliament. Similar powers are expressly conferred upon the Dominion Parliament. Weights and measures, bills of exchange, etc.

Bankruptcy and insolvency are Federal powers in Canada [1] and Australia. Bankruptcy and insolvency.

The power in the United States has been already referred [2] to.

Copyrights, patents of inventions, and designs and trade marks are Commonwealth powers. [3] Copyright is a Dominion power, and so also is the power to legislate in respect of patents of invention and discovery. The power over copyrights, patents of invention, obviously intrude in Canada upon Provincial rights, since it is impossible for the Dominion Parliament to pass legislation without affecting "property and civil rights" in the Provinces. Nevertheless, it has been decided by necessary implication, that the Copyrights, patents of invention, designs, and trade marks.

---

[1] *Ante*, p. 252.
[2] *Ante*, p. 17.
[3] Acts have been passed dealing with Patents, Trade Marks, Copyrights and Designs.

Dominion power in these matters is destructive of any Provincial power.

Naturalisation. Aliens. Legislation over naturalisation and aliens are powers assigned to the Commonwealth Parliament as they are in Canada to the Dominion Parliament.[1] The power possessed by Congress to establish a uniform rule of naturalisation throughout the United States has already been referred to.[2] The Commonwealth Parliament has legislated under its power by passing a Naturalisation Act, in 1903, and an Immigration Restriction Amendment Act, in 1905.

In United States.

Foreign corporations, trading and financial. Power to legislate in respect of foreign corporations and trading or financial corporations, formed within the limits of the Commonwealth, is another power assigned to the Commonwealth Parliament. The right of foreign corporations to carry on business in England without the necessity of obtaining Parliamentary or Ministerial sanction has long been recognised in the United Kingdom. This right has been recognised as well by the comity of nations as by international conventions. Foreign corporations carrying on business in Australia would be liable to Federal taxation.

Marriage and divorce. The powers to legislate in respect of marriage and divorce are powers of the Commonwealth Parliament, as they are of the Canadian Parliament;[3] In Canada the power is not unqualified. They are State powers in the United States.

The subjects of divorce and matrimonial causes and, in relation thereto, parental rights and the custody and guardianship of infants are Commonwealth powers. In the United States, Congress possesses no such powers. Therefore, persons removing from one State and becoming domiciled in another where facilities are easy can obtain divorces, which they would not have been able to have obtained had they continued to live in their own States.[4]

Invalid and old-age pensions. The Commonwealth Parliament can legislate in respect of invalid and old-age pensions. This is a power which does not appear in either of the older Constitutions. One reason urged why the Federal authority should possess it instead of the State authority was because within the bounds

[1] *Ante*, p. 252. [2] *Ante*, p. 97. [3] *Ante*, p. 252. [4] *Ante*, p. 115.

of Federated Australia a law could be enacted compelling that individual who was to receive the benefit to
contribute to the fund in which he was to participate in
old age.

Another Federal power which is not found in either the Service of
United States' Constitution or in that of Canada is that civil powers
conferring upon the Parliament the right to legislate for Australia.
the service and execution throughout the Commonwealth
of civil and criminal process and the judgments of the
Courts of the States ; the necessity for this power became
evident from the decisions of the State Courts prior to
Federation.   In many cases, provision had been made by
Australian legislatures for an ex-territorial service of civil
process, notably by the legislatures of Victoria, South
Australia, and New South Wales ; but these Colonies,
according to international law, were as much apart as if
they were foreign States.   The Inter-Colonial Debts Act,
which had made provision for a measure of inter-Colonial
reciprocity, could not make a Victorian subject amenable
to a judgment obtained in a South Australian Court, if he
had never submitted to the jurisdiction, was domiciled in
Victoria, and had never been in South Australia at all.[1]
It necessarily followed, from the grant of a power to legislate
for service, that there should also be a power to legislate
as to execution.

Such a power existed in the United Kingdom ; where, by Scotch and
following a certain procedure, a Scotch or Irish judgment judgments.
may be enforced as if it were an English judgment under
the Judgments Extension Act of 1868.

The Federal power over criminal process permits a person Criminal
charged in one State with a crime to be brought before the process.
Courts of the State that has jurisdiction over him.   Formerly an offender against justice, escaping to another portion
of the British Dominions from that in which he had committed the offence could defy the authority of the State
seeking to extradite him.   The Supreme Court of New Zealand
decided that a Colonial legislature had no power under its

[1] 22, A.L.T., p. 34.

Constitution to authorise the conveyance on the high sea of any person whatever to another Colony, and that such a power must be exercised either directly or indirectly under the authority of an Imperial Act.

Fugitive Offenders Act. · In consequence of this decision, the Fugitive Offenders Act was passed by the Imperial Parliament. The power of the Commonwealth Parliament over criminal process Surrender dependent upon Executive power in the United States. extends only to the Commonwealth. In the United States the return of a fugitive offender from one State to another does not depend upon legislation but on the executive Government of the State in which he is found.

In Australia his return is a judicial proceeding. An Extradition Act was passed by the Commonwealth Parliament in 1903. Another power given to the Commonwealth Parliament enables it to legislate throughout the Commonwealth for the laws, the public Acts and records, and the judicial Similarity of Australian and United States' Constitutions. proceedings of the States. Section 118 of the Constitution declares that full faith and credit shall be given throughout the Commonwealth to the laws, the public Acts and records, and the judicial proceedings of the States. This provision is similar to one in the United States' Constitution.

Powers over immigration and emigration. Before referring to the Commonwealth Parliaments' powers over immigration and emigration, a special power must be mentioned, that is, the power to legislate for the people of any race, other than the aboriginal race, in any State, for whom it is deemed necessary to make special laws. At first sight, it would appear as if this power might have reference to emigration; but as a special power is given over immigration and emigration, this is not the case.

White man's Australia. Australia has accepted the idea that Australia should be a white man's country.

Decisions in case of Chun Teung Toy. From a legal point of view, her position is unassailable. Whether an alien is entitled as of right to enter British territory was considered in the well-known case of Chung Toy v. Musgrave, which was decided by the Judicial Committee of the Privy Council in 1891. Their lordships observed that " the facts, quite apart from the statutes referred to, raise a grave question as to the plaintiff's right to maintain the action. He can only do so if he can establish that an alien has a legal right, enforceable by action to enter British territory. No authority exists for the proposition that an alien has any such right. Circumstances may occur in which the refusal to permit an alien to land might be such an interference with international comity as would properly give rise to diplomatic remonstrance from the country of which he was a native ; but it is quite another thing to assert that an alien excluded from any part of Her Majesty's dominions by the executive Government there, can maintain an action in a British Court and raise such questions as were argued before their lordships on the present appeal—whether the proper officer for giving or refusing access to the country has been duly authorised by his own Colonial Government, whether the Colonial Government has received sufficient delegated authority from the Crown to exercise the authority which the Crown had a right to exercise through the Colonial Government if properly communicated to it ; and whether the Crown has the right, without Parliamentary authority, to exclude an alien."

In Canada, the Dominions and Provinces possess con-current powers of legislation on the subject of immigration ; but any Provincial law repugnant to Dominion legislation is void. _{Concurrent power in Canada.}

In 1878 British Columbia passed an Act requiring every Chinaman above the age of twelve to take out a quarterly licence, for which he was charged $10. This licence fee was in substitution for general taxation. The Supreme Court of British Columbia declared the tax void as beyond the power of the Province, since it was at variance with the treaty obligations of Great Britain and China, and also interfered with the Dominion trade and commerce power. The Act was subsequently disallowed by the Governor-General in Council.

In 1885 the Dominion Parliament passed an Act to regulate and restrict Chinese immigration. A poll tax of _{Regulation of Chinese immigration.}

$50 was imposed on every Chinaman landing, and no vessel was allowed to carry more than one Chinaman to every 50 tons of its tonnage. A Chinaman leaving with the intention of returning was required to give notice of his intention at the port of his departure and on giving up his certificate of entry or of residence, to receive, on payment of a fee of $1, a certificate of leave to depart and return.

In the United States, difficulties similar to those encountered in Australia and Canada in respect to Chinese immigration have been dealt with by Congress. State laws that have attempted to regulate it have been declared unconstitutional, generally on the ground that they have interfered with existing treaties between the United States and China. The power of Congress to interfere has been denied, since the power of modifying treaties rests with the Executive.

In 1888 a provisional treaty was entered into between the United States and China, providing against the admission of any Chinaman into the States, but was not ratified as the Senate amended it, and the Chinese Government refused to accept it.

Mr. Chamberlain's views. In 1897, when the Australian Premiers were in London, Mr. Chamberlain expressed entire sympathy with the determination of the Australian Colonies to prevent the influx of people who were alien in civilisation, in religion, and in customs, and who interfered with the legitimate rights of the existing labouring population. Such an influx must be prevented at all hazards ; but he asked the Premiers to remember the traditions of the Empire, which made no distinctions of race or colour ; and pointed out that the exclusion of all Her Majesty's Indian subjects or even of all Asiatics, would be so offensive to those people, that it would be most painful to Her Majesty to sanction it. He, therefore, urged them to base their prohibitive legislation not upon race or colour, but upon the really objectionable characteristics of the immigrants legislated against ; and he instanced, as a type of legislation which the Imperial

Government would think satisfactory, the Immigration Restriction Act of 1897, recently passed in Natal—a measure which was being found adequate in that Colony to meet the same evil." [1]

The Commonwealth Parliament has power to legislate over external affairs. The meaning to be attached to this grant of power is generally considered to be doubtful. *External affairs.*

The authors of the *Annotated Constitutions of the Australian Commonwealth* consider that the power applies to the external representation of the Commonwealth by accredited agents where required ; the conduct of the business and promotion of the interests of the Commonwealth in outside countries, and the extradition of fugitive offenders from outside countries. The Extradition Act of 1903 and the High Commissioners Act of 1909 have been passed under the authority of this power.

Reference has already been made to the powers of the Dominion Governments with reference to the negotiation of commercial treaties. [2]

The Commonwealth Parliament is empowered to legislate with reference to the relations of the Commonwealth with the islands of the Pacific. *The Commonwealth and the islands of the Pacific.*

The islands of the Pacific, south of the Equator, which belonged to Great Britain or were under her protection when the Commonwealth Act was passed, were South-Eastern New Guinea, Southern Solomon Islands, Gilbert Islands, Ellice Islands, Phœnix Islands, Tokelau Islands, New Hebrides (dual control with France), Fiji Islands, Tonga Islands, Savage Islands, and Cook Islands.

Legislation dealing with labourers in these islands was passed in 1901 and 1906.

A power is given to the Commonwealth Parliament to legislate for the acquisition of property, on just terms, from any State or person for any purpose in respect of which the Parliament has power to make laws. *power to acquire land from States.*

---

[1] Quick and Garran's *The Annotated Constitution of the Australian Commonwealth*, pp. 626-627.
[2] *Ante*, p. 210, *et seq.*

Origin of power in the United States.

In the United States, such a power was implied from the power which enabled Congress to make all laws which might be necessary for carrying into execution any of the federal powers ; as the power to acquire land in any State was an incident of sovereignty, it could, therefore, be exercised, notwithstanding the opposition of the State. The branch of law on this subject is known as the law of eminent domain.

Limitation of Commonwealth power.

The exercise of the Commonwealth power is confined to any of the purposes in respect of which the Parliament is empowered to make laws.

Control of railways for military purposes.

A power is granted to Parliament over the control of railways with respect to transport for the naval and military purposes of the Commonwealth ; and is therefore a power ancillary to the war power.

States own railways.

Most of the railways in Australia are State-owned railways and the Commonwealth power does not extend to control the working or management of these, except for the purposes stated in the power.

Power to acquire with State consent.

Another power entitles the Parliament to legislate for the acquisition of any State railways, with the consent of the State on terms arranged between the Commonwealth and the State. Railway construction and extension in any State can also be a subject for Commonwealth legislation with the consent of the State.

Power in Canada contrasted.

In Canada the Provincial legislatures are exclusively empowered to make laws in relation to local works and undertakings other than such as are of the following classes—

Lines of steam or other ships, railways, canals, telegraphs, and other works and undertakings connecting the Province with any other or others of the Provinces or extending beyond the limits of the Province. There is, therefore, a wide difference between the Dominion power in Canada and the Commonwealth power in Australia. The State power over railways in Australia is subject to the Commonwealth power to legislate with respect to trade and commerce. The power was expressly given to prevent any doubts arising as to whether the trade and commerce power extended to railways owned by the State.

Parliament has power to legislate in respect of conciliation and arbitration for the prevention and settlement of industrial disputes extending beyond the limits of any one State. *Conciliation and arbitration for settlement of trade disputes.*

This power has already been the subject of legislation.

In 1904 the Commonwealth Legislature passed the Commonwealth Conciliation and Arbitration Act, which has since been declared to be invalid so far as it affects State railways.[1] Other sections of this Act have also been declared void, in so far as they purported to empower the Court of Conciliation and Arbitration to make a common rule in respect of any industry.[2]

Parliament possesses the power to legislate in matters in respect of which the Constitution makes provision "until the Parliament otherwise provides." "Until the Parliament otherwise provides" is a proviso common to all the Imperial Federations, and where the power is expressly given, it enables amendments of the Constitution to be made solely by force of the legislative authority. *Until Parliament otherwise provides.* *An amending power.*

" There are no less than twenty-two provisions in the Constitution where it is enacted that the law of the Constitution shall be as it is stated in the Constitution, " until the Parliament otherwise provides."[3] They relate to the Governor's salary, Senate electorates, Queensland Senatorial divisions, number of Senators, State electoral laws regulating the election of Senators, quorum of Senate, mode of ascertaining the quota for election of members of the House of Representatives, electoral divisions, qualification of electors, State electoral laws regulating the election of the Members of the House of Representatives, qualification of Members, quorum of the House of Representatives, penalty for sitting when disqualified, mode of

[1] The Federated Amalgamated Government Railway and Transport Service Association *v.* the N.S.W. Railway Traffic Employers' Association, 4 C.L.R. 488.

[2] Australian Boot Trade Employees Federation *v.* Whybrow and others, Vol. II, C.L.R. (1910), p. 1.

[3] Quick and Garran's *Commentaries on the Constitutions*, p. 647.

settling disputed elections, payment of Members, number of Ministers, salaries of Ministers, appointment and removal of non-political officers, conditions and restrictions on appeals, application of Customs and Excise revenues, financial assistance to States, and audit.[1]

Power to legislate on reference by State Parliament. The Commonwealth Parliament is empowered to legislate on matters which a Parliament of a State or the Parliaments of the States may refer to it ; but so that the law shall extend only to the States by whose Parliaments the matter is referred, or which afterwards adopt the law.

When power comes into force. This power can only come into existence where State Parliaments desire some general law, which the Commonwealth Parliament under its existing powers is unable to pass.

Applicable to Imperial Federal scheme. The power seems more applicable to a Confederation than to a Federation : but in any scheme of Imperial Federation, the grant of a similar power to a central body to legislate for matters common to the Empire might prove of considerable value.

Power to legislate is given also to the Commonwealth Parliament in respect of the exercise within the Commonwealth, at the request or with the concurrence of the Parliaments of all the States directly concerned, of any power which could, at the establishment of the Constitution, have been exercised only by the Parliament of the United Kingdom or by the Federal Council of Australasia.

Matters incidental to the powers. The last of the thirty-nine powers of legislation expressly conferred by the 51st section of the Constitution Act on the Commonwealth Parliament is a power to legislate on matters incidental to the execution of any power vested by the Constitution in the Parliament or in either House thereof, or in the Government of the Commonwealth, or in the Federal Judicature, or in any department or officer of the Commonwealth. This power is complementary to all the other powers, and enables the Commonwealth Parliament to give full effect to any of the powers which have been expressly conferred upon it by the Constitution.

[1] *Ibid.*, p. 648.

In addition to the Commonwealth Parliament's powers _{Exclusive} of legislation over the numerous subjects already referred _{powers of legislation.} to, Parliament has certain exclusive powers of legislation ; thus it may legislate in respect of the seat of Government and all places acquired by the Commonwealth for public purposes.

In 1908 an Act was passed to acquire a seat of Government and a further Act in 1909. It was necessary by the Constitution that the seat of Government should be on territory acquired by the Government, and not nearer than 100 miles from Sydney. A site in the district of Yass Canberra, in accordance with these conditions, was fixed upon.

It was provided that the area of land acquired should not be less than 100 square miles, and within its border the State out of which it was carved should possess no powers even of a local nature. The first stone of the commencement column of Australia's Capital was laid on the 12th of March, 1913, by Lord Denman, the Governor-General, the second by the Prime Minister, the Right Hon. A. Fisher, and the third by the Hon. King O'Malley, Minister for Home Affairs. The name of the capital was drawn from a casket by Lady Denman, the wife of the Governor-General who declared it to be " Canberra."

Another exclusive power vested in the Commonwealth Parliament is that over matters relating to any department of public service, the control of which was by the Constitution transferred to the executive Government of the Commonwealth and in respect of other matters than declared by the Constitution to be within the exclusive power of the Parliament.

The meaning of an exclusive power has been often dis- _{Meaning of exclusive power.} cussed by the Supreme Court of the United States, and also in Canada ; but the point is not of such great importance in the Australian Constitution, since the distinction between Federal powers and State powers is more clearly drawn. [1]

[1] See States *post*, p. 351.

CHAPTER XXIX

THE JUDICIAL POWER

Early
Judiciary.

THE first authority for the erection of a Court of Law in Australia appears in the statute 27 Geo. III, c. 2. By this Act, the Crown was authorised by letters patent to erect a Court of Criminal Jurisdiction on the east coast of New South Wales, and the parts adjacent thereto, for the trial of treasons, felonies, and misdemeanours.

Court of
Civil
Jurisdiction.

In 1787, relying apparently on the supposed prerogative of the Crown, a Court, with a limited jurisdiction in civil matters, was established.

Court of
Criminal
Jurisdiction.

The Criminal Court constituted consisted of a Judge-Advocate and six naval or military officers selected by the Governor, whilst the Civil Court was composed of the Judge-Advocate and two inhabitants similarly selected.

New Federal
system.

These Courts continued in force until May 17th, 1823, when, by virtue of an Act which had been passed in the previous year, a Charter of Justice was issued, which abolished the old military courts and set up a Supreme Court and Court of Appeal on the English system, with an ultimate right in certain cases to appeal to the Judicial Committee of the Privy Council. From this time onwards the judicial system of Australia has steadily progressed side by side with her constitutional development. One of the proposed advantages of Federation held out to the people of Australia was the establishment of a final Court of Appeal, and when the Constitution was framed this Court of Appeal was created, both of a Federal and final nature. [1]

Vesting of the
Judicial power
of the
Common-
wealth.
Composition
of High Court.

The judicial power of the Commonwealth is now vested in this Court, which is called the High Court of Australia, and also in such other Federal Courts as Parliament chooses to create, and in such other Courts as it invests with Federal jurisdiction.

[1] *Post*, p. 345.

The High Court is required to be constituted with a Chief Justice and as many other justices—not less than two—as Parliament may prescribe. It now possesses seven judges. The Chief Justice receives a salary of £3,500 and the other judges £3,000.

The provisions relating to the judicial power bear a close resemblance to those of the United States. In the United States it was decided early in its history that the divisions created by its Constitution impliedly prohibited the one encroaching upon the other, and that neither the legislative nor the executive branches of a Government could constitutionally assign to the Judiciary any duties but such as were properly judicial and to be performed in a judicial manner. It was also decided that neither the executive nor legislative departments could review or sit as a court of error on the judicial acts or opinions of the Courts of the United States.[1] Questions may arise as to the extent of the judicial power in Australia. Do the judges of the High Court possess such powers as those of the Supreme Court of Washington? It may be claimed that the Judiciary in Australia is no mere auxiliary of the Parliament and the Executive Government. It has possibly, like them, an independent duty, but only within its own sphere of judicial power, to uphold and maintain the Constitution against all attacks, whether from the Commonwealth Executive, or Legislative departments, or from the States Governments.

The origin of the judicial power, both in the United States and in Australia, must be looked for in the controlling *Origin of power.* powers that were exercised by the King in Council in respect to subordinate Constitutions. The grant of such Constitutions in North America, establishing legislatures with power to legislate not contrary to the grant, necessitated the existence of some controlling power to see that the power conferred was not exceeded. Such a power was naturally found in the King in Council who had made the grant. In the same way that courts of law in the United Kingdom will now examine the nature of the powers of corporations to

---

[1] Baker's *Annotated Constitution of the U.S.*, p. 21.

see whether the exercise of a particular authority has been exceeded or not, the King in Council was accustomed to examine the charters under which the Plantations were established for a like purpose.

By the time of Charles II, the power of the King to control legislation in Great Britain had ceased, for by this period the Parliament had established its independence of all controlling, prerogative rights ; but with regard to the Colonies, the royal jurisdiction was left untouched. Many of the Colonies were in the nature of corporations. The King, it was therefore said, could enquire as to whether they had properly discharged their corporate privileges. In England, about the same time, the royal power was judicially held to be competent, by information *quo warranto*, to suspend corporate rights. The corporate rights of the City of London were suspended, and when this precedent had been established, Judge Jeffreys, " made all the charters like the walls of Jericho fall down before him, and returned laden with the spoils."[1]

Jurisdiction of King in Council must not be confused.

This jurisdiction to examine as to whether an Act of a subordinate legislature was in excess of its authority must not be confused with the right of appeal to the King in Council, for both matters came before the King in Council.

The people of the United States were so familiar with the exercise of this jurisdiction that when they established their Supreme Court it was their intention that it should exercise a jurisdiction of a similar character but strictly judicial over both Federal and State laws.

The justices of the High Court of Australia and of other courts created by Parliament are appointed by the Governor-General in Council ; a judge is not removable except on addresses from both Houses of Parliament, presented in the same session, praying for his removal on the ground of proved misbehaviour or incapacity. The salary of a Judge cannot be diminished during his continuance in office. · ·

Similar provisions in Canada and South Africa have

[1] Hallam's *Constitutional History*, 8th Edition, Vol. II, p. 451.

ensured the independence of the Judiciary. The use of the words " proved misbehaviour or incapacity " in the Australian Constitution assures that a judge shall be first tried before he is condemned. The necessity for the insertion of these words was occasioned by the existence of the Act 22 George III, c. 75, which enabled a Governor to remove a Colonial Judge from office for absence without reasonable cause, or neglect, or misbehaviour.

The High Court has jurisdiction, subject to such excep- *Jurisdiction of High Court.* tions and subject to such regulations as Parliament may prescribe, to hear and determine appeals from all judgments, decrees, orders, and sentences—

(1) of any justice or justices exercising the original jurisdiction of the High Court ;

(2) of any other Federal Court or Court exercising Federal jurisdiction, or of the Supreme Court of any State, or of any other Court of any State from which at the establishment of the Commonwealth an appeal lies to the King in Council ;

(3) of the inter-State Commission, but as to questions of law only.

·Parliament has legislated in respect of the first two of these matters and has passed Judiciary Acts ; a judgment of the High Court is now final and conclusive in these cases. There is no appeal to the Judicial Committee as of right ; but since the King's prerogative right to admit an appeal is not taken away by express words, it therefore, remains, and is exercisable by special leave of the Judicial Committee.

The High Court is a Supreme Court of Federal jurisdic- *High Court supreme* tion, and is also a general Court of final Appeal for Australia. *Court of Federal* In the United States the Supreme Court is the highest *jurisdiction.* Federal Court, but is not a Court of final Appeal for other matters ; and, although the Supreme Court of Canada exercises Federal jurisdiction, it is, in its nature, mainly a general Court of final Appeal for Canada.

In 1903 the Federal Parliament passed a Judiciary *Judiciary* Act and a High Court of Practice and Procedure Act, *Act.*

regulating the legal constitution and organisation of the
High Court, and the distribution of the judicial power
between the High Court and the State Courts.

Congress passed a somewhat similar Act in 1789.

Section 74.   Section 74 of the Australian Constitution, the section that
was so much under debate when the Constitution Act was
before the Imperial Parliament, provides " that no appeal
shall be permitted to the King in Council from a decision
of the High Court upon a question howsoever arising as
to the limits *inter se* of the Constitutional powers of the
Commonwealth and those of any State or States, or as to
the limits *inter se* of the Constitutional powers of any
two or more States, unless the High Court shall certify,
that the question is one which ought to be determined by
his Majesty in Council. The High Court may so certify
if satisfied that for any special reason the certificate
shall be granted, and thereupon an appeal shall lie to
His Majesty in Council on the question without further
leave.

Except as provided in this section, this Constitution
shall not impair any right which the King may be pleased
to exercise by virtue of His Royal prerogative to grant
special leave of appeal from the High Court to His Majesty
in Council."

Parliament is empowered to " make laws limiting the
matters in which such leave may be asked ; but proposed
laws containing any such limitation must be reserved by
the Governor-General for His Majesty's pleasure."

Importance of   This section, which has given rise to much controversy,
Section 74.   marked the desire of Australia to act as the interpreters of
her own Constitution.   It has been said that neither English
judges nor lawyers, as a rule, were familiar with Federal law,
and the criticism was no doubt just.   Federal law in the
United States has ramified in thousands of ways, and given
rise to endless controversies and innumerable decisions, but
in England there has been little occasion, except in the
Canadian cases, to discuss its principles.   No University of
Law at present exists.   Colonial Constitutional law, as a

branch of study, is but little known. The Imperial Court
of Appeal, although its establishment has been promised
largely on the initiation of Australia at present, is not yet
established. ·If it should number, and it possibly may, in
the future, an adequate representation of the great Judges
of the Dominion among its members, controversies may
arise when the High Court may consider that Imperial
interests, or even the interests of Australia, may be so
affected, as to grant a certificate of leave to appeal, a course
that so far they have not adopted.

The High Court possesses original jurisdiction in all Original
jurisdiction.
matters (1) arising under any treaty ; (2) affecting consuls
or other representatives of other countries ; (3) in which
the Commonwealth, or a person suing or being sued on
behalf of the Commonwealth, is a party ; (4) between States
or between residents of different States, or between a State
and a resident of another State ; (5) in which a writ of
mandamus, or prohibition, or an injunction, is sought
against an officer of the Commonwealth.

Parliament may make laws conferring original jurisdiction
on the High Court in any matter—

(1) arising under the Constitution or involving its Parliament's
power to
confer
original
jurisdiction.
interpretation ;

(2) arising under any laws made by Parliament ;

(3) of Admiralty and maritime jurisdiction ;

(4) relating to the same subject-matter claimed under
the laws of different States.

With respect to any of the matters over which the High
Court has original jurisdiction, or in respect of any of the
matters of conferred jurisdiction, Parliament is empowered
to make laws (1) defining the jurisdiction of any Federal
Court other than the High Court ; (2) defining the extent
to which the jurisdiction of any Federal Court shall be
exclusive of that which belongs to or is invested in the
Courts of the States ; (3) investing any Court of a State
with Federal jurisdiction.

Parliament has legislated by the Judiciary Acts, 1903– Parliamentary
legislation
conferring
jurisdiction.
10, fixing the appointment and remuneration of the judges,

and excluding the jurisdiction of State Courts and investing State Courts with Federal jurisdiction and other matters. The appellate jurisdiction of the High Court in Australia includes jurisdiction to hear appeals from all judgments, decrees, orders, and sentences of the Central Court of the territory of Papua and appeals under the Land Tax Assessment Act of 1910. In numerous matters arising under laws made by the Commonwealth Parliament, including the Referendum Act, Parliament has also legislated.

Jurisdiction conferred to hear and determine questions of law. A new function was added to the judicial duties of the Judges by the Judiciary Act of 1910, which confers jurisdiction on the High Court to hear and determine any question of law as to the validity of any Act or enactment of Parliament. The matter must be heard and determined by a full Court, consisting of all the justices, except in cases where all cannot be present owing to illness.

Procedure. The Attorney-General of each State must be notified of the hearing of the matter, and he is entitled to appear or be represented in Court. The High Court of Justice may also direct that any person or class of persons, or associations claiming to be interested in the matter, shall be notified of the hearing of the matter, and be entitled to appear or be represented at the hearing.

Determination. The determination of the Court upon any matter shall be final and conclusive, and not subject to any appeal.

Canadian practice. The provisions of this Act bear some resemblance to Canadian Acts, passed with a view of ascertaining the likely validity of Dominion Acts, and doubtless it was directed to ensure a[1] reasonable measure of confidence in the Federal Legislature that the legislation passed by them was sound.

United States. The Supreme Court of the United States declines to entertain questions which do not arise directly out of litigation.[2] But a different course has been adopted in Canada, not without protest. The Commonwealth Parliament is empowered to make any laws conferring rights to proceed against the Commonwealth or a State in respect

[1] *Ante,* p. 224.
[2] *Ante,* pp. 80, 223.

of matters withing the limits of the Judicial Power. Legislation has been passed on these subjects.[1]

The trial on an indictment of any offence against any law of the Commonwealth must be by jury, and must be held in the State where the offence is committed. If not committed within any State, the trial must be held at such place or places as Parliament may prescribe.

Trial on indictment by jury.

[1] Claims against the Commonwealth Act. No. 21, 1902. Judiciary Act, 1903, No. 6, 1903.

The States. THE six States of Australia lost by Federation some portions of their power by voluntary surrender to the Federal Government in the same way as did the thirteen States of the United States in 1789.

Authority of the Constitution. The Constitution Act, however, which represents the Federal pact, is unlike the United States' Constitution, since it possesses no higher force than that which belongs to an Act of the Imperial Parliament. The declaration in the United States' Constitution states that the Constitution and the laws of the United States which shall be made in pursuance thereof and all Treaties made or which shall be made under the authority of the United States shall be the supreme law of the land. No such declaration as this is embodied in the Australian Constitution. The Constitution Act is not the only Act in force in Australia. Acts of the Imperial Parliament are in force, and it may be assumed that the Colonial Laws Validity Act applies to the Constitution.

States not created by the Constitution. The State Constitutions, like the States of the American Republic, were not created by the Constitution Act ; therefore, within their sphere, the State legislatures still possess, the amplest powers of legislation, subject only to the limits imposed by the Constitution. Every State has its executive power, legislative and judiciary ; but its executive and judiciary are not independent of the legislative, but subordinate to it. In this respect the Australian State is again unlike the State in the United States. The Constitution Act provided that the Constitution and all laws made by the Parliament of the Commonwealth, under the Constitution, should be binding on the Courts, judges, and people of every State, and of every part of the Commonwealth, notwithstanding anything in the laws of any State.

On the passing of the Constitution Act, the six Colonies of Australia immediately became States. As each Colony prior to Federation possessed a Constitution, so after Federation the Constitution of each State continued subject to the Constitution as at the establishment of the Common- wealth, or as at the admission or establishment of the State (as the case might be), until altered in accordance with the Constitution of the State. As has been previously pointed out,[1] every power of the Parliament of a State, unless the Constitution exclusively vests it in the Parliament of the Commonwealth, or withdraws it from the Parliament of the State, continues as at the establishment of the Common- wealth, or as at the admission or establishment of the State, as the case may be.

The Constitution Act took away certain definite portion of the States' powers, some of those termed exclusive, or which were necessarily exclusive became vested in the Commonwealth Parliament, and over this exclusive domain of Federal legislation the State Parliaments must not intrude.

In respect of another class of powers termed concurrent, that is to say, powers that are exercisable both by the Federal and State authorities, as soon as the Commonwealth Parliament passes legislation, the particular power to legis- late on the same subject is withdrawn from the State Parlia- ment ; but until the power has been exercised, State laws relating to any matter within the powers of the Parliament of the Commonwealth, in force as laws of the Colony before the Colony became a State, subject to the Con- stitution, still continue in force in the States ; and until pro- vision is made in that behalf by the Commonwealth, the State Parliaments possess such powers of alteration and repeal as the Parliament of a Colony had before it became a State. The States, therefore, as the Commonwealth Parliament exercises its powers by legislation, gradually lose some of these powers.

But when the exclusive and concurrent powers are deducted from the mass of powers, most of which were

[1] *Ante*, p. 323.

formerly exercised by the States, a large and ample area of
residuary power still remains with the States. Within this
area Commonwealth legislation is unable to intrude.

Extent of.

The residuary powers, amongst others, include control
over agriculture, education, State banking, borrowing of
money for State purposes ; corporations other than foreign
corporations and trading or financial corporations formed
within the limits of the Commonwealth, trade and commerce
within the States, taxation and inspection of goods to detect
fraud or to prevent infection, factories, licences, mines and
mining control and constitution of State railways, and many
other numerous and important powers.

Inconsistency
of laws.

To prevent a conflict which might arise from Commonwealth and State legislation, operating on the same subject
matter when a State law is inconsistent with a valid law of
the Commonwealth, the State law to the extent of the
inconsistency is invalid.

Power to
surrender
portion of a
State.

One power that was conferred upon a State Parliament
was the power to surrender any part of the State to the
Commonwealth, and upon such surrender and its acceptance by the Commonwealth, the part of the State surrendered
became subject to the exclusive jurisdiction of the
Commonwealth.

The Northern
Territories.

An instance of the exercise of this power is found in the
recent surrender of the Northern Territory to the Commonwealth by an Act of the Parliament of South Australia in
1907.

Common-
wealth Acts.

In 1910 the Commonwealth Government passed an Act[1]
taking over this territory ; and with it accepted some very
heavy liabilities. By the Northern Territory Acceptance
Act they defined the limits of the Northern Territory, ratified and approved an agreement between the two Governments, and constituted it a territory under the authority
of the Commonwealth.

Organisation
of Northern
Territory.

By another Act, the Northern Territory (Administration) Act,[2] they provided for its administration by an

[1] Northern Territory Acceptance, No. 20, 1910.
[2] No. 27 cf. 1910.

administrator to hold office for five years, appointed by the Governor-General by commission under the seal of the Commonwealth.

The States are entitled to levy on imports or exports, or Charges for on goods passing into or out of the States, such charges inspection laws. as may be necessary for executing the inspection laws of the State; but the net produce of all charges so levied are prescribed to be for the use of the Commonwealth.[1] The Commonwealth Parliament possesses power to annul any such inspection laws.

The provision resembles one in the United States Constitution.[2]

Fermented, distilled, or other intoxicating liquids passing Fermented liquids. into any State, or remaining therein for use, consumption, sale, or storage, are subject to the laws of the States, as if they had been produced in the States. Liquids answering this description are, therefore, subject to the licensing laws of the States.

The States are prohibited from raising or maintaining Prohibition against any naval or military forces, or from imposing any tax on raising naval property of any kind belonging to the Commonwealth, or military forces. without the consent of the Commonwealth Parliament; on the other hand, there is a corresponding duty on the part of the Commonwealth to protect every State from invasion Duty of Common- and, on the application of its Executive, from domestic wealth. violence. This provision is similar to one in the Constitution of the United States; but the State power to apply is there vested in the State Legislature and not in the executive, except when the Legislature is not sitting. In the United States there is what is known as " a peace of the United States;[3] therefore, the Federal Executive has a corresponding power to intervene to protect itself when domestic violence within the State interferes with Federal agencies, such as the carriage of mails or inter-State commerce." It was said " that the strong arm of the National

---

[1] Commonwealth of Australia Constitution Act, Sect. 112.
[2] *Ante*, p. 93.
[3] *Re* Neagle, 135, U.S. 1.

Government may be put forth to brush away all obstructions to the freedom of inter-State commerce or the transportation of the mails. If the emergency arises, the Army of the nation and all its Militia are at the service of the nation to compel obedience to its law. Is the army the only instrument by which the rights of the public can be enforced and the peace of the nation preserved ? Grant that any public nuisance may be forcibly abated either at the instance of the authorities or by any individual suffering private damage therefrom, the existence of this right of forcible abatement is not inconsistent with, nor does it destroy, the right of appeal in an orderly way to the courts for a judicial determination, and an exercise of their powers by writ of injunction and otherwise to accomplish the same results."[1]

Protection of States. The words " shall protect every State " cast a mandatory duty on the Commonwealth to protect the States against domestic violence. But could such a duty be legally enforced on the Commonwealth, if the Commonwealth declined to interfere ?

State property not taxable. The Commonwealth may not impose any tax on any property of the State.

Protection against State coinage. A prohibition in favour of the Federal powers is imposed by the prohibition that a State shall not coin money, nor make anything but gold and silver coin a legal tender in payment of debts. A prohibition is also imposed on the Commonwealth by a provision which, on the other hand, forbids the making of any law for establishing any religion or for imposing any religious observance, or for prohibiting the free exercise of any religion : no religious test can be required as a qualification for any office of public trust under the Commonwealth.

Rights of residents in States. The rights of residents in States are protected, since the Constitution declares that a subject of the King resident in any State shall not be subject to any disability or discrimination which would not be equally applicable to him if he were a subject of the King resident in such other

[1] Per Brewer, *Re* Debs., 158 U.S., 582.

State.[1] This provision is one of the few provisions that impede the State powers, which are limited at fewer points than are those of the legislatures of the American States. In the United States the Supreme Court has refused assent to the doctrine that the citizens of the several States are entitled to participate in all rights exclusively belonging to the citizens of another State, merely on the ground that they were enjoyed by those citizens.

A law of Virginia has accordingly been held valid that limited the enjoyment of the oyster fishery in Virginia to citizens of Virginia.[2]

The recognition of the laws of a State in another State *Recognition of State Laws.* is a matter of considerable importance. This recognition has been established by a provision which declares that full faith and credit shall be given throughout the Commonwealth to the laws, the public Acts and records, and the judicial proceedings of every State. The declaration conceives an inter-State official and judicial reciprocity of great value, capable of enforcement both by Commonwealth and State legislation.

All the States of Australia possess Governors appointed *State Constitutions.* by the Crown and bicameral legislatures. Since after Federation as many of their functions of Government devolved upon the Commonwealth, it was found desirable to limit the existing number of Ministers in some of the legislatures, and these have been accordingly reduced in the State House.

The Victorian Constitution Act of 1903, for instance, reduced the numbers of the Ministry from ten to eight, and the number of members in its Legislative Council from forty-eight to thirty-five. It, however, increased the number of the electoral provinces.

The Constitutions of the six States of Australia are not in all respects similar, since each State has been at liberty to alter its own Constitution. The States composing the United States possess a similar liberty. Any Bill, however,

---

[1] *Ante* United States' Constitution, p. 153; see also p. 157.
[2] McCready *v.* Virginia, 94, U.S. 391.

that alters an Australian State Constitution requires reservation for the King's pleasure when it alters the Constitution of the legislature of the State or of either of its Houses, affects the Governor's salary, or is under any Act of the legislature of the State passed after the passing of the Australian States' Constitution Act, 1907[1] or under any provision contained in the Bill itself required to be reserved. Nothing in the Act affects the reservation of Bills, in accordance with instructions given by His Majesty to the Governor, nor does the Act affect cases where it has been necessary to pass a temporary law which the Governor expressly declares necessary to be assented to forthwith by reason of some public and pressing emergency. Nor is it necessary to reserve any Bill when the Governor declares that he withholds His Majesty's Assent, or if he has previously received instructions from His Majesty to assent and does assent accordingly to the Bill. The Act further explains the nature of the alterations of the legislature of a State or of either House which require the reservation of the Bill.

The State Parliaments of Australia are utterly unlike the Provincial legislatures of Canada. The Provincial legislatures of Canada possess certain enumerated powers, which are subject to control by the Dominion Government and by the Judiciary if they are exceeded ; they also have no direct right of communication to the King through their Lieutenant-Governors, as the Australian States have through their Governors. The Secretary of State for the Dominion occupies the same position towards them that the Secretary of State for the Imperial Government exercises towards the Australian States.

With one exception, the many restraints imposed by the United States' Constitution on State action in the interest of personal liberty are absent from the Australian Constitution ; consequently the States' Parliaments enjoy the fullest powers not impliedly prohibited by the sharp distinctions existing between the executive, the legislative, and judicial powers in America.

[1] 7 Edward VII, c. 67.

As in all Federal Constitutions, there was a transition period whilst the State agencies which devolve upon the Commonwealth by the Constitution Act were in course of transference. Financial provisions of considerable import- Financial provisions of the Constitution. ance, therefore, required to be inserted in the Constitution Act. The creation of a Commonwealth consolidation fund, subject to appropriations at law by the Commonwealth Parliament, necessarily diminished the States' financial resources, as they were consequently deprived of certain revenues which had hitherto been controlled by the State Parliaments, such as Customs and Excise. Until the imposition of uniform duties of Customs, which were imposed within two years, the Commonwealth was required to credit to each State, month by month, the revenues collected by the Commonwealth in that State, after debiting it with (1) the expenditure of the Commonwealth, incurred solely for the maintenance or continuance, as at the time of transfer, of any transferred department ; (2) the proportion of the State, according to the number of its people, in the other expenditure of the Commonwealth. Provision was also made for the payment, month by month, of the balance (if any) in favour of the States.

During the first five years after the imposition of uniform duties of Customs, until the Commonwealth Parliament " Braddon Clause." otherwise provided, the credit basis of the State was not the collection of duties of Customs and excise, but consumption of imports or goods·produced or manufactured in the State. After five years from the imposition of uniform duties of Customs, the Commonwealth Parliament could provide, on such bases as it thought fair, for the monthly payment to the several States of the surplus revenue to the Commonwealth. Certain provisions were made in favour of Western Australia. During a period of ten years from the establishment of the Constitution, it was required that not more than one-fourth of the net revenue of the Commonwealth from duties of Customs and Excise should be applied by the Commonwealth towards its expenditure. The balance was to be paid, in accordance with the

Constitution, to the several States, or to the payment of interest on the debts taken over by the Commonwealth.

The Braddon clause, as this was called, gave rise to endless discussions, and no less than eleven conferences took place, during 1901 and 1909, between State Ministers and, occasionally, Commonwealth Ministers, on this subject.

In August, 1909, a final agreement was reached; and although the terms of this agreement were rejected at a Referendum, they were embodied in the Surplus Revenue Bill, which received the Royal Assent on September 2nd, 1910. This Act repealed the Braddon Clause, so far as it affected the power of the Commonwealth to apply any portion of the net revenue of Customs and Excise towards its expenditure, and also so far as it affected the payment of any balance by the Commonwealth to the several States, or the application of such balance towards the payment of interest on the debts of the several States taken over by the Commonwealth; and substituted provisions under which the Commonwealth now pays to each State, for a period of ten years, as from July 1st, 1910, and thereafter, until Parliament otherwise provides, an annual sum amounting to 25s. per head of the number of the people of the States. In addition, Western Australia receives £250,000, payable by monthly instalments, to be progressively diminished in each subsequent year by £10,000.

Revenue of State Governments. The State finances consist of these payments from the Commonwealth and revenue derived from State taxation and other sources. With reference to the State debts, the Commonwealth Parliament may take them as they existed at the time of the establishment of the Commonwealth, or a proportion of them, according to the respective numbers of the people, as shown by the latest statistics of the Commonwealth; and may convert, renew, or consolidate such debts or any part thereof. The States, however, must indemnify the Commonwealth in respect of the debts taken over, and thereafter the interest payable in respect of the debts taken over must be deducted and retained from the portions of the surplus revenue of the Commonwealth payable to the several States, or if such surplus be insufficient, or if there is no surplus, then the deficiency or the whole amount must be paid by the several States.

An appeal lies direct from the State Courts to the Judicial Committee where an appeal lies other than on Federal matters which come within the provisions of section 74.

CHAPTER XXXI

THE AMENDMENT OF THE CONSTITUTION AND
CREATION OF NEW STATES

The Referendum. THE Constitution cannot be altered in its main features except by the Referendum, but Parliament may make some changes in it, where the power has been expressly conferred *Provisions of Referendum.* upon it.[1] The Referendum was introduced for the purpose *After passing of the pro-* of obtaining the considered opinion of the people on pro-*posed law by absolute* posed alterations. The Constitution Act declares that any *majority of both Houses.* proposed law for the alteration of the Constitution must be passed by an absolute majority of each of the Houses of the Federal Parliament and not less than two or more than six months after its passage through both Houses the pro-*Submission to* posed law must be submitted in each State to the electors *the electors of each State.* qualified to vote for the election of members of the House of Representatives.

Where one House fails to pass. Should either House pass any such proposed law by an absolute majority and the other House reject or fail to pass it or pass it with any Amendment to which the first men-*Deadlock provisions.* tioned House will not agree, and then if after an interval of three months the first-mentioned House in the same or the next session again passes the proposed law by an absolute majority with or without any amendment which has been made or agreed to by the other House and such other House rejects or fails to pass it or passes it with any amendment to which the first-mentioned House will not agree the *Submission to the* Governor-General may submit the proposed law as last *electors of each State.* proposed by the first-mentioned House, and either with or without amendments subsequently agreed to by both Houses to the electors in each State qualified to vote for the election of the House of Representatives. The voting takes place in the manner prescribed by Parliament. If *Majorities required.* in a majority of the States a majority of the electors voting approve the proposed law, and if a majority of all the electors

[1] *Ante,* p. 339.

voting also approve the proposed **law** it must be presented to the Governor-General for the Royal Assent.

The provisions that protect the representation of individual States in the Federal Parliament have already been referred to.[1]

It will be observed that the sole initiation of amendments to the Constitution in either House is left to the Government of the Commonwealth, and that the State Parliaments cannot propose amendments to the Constitution as in the United States. Again, an absolute majority in both Houses of Parliament is required. Two-thirds is necessary in the United States' Congress, or the concurrence of three-fourths of the State legislatures when the proposal is initiated by them. *Compared with United States.*

Whilst the deadlock provisions with reference to proposed laws apply to proposed laws originated by the House of Representatives only, the deadlock provisions relating to constitutional amendments apply to proposed laws originating in the one House, and rejected by the other. The reason for this may be found in the fact that the Senate takes to some extent the place of the State legislatures in the United States and for this reason possesses a power of originating amendments to the Constitution on behalf of the States.

Federal and democratic principles are strikingly in evidence in the submission of the question to the people of the States.

If in a majority of the States a majority of the electors voting approve the proposed law and a majority of all the electors of Australia voting approve, the proposed law must then be presented to the Governor-General for the King's Assent.

The most extensive powers are conferred on the people by these provisions for amendment, and possibly the Constitution itself might be repealed under them. *Extensive power.*

Acts have been passed providing for the taking of the Referendum.[2] In 1911, owing to decisions of the High *Referendum Acts. Referendum of 1911.*

---

[1] *Ante*, p. 303.
[2] Referendum (Constitution Alteration) Acts, 1906-10.

Court on questions of trade and labour, Referenda were taken on two Bills altering the Constitution—the Legislative Powers Bill and the Taking Over of Monopolies. The Government proposals, however, were defeated by large majorities in all the States except Western Australia.

The defeat of these proposals at the Referendum has been explained in many ways. In the main it probably indicated a desire on the part of the people not to interfere with the powers of the States and the Constitution.

Altering boundaries of States.
The democratic principle of consulting the people is not confined solely to constitutional amendments. In addition to those already stated, when the Parliament of the Commonwealth, with the consent of the Parliament of a State, proposes to increase, diminish, or otherwise alter the limits of the State upon such terms and conditions as may be agreed on, the approval of the majority of the electors of the State voting upon the question is required.

Establishment of new States.
Provision is made by the Constitution for the admission or establishment of new States. The power is somewhat similar to one in the Constitution of the United States, but it is more extensive. In Canada provinces existing at the time of Federation were admitted on addresses by the Canadian and Provincial Parliaments, subject, however, to Royal approval.

Authority of Parliament.
On the admission or on the establishment of a new State, the Commonwealth Parliament may make or impose such terms and conditions, including the extent of representation in either House of the Parliament as it may think fit.

A new State may be formed by separation of territory from a State, but only with the consent of its Parliament ; and a new State may be formed by the union of two or more States or parts of States, but only with the consent of the Parliament of the States affected.

Classes of States.
The Constitution recognises the existence of two classes of States : (1) Original States, and (2) New States.

The first class consists of the present six Australian States and New Zealand, which were qualified to form the Federation. The second class consists of States which may be subsequently admitted or established   The States capable of admission are New Zealand, Fiji, and New Guinea, and any other political communities already in existence at the time of Federation, and in addition any other colonies which have since sprung into existence.   The establishment of new States also contemplates their formation out of Federal territory, as, for instance, out of the Northern territory, or by partition of a State and the erection of its several parts into new States, or by a union of two States, or by junction of adjacent portions of two or more States forming one State.

At the present time New Zealand is not entitled to join the Australian Federation as of right.   Her admission would be dependent upon the will of the Federal Parliament.

In the United States no new State can be formed or erected within the jurisdiction of any other State nor any State be formed by the junction of two or more States without the consent of the Legislatures of the States concerned, as well as of Congress.   The Australian Constitution, with its more democratic principles, requires the consent of the people.

The territories of the Commonwealth include the south-eastern portion of New Guinea nearest Australia, called Papua, which was transferred from Queensland to the Commonwealth by proclamation on 1st Sept., 1906, under the authority of the Papua Act (Commonwealth Act), 1905, and the islands of Trobriand, Woodlark, D'Entrecasteaux, and the Louisiada, and the newly acquired Northern Territory.

CHAPTER XXXII

THE NATURE OF THE AUSTRALIAN CONSTITUTION

THE Australian Constitution is a great Federal instrument, in many respects modelled upon the Constitution of the United States, yet in many matters distinguishable. It was founded on agreement, and therefore partakes both of the character of an Act of Parliament and of an international agreement made between the people of the self-governing Australian Colonies, and also between the people of the Colonies and the United Kingdom. For the Preamble recites that the people of New South Wales, Victoria, South Australia, Queensland, and Tasmania, humbly relying on the blessings of the Almighty God, have agreed to unite in one indissoluble Federal Commonwealth, under the Crown of the United Kingdom of Great Britain and Ireland, and under the Constitution hereby established.

The object of the advocates of Federation was not to establish a sort of municipal union government by a joint committee, like the Union of Parishes for the administration of the Poor Laws, say, in the Isle of Wight, but the foundation of an Australian Commonwealth embracing the whole Continent with Tasmania, having a national character and exercising the most ample powers of self-government consistent with allegiance to the British Crown.

Characteristics of Commonwealth. The four main characteristics of the Commonwealth, according to Professor Dicey, are, first, a Federal form of Government; secondly, a Parliamentary Executive; thirdly, an effective method for amending the Constitution; fourthly, the maintenance of the relation which exists between the United Kingdom and a self-governing colony.

The Australian Federation is one of the best examples of a purely Federal Government in fixing the respective limits of Federal and State Government. As in the United States, the powers of the Federal Government are defined but the powers of the States are not defined. The residue of power is, therefore, left with the State Governments. The Federal principle is evidenced in the composition of the Senate and the equality of State representation, whilst the national principle finds expression in the House of Representatives. No Federal veto exists, as in Canada, and unless the Federal power in respect of legislation is transcended by State laws, State laws possess as much force and validity as Federal laws.

The Australian Constitution has largely followed the United States' Constitution, but after over one hundred years of the working of the latter, the framers of the former were able to observe and largely obviate its imperfections.

In the Australian Constitution the powers are far more fully enumerated than in the United States' Constitution. Although the latter Constitution is one of enumerated powers, yet so few powers were at the time enumerated that it was necessary to discover or invent implied powers and implied prohibitions to create a proper working system.

Although a Constitution it is a legislative enactment and must be interpreted according to the rules which relate to the interpretation of Constitutions. In Australia the legislative powers either belong to the Parliament of the Commonwealth or the Parliament of the State, and there is no further reservation, as in the United States' Constitution, to the people. It has been pointed out that owing to the reservation of power to the States or the people in America, it was possible to infer powers not otherwise expressed, and such as the Judges thought necessary for the purposes of the National Government.[1] The full enumeration of powers in the Australian Constitution leaves little room either for implied powers or implied prohibitions, therefore, in examining the decisions of the Supreme Court of the United States modern decisions require to be traced back to their source to see how far they are applicable to the interpretation of powers in the Australian Constitution. The people willed the United States' Constitution, in other

Implied powers and prohibitions.

[1] *Ante*, p. 87.

words they enacted it. In the Australian Constitution, although the people willed it they did not enact it. As the States were parties to the surrender of their powers expressed through the consent of the people, the Constitution is a treaty or pact, which cannot be altered so far as the powers of the Commonwealth or the States are concerned without the consent of the people expressed through the medium of the Referendum, nor till the Commonwealth or one of the contracting parties chooses to submit the issue to the people.

The Australian Constitution is by far the most democratic of all the four Constitutions, and this is seen by the Referendum provisions, and the special provisions which exist compelling a reference of certain questions to the people of the States, such as alteration of State boundaries. It is also seen in the method of direct election to the Senate, by the people of the States.

The Constitution contains the well-known triple division of powers, but the powers of the Executive, Legislative and Judicial departments are not so sharply defined as in the United States' Constitution.

Whilst the Constitution may be stated to be a rigid one in the sense that it is incapable of any fundamental alteration by Parliament, it can be altered in many respects by Parliamentary legislation.

. Responsible Government and the Parliamentary Cabinet also distinguish it from the United States' Constitution.

On the other hand, the Australian Constitution contains no declaration of rights guaranteeing individual liberty such as is embodied in the United States' Constitution. It was unnecessary.

As a Constitution, however, it enacts the principles of Government borrowed from the Mother Country, and in some instances considerably improves upon them, and with the English Common law contains every safeguard of personal freedom.

Like the Canadian Constitution, it recognises the relationship with the Mother Country, and its maintenance. " The founders of the Commonwealth have admittedly been influenced at once by a growing sense of Australian nationality, and by an enduring or even increasing loyalty to the Motherland."[1]

The Australian Constitution is a great Imperial Constitution, and as an instrument of government a work of the greatest skill. It was fashioned by Australian statesmen after a long deliberation and an exhaustive examination into the merits of other Constitutions.

Its language is generally clear and well chosen, and amongst Federal Constitutions it must always take the very highest rank.

[1] Dicey, 6th Edition, p. 483.

CHAPTER XXXIII

THE CONSTITUTIONAL DEVELOPMENT OF SOUTH AFRICA

Surrender of South Africa by Dutch. THE surrender of Cape Colony by the Dutch on the **16th** September, **1795,** brought together two branches of **the** same race : conquerors and conquered were of the same stock. During the centuries, however, that had separated them, their training had been different, so that many slight variations had arisen. In the most important features their characters were the same ; each regarded the variations in the other as blemishes, and often made more of them than they merited.[1] After the surrender for a time the **Government of new Colony.** government of the newly-acquired colony was carried out by the naval and military authorities, Admiral Elphinstone and Generals Clarke and Craig acting conjointly. A joint proclamation issued soon after appointed Major Craig commandant of the Cape of Good Hope. The government carried on by him was despotic but fair. In **1796** Earl Macartney was appointed by King George III as the first Governor. He was invested with almost absolute power, subject, however, to the controlling authority of the Home Government.

The Treaty of Amiens. By the Treaty of Amiens on the **27th March, 1802,** the Cape of Good Hope was restored by the British Government to the Batavian Republic. On the **30th** of December, General Dundas, the then Governor, issued a proclamation absolving the people of the Colony from their allegiance to the Crown as from **1st** Jan., **1803.** The formal cession, however, of the Colony by the British did not take place till **20th** Feb., **1803.**

Recapture of Colony. Final surrender of the Cape, 1814. In **1806** the Colony was recaptured by British forces under Major-General Baird, and in **1814,** by a Convention, the newly restored Sovereign of the Netherlands, restored on the fall of Napoleon, finally ceded the Cape to Great Britain,

[1] Theal's *History of South Africa,* Vol. III, pp. 1-2.

and it has ever since remained a portion of the Imperial dominions.

For some few years after 1814, with the exception of some British officials and soldiers, and a few merchants and missionaries, the Dutch constituted the large bulk of the population. In the year 1819–1820 about 5,000 British emigrants were brought from the Motherland and settled in the country between Port Elizabeth and Grahamstown. To these colonists is due the predominance of British nationality in the eastern districts of the Cape Provinces. [1]

In 1825 the Government of the country, which up till then had been carried on by a succession of Governors who were practically absolute, was altered, and a Council of six was appointed to advise the Governor, who was required to submit to the Council ordinances, public orders, and proclamations. The Governor, however, was empowered for good reason to act in opposition to the opinion of a majority of the Council. The Council could discuss no question unless it had been proposed by the Governor. The Governor had the further power of dismissing any member of the Council that he wished, so that on the whole there was very little advance made on the road to self-government.

Council established.

In 1825 it was proposed to divide the Colony into two provinces, and Major-General Bourke was, in fact, appointed the Lieutenant-Governor of the eastern portion. The proposed division was abandoned before it was actually carried out. In 1828 a Supreme Court was established, consisting of a Chief Justice and three puisne judges. Circuit Courts were also directed to be held twice a year in the chief villages throughout the Colony, and at the same time the Colony was divided into the Eastern and Western Provinces.

Proposal to divide Colony.

Establishment of Supreme Court.

After the failure of two attempts on the part of the Colonists to obtain a Representative Government by petition to the Imperial Parliament, in 1831, they appealed to the King in Council, praying for the form of government that could be granted by an exercise of the Royal Prerogative,

Appeal for King's prerogative Government.

[1] Worsfold, *The Union of South Africa*, p. 104.

24—(2125)

and which had in former times been granted to the American Plantations, namely, a Governor and an Executive Council appointed by the Crown, and a Legislative Assembly chosen by the people. In 1833 slavery was abolished.

Changes
in 1833.
In the same year a constitutional change took place. A Legislative Council was established consisting of not less than ten nor more than twelve members, exclusive of the Governor. Certain officials were entitled to seats on this body by virtue of their offices. For the remaining seats members were selected by the Governor, to hold office during residence and good behaviour, unless their appointments were disallowed by the Secretary of State within two years from the date of their nomination. An Executive Council was also established at this time. In 1835 the Great Trek took place. The Boers in the Eastern districts of the Colony resolved to leave their lands and divest themselves of their allegiance to the British Government. Amongst other reasons which induced this step may be given: the abolition of slavery; the continual depredations of the Kaffirs, their overbearing conduct, and their being placed on an equal footing with Christians. The motives of the Great Trek were placed on record by Piet Retief, an exact translation of which was published in the *Grahamstown Journal* of February 2nd, 1837; although the Boers emigrated they received no official status till the Conventions of 1852 and 1854 were signed. It is estimated that 10,000 men, women and children left the Cape between 1835 to 1838.[1]

The signing of the two Conventions, known as the Sand River in 1852 and Bloemfontein 1854, granted internal
Constitution
of 1853.
independence to the Boers. In 1853 a new Constitution was introduced at the Cape under which the legislative authority was declared to consist of a Governor appointed by the Crown for six years, and two Chambers, an Upper House or Legislative Council, and a Lower House or House of Assembly. Both Houses were elected by the people, and the former body up till 1874 continued to be composed of eleven members who sat for the Western, and ten who sat

[1] Worsfold, *The Union of South Africa*, p. 107.

for the Eastern Province, elected by the whole body of the electors.

In 1874 the country was divided into seven electoral provinces. Each of the new divisions returned three members to the Legislative Council; a property qualification was required of candidates, and it was also necessary that a candidate should be thirty years of age, and invited to stand on the written requisition of not less than twenty-five electors. The practice of cumulative voting was introduced. Members of the Council were elected for a term of ten years, and the rota principle adopted, under which half of the Council retired at the end of five years. Division into provinces. Alterations in 1874.

No property qualification was required by candidates for the House of Assembly. The members of this House were chosen by the electors of towns and by the electors of electoral districts, to serve as representatives for a period of five years. The Chamber consisted of sixty-eight members. Responsible Government had been already introduced into this Colony in 1872, two years prior to these important changes taking place. No property qualification required for membership of the House of Assembly.

The electoral franchise was fixed by the Constitution for both Houses. The qualification required was the occupation of fixed property worth £25, or the receipt of wages of not less than £50 a year. Franchise.

The earliest settlers in Natal were Englishmen who settled at Durban in 1824. Between 1848 and 1850 some 4,000 British immigrants were introduced.

Natal was annexed as a district to Cape Colony in August, 1845. In the November following it received a separate government, which was administered by a Lieutenant-Governor, under the general control of the Governor of Cape Colony. The Executive Council of Natal was composed of the Lieutenant-Governor and four chief officials who formed the Executive Council. The Legislative Council consisted of the Lieutenant-Governor and three principal officers. In 1856 Natal was separated from Cape Colony, and received a Legislative Council that consisted of sixteen members, twelve of whom were elected and four of whom Annexation of Natal, 1845. Alteration in Government of Natal.

were nominated. In 1869 the Governor received power to add two elected members of the Legislative Council to the Executive Council. In 1883 the Legislative Council consisted of thirty members, twenty-three elected, seven nominated ; two of the latter, however, held office during the Royal pleasure.

In 1893 the Natal Act, No. 14, established a new Constitution. The Act was entitled " An Act to provide for the Establishment of Responsible Government in Natal." A Legislative Council of eleven, which was subsequently altered in 1898 to twelve members, was chosen by the Governor in Council and formed the Upper House. The qualification of a candidate was a ten years' residence in the Colony, a property qualification and age qualification (a member could not be less than thirty years old). A member was nominated for a period of ten years. The rota principle was adopted, by which half the members retired at the end of the fifth year.

The Legislative Assembly consisted of thirty-seven members, which was increased to thirty-nine in 1898.

In 1877 the Transvaal was annexed, but in 1880 the revolt of the Transvaal Boers led to the Convention of Pretoria. The subsequent history of the Boer Republics embraces the years of the Jameson raid, the premiership of Rhodes, the Boer war and the Governorship of Lord Milner.

The Transvaal and Orange River Colonies, which passed under Imperial domination at the close of the Boer War, had been promised the right of self-government as one of the terms of peace. The Imperial Government fulfilled its promise by giving to the Transvaal a representative Government consisting of a Single Chamber with the addition of nominee members.

In 1906 Responsible Government in the Transvaal was created under letters patent. A year later Responsible Government was given to the Orange River Colony.

Important features of the self-governing instruments were the reservation of native affairs to the Governor, who acted independently of his Ministers in respect of labour

1883.

Constitution of 1893.

Transvaal and Orange River.

Introduction of Responsible Government.

Features of.

carried on under conditions of servitude, and the commission to him of the Land Settlement policy for a period of five years.

In **1877** an Imperial Act had been passed which had provided for the Union under one Government of such of the South African Colonies and States as might agree thereto, and for the Government of such Union. The Act, however, never came into operation. It provided for a voluntary Union enabling any two or more of the Colonies or States of South Africa to join or confederate together in one Union under one general Government and Legislation. The Union proposed for establishment bore a resemblance to that at present in existence in Canada, the distribution of legislative powers between the Union Parliament and Provinces closely following that of the British North America Act, but there was an absence of all concurrent powers, with the solitary exception of immigration. A special power, however, was given to vary the distribution of powers by order in Council by the adoption of a certain stated procedure. Act of 1877.

The desire for closer Union which had failed to be realised under the Act of **1877** became keen at the close of the war. There was the wish to reconcile the two English and Dutch races under the Crown. Disunion could not for ever prevail. Whilst the two races were closely allied in kinship they were not separated as in Canada by such strong dividing ties of race and religion. Both races were mainly of the Protestant faith, and Briton and Boer, in many an ensanguined field, had learned the lesson how to respect each other.

No long years were to elapse in the making of a **Constitution**. One hundred and fourteen years from the time that the British flag flew at the Cape, South Africa in Union was prepared to take her place as one of the great dominions or Sister States of the Empire.

Failure of
Earl
Carnarvon's
proposals.

As early as in **1858** the Orange Free State desired Federation,
and the question was again to the fore in **1871** on the discussion of self-government for the Cape. In **1875** Lord
Carnarvon made proposals for a Federation, but with the
same result that followed Earl Grey's suggestions for
Federation in Australia. The movement did not originate
in the universal desire of the Colonies themselves and consequently failed. The Federal idea requires to be slowly
instilled into the minds of the people by the consciousness
of its advantages brought home to them by their necessities.

Position
in 1875.

In **1875** neither the Orange Free State nor the Transvaal
were prepared to abate one jot of their independence.
Natal did not possess Responsible Government, and the
Cape of Good Hope had but recently obtained a new
Constitution.

Lord Carnarvon's proposals were not statesmanlike.
The Cape considered that they should have been left to
decide the number of their representatives and their manner
of selection to any Conference called for the purpose of
Federation, and not be left merely to assent to an already
prepared scheme.

Froude's
part in
negotiations.

In the negotiations which followed in South Africa
Mr. Froude took a prominent part, but his actions were
unhappily marred by indiscretions. The rebellion in the
Transvaal and the subsequent alteration of affairs that then
took place for the time being put an end to all hopes of Union.

Movement
practical at
close of
Boer War.

·At the close of the Boer War, however, Federation once
more became a practical question.

Two steps in advance had then been taken, the formation
of an Intercolonial Council providing for a common administration of the railways of the Transvaal and Orange River,

and for the expenditure of the South African Constabulary and the establishment of a Customs Union for the four colonies and Rhodesia, together with the territories administered by the High Commissioner for South Africa.

The Intercolonial Council, however, did not gain in public estimation and was ultimately dissolved. *Failure of Intercolonial Council.*

The subsequent rapid acceleration of the Union Movement was due as in the case of the United States prior to 1789, to financial difficulties, and in addition to railway disputes, and fears of native rebellions.

In 1906, the Customs Union Convention was renewed for two years. In the same year Mr. Lionel Curtis, the Assistant *Meeting of the Convention.* Colonial Secretary for Urban Affairs in the Transvaal Crown Colony Administration, with the aid of his colleagues drew up a statement showing the urgent necessity for administrative union. The work of Mr. Lionel Curtis was embodied in a memorandum which was sent to the South African Governments on Jan. 7th, 1907, and published for the use of the general public in the following July. On the assembly of the Intercolonial Conference on Customs and Railway Rates to provide for its renewal, it became apparent that some forward step must be taken ; for the Transvaal Government had given notice of its intention of retiring from the Customs Union. Under these circumstances the representatives of the four self-governing Colonies passed a series of resolutions pledging their respective Governments to take steps to create a Central Government. A National Convention was summoned and met at Durban on October 8th. Amongst the distinguished men who assembled as delegates of the Colonies were Mr. Merriman (Prime Minister) Mr. Malan, Sir Henry (now Lord) de Villiers (President of the Convention), and Sir Starr Jameson, from the Cape. Natal was represented by her Prime Minister, Mr. Moor. From the Transvaal came General Louis Botha (Prime Minister), General J. C. Smuts, Sir George Farrar and Sir Percy Fitzpatrick ; from the Orange River Colony came Mr. Fischer (Prime Minister) and ex-President Steyn.

Rhodesia sent Sir William Milton (the Administrator) and Sir Lewis Mitchell (a director of the Chartered Company). One of the many problems that the Convention had to discuss was whether to recommend a federal system or a more unified form of government. The leanings of so many of the delegates were in favour of a more unified form of government that Mr. Jan Hofmeyr, the veteran leader of the Afrikander Bond in the Cape Colony, was understood to have refused nomination on the ground of his well-known preference for a federal Union.[1] Unification was strongly urged by the Transvaal delegates, and ultimately a legislative Union was adopted such as exists at the present moment in the United Kingdom. As in the United Kingdom so in South Africa, there is a recognition of the federal principle in the composition of the Second Chamber, but there is a difference in the Constitution, for a form of Home Rule was conferred upon the Provinces.

The delegates, after sitting at Durban and Cape Town, in the early months of 1909 produced a Bill for the Union of South Africa.

Proposed Act laid before Parliaments. The proposed Act was shortly afterwards laid before the four Colonial Parliaments of the Cape, Natal, Transvaal, and Orange River, and amendments were discussed.

Referendum in Natal. In Natal there were several amendments proposed, and the Government insisted on a Referendum being taken in that Colony.

Further meeting of the Convention. The Convention again met at Bloemfontein in May, and considered the proposed amendments, and then reaffirmed the draft Bill with alterations. Except in the case of Natal no Referendum was ever taken.

Delegates appointed to proceed to England. Delegates were appointed by the Parliaments to proceed to England, and subsequently the Bill was translated into an Act by the Imperial Parliament.

Writing of the formation of the Union, Mr. Keith offers an undoubtedly just criticism : " It must be confessed that the precedents were in favour of a fuller consultation of the electors than was in this case required. It must be admitted,

---

[1] Worsfold, *The Union of South Africa*, p. 125.

moreover, that the Parliaments then existing were not elected
with a view to Union or Federation, and that it is somewhat
contrary to principle that Parliaments elected merely for
the ordinary conduct of public affairs should accept an
arrangement which sanctions the abolition of their separate
existence."[1]

[1] Keith's *Responsible Government in the Dominions* (1912), pp. 949-50.

CHAPTER XXXV

THE UNION EXECUTIVE POWER

Executive power; how styled.
" THE Executive power " is termed " the Executive Government." In the Union of South Africa it may be administered *By whom exercised.* by the King in person or by a Governor-General as his representative. The Governor-General receives an annual salary of ten thousand pounds, which is payable to the King out of the Consolidated Revenue of the Union. This sum cannot be altered during his continuance in office.

The general powers of a Governor-General have been dealt with elsewhere.[1] The Governor-General of the Union of South Africa, however, possesses certain special powers, and his authority is subject to some special limitations.

Power to dissolve Senates.
Thus, his power of dissolving the Senate is limited, since he cannot dissolve it until the expiration of ten years from the establishment of the Union.[2]

When Royal authority required.
The provisions of the Union Act relative to the Governor-General apply to the Governor-General for the time being, or to such person as the King may appoint to administer the affairs of the Union. The Royal authority must be obtained should the Governor-General desire to appoint any person to be his deputy within the Union during his temporary absence. A Deputy Governor may exercise such of the powers and authorities vested in the Governor-General as the Governor-*Effect of appointment of deputy.* General may assign him, subject to any limitations expressed or directions given by the King. An appointment of a deputy, however, does not affect the exercise by the Governor-General himself of any power or function.

Executive Council.
In discharge of his functions in the Government of the Union the Governor-General is advised by an Executive Council. The Governor-General, when acting with their advice, is described as the Governor-General in Council.

[1] *Ante,* p. 201.
[2] See *post,* the Legislative Power, p. 388.

378

The members of this Council are chosen by and summoned by the Governor-General, and sworn as executive Councillors. They hold office during his pleasure.

The Governor-General appoints the Ministry, but by the theory of Responsible Government its members must be chosen from the party which is in power. The Ministry must not exceed ten in number, and ministers administer such departments of State of the Union as the Governor-General in Council establishes. Ministers must be members of the Executive Council. The first ministry was constituted as follows : Prime Minister and Minister of Agriculture, General the Right Hon. L. Botha ; Minister of Railways and Harbours, the Hon. T. W. Sauer ; the Minister of the Interior, Minister of Mines and Minister of Defence, General the Hon. J. C. Smuts ; Minister of Justice, the Hon. J. B. M. Hertzog ; Minister of Education, the Hon. F. S. Malan ; Minister of Finance, the Hon. H. C. Hull ; Minister of Lands, the Hon. A. Fischer ; Minister of Native Affairs, the Hon. H. Burton ; Minister of Commerce and Industries, Colonel the Hon. G. Leuchars ; Minister of Public Works and Minister of Posts and Telegraphs, the Hon. Sir D. P. de V. Graaf ; Minister without Portfolio, Senator the Hon. Dr. C. O'Grady Gubbins. The addition of an honorary minister or ministers without a portfolio does not affect the rule that there must be only ten ministers. No minister can hold office for longer than three months unless he is or becomes a member of either House of Parliament. The administration of justice is specially controlled by a Minister of State, in whom vests all powers, authorities, and functions which were at the establishment of the Union vested in the Attorney-General of the Colonies, except the powers, authorities, and functions relating to the prosecution of crimes and offences. These particular powers are now vested in the Attorney-Generals of the Provinces, who are appointed by the Governor-General in Council. The Attorney-Generals must discharge such other duties as may be assigned to them.

The appointment and removal of all officers in the Public

Number of Ministry.

Must be Members of Executive Council.

Minister of Justice.

Appointment and removal of all officers in the Public Service. Service is vested in the Governor-General in Council, unless the appointment is delegated by the Governor-General in Council, or by the Union Act, or by a law of the Parliament to some other authority.

Powers, authorities, and functions of Government. On the establishment of the Union all powers, authorities, and functions which were formerly vested in the Governor or in the Governor in Council, or in any authority of the Colony, so far as they continue to exist and were capable of exercise, become vested in the Governor-General or the Governor-General in Council, except such of the powers as may by the Constitution Act or a law of the Parliament, be vested in some other authority.

Seats of Executive and Legislature. The seat of the Executive Government is fixed at Pretoria, and is apart from the seat of the Legislature which meets at Cape Town. This was the result of a compromise to avoid the difficulties attendant on the fixing of a federal capital.

The Governor-General possesses certain duties in relation to the issue of commissions for the delimitation of electoral divisions. [1]

With regard to Bills presented to him for the King's Assent, he must declare according to his discretion but subject to the provisions of the Constitution Act, and the instructions that he receives from time to time from the Imperial Government that he assents in the King's name or that he withholds assent or that he reserves the Bill for the signification of the King's pleasure.

What Bills require reservation. All Bills repealing or amending any provisions as to the assent or dissent or reservation of Bills must be reserved, so must any Bill which affects to repeal or amend any of the provisions relative to the House of Assembly, or Bills abolishing provincial Councils or abridging the powers conferred upon them otherwise than in accordance with the provisions of section 85 of the Act, under which the powers of Provincial Councils were established.

Power to suggest amendments. The Governor-General has authority to return to the House in which it originated any such Bill so presented to

[1] *Post,* p. 396.

him, and at the same time may transmit any amendments which he may recommend and the House may deal with his recommendations.

A power to suggest amendments to a Bill was conferred by the Constitution Act on the Governor-General of the Australian Commonwealth.[1]

The King may disallow any law within one year after it has been assented to by the Governor-General and on such disallowance being made known by the Governor-General by speech or message to each of the Houses of Parliament, or by proclamation, the law is annulled from the day when the disallowance is so made known. *Disallowance.*

A Bill reserved for the King's pleasure possesses no force, unless and until one year from the day on which it was presented to the Governor-General for the King's Assent, the Governor-General makes known by speech or message to each of the Houses of Parliament or by proclamation that it has received the King's Assent. *Reservation when Bill comes into force.*

When a law is assented to, whether reserved or not, the Clerk of the House of Assembly must cause two fair copies of the law, one in English and one in Dutch, to be enrolled of record in the office of the Registrar of the Appellate Division of the Supreme Court of South Africa. One copy must be signed by the Governor-General. *Duty of Clerk of the House.*

The copies are conclusive evidence as to the provisions of the law, and in case of conflict between the two deposited copies, the copy signed by the Governor-General is accepted as authoritative. *Copies conclusive evidence.*

All revenues from whatever source they arise over which the Colonies had at the time of the Union powers of appropriation now vest in the Governor-General in Council, but that portion of revenue raised from the administration of railways, ports, and harbours which is received by the Governor-General in Council, is paid into a Railway and Harbour Fund. Parliament can exercise a power of appropriation over this fund for the purposes of the railways, ports, and harbours. But those undertakings under the *Vesting of revenues in Governor-General, in Council.* *Revenues from railway administration, etc.*

---

[1] *Ante,* p. 295.

Harbour and Railways Board. control and management of a Harbour and Railways Board, are subject, however, to the authority of the Governor-General in Council.

This Board consists of not more than three commissioners, appointed by the Governor-General in Council and a Minister of State is its Chairman. The Commissioners are appointed for five years, but are not removable except by the Governor-General in Council, for cause assigned, information as to which must be communicated to Parliament within a week of removal if Parliament is sitting, if not then a week after the commencement of the ensuing session.

Duration of term of Commissioners eligible for re-appointment. The Commissioners are eligible for re-appointment. Parliament fixes their salaries, and these are not subject to reduction during their term of office.

Vesting of ports, harbours, and railways in Governor-General in Council. All the ports, harbours, and railways that belonged to the several Colonies before the Union are now vested in the Governor-General in Council, and no railway for the conveyance of public traffic, and no ports, harbours, or similar works can be constructed without Parliamentary sanction. These great undertakings of the Union are directed by the Constitution to be administered on business principles but with due regard to agricultural and industrial development, and promotion by means of cheap transport of the settlement of an agricultural and industrial population in the inland portions of all provinces of the Union.

Provisions for cheap transport. Cheap transport seems to have been so clearly desired that special provisions have been made for its encouragement. It is declared that the total earnings of these undertakings shall be not more than are sufficient to meet the necessary outlays for working, maintenance, betterment, depreciation, and the payment of interest due on capital, not being capital contributed out of railway and harbour revenue, nor any sums payable out of the Consolidated Revenue Fund.[1]

Interest on invested capital. The interest due on invested capital is paid from the Railway and Harbour Fund into the Consolidated Revenue Fund.

[1] *Post,* p. 384.

This Board is further empowered to establish a fund for maintaining uniform railway rates, notwithstanding fluctuations in traffic. This fund is created out of the Railway and Harbour Revenue.

Every proposal for the construction of any port or harbour works, or of any line of railway, before it is submitted to Parliament must be considered by the Board which must make a report upon it, and advise whether it shall be constructed or not, if any of these undertakings are constructed contrary to the advice of the Board, where the Board has come to the conclusion that the revenue from the operation of the work or line will be insufficient to meet the costs of its working and maintenance, and of interest on the capital invested in it the Board must frame an estimate of the probable annual loss which in their opinion is likely to result from the operation. When this estimate has been examined and approved by the Controller and Auditor-General, the amount of the estimate then becomes payable annually out of the Consolidated Revenue Fund to the Railway and Harbour Fund, but if the actual loss is less than the estimate then the amount paid over in respect of that year is reduced accordingly so as not to exceed the actual loss incurred. In calculating the loss from the operation of any work or line the Board must have regard to the value of any contributions of traffic to other parts of the system which may be due to the operation of such work or line.

A deficiency also in the Railway Fund must be made good, when the Board has been required by the Governor-General in Council or by an Act of Parliament or resolution of both Houses to provide any services or facilities either gratuitously or at a rate of charge which is insufficient to meet the costs involved in providing them, the statement of the amount of loss which has been incurred in consequence must be presented to Parliament as approved by the Controller and Auditor-General. It then becomes payable out of the Consolidated Fund.

The Board controls and manages as from the establishment of the Union all balances standing to the credit of any fund which was established in any of the Colonies composing the Union for railway or harbour purposes. The balances were deemed to have been appropriated by Parliament for the respective purposes for which they had been provided.

These provisions of the Constitution with regard to the administration of these great public undertakings were devised by the framers of the Constitution for the purpose of ending the practice of treating them as agencies of taxation and so solving the practical obstacles to administrative unity, which arose from the difficulty of ascertaining what was the real value of the revenue of that part of the assets of the provinces which was made up of their railway systems. To have attempted to apportion them would have been difficult if not unpracticable. The Convention followed the course which Lord Milner had adopted when dealing with the earnings of the railways of the Transvaal and Orange River: He constituted an Intercolonial Council to administer the railways as a joint concern and to apply the revenue to maintain a common service. In addition to railways, ports and harbours seemed suitable subjects for an administrative control largely removed from popular influences.

Whilst these great South African undertakings are worked for the benefit of the whole the other provisions with regard to revenue raised from taxation ensure its fair division between the four provinces.

The Consolidated Revenue Fund consists of all other than the revenue arising from the administration of the railways, ports, and harbours raised or received by the Governor-General in Council. This sum is subject to appropriation by Parliament in accordance with the Union Act subject to certain charges: the annual interest on the public debts of the Colonies and any sinking funds constituted by law at the establishment of the Union forming a first charge on this fund.

Consolidated Revenue Fund.

No money may be withdrawn from the Consolidated Revenue Funds or the Railway and Harbour Fund except under appropriation made by law.

Appropriation required prior to withdrawal.

The stocks, cash, bankers' balances, and securities for

money belonging to each of the Colonies at the establishment Stock, cash, etc., of
of the Union became the property of the Union, but the Colonies now property of
balance of any funds, raised at the establishment of the Union.
Union by law for any special purposes in any of the Colonies
are deemed to have been appropriated by Parliament for
the purposes for which they were provided.

Crown Lands, public works, and all property throughout Crown Lands, public works,
the Union, movable or immovable, and all rights of whatever etc.
description that belonged to the Colonies prior to the
Union, now vest in the Governor-General in Council, subject
to any debt or liability specifically charged on them.

All rights in and to mines and minerals, and all rights Vesting of mines,
in connection with the searching for, working for, or dispos- minerals and mining rights
ing of minerals or precious stones which, at the establish- in Governor-General in
ment of the Union, vested in the Government of any of the Council.
Colonies, are now vested in the Governor-General in Council.

The Union in consideration of the transfer of the property Debts of Colonies
of the Colonies, assumed all the debts and liabilities of the assumed by Union.
Colonies existing at the time of the Union, subject to the
conditions imposed by any law under which they were
raised or incurred, and without prejudice to any rights of
security or priority in respect of the payment of principle,
interest, sinking fund, and other charges conferred on the
creditors of any of the Colonies.   Subject to such conditions
and rights the Union is entitled to convert, renew, or
consolidate such debts.

The financial controller of the Union is the Controller The Auditor-General.
and Auditor-General, who holds office during good behaviour.
He is appointed and is subject to removal by the Governor-
General in Council on addresses praying for his removal from
both Houses.   When Parliament is not sitting the Governor-
General has the right to suspend him on the ground of Suspension of.
incompetence and misbehaviour, but Parliament is entitled
to a statement, within fourteen days after its meeting, of the
circumstances under which such suspension took place, and
can present addresses during the session to the Governor-
General, praying for his restoration to office, on receipt of
which the Governor must restore him.   Failing any such

request for restoration, the suspension is confirmed and the office thereupon becomes vacant.

Until Parliament otherwise provides, the Controller and Auditor-General must exercise such powers and duties and undertake such functions as the Governor-General in Council may assign him by regulations framed for that purpose.

One object earnestly discussed prior to the Union was the organisation of the Civil Service of South Africa.

To carry this into effect the Constitution provided for the appointment of a Public Service Commission to make recommendations for reorganisation and readjustment of such of the public service departments as might be necessary, and for the assignment of officers to the several Provinces, and empowered the Governor-General in Council after the Commission had reported to assign the necessary officers to the

Provinces. The power, however, was not to apply to any service or department under the control of the Railway or Harbour Board.

Provision was also made for the appointment of a permanent Public Service Commission with such powers and duties relating to the appointment, discipline, retirement and superannuation of officers as Parliament should determine. Provision was also made for the tenure of existing offices, and forbidding the dismissal of persons for ignorance of the English or Dutch languages.

One of the most important functions possessed by the Governor-General in Council is the control and administration of native affairs and of all matters specially or differentially affecting Asiatics. He exercises also all special powers in regard to native administration formerly vested in the Governors of the Colonies or exercised by them as supreme chiefs. The lands vested in Governors of Colonies or Governors and Executive Councils for the purpose of reserves for native location are now vested in the Governor-General in Council, who exercises all special powers that were formerly exercised by Governors and Executive Councils. All such lands as could not formerly be alienated except by

the Acts of Colonial Parliaments, cannot now be alienated

or in any way diverted except by an Act of the Union Parliament.

It will be observed how the Governor-General of South Africa is made in a particular way the guardian of the native races.   In this respect he specially represents the Imperial Government.   How important this is will be seen from the fact that within the last thirty years Bechuanaland, Mashonaland and the subsequent foundation of Southern Rhodesia have enormously added to the number of the native races under the control of the Imperial Authority.   To-day the Union Government approximately has 4,680,474 natives under its control, and if these who are outside the Union are counted in Basutoland, Swaziland, the Bechuanaland Protectorate and Southern Rhodesia, the total aggregates 6,000,000, whilst in the territory north of the Zambezi, there are some 1,000,000 of Bantu population in the territory of the Chartered Company, making a grand total of about 7,000,000 natives. [1]

[1] Worsfold, *Union of South Africa*, pp. 43, 44.

CHAPTER XXXVI

CONSTITUTION OF THE LEGISLATIVE POWER

Legislative power in Union Parliament.

THE legislative power of the Union of South Africa is vested in the Union Parliament, which consists of the King, a Senate, and a House of Assembly.

The Governor-General appoints the times for holding sessions of Parliament. He is empowered from time to time by proclamation or otherwise to prorogue Parliament and to dissolve the Senate and the House of Assembly simultaneously, or the House of Assembly alone, but the Senate, as previously stated, cannot be dissolved within ten years after the establishment of the Union. [1] The dissolution of the Senate, however, does not affect the position of any Senators who have been nominated by the Governor-General in Council.

Two-Chamber Government.

In this Constitution, as in others dealt with, the system of two-Chamber Government is established. The power to dissolve the Senate and House of Assembly simultaneously

Power of Governor-General.

places considerably more power in the hands of the Governor-General than a Governor-General possesses under any of the other Federal Constitutions. Since a Governor-General acts mainly upon the advice of his Ministers, though not entirely, the Ministry consequently has more power than a Ministry under any of the other Constitutions. A dissolution of the Senate in the United States or Canada is impossible. In Australia the power to dissolve only exists after a disagreement has taken place between the two branches of the Legislature, which has resulted in a deadlock.

Annual meeting of Parliament.

A provision, which is also common to the Canadian and Australian Constitutions, requires that there shall be an annual Session of Parliament so that a period of twelve months shall not intervene between the last sitting of Parliament in one session and its first sitting in the next session. [2]

[1] *Ante*, p. 378. [2] *Ante*, pp. 228, 301.

The seat of the Union was fixed at Cape Town. The The Seat of the Union. Constitution of the Senate for ten years after its establishment in respect of the original provinces was thus provided for: the Governor-General in Council nominated eight Nominated Senators: Senators for each, and each original province elected eight. grounds for selection. Those nominated hold their seats for ten years. One-half of these nominee members were required to be selected on the ground mainly of their thorough acquaintance by reason of their official experience or otherwise with the reasonable wants and wishes of the coloured races in South Africa. When the seat of a nominated Senator falls vacant, it is When vacancy filled by the Governor-General in Council, who is required occurs. to nominate another Senator, to hold his seat for ten years.

The first choice of Senators by the Provinces took place First choice of Senators after the passing of the Act, and before the day appointed by both branches of for the establishment of the Union. The method of their Provincial Legislatures. election was as follows: the Governors of each of the four Colonies of the Cape of Good Hope, Natal, Transvaal, and Orange Free State summoned a special sitting of both Houses of their respective Colonial Legislatures, which sat in each Colony as one body. The Speaker of the Legislative Assembly presided. The Colonial Legislatures proceeded to elect eight Senators for each province. The Senators thus chosen were entitled to hold their seats for ten years.

Subsequent vacancies in the membership of the elected Vacancies in Senate. portion of the Senate are now filled by the Provincial Council voting together with the Members of the House of Assembly elected for the province, who choose a senator to fill any vacant place for the unexpired period for which the elected Senator was chosen.

It will be seen that the first Senate was chosen on the United States' model by the State or Provincial Legislatures. Subsequent elections will be distinguishable.

In the United States the State Executive receives only a power to make temporary appointments to the Senate until the State Legislature meets. In the event of an election of Senators in South Africa the election is conducted on the principle of proportional representation.

The periods of senatorial service vary in the four Federal Constitutions, whilst the American and Australian Senator is chosen for six years, the Canadian is nominated for life. The South African sits for a period of ten years. In one Constitution only, that of Australia, is a Senator directly elected by the people. The addition of nominated Senators with a view to the interests of the coloured races is a strong distinguishing feature of the South African Constitution.

Equality of State Representation. Equality of State representation was originally an accepted principle of all these Constitutions, although it has since been departed from in Canada. 40

The Union Senate consists of 64 Senators, the Australian of 48. The principle of a small Senate, having regard to the deadlock provisions, is a feature of the Australian Constitution. Consequently S. Africa has the smallest of all the Senates.

Power to alter. The Union Parliament, at the expiration of ten years, may provide for the manner in which a future Senate shall be constituted. The permanency of its Constitution is, therefore, not assured.

Senatorial qualification. As in the United States and Canada the Senatorial qualification as to age is fixed at not less than thirty; whilst in Australia, on the other hand, a Senator is qualified if he be only twenty-one. The electoral qualification for the office of Senator demands that the candidate should be registered as a voter qualified to vote for the election of Members of the Union House of Assembly in one of the Provinces. [1] Further, he must have resided for five years within the limits of the Union as existing at the time of his election or nomination, as the case may be. He must also be a British subject of European descent, and if an elected Senator he must be the registered owner of immovable property within the Union of the value of not less than five hundred pounds over and above any special mortgages thereon. Neither the United States nor the Australian Property qualification. Constitutions prescribe property qualifications. The American Constitution requires a candidate for the Senate

[1] *Post*, pp. 394, 395.

to have been for nine years preceding his election a citizen of the United States. On the other hand, in Canada it is sufficient if the proposed Senator is a natural born or a naturalised subject. In Australia he must have been a resident within the limits of the Commonwealth for at least three years.

In South Africa residence in and property situated within a colony before its incorporation in the Union are treated as residence in, and properly situated within the Union.

When the Senate first meets before proceeding to the despatch of any other business, its first duty is to nominate a Senator to be President of the Senate, and as often as the office becomes vacant it must nominate a Senator in his stead. A President becomes disqualified for his office by ceasing to be a Senator. He is only removable from office by a vote of the Senate, but may resign by writing under his hand addressed to the Governor-General. *Election of President.* *Grounds of disqualification of.*

Prior to or during any absence of the President the Senate may choose a Senator to perform his duties in his absence. In Canada the Speaker of the Senate in the Dominion House is appointed by the Governor-General, with whom rests the power of removal. The method of choosing a Speaker adopted in South Africa is similar to that which exists in the Australian Senate. *Appointment of Senator in absence of Speaker.*

A Senator may resign by writing under his hand. The Governor-General must then, as soon as practicable, cause steps to be taken to fill the vacancy.

Twelve Senators at least must be present to constitute a quorum. Till the Commonwealth Parliament otherwise provided a third of the Senate was necessary under the Australian Constitution. A majority constitutes a quorum in the United States. Fifteen Senators, including the Speaker, were requisite to make a quorum in the Canadian Senate until the Parliament of Canada otherwise provided. *Quorum.*

All questions in the Senate are determined by a majority of the votes of the Senators present other than the President or the presiding Senator, but the President as presiding *Majority vote.*

Casting-
vote of
President.
Senator possesses a casting-vote in the case of an equality of votes. This provision follows the provision in the United States' Constitution, which awards the President of the Senate a casting-vote, but is contrary to the provisions both of the Canadian and Australian Constitutions. It has before been pointed out that the President of the Senate of the United States is not a State representative, whereas in South Africa he may be, with the result that his vote on a division in the majority of cases may be lost to his Province. On the other hand, the existence of a nominee element to some extent reduces the risk, since it is possible to elect a nominee Senator President of the Senate. As to the oath and affirmation required of a Senator, his disqualification, etc.[1]

THE HOUSE OF ASSEMBLY

House of
Assembly.
The House of Assembly is a title which distinguishes the first Chamber in South Africa from the first Chambers in three Federal Constitutions of the United States, Canada, and Australia.

Composition
of House.
The House is composed (and will continue so to exist until altered in accordance with the Union Act) of fifty-one members for the Cape of Good Hope, seventeen for Natal, thirty-six for the Transvaal, and seventeen for the Orange Free State.

When can be
diminished.
The number of representatives may be increased but not diminished in any original Province until the total number of members of the House of Assembly for these Provinces reaches one hundred and fifty or till ten years has elapsed from the establishment of the Union, whichever is the longer period.

Provisions for
increase.
The number of members must be increased in accordance with the following provisions—

(1) The quota of the Union must be obtained by dividing the total number of European male adults in the Union, as ascertained by the Census of 1904, by the total number of Members of the House of Assembly, as constituted at the establishment of the Union.

[1] *Post*, p. 398.

(2) In 1911 and in every five years subsequently, a Census of the European population of the Union must be taken.

(3) After any such Census the number of European male adults in each Province must be compared with the number of European males as ascertained at the Census of 1904, and in the case of any Province where there appears an increase as compared with the Census of 1904 equal to the quota of the Union or any multiple thereof, the number of members allotted to such Province must be increased by an additional member, or an additional number of members equal to such multiple as the case may be.

(4) No additional member must be allotted to any Province until the total number of European male adults in such Province exceeds the quota of the Union multiplied by the number of members allotted to such Province for the time being, and thereupon additional members must be allotted to such Province in respect only of such excess.

(5) When the number of members of the House of Assembly elected in the original Provinces reaches one hundred and fifty, no further increase of membership may be made unless by Parliamentary legislation and subject to the provisions of the last preceding section.[1] The distribution of members among the Provinces must be such that the proportion between the number of members to be elected at any time in each Province and the number of European male adults in such Province as ascertained at the last preceding Census shall as far as possible be identical throughout the Union.

The number of European male adults at the Census of 1904 were : for the Cape, 167,546 ; for Natal, 34,784 ; for the Transvaal, 106,493 ; for the Orange Free State,

Census of 1904.

---

[1] Sect. 33, South Africa Act, 1909 : The number of members to be elected in the original provinces at the first election and until the number is altered in accordance with the provisions of this Act shall be as follows :—
Cape of Good Hope, 51, Natal 17, Transvaal 36, Orange Free State 17. These numbers may be increased as provided in the next succeeding section but shall not in the case of any original province be diminished until the total number of members of the House of Assembly in respect of the province herein provided for reaches one hundred and fifty, or a period of ten years has elapsed after the establishment of the Union, whichever is the longer period.

41,014. European male adults are males of twenty-one years or upwards, not being members of His Majesty's Regular Forces.

To find the quota referred to, the total number of male adults in 1904 must be added up and divided by the number of members allotted at the time of the Union.

Thus, 349,837 ÷ 121 makes 2891·26, to be the quota of the Union.

Automatical redistribution of seats.

If the Cape Province, with 167,546, be taken, it was actually entitled to fifty-seven seats, thus : $\dfrac{167,546}{2,891\cdot2} = 57$.

Natal received seventeen but was only entitled to twelve, and the Orange Free State fourteen, whilst it received seventeen, with the result that the smaller provinces were over-represented.

The system of an automatical redistribution for membership of the Lower House follows precedents set by the Constitutions of Canada and Australia.

The Union Franchise. Restriction on Parliamentary legislation.

The Union Parliament possesses power to prescribe the qualifications necessary to entitle persons to vote at elections for members of the House of Assembly, but no legislation may disqualify any person in the Province of the Cape of Good Hope, who, under the laws existing in the Colony at the establishment of the Union, at present is, or in future may be, capable of becoming a registered voter, from being registered on the ground of race or colour only, unless such legislation be passed by both Houses of the Union Legislature sitting together, and the third reading is agreed to by two-thirds of the total number of members of both Houses of Parliament.

Restriction against removal of persons on the register.

This and another provision which declared that no person who, at the time of the passing of such legislation, is a registered voter shall be removable from the register by reason of any disqualification based on race and colour, marked the general desire on the part of the framers of the Constitution to safeguard the electoral rights of the coloured races of the Cape of Good Hope. As in Canada and Australia, Parliament is entitled to create a Federal or Union franchise, but until it does so, subject to the provisions against disqualification already referred to with regard to the coloured races, the Federal or Union franchise is the existing franchise in force for the provincial elections for Provincial Assemblies. In the United States the fixing of the State franchises as the Federal franchise ultimately enabled some of the States to discriminate against the African population after the Civil War. The power of disqualification by discrimination was substantially redressed by the passing of the 14th and 15th Amendments to the Constitution.[1] No member of His Majesty's Regular Forces on full pay is entitled to be on the voters' register. *In the United States.*

The procedure on elections for the House of Assembly, including the registration of voters, oaths and declarations to be taken by voters, returning officers, their powers and duties, the proceedings in connection with elections, election expenses, corrupt and illegal practices, the hearing of election petitions and incidental proceedings, the vacating of seats of members, and the proceedings necessary for filling such vacancies are regulated by the laws which were in force relative to elections for the more numerous Houses of Parliament in the Provinces,[2] subject, however, to the provisions of the Union Act. *Electoral law.*

The poll throughout the Union takes place on one day, which the Governor-General in Council appoints.[3] *Poll on one day.*

The first electoral divisions of the four Colonies which became Provinces under the Constitution were made by a Joint Commission of Judges, each Province appointing one judge of its Supreme or High Court for this purpose. The principle of single electoral areas was ordained by the Constitution Act, and one member was to be returnable for each division. The Commission, in fixing the divisions, was directed to give due consideration to the community or diversity of interests, means of communication, physical features, existing electoral boundaries, and sparsity or density of population in such manner that while taking the quota of voters on the register as the basis of division they might, *Electoral divisions.*

[1] *Ante*, p. 153. [2] *Ante*, p. 314. [3] *Ante*, p. 297.

whenever they thought it necessary, depart from it, but in no case to any greater extent than 15 per centum more or less than the quota. Future electoral redistributions were provided for as follows.

The Governor-General in Council after each quinquennial Census, is required to appoint a commission of three Judges of the Supreme Court of South Africa to carry out any re-division which may have become necessary as between the different electoral divisions in each Province and to provide for the consequent allocation of the number of members to which each Province may have become entitled. The Commission must proceed on the same principles as were laid down in the case of the first Commission.

As soon as the Commission has finished its labours, it must submit to the Governor-General in Council, a list of electoral divisions, with the names that the Commission has given them and a description of their boundaries, with a map or maps showing the electoral divisions into which the Province has been divided, together with such further particulars as the Commission deems necessary. In the event of any discrepancy existing between the description and the maps, the description must be taken as correct. The Governor-General in Council must proclaim the names and boundaries of the electoral divisions as settled and certified by the Judges.

Whenever an alteration in the number of members of the House or re-division of the Provinces takes place its operation is deferred till the next General Election, held after the completion of the re-division or of any allocation consequent upon such alteration, but not at an earlier period.

The whole of these provisions with reference to the fixing of electoral areas and redistribution shows the desire of the framers of the Constitution to remove these matters from the area of party controversy. Where the ascendancy of one of two races may perhaps be assured by its power of fixing electoral divisions to suit its exigencies, the wisdom of a Commission of Judges removing the question from the political sphere is obvious.

In the United States, what is known as the practice of Gerry-mandering. gerrymandering the constituencies, at one time was reduced to a fine art. The expression " gerrymander " owed its meaning to the action of Elbridge Gerry, Democratic Governor of Massachusetts, in 1812. To insure an increased representation for his party in the State Senate, he formed the State districts in such a way that the shapes of the towns forming such a district in Essex County brought out a territory of regular outline. On Sheard, the painter, observing the map on which this was outlined in the office of Russell, the editor of *The Continent*, he added a head, ring, and claws, remarking that it would do for a salamander. " Gerrymander," said Russell, and the expression became proverbial.

To sit in the House of Assembly a person must be qualified Qualification for seat in the House of Assembly. to be registered as an elector for Members of the House of Assembly in one of the Provinces. He must also have resided for five years within the limits of the Union as existing at the time of his election. In addition, he must be a British subject of European descent, but residence in the Colony before the Union is treated as residence in the Union.[1]

The House of Assembly continues for five years from its first meeting unless sooner dissolved by the Governor-General.

The first business of the House of Assembly on its meeting Appointment of Speaker. is to appoint a Speaker, and whenever his office becomes vacant a fresh Speaker must be chosen. The Speaker is entitled to hold office only so long as he is a Member of the House.

He may be removed by a vote of the House or he may How removable. resign his office or his seat by writing under his hand addressed to the Governor-General. Prior to his election or during his absence the House may choose a Member to perform his duties.

A Member of the House may resign at any time by writing How Members may resign. under his hand addressed to the Speaker, or if there be no

[1] *Ante*, p. 390.

Speaker, or the Speaker be absent from the Union, he may place his resignation in the hands of the Governor-General, and on so doing his seat becomes immediately vacant.

Quorum of the House. Thirty members of the House constitute a quorum for the exercise of its powers. A third is necessary in the Australian House of Representatives. [1]

Majority of House. A majority of votes of the members present determines questions, excluding the Speaker or the presiding member.

Casting-vote of 'Speaker. The Speaker or the presiding Member may exercise a casting-vote when the votes are equal. [2]

Provisions affecting Members of both Houses. There are certain provisions of the Union Act which affect Members of both Houses of Parliament. Every Member must make and subscribe before the Governor-General or some person authorised by him an oath or affirmation of allegiance before taking his seat.

The oath required is as follows—

Oath of allegiance, Form of. " I, A B, do swear that I will be faithful and bear true allegiance to His Majesty [*here insert the name of the King or Queen of the United Kingdom of Great Britain and Ireland for the time being*], His [or Her] heirs and successors according to law. So help me God."

AFFIRMATION

Affirmation. " I, A B, do solemnly and sincerely affirm and declare that I will be faithful and bear true allegiance to His Majesty [*here insert the name of the King or Queen of the United Kingdom of Great Britain and Ireland for the time being*], His [or Her] heirs and successors according to law."

Right of Ministers to speak and sit in either House. A provision in the Constitution common to the two other Imperial Federations applies to disqualify a Member of either House of Parliament being a member of the other, but a Minister of State who is a member of either House possesses the right to sit and speak in the Senate and the House of Assembly, but he is only entitled to vote in the House of which he is a member.

Advantages and disadvantages of 'practice. This provision is not to be found in either the Canadian or Australian Constitutions, nor is it to be found in the

[1] *Ante,* p. 316. [2] *Ante,* p. 316.

Constitution of the United Kingdom. One possible objection to this practice may be its tendency to exclude members of the Senate from ministerial offices with the consequent diminution of the importance of the Second Chamber. On the other hand, considerable compensatory advantages spring from the fact that a Minister is able to explain his policy in both Chambers first hand.

The actual disqualifications attaching to Members of both Houses which would prevent them either from being capable of being chosen or of sitting are : (1) conviction at any time of any crime or offence in respect of which the convicted person has been sentenced to imprisonment without the option of a fine for a term of not less than twelve months. The disqualification, however, does not attach when the convicted person has received a grant of amnesty or a free pardon, or where the imprisonment has expired at least five years before the date of his election, (2) the fact that the Member is an unrehabilitated insolvent, (3) or is of unsound mind so declared by a competent court, or (4) that he holds any office of profit under the Crown within the Union, but Ministers of State for the Union, persons in receipt of a pension from the Crown, officers or members of His Majesty's naval or military forces on retired or half-pay, or an officer or member of the naval or military forces of the Union whose services are not wholly employed by the Union, are exempted from this disability. *Disqualifications.*

The seat of a Senator or Member of the House of Assembly becomes vacant whenever he becomes subject to any of the above-mentioned disabilities, or when he ceases to possess his legal qualification, or if he fail for a whole ordinary session to attend the House without the special leave of the Senate or the House of Assembly as the case may be. *When vacancy occurs.*

A penalty of one hundred pounds a day may be imposed on any person who, although by law incapable of sitting as a Senator or Member of the House of Assembly, sits or votes whilst he is disqualified but he must know or have reasonable grounds for knowing of his disqualification. The penalty is recoverable on behalf of the Treasury *Penalties.*

of the Union by action in any Superior Court of the Union.

Payment of Members. Members of both Houses receive a payment of £400 a year.   This was the original remuneration that was attached to the position of members of the Commonwealth Parliament, and the remuneration is the same as that now paid to Members of the Imperial Parliament.   The amount is computed from the date that a Member takes his seat. The allowance is recoverable under rules framed by Parliament.   A deduction of £3 from a Member's salary is made in respect of every day of his absence.   No allowances are paid to Ministers of the Crown in receipt of a salary, nor to the President of the Senate nor the Speaker of the House of Assembly.

A day of the session means in respect of a Member any day during a session on which the House of which he is a member or any committee of which he is a member meets.

Powers and privileges of Senate and House of Assembly. The powers, privileges, and immunities of the Senate and of the House of Assembly and their Members and committees, subject to the South Africa Act, are such as the South African Parliament declares, till such declaration they are those of the House of Assembly of the Cape of Good Hope and of its members and committees as at the establishment of the Union.   They are not so great as those of the Commonwealth Parliament of Australia.

Powers of each House. Each House of Parliament possesses the power to make rules and orders with respect to the order and conduct of its business and proceedings.   Until they are made, the rules and orders of the Legislative Council and House of Assembly of the Cape of Good Hope at the establishment of the Union, *mutatis mutandis* apply to both Houses.

Joint sittings. Joint sittings of the Union Parliament may be held for many purposes ; amongst others, for altering certain portions of the Constitution.   Thus they must be held when it is proposed to repeal or alter the number of Members to be **Alteration of number of House of Assembly.** elected to the House of Assembly, but no repeal or alteration is possible until the House of Assembly has reached its prescribed limit of Members (one hundred and fifty), or until ten years have elapsed after the establishment of the Union, whichever is the longer period. They must also be held when Parliament introduces a law to alter or repeal the provisions of the Constitution with reference to section 35 of the Act which refers to the qualification of voters ; when it is proposed to alter the provisions as to the use of the English to Dutch languages ; or to alter any of the provisions with regard to the Amendment of the Act. The third reading of a Bill in all these cases must be agreed to by not less than two-thirds of the total number of Members of both Houses sitting together. A Bill passed in this way is taken to be duly passed by both Houses of Parliament. *When a law introducing disqualification.*

Numbers on third reading.

Where a joint sitting of both Houses is required the Governor-General convenes it by message to both Houses. *How joint sitting convened.*

The Speaker of the House of Assembly then presides over the joint sitting, and the rules of that House as far as practicable apply to the proceedings. In all other respects but subject, however, to reservation in some cases Parliament can alter the Constitution as it chooses. *Speaker of House of Assembly presides.*

In the occasions and purposes for which a joint sitting may be held, the Constitution, compared with other Federal Constitutions is unique. The provisions as to the amendment of the Constitution show how different it is from the three other Federal Constitutions, two of which require the direct assent of the people, and the other of an Imperial Act. The principle asserted that a Parliament has the power to alter a Constitution without a special reference to the people whose Government they propose to change is one requiring some consideration. It has always been admitted that Parliament is entitled to make some amendments of the Constitution, and in the Imperial Constitutions the words " until Parliament otherwise provides " are familiar to students of Constitutional History, but that the power should be invoked to alter the relations of the central and local authorities, or alter the fundamental bases of the Constitution, seems a doubtful proposition. If the people are not mere chattels to be transferred from one form of Government to another at the bidding of the Representatives *Criticism on amending powers.*

whom they have elected they surely possess a right to be consulted, and no plan seems better devised for this purpose than the referendum which has been adopted by the Australian people, otherwise the representatives and not the people are masters of the situation which seems a *reductio ad absurdum*.

CHAPTER XXXVII

THE JUDICIAL POWER

THE Union Act established a Supreme Court of South Africa Supreme Court of South Africa. consisting of a Chief Justice of South Africa, the ordinary judges of appeal, and the other judges of the several divisions of the Supreme Court of South Africa in the Provinces.

Prior to the Union the Cape of Good Hope, Natal, and the Existence of Supreme Courts prior to Union. Transvaal possessed Supreme Courts, and the Orange River Colony a High Court. On the establishment of the Union these courts at once became provincial divisions of the Supreme Court of South Africa within their respective Provinces, presided over by Judge-Presidents.

The Appellate Division of the Supreme Court now consists Composition of Court. of the Chief Justice of South Africa, two ordinary Judges of Appeal, and two additional judges. These additional judges are assigned to the Supreme Court, from the provincial or local divisions of the Supreme Court. When not sitting in the Appellate Court, these judges must continue to perform their ordinary duties.

The Courts of the Eastern Districts of the Cape of Good Local divisions of Supreme Court. Hope, the High Court of Griqualand, the High Court of Witwatersrand, and the several Circuit Courts of the Union became local divisions of the Supreme Court within the respective areas of their jurisdiction as existing at the establishment of the Union.

In addition to any original jurisdiction exercised by the Additional jurisdiction. corresponding Courts of the Colonies at the establishment of the Union, the Provincial and Local Divisions Courts, which are termed Superior Courts in the Act, received jurisdiction in all matters.

(a) In which the Government of the Union or a person suing or being sued on behalf of such Government is a party.

(b) In which the validity of any provincial ordinance comes into question.

Jurisdiction as to validity of elections. Till the Legislature makes other provisions, the Superior Courts possess jurisdiction affecting the validity of elections of members of the House of Assembly and Provincial Councils, as the Corresponding Courts of the Colonies had at the establishment of the Union in regard to Parliamentary elections in such Colonies.

Changes in position of judges. All Judges of the Supreme Courts of the Colonies holding office at the time of the Union, including the Judges of the High Court of the Orange River Colony, became Judges of the Supreme Court of South Africa assigned to the divisions of the Supreme Court in the respective Provinces, retaining all such rights in regard to salaries and pensions as they possessed at the establishment of the Union. The Chief Justices of the Colonies holding office at its establishment and the Judges-President of the divisions of the Supreme Court in the respective Provinces retain the titles of Chief Justices of their respective Provinces so long as they hold office.

Subsequent appointments of judges vested in Governor-General in Council. The appointment of a Chief Justice of South Africa, of the ordinary Judges of Appeal, and all other Judges of the Supreme Court of South Africa is now vested in the Governor-General in Council, but Parliament fixes their remuneration, although it has no power to diminish it during their continuance in office.

Provisions as to removal of judges. Neither the Chief Justice of South Africa nor the other Judges of the Supreme Court of South Africa are removable from office, except by the Governor-General in Council on an address from both Houses of Parliament in the same session, praying for such removal on the ground of misbehaviour or incapacity.[1]

The provision as to diminution of salary and the requirement of addresses from both Houses in the same session establishes and preserves the independence of the Judicial Bench.

Power to postpone the filling of vacancies on Judicial Bench. The Governor-General in Council possesses power to postpone filling a vacancy occurring in any Division of the Supreme Court of Africa other than the Appellate Division,

[1] *Ante*, p. 345.

when he thinks it advantageous in the public interest to do so until Parliament determines whether a reduction in numbers shall take place.

Appeals must now be brought to the Appellate Division Appeals brought to Appellate Division of Supreme Court of the Union. of the Supreme Court of the Union in civil cases, where formerly they might have been brought to the Supreme Court of any Colony from a Superior Court in any of the Colonies, or from the High Court of Southern Rhodesia, except in cases of orders or judgments given by a single judge upon applications by way of motion or petition, or on summons for provisional sentence or judgment as to costs only, which by law are left to the discretion of the Court. Appeals Exceptions. from any such orders or judgments as well as any appeal in criminal cases, from any such Superior Court, or the special reference by any such Court of any point of law in a criminal case, must be made to the provincial division corresponding to the Court which before the establishment of the Union would have had jurisdiction in the matter. There is no further appeal against any judgment given on appeal by such provincial division except to the Appellate Division, and then only where the Appellate Division shall have given special leave to appeal.

Where at the establishment of the Union an appeal might Appeals formerly brought to King in Council. How now brought to Appellate Division. have been brought from the Supreme Court of any of the Colonies or from the High Court of the Orange River, to the King in Council, the appeal must now be made to the Appellate Division, but the right of appeal in any civil suit is not limited by reason only of the value of the matter in dispute or the amount claimed or awarded in such suit, and where an appeal might have been made formerly from a resident magistrate or other inferior court to a Superior Court in any of the Colonies, the appeal must be made to the Appeals from resident magistrates and other inferior courts. corresponding division of the Supreme Court of South Africa. Any further appeal can only be brought by special leave of the Appellate Division to which the appeal must be brought.

No appeal lies from the Supreme Court of South Africa, or from any division thereof to the King in Council, but the

Union Act declares that nothing shall be construed to impair any right which the King in Council may be pleased to exercise to grant special leave to appeal from the Appellate Division to the King in Council.

Special leave.

These words do not, therefore, limit the King's prerogative right to admit appeals from the Supreme Court. The right, therefore, to appeal by special leave of the Judicial Committee is not taken away, as it was under the Australian Constitution Act under the provisions of section 74. The Union Parliament has power, however, to limit the matters in respect of which such special leave may be asked, but Bills containing any such limitations must be reserved by the Governor-General for the signification of the Sovereign's pleasure.[1]

Bills limiting special leave.

The Appellate Division sits at Bloemfontein, but it may hold sittings elsewhere within the Union. Five judges constitute a quorum to hear appeals from a Court which consists of two or more judges ; but on the hearing of appeals from a single judge, three judges of the Appellate Division form a quorum. No judge may take part in the hearing of an appeal against the judgment given in a case heard before him.

Appellate Division sits at Bloemfontein.

Quorum of judges.

The process of the Appellate Divisions runs throughout the Union, and all its judgments or orders have full force and effect in every Province, and are executed as if they were original judgments or orders of the provincial division of the Supreme Court of South Africa in such Province.

Process of Appellate Division runs through Union.

Judgments or orders of a Provincial Court can be executed throughout the Provinces by the adoption of an extremely simple procedure. The Registrar of every Provincial Division of the Supreme Court of South Africa if requested by the party in whose favour the judgment or order has been given or made by any other division, must issue a writ or other process for the execution of such judgment or order, and thereupon it must be executed in like manner as if it had been issued from the division of which he was registrar. An authenticated copy of the judgment or order must be

Judgments or orders of Supreme Courts.

[1] *Ante*, p. 346.

deposited with him, and proof must be given that it is unsatisfied.

Civil suits for convenience are transferable from any Transfer of civil suits. Provincial or local division to any other division. The Judicial system of the Union has been well devised and is extremely simple. The Judiciary, however, will not be called upon to decide any of these great federal questions which are constantly before the courts in the United States, Canada and Australia.

CHAPTER XXXVIII

POWERS OF LEGISLATION

THE Parliament of the Union of South Africa possesses power to make laws for the peace, order, and good government of the Union ; no other power is conferred. Any subsequent enumeration of powers would have only
weakened this grant of a great general power. It is the widest authority that could have been conferred compatible with Imperial supremacy, and exceeds any of the powers granted to the Federal Government in any of the Imperial Federal Constitutions. It is only limited, on the one hand, by the words by which it is granted. If it does not confer the highest attributes of sovereignty, it extends over and pervades the whole Union of South Africa, and is only restricted in the Union by the extremely limited powers which have been granted to the Provinces to make ordinances falling within a certain class of subjects. Even these Provincial powers are limited by a provision which declares that : " An ordinance made by a Provincial Council has effect in and for the Province, so long and as far only as it is not repugnant to any Act of Parliament." To fully understand the plenitude of the Union Parliaments' legislative powers, the powers of the Provincial Councils require to be examined.

They possess powers to make ordinances in relation to matters coming within the following classes of subjects (that is to say)—

(1) Direct taxation within the Province, in order to raise a revenue for provincial purposes.

(2) The borrowing of money on the sole credit of the Province, with the consent of the Governor-General in Council and in accordance with regulations framed by Parliament.

(3) Education, other than higher education, for a period

of five years and thereafter until Parliament otherwise provides.

(4) Agriculture to the extent and subject to the conditions to be defined by Parliament.

(5) The establishment, maintenance, and management of hospitals and charitable institutions.

(6) Municipal institutions, divisional councils, and other local institutions of a similar nature.

(7) Local works and undertakings within the Province, other than railways and harbours, and other than such works as extend beyond the borders of the Province, and subject to the power of Parliament to declare any work a national work and to provide for its construction by arrangement with the Provincial Council or otherwise.

(8) Roads, outspans, ponts, and bridges other than bridges connecting two Provinces.

(9) Markets and pounds.

(10) Fish and game preservation.

(11) The imposition of punishment by fine, penalty, or imprisonment for enforcing any law or any ordinance of the Province made in relation to any matter coming within any of the classes of subjects enumerated in this section.

(12) Generally all matters which in the opinion of the Governor-General in Council are of a merely local or private nature in the Province.

(13) All other subjects in respect of which Parliament shall by law delegate the power of making ordinances to the Provincial Council.

None of these powers exceed those that might be granted to a County Council in England. A County Council has no power to tax, although it can levy a rate; whilst a Provincial Council has powers of direct taxation given, but only in the Province. A Provincial Council, like a County Council, can borrow money, but again its power is restricted; for its borrowings must be in accordance with Parliamentary regulations; and, subject to the consent of the Governor-General in Council: no such restriction as this applies to the grant of similar powers to the Provinces of Canada.

Compared with Count Councils in England. y

Compared with powers of Canadian Provinces.

No such power is given to Provincial Councils as is given in the Provinces of the Dominion to impose shop, saloon, tavern, and other licences for the purpose of revenue; nor is a power given to incorporate companies for provincial objects. Even the Provincial Councils' authority over agriculture, which is usually conceded to be a matter of State or Provincial concern, is only granted by the Constitution to the extent and subject to the conditions to be defined by Parliament.

Position of Union Parliament in South Africa.

In so far as South Africa is concerned, the Union Parliament holds a position but little short of that held by the Imperial Parliament of the United Kingdom. In treating of the Provinces, it will be subsequently shown how their powers of making ordinances are further curtailed by other provisions of the Constitution, which still further limit their authority.

Appropriation Bills.

In the Union Parliament, Bills which appropriate revenue, or moneys, or impose taxation, must originate in the House of Assembly; a Bill, however, neither appropriates revenue nor moneys, or imposes taxation by reason only that it contains provisions for the imposition or appropriation of fines or other pecuniary penalties.

Powers of Senate.

The Senate is not entitled to amend any Bills so far as they impose taxation, or appropriate revenue or moneys for the services of the Government. Neither must it amend any Bill so as to increase any proposed charge or burden on the people.

Separate appropriation.

Another Constitutional provision to prevent tacking provides that any Bill which appropriates revenue or moneys for the ordinary annual services of the Government shall deal only with such appropriation.

Appropriation of public revenue recommended by the Governor.

The House of Assembly cannot originate or pass any vote, resolution, address, or Bill for the appropriation of any part of the public revenue, or of any tax or impost to any purpose, unless such appropriation has been recommended by message from the Governor-General during the Session in which the vote, resolution, address, or Bill is proposed.

Disagreements between the two Houses are provided Disagreements between Houses. for as follows : If the House of Assembly passes any Bill which the Senate rejects, or fails to pass, or passes with amendments, and if the House of Assembly will not agree, and the House of Assembly, in the next Session, again passes the Bill with or without any of the amendments, which Passing the Bill in second Session. have been made or agreed to by the Senate, and the Senate then rejects or fails to pass it or passes it with amendments to which the House of Assembly will not agree, the Governor-General may, during that Session convene a joint sitting of the Members of both Houses. [1]

At this joint sitting the Members present may deliberate, Joint sitting. Voting together. and must vote together upon the Bill as it was last proposed by the House of Assembly, and upon amendments, if any, which have been made therein by one House of Parliament and not agreed to by the other ; and any such amendments which are affirmed by a majority of Members of the Senate and the House of Assembly present at such sitting must be taken to have duly been carried by both Houses of Parliament, and if the Bill with amendments, if any, is affirmed by a majority of the Members of the Senate and House of Assembly present at such sitting it shall be taken to have been duly passed by both Houses of Parliament. ·

If the Senate reject or fail to pass any Bill dealing with Joint sitting in first Session in case of rejection of appropriation Bill. the appropriation of revenue or moneys for the public service, a joint sitting may be convened during the same Session in which the Senate rejects or fails to pass the Bill. [2]

---

[1] *Ante*, p. 320. [2] *Ante*, p. 318.

CHAPTER XXXIX

THE PROVINCES

Chief Executive Officer of Province. THE chief Executive Officer of the Provinces is styled the administrator of the Province. He is appointed by the Governor-General. In his name all the executive Acts relating to Provincial affairs are done.

Choice of administrator. In choosing an administrator of the Province, the Governor-General in Council, as far as practicable, must give preference to persons resident in the Province.

Term of office of. When appointed, an administrator holds office for a term of five years, and is not removable except by the Governor-General for cause assigned, which must be com-**Cause of removal.** municated by message to both Houses of Parliament within one week after the removal, if Parliament is then in Session ; but if Parliament is not sitting, then within a week after the commencement of the next ensuing Session.[1]

Deputy Administrator. The Governor-General in Council also possesses a power to appoint a deputy administrator to execute the office and functions of the administrator during his absence, illness, or other inability. In the provisions relative to this appointment and removal from office, the provisions of the Canadian Constitution with reference to the appointment of the Lieutenant-Governors of the Provinces of Canada have been closely followed. The appointment of an Administrator, **Compared with Lieutenant-Governors in Canada.** like the appointment of a Lieutenant-Governor, vests, in practice, in the Ministry of the day ; and his salary, like the salary of the Lieutenant-Governor in Canada, is fixed and provided for by Parliament.[2]

Nature of Provincial Councils. Provincial Councils are elected bodies. A Council is constituted for each of the four Provinces. Each of the Councils consist of the same number of members as those elected by the Province to the House of Assembly ; but where any Province would, according to this rule, possess a less

[1] *Ante,* p. 265. [2] *Ante,* p. 265.

representation than twenty-five, the Provincial Council must consist of not less than twenty-five members. Number of Members.

The qualification of a Provincial Councillor is the same as that of a person entitled to vote for a Provincial Councillor. The qualification, until altered, would, therefore, be the qualification which is required to entitle a person to vote for a Member of the House of Assembly. Qualification of Councillors.

Provincial Councillors are elected by persons who are qualified to vote for the Members of the House of Assembly in the Province voting in the same electoral divisions as are delimited for the election of Members of the House of Assembly. Franchise.

In any Province, however, in which less than twenty-five Members are elected to the House of Assembly, the delimitation of the electoral divisions, and any necessary re-allocation of Members or adjustment of electoral divisions, must be effected by the same Commission, and on the same principles as are prescribed in regard to the electoral divisions for the House of Assembly.[1] When less than twenty-five members are returned to the House of Assembly.

Any alteration in the number of members of the Provincial Council, and any re-division of the Province into electoral divisions, comes into operation at the next General Election for the Council, held after the completion of such re-division or of any allocation consequent upon such alteration, and not earlier. Alteration in numbers of Members.

The Administrator fixes by Proclamation the date of the elections. Duty of administration with respect to elections.

The electoral law, applicable to such elections, is the same as that which applies to elections for Members of the House of Assembly, that is to say, the law which was in force in each Colony at the date of the Union.[2] Electoral laws.

All elections throughout the Provinces take place on the same day. Elections on same day.

The provisions relative to the disqualifications for membership of either House of Parliament, the vacating of seats, and the liabilities to penalties for sitting or voting when disqualified, apply to Provincial Councillors. Disqualifications.

---

[1] *Ante,* p. 396.   [2] *Ante,* p. 395.

On becoming a Member of Parliament. A Provincial Councillor, on his becoming a Member of Parliament, ceases to be a Councillor.

Duration of Councils. Provincial Councils continue for three years from the date of their first meeting ; they are not subject to dissolution.

Times of Meetings. The Administrator, by Proclamation, fixes the times for their meetings as he thinks fit. He is entitled to prorogue **One meeting in each year.** the Council, but there must be one meeting in each year, and twelve months must not intervene between its meetings.

Presiding officer chairman. The presiding officer of the Provincial Council is the chairman, who is elected by the members.

Rules for conduct of business. A Council is entitled to make its own rules for the conduct of its proceedings. The proposed rules, however, must be transmitted to the Governor-General by the Administrator ; they possess full force and effect, unless they are disapproved by the Governor-General in writing addressed to the Administrator.

Allowance for services. Members receive such allowance for their services as Councillors as the Governor-General in Council determines.

Freedom of speech and action. Freedom of speech in Council is accorded to every Councillor, nor is he liable to any action in any Court by reason of his speech or vote in Council.

The Executive Committee for the Province. When the Provincial Councils first met they were charged with the duty of electing from their members four persons, who, with the Administrator as their chairman, were to constitute an Executive Committee for the Province. The members of this Committee other than the Administrator were directed to continue to hold office until the election of their successors in the same manner.

Fresh Executive Committee after three years. It therefore follows that every three years after the election of a Provincial Council, a fresh Executive Committee must be chosen. The Committee is elected on the principle of proportional representation.

Remuneration of Executive Committee. The members of the Executive Committee receive such remuneration as the Provincial Council, with the approval of the Governor-General, determines.

No disqualification. No disqualification attaches to membership of a Provincial Council by reason of a Provincial Councillor being chosen as a member of the Executive Committee.

Casual vacancies on the Executive Committee are filled up by elections by the Provincial Council, if it is then in session ; but if not in session, a person is temporarily appointed by the Executive Committee to hold office pending the election by the Council.

The Administrator and any other member of the Execu- tive Committee of a Province, who is not a member of the Provincial Council, can take part in the proceedings of the Council, but has no right to vote.

It is the duty of the Executive Committee to carry out the administration of provincial affairs on behalf of the Provincial Council. When, however, a quorum of the Committee cannot be constituted according to the rules of the Committee, the Administrator must, as soon as practicable, convene a meeting of the Provincial Council for the purpose of electing a member or members to fill any vacancies. Until such vacancies are filled, the Administrator must act alone.

Except where the Union Act has expressly provided for an alteration or modification of the powers, authorities, and functions, which at the date of the establishment of the Union were vested in or exercised by the Governor or the Governor in Council of any of the Colonies, or in any Minister of the Colony, all such powers, authorities, and functions are now vested in the Executive Committee of the Province, but only in so far as they refer to matters in respect of which the Provincial Council are competent to make ordinances.

Questions arising in the Executive Committee are deter- mined by a majority of the votes of the members present, but in cases of equality the Administrator also possesses a casting-vote.

With the approval of the Governor-General in Council, the Executive Committee is empowered to make rules for the conduct of its proceedings.

Whilst Parliament can legislate regulating the conditions of appointment, tenure of office, retirement and super- annuation of public officers, the power is given to the

Executive Committee, subject to the provisions of any such law, to appoint such officers as may be necessary, in addition to any officers assigned to the Province whose appointment rests with the Governor-General in Council.

Appointment and duties of officer.

·The officers appointed by the Executive Committee are appointed to carry out the services entrusted to them ; and, when appointed, they are subject to regulations made for their organisation and discipline by the Committee.

When Administrator acts without Executive Committee.

The Administrator of a Province, in all matters in respect of which no powers are reserved or delegated to the Provincial Council, acts on behalf of the Governor-General in Council when required so to do. When he acts on behalf of the Governor-General he performs his duties without reference to the other members of the Executive Committee. He is, therefore, in his nature, both a Union and a Provincial officer ; as a Union officer his duties would be mainly in regard to the native races.

Auditor for Province. How appointed.

Each Province possesses an Auditor of Accounts, whose appointment is made by the Governor-General in Council.

The Auditor of Accounts is not removable from office except by the Governor-General for cause assigned, communicated by message to both Houses of Parliament within one week after the removal of Parliament, if in session ; if not, then within one week after the commencement of the next ensuing session.

Salary of.

The Auditors receive a salary paid out of the Consolidated Revenue Fund. The amount is determined by the Governor-General in Council, with the approval of Parliament.

Duties of Auditor.

An Auditor's duties are defined. He is required to examine and audit the accounts of the Province to which he is assigned, subject to regulations and orders framed by the Governor-General in Council and approved by Parliament.

Warrants for issue of money must be signed by Auditor.

Any warrant signed by the Administrator of a Province which authorises the issue of money is of no effect, unless it is countersigned by the Auditor.

The powers, authorities and functions exercised at the

establishment of the Union by Divisional or Municipal Councils, or any other duly constituted Local Authority continue in force until waived or withdrawn by Parliament or by a Provincial Council having power.

A less power of legislation is conferred upon the Provinces than is conferred under any of the three Federations upon the States or Provinces composing the Federation. Thus they only possess a limited power not to make laws, but to pass ordinances as has already been shown. *Modified powers of provincial legislation.*

" The difference between these two modes of legislation in England is described by Dr. Stubbs as being differences partly of form, partly of character. The ordinance is put forth in letters patent or charter, and is not engrossed on the Statute Roll; it is an act of the King or of the King in Council. The statute is the Act of the Crown, Lords and Commons; it is engrossed on the Statute Roll; it is meant to be a permanent addition to the law of the land; it can only be revoked by the same body that made it and in the same form." [1] *Distinctions between ordinances and laws.*

The power of the Provincial Councils in South Africa to make ordinances denotes the minor character of the authority conferred. This form of legislative power has hitherto been assumed to be originally founded on and justified by the prerogative of the Crown. It has, however, for many years been the subject of express consent by the Imperial Parliament, and when so granted probably means a subordinate or inferior power of legislation.

An ordinance assented to by the Governor-General in Council and promulgated by the Administrator, subject to the provisions of the Union Act, has the force of law within the Province. *Effect of ordinance assented to by Governor.*

It is the Administrator's duty to cause two fair copies of every ordinance to be made: one in the English and the other in the Dutch language. One of these copies must be signed by the Governor-General, and be enrolled of record in the office of the Registrar of the Appellate Division of the Supreme Court of South Africa. The copies *Copies of ordinances.*

[1] Anson, *Law and Custom of the Constitution*, 3rd ed., p. 236.

are conclusive evidence as to the provisions of such ordinance. In cases of a conflict between the two copies which are thus deposited, the copy which is signed by the Governor-General prevails. This provision is analogous to that which prescribes for the publication of laws passed by the Union Parliament.[1]

Governor-General's assent required.

A proposed ordinance, after it has passed the Provincial Council, must be presented by the Administrator to the Governor-General in Council for his assent who must declare

Provisions as to.

within one month of its presentation to him whether he assents to it or withholds his assent, or whether he reserves it for further consideration. If a proposed ordinance is reserved it possesses no force unless and until within one year from the day of its presentation to him the Governor-General makes known by Proclamation that it has received his assent.

Provincial revenue.

A fund for the purposes of provincial revenue is formed in every province. Into this fund all revenue raised by or accruing to the Provincial Council, and all moneys paid over by the Governor-General are paid. Till the financial relations between the Union and Provinces were adjusted, and until Parliament made other provision, the Provinces were to receive annual grants out of the Consolidated Revenue Fund of the Union, but were bound to submit estimates of their expenditure for the approval of the Governor-General in Council.

Grants.

These grants consist of (a) amounts equal to the sum provided in the estimates for education—other than higher education—in respect of the financial year 1908-9, as voted by the legislature of the corresponding Colony during the year 1908 ; (b) such further sums as the Governor-General in Council might consider necessary for the due performance of the services and duties assigned to the Provinces respectively.

Provincial funds.

The Provincial fund, which is thus made up of revenue raised by direct taxation by the Council in the Province, or revenue accruing due, and annual grants from the Consolidated Fund paid over by the Governor-General, is subject

[1] *Ante*, p. 381.

to appropriation by the Provincial Council by ordinance for purposes of Provincial administration generally ; but where any moneys are paid over by the Governor-General in Council for particular purposes only, then only for such purposes.

An ordinance appropriating money can only be passed by a Provincial Council when the Administrator has first recommended to the Council to make provision for the specific service for which the appropriation is to be made. *Ordinances appropriating money.*

No money may be issued from the Provincial Revenue Fund except in accordance with such appropriation and under warrant signed by the Administrator.[1] *Warrant of administrator.*

The matters falling within the classes of cases in which ordinances can be made have been stated already,[2] and it is unnecessary to recapitulate them.

In addition to its other powers, a Provincial Council may recommend Parliament to pass any law relating to any matter in which the Council is not competent to make ordinances. *Recommendatory power.*

A means of lightening the labours of the Union Parliament in respect of a class of work which entails much labour on the Imperial House of Commons is found in the provisions that when any matter requires to be dealt with by a private Act of Parliament, the Provincial Council of the Province to which the matter relates may, subject to the procedure prescribed by Parliament, take evidence by means of a Select Committee, or otherwise, for and against the passing of such law ; and upon receipt of a report from the Council, with the evidence on which it was founded, Parliament may pass the Act without taking further evidence in support. *Taking evidence.*

The four provincial seats of Government are : Cape Town for the Cape of Good Hope ; Pietermaritzburg for Natal ; Pretoria for the Transvaal ; and Bloemfontein for the Orange Free State. *Provincial seats of Government.*

The system of Provincial Councils established by the

---

[1] An administrator was entitled to expend money for provincial services until the expiration of one month after the first meeting of the Provincial Council.

[2] *Ante,* p. 416.

Powers of Provincial Councils does not interfere with the powers of Divisional or Municipal Councils.

Union Act does not interfere with the powers, authorities, and functions lawfully exercised by Divisional or Municipal Councils, or other duly constituted local authorities in the Union. Such authorities continue to exist, and remain to provide for municipal and local government purposes.

But the Union Parliament may vary or alter the powers of these bodies, and so may Provincial Councils, since municipal institutions, divisional councils, and other local institutions of a similar nature are matters on which legislation by ordinance can be passed by a Provincial Council.

CHAPTER XL

NEW PROVINCES AND TERRITORIES

THE Union Parliament is entitled to alter the boundaries Division of provinces. of any provinces, to divide a province into two or more provinces or to form a new province out of provinces within the Union on the petition of the Provincial Council of every province whose boundaries are affected by the proposed change. The simplicity of the process shows how markedly unified the Constitution is, no such requirement is demanded as is demanded by the Australian Constitution, the principle that the people shall be directly consulted and that a majority shall approve of the change is not adopted.

If both Houses of Parliament present addresses to the Admission of territories to the Union. King, the King with the advice of His Privy Council may admit into the Union the territories administered by the British South Africa Company, on such terms and conditions as to representation and otherwise in each case as are expressed in the addresses and approved by the King. The provision is similar to that in the Canadian Constitution, but again singularly unlike the provisions in the Australian Constitution. Any Order in Council for the purpose of carrying out the admission possesses the force of an Act of Parliament. At present Rhodesia is administered by the Chartered Company, and apparently there are three alternatives open for it in the future. It may join the Union, it may become a Crown Colony, or it may continue under the Administration of the Chartered Company for some years. The matter rests with the King in Council, for even if the Union Parliament should present addresses to the Crown praying for its admission, the Crown has power to decline to admit it. Although no provision is made requiring the assent of the people of Rhodesia to any transfer of their Government, no doubt the wishes of the people would be Territories occupied by natives. carefully consulted. By the adoption of a similar procedure, the government of territories inhabited wholly or in part by natives, and under British protection, may be transferred, and on the transfer the Governor in Council may undertake the government of such territory upon the terms and conditions embodied in the schedule to the Union Act.

CHAPTER XLI

THE NATURE OF THE UNION CONSTITUTION

ALTHOUGH the Act constituting the Union of South Africa Legislative Union. contains many provisions which are in accordance with the principles of Federalism, the Constitution is in reality a Legislative Union. The preamble of the South African Act does not state that the Union is Federal, but it expressly declares that it is desirable for the welfare and future progress of South Africa that the several British Colonies therein should be united under one Government in a legislative union under the Crown of Great Britain. The Constitution of South Africa is, therefore, unlike any of the great Federal Constitutions which avowedly adopt the Federal principle as the basis of their Constitution.

The Federal principle, however, does exist and is in Existence of Federal principle. evidence in the composition of the Senate, which was chosen at the outset, but only partially, on the method adopted for the election of Senators in the United States. The four Provinces in the Senate, also, possess an equality of representation, which is a feature in all the Federal Constitutions except Canada.

The difficulties which have been attendant on a Legislative Union in the United Kingdom and in Canada under the Constitution of 1840, where it will be remembered that it was attempted to bring two races in one Legislative Union only for the attempt to fail[1] seems to have been present to the minds of the framers of the Constitution. Instead of endowing the Union Parliament with all the powers that the Imperial Parliament possesses in Great Britain and Ireland, they relieved it of some of the functions by the establishment of Provincial Councils.

The Imperial Parliament legislates for all the wants of England, Scotland, Ireland and Wales, sometimes by separate

[1] *Ante,* p. 186.

Acts, with the result that the legislative machine is clogged and weary legislators surrender their legislative powers to non-representative bodies empowered to make rules and regulations with the force of laws—whether sufficient power has been given to the Councils in South Africa or whether the Union Parliament will not deprive them of the possession of what they now possess time alone will show. The school of thought that sees perfection only in a unified Constitution forgets the value of local legislatures the better to unite in one general Government two or more different races. Whether the problem has been as successfully solved in South Africa as it has been in Canada is somewhat doubtful.

Senate.

The Senatorial electorate in South Africa is a State electorate, since it consists of members of the Provincial Councils, who vote with the Members of the House of Assembly for each Province. The plan thus adopted consequently makes the Members of the first Chamber in a large measure responsible for the election of the Second Chamber, but at the same time it may be said that it assures a State representation. The method in force prescribed by the Constitution, however, may be of only a temporary character, since Parliament possesses the power to constitute the Senate in a different manner at the expiration of ten years. The Federal principle may also be recognised in the acceptance by the Central Government of the existing provincial franchise but with some modifications, as the qualification for the Union Parliamentary franchise.

Acceptance of Provincial franchise.

The acceptance of the State or Provincial franchise as the qualification for the Federal franchise is, as has already been pointed out, a common feature in all the four Constitutions.

The Constitution is in no wise such a democratic Constitution as that of the United States or Australia. One instance of this has been seen in the way that the boundaries of provinces may be changed without a direct vote of the people concerned.

Likeness to Canada.

In many respects it shows a considerable likeness to the Constitution of Canada, but in the distribution of power between the Provinces and the Central Authority the least possible authority has been given to Provincial Councils, and far less than has been given to the Provinces in Canada. Again, the chief Executive officer, the administrator, is of far less importance as his title denotes than the Lieutenant-Governor of a Canadian Province, for the Provincial Councils are very little more than Local Government Councils ; a Provincial Council cannot make laws, but only ordinances, assent to which is given by the Governor-General in Council, and not as in the case of Canada by a Lieutenant-Governor, who is the Royal Representative of the Province. Any ordinances when assented cease to be operative if repugnant to any Act of Parliament.

The establishment by the Constitution of a Harbour and Railway Board acts as a check upon the power of Parliament in matters of administration, and it was no doubt advisable to remove the great enterprises it controls from the direct control of Parl ament.

In many of its provisions the Union Act has regard to the existence of the two nations which it unites. Thus it places the English and Dutch languages on terms of equality, and continues existing systems of laws, although it enables alterations to be effected. · · *Administrative check on Parliament. Reference to existence of two nations.*

Perhaps its most marked characteristics is the regard that it pays to the interests of the native races, instanced in the provisions against electoral disqualification in the Cape of Good Hope on the grounds of race and colour, and by the other safeguards enacted against abuse of the natives, by vesting the control and administration of native affairs in the Governor in Council. *Interests of native races.*

Whilst in many important matters Canada is unable to alter her Constitution except by means of an Imperial Act, the South African Parliament is empowered to repeal or alter any of the provisions of her Constitution Act, although no alteration or repeal may take place in many notable instances until the Act has been in force ten years. In other instances the alteration or repealing power can only be used when the Bill making the Constitutional *Amendment of Constitution.*

change has been carried on a third reading by a two-thirds majority of members of both Houses at a joint sitting. The Constitution cannot be said to be in any way rigid. Compared with the process of alteration and amendment in the Union of South Africa how different seems the methods of amendment prescribed by the other three Federal Constitutions.

The Judiciary. The Judiciary, unlike that of Canada, is established by the terms of the Constitution, and is not left to Parliament to organise. In this respect the South African Constitution Federal jurisdiction. resembles the Constitution of the United States and Australia. Its Courts, as in Australia, exercise both Appellate and Federal jurisdiction, but the Federal jurisdiction is confined to the ascertainment of the validity of a provincial ordinance, when it comes in question. The Federal jurisdiction is, therefore, of very small importance when compared with the jurisdiction exercised in the United States or Australia. Again, it is far less than that exercised by the Courts of Canada.

New territories. In the provisions relating to the admission of new territories to the Union, some likeness is seen to the procedure required to be adopted in similar cases in Canada ; but in Canada it was unnecessary to take the elaborate precautions required for the benefit of the native races.

Free trade. Free trade exists throughout the Union, but the Constitution provided that the duties of Customs and Excise should remain as they were in the Colonies composing the Union until altered by Parliament.

CHAPTER XLII

COMPARISON OF FEDERAL CONSTITUTIONS

IT has been necessary from time to time to institute com- Impulses of Federation. parisons between the four Constitutions. There are, however, important matters that have not been contrasted in detail. One of these is a consideration of the impulses that brought about Federation. It has been pointed out that this impulse was supplied originally by trade in Australia, but the appearance of foreign Powers in the waters of the Pacific quickened the movement into strong vitality. In the case of South Africa, it was only when exhausted by wars between her peoples that she found at last to her cost that she had neglected her task of unifying herself so long that it must be done at once. In Canada the Federal movement was completed by the threats of a Fenian invasion following on the warning spectacle of the War of Secession in her neighbour State. The old Confederation of the United States was based solely upon the necessities of a Defence without which it could never have had an existence, and the present Federation was the outcome of the failure of its predecessor.

In all the three Imperial Constitutions it will be found Movement from the people. that the movement has always sprung from the people of the States and not from above. Earl Grey could not, although he evidently wished it, found a Federated Australia. The time was not yet come, and a Federal Constitution could not be made by any outside impulse in advance of Australian national destiny. Again, the Earl of Carnarvon cordially welcomed whilst he did not frame the Dominion Act or even suggest it. That was the work of Canadian statesmen. Flushed with the part he played as Colonial Secretary in the work of Canadian Federation, he longed to repeat his triumph in creating a Federated South Africa to be united on the Canadian model, but South

427

Africa was deaf to outside inspiration. Mr. Froude, who journeyed out to South Africa at Earl Carnarvon's request as an unofficial Federal plenipotentiary, returned disappointed in his high hopes.

Another important aspect of Federation is to be found in the signification of a general desire and consent of the peoples of the various States, Provinces, or Colonies, for Federation. Till there is a general union and a free consent, no perfect Union can be established.

Two of the thirteen States of America did not join the Union till after its formation, although some pressure was employed no coercive force was used. ·When these States joined it was as willing members. Not. all the Provinces of Canada joined the Confederation at once, but no bitterness was created. The door was left open and they all eventually came in but Newfoundland, which up till this day stands out in solitary dignity. In Australia, Western Australia did not join till late, and New Zealand has never become a member of the Federation. In South Africa, Natal expressed a wish that the people should be consulted, and a Referendum was taken, but no resentment was shown. Her right was admitted and hereby the great principle was approved that all the people must be consulted when they are asked to place themselves under a new form of government. ·

Thus, Federation has always rested on a brotherly pact to live henceforth in amity, the true foundation of which has been the uncoerced and reasoned consent of the people of every part of the Federation.

The mandate of the people in the United States and Australia was given by the Governments and the people. In Canada by the legislative Authority and in South Africa by all the Legislatures, except Natal, where both the people and Legislature assented.

In comparing the four Constitutions, the amending powers show striking diversities. Whilst the amendment of the United States' Constitution is essentially slow in action and surrounded by difficulties, the Constitution of

Marginal notes:

Based upon free consent.

Basis of Federal assent.

Mandate for.

Amending powers.

Canada, except so far as it contains amending powers in itself, is incapable of amendment except by an amending Act of the Imperial Government. In Australia the amendment of the Constitution rests with the people under referendum provisions, whilst in South Africa the amending power remains with her Parliament.

In the United States and Australia the President and the Governor-General are trusted to suggest alterations and amendments to proposed legislation, but neither Canada nor South Africa entrust him with such authority.

Again, a comparison of the Second Chambers exhibits *Second Chambers.* remarkable diversities. The Senate of the United States is neither an hereditary Second Chamber, nor is it nominated nor directly elected by the popular vote.[1] Nevertheless, it has been accorded general approval as a revising Chamber, whilst it has in the main fulfilled its function as a State representation embodying the Federal principle. To quote Sir Henry Maine, it is the one thoroughly successful institu- *Sir Henry Maine's views.* tion which has been established since the tide of modern democracy began to run.

What is the reason ? Though not popularly elected, it has yet had a sufficiency of support behind it to hold its own with the popular Chamber. In a large measure this has been due to the fact that it is a State representation. A *State representation.* Senator is armed with the consciousness that he is the chosen of two branches of his State Legislature. The moral force behind him is consequently very great. If a representative of the popular Assembly can rely on the fact that he is chosen of the people of the United States, a Senator can rely with equal confidence on his choice by the considered judgment of his State Legislature.

Would this apply as an argument with equal force if *Rota principle.* Senators were all elected at one and the same time for six years ? Probably not, since it then might be urged by a representative fresh from his constituency that the popular opinion had changed in six years. Whatever a Senator once was at the end of his term he was no more than the

[1] *Ante,* p. 48.

mere reflection of a dead public opinion. The fact that one-third of the Senate is renewed every two years renders such an argument impossible. If any great change has come over the political ideas of the country, the signs are reflected in an alteration of the composition of the Senate. Like the fabled Giant who was thrown to Mother Earth, and at each fall renewed his vigour, so the Senate constantly revivifies itself each two years by the State's mandate. Other Senates may have the respect of years behind them, public service, long experience, honours, wealth. All these advantages the American Senate possesses. They are but additional qualifications of respect to commend it to the citizens. Yet if they stood by themselves they would be of insufficient authority to counterbalance the overwhelming weight of a popularly elected Chamber.

Canadian
Senate.

The Canadian Senate is nominated. Consequently it does not rest on such a solid basis as does an elected Chamber. The Governor-General is the nominating authority, and therefore theoretically the Chamber should be an impartial one as nominated by an impartial authority. Owing, however, to the workings of Responsible Government, it has proved a partisan body. Sir John Macdonald, who was Prime Minister for nearly thirty years after 1867, insisted that the Governor-General should fill up vacancies in the Senate according to the advice of the Government with the result that Canadian Senators have become mere nominees of the ruling party. Since the office was for life, the advent of the Opposition to power exhibited the spectacle of the two Houses holding antagonistic views. Sir John Macdonald, during his premiership, is said to have appointed one Liberal to the Senate ; Sir Wilfrid Laurier appointed no Conservative. Owing to the workings of Responsible Government, it is difficult to see how either statesmen could have acted otherwise.

Again, the numbers of the Canadian Senate are strictly limited, and cannot be increased except by Imperial legislation ; the situation, therefore, forbids the exercise of political generosity. If a Senator resigns or dies his place must by the exigencies of the case be filled by an adherent of the party in power. It is impossible, as in the United Kingdom, to use the threat to swamp the Second Chamber with new Senators. The Canadian Government in power, if it so long lasts, must bide its time till Senatorial vacancies occur. The smoothness of the running of the legislative machine is, therefore, necessarily largely dependent upon the vitality or staying powers of Opposition Senators, who are generally indisposed to resign to oblige the Government. A loyal party Senator, indeed, would adopt the Fabian policy of delaying an intended resignation. Even the exigencies of the State will not move a Senator convinced of his political indispensability. If quick changes of Government should happen in Canada, it is difficult to prophecy how the legislative machinery would work.

By reason of the method of its composition, the Senate largely loses its value as a revising Chamber. The best criticism of a measure comes from its opponents or sometimes from disappointed friends. There is no necessity for the latter in the Canadian Senate, and as for the former the longer the one party is in power the smaller in numbers is the other. In fact, during the Macdonald and Laurier administrations, Canada was virtually under unicameral Government.

Again, though the original tripartite division of the Dominion Senate suggested the Federal idea of the equality of States, the Senate is not now genuinely representative of equal State Representation. It does not even indicate it. With the addition of new Provinces this idea has practically disappeared. Federal principle.

In Australia the Senate is akin to the United States' model, although there are important variations. Equality of State representation is kept, but the method of select appointment is absent. The people of the States elect the Senate, therefore the Senate is directly chosen. An election for a whole State admits of a platform being put forward which may not have the remotest connection Australian Senate.

with State interests. Again, the election for six years
with one-half of the Senate retiring at the end of the third
year, does not seem, from a democratic view, an improvement on the third retiring at the end of two years as in the
United States.

In one respect the Australian Senate and that of the
Union of South Africa are better than those of the older
Constitutions. They recognise the possibility of a deadlock
between the two legislative chambers and make provision
for it. The Australian Constitution is, however, the sounder
of the two, for it prohibits tacking, and forbids the amendment of money Bills or Bills imposing taxation by the
Senate, but allows the Senate to suggest and reject alterations in any such Bills. It thus recognises the principle
of the equality of representative authority. It provides
for the termination of a deadlock after an interval for
reflection by dissolution, and, in the event of the continuance of the deadlock, provides for a joint sitting, and a final
decision by an absolute majority of both Houses voting
together as one body.

Deadlock provisions.

The South African Senate, at any rate for the first ten years
of its existence, contains the nominated as well as the elected
element. In respect of all the first elected members, it
adopted the system of the United States in that the Senators
were chosen by the Colonial Legislatures of the Provinces.
What system may be ultimately adopted time alone will
show. Until a change is made future Senators of the Union
will be elected by members of the Provincial Council of a
Province, together with the Members of the House of
Assembly for the Province. So far the method of a select
appointment of Senators by representative bodies distinguishes the method of choosing the Senate from the far
more democratic system of Australia.

The South African Senate.

The South African Constitution omits the provision which
enables the Governor-General of Australia to dissolve both
Houses. It, however, adopts the idea of both Houses
sitting together, and voting, and the attainment of a final
decision by a majority of the joint Houses. It does not,

however, adopt the rota principle of the United States and
Australia, but leaves its Senators in possession of their seats
for ten years, thus avoiding the difficulty created by the life
Senate of Canada. It would seem that through the Provincial Councils the future Senate may be likely to acquire
a considerable strength as a State representation, that might
eventually be used to increase the power of the Councils.
On the other hand, if they fail to establish their popularity
it is not unlikely that the votes of Members of the
Assembly for the Provinces voting with the councillors,
may so leaven the Senate as to make the Second Chamber
a mere reflex of the First Chamber. Again, since a Senator
is elected by a voting on the proportional system, each voter
having one transferable vote, an election is bound to be a
source of a good deal of bargaining amongst politicians,
suggesting compromises which in their turn may lead to a
diminution of the respect that the Second Chamber should
always hope to obtain. "The exact functions," says
Mr. Keith, "which will be performed by so remarkably
constituted a body it is difficult to foretell."[1]

· There is no power in the Senate to suggest amendments to
Money Bills. The power of rejection, however, remains
and could be used except in respect of annual Appropriation Bills. In the method of choice of this Senate and by
reason of its duration it will fail to give full effect to the only
true conservatism in a democracy, that is the conservatism
of second thoughts obtained by the adoption of the rota
principle. Nor does it adequately provide for an independent
State representation.

In a unified Constitution, the idea may be suggested
that the best Second Chamber would be an elected Chamber.
The franchise, which might be the same as for the first,
would contain an electorate of double the size, obtained by
the grouping of two ordinary constituencies together. The
adoption of the rota principle under which one-third of the
Second Chamber should retire at the end of each two years
would ensure its always being in touch with the trend of

---

[1] Keith's *Responsible Government*, Vol. II, p. 640.

public opinion. Possibly the deadlock principles of the South African Constitution might be introduced to avoid conflicts between the two Houses, to prevent those too frequent appeals to the people, which are always a source of embarrassment to an Executive.

Distribution of powers.

In the distribution of the powers of government, the Constitutions of the United States and Australia recognise the importance of the States as component parts of the Federal Union. In Canada and South Africa, the Provinces are of less importance. A Single Chamber is sufficient in the majority of the Provinces for all provincial purposes in Canada, a Council in South Africa. Under the Imperial system, nothing better shows the importance of the States of Australia than the existence of the Royal Governor, directly chosen by, and responsible in his Imperial capacity to the Crown. The Provinces of South Africa only possess an Administrator appointed by the Governor in Council, that is, by the Government in power. In Canada the appointment of Lieutenant-Governors is similarly made, the Lieutenant-Governor receiving his instructions from the Dominion Secretary of State. In the United States the people of the States choose their own Governors. A choice of Governors by the people of the Australian States would directly tend to weaken the authority of the State in Imperial Councils.

Nature of criticism.

It must be presumed that the people are satisfied with the Constitutions that they possess. Therefore, criticism must be largely directed by a critic's individual point of view, according to whether he believes in a pure Democracy as the best of governments or not. Any other views must be expressed by writers and persons familiar with the workings of the Constitution under which they live.

If the time occupied by the statesmen engaged and a knowledge of the working of other Constitutions, should have made a Constitution perfect, then the Australian Constitution should be the best of the three.

Is it so ? An admirer of Federal institutions would say " Yes ! As a Constitution it is superior to that of the

United States. It corrects the faults of that Constitution, yet conserves the individualism of the State."

An admirer of a unified Government would say " No," and would argue : " What advantages does a Federal Constitution confer ? Governments within a Government, conflicts of jurisdiction and jealousies, a duplicated Parliamentary machinery and a double citizenship."

The admirer of Federal institutions, whilst admitting some disadvantages, will reply that no system of government ever devised is perfect, but will enquire if the Federal principle does not confer compensating advantages greater than its disadvantages ? For an increased cost of administration there is greater efficiency and more control by the people. A unified Government may legislate for millions over vast areas, under different climates, but it cannot legislate without losing touch of its constituents.

The British Parliament during the eighteenth century Failure of Imperial signally failed to govern the Empire. During the nineteenth Parliament. century it met with but small success. The loosening of Imperial Parliamentary control was not a weakening of bonds, but instead was a tightening of them.

Mr. Bryce considers that the faults generally charged on Mr. Bryce on faults of Federations as compared with unified Governments are Federalism. the following—

(1) Weakness in the conduct of foreign affairs.

(2) Weakness in Home Government, that is to say, deficient authority over the component States and the individual citizens.

(3) Liability to dissolution by the secession and rebellion of States.

(4) Liability to division into groups and factions by the formation of separate combinations of the component States.

(5) Want of uniformity among the States in legislation and administration.

(6) Trouble, expense, and delay due to the complexity of a double system of legislation and administration.

Whilst all of these faults at some time or other have shown

Fault not of system but of Constitutional machinery. themselves in the United States, and some still exist and call for a remedy, it has not been so much the system as the workings of the machinery that has been in fault. They have so far been less evident in the three Imperial Constitutions.

Value of Federalism to the Empire. Federalism has undoubtedly been the means of uniting adjacent Colonies and Provinces of the Empire, and, contrary to expectation, has increased, and not diminished, the feelings of attachment to the Motherland. It has proved the best means of developing new areas which other-

Advantages of Federalism. wise would have developed more slowly under a bureaucratic administration ; since it has allowed the inhabitants who knew their needs to develop them in accordance with their experience.

Healthy rivalry. Where a number of States are united under Federalism a healthy rivalry springs up. Legislative experiments are watched with the keenest interest ; nor does their failure result in disaster as it would in an old country.

Avoidance of bureaucracy. It is an old maxim that a delegated authority cannot be delegated, and perhaps this should apply with the greatest force to Governments who are elected to legislate and not to depute their trust to an irresponsible body. Yet how is it possible for one legislative authority whose power stretches over thousands of miles to avoid breaking this rule ! The delegation of power to a body, empowered to legislate by making orders, rules, and regulations as they please, constitutes a bureaucracy ; Federalism, and on a smaller scale, Local Government, avoids the necessity for delegations of this character, providing in its place Government of the people by the people.

Checks on over-centralisation. In the four Constitutions, the Provinces and States of Australia, Canada, and South Africa, may be trusted to satisfactorily discharge their functions as parts of the unit, bulwarks against the rise of a despotic central power, and citadels of freedom for the individual citizen.

Truer Federalism amongst people of the same race, It is curious and perhaps not a coincidence, to notice the ampler powers possessed by the States, where the people have been practically all of one race and religion, as in the United States and Australia, and how a lesser power has been given to Provinces uniting where there have been two races joined in Union, as in Canada and South Africa. Questions of race and religion might snap the golden chain that bound, therefore, to avoid such a calamity the central power has been proportionately strengthened. It is true that a union may be dissolved by people of the same race, as it once was for a time in the United States, but such a possibility must always seem remote.

CHAPTER XLIII

THE UNITED KINGDOM AND ITS RELATIONS WITH
THE GROWTH OF THE EMPIRE (*continued*)

THE close of the second period, that ended with the Golden
Jubilee of Queen Victoria in 1887, shows a very slow approx-
imation towards Imperial ideals by the peoples of the
Empire. The apostles of Imperialism were discouraged.

Froude, in the pages of *Oceana,* cannot discern whether
the Empire will ever take form. Indeed the Colonies were

like ships at sea, tossed about and buffetted by the waves,
but steering no common course and apparently bound for no
common destination. Will they ever reach the haven of a
United Empire, a haven that promises peace, happiness and
security for all ? Froude cannot say. The historical
aspect of the Colonies rivets his vision. Like a stately
procession of Tudor times, there passes before his eyes:
the men of the *Mayflower,* who fled from oppressive laws
to the Plantations making the lusty life of New England.
There were Australia and South Africa, lands of ample
promise, but there was also the past folly of British statesmanship. Had the Mother Country yet learned her lesson ?
Would nothing wake her from her lotus dreams ? It was
true that there was hope but it was mingled with grave
doubt ! Had much legislated Australia forgiven the planting
of convict stations on her shores, the favouritism and the
blundering of the Colonial Office ? Perhaps, but slowly,
for people have long memories. Froude, sailing round the
Empire, found in the Oversea dominions statesmen no whit
inferior to those he had mixed with in the councils of the
Mother Country. At Melbourne, where he stopped for a
while, he met Mr. Service, the Premier of Victoria, and was
charmed ; outside the United Kingdom the men were more
loyal to the Empire's ideal than those within its borders.
The book of fate was closed to Froude, but the lessons that

he and others taught were not lost. The poets and the
writers of the Victorian age were like the birds that sing
with the first breaking of the dawn, heralding sunshine,
and the promise of a glorious day !

The second Colonial Conference met outside Great Britain *Second Colonial Conference.*
at Ottawa in 1894, at the invitation of the Canadian Govern-
ment. The Conference discussed many things of moment,
but chiefly the question of reciprocal trade within the *Colonial Conference*
Empire. In 1897 the third, or the second Colonial Confer- *of 1897.*
ence, as it is generally called, met in London. In 1902 the
Colonial Conference, which again met in London, began to *Growing importance of*
take form as an Imperial body of great weight. It then *Conference.*
resolved that it was for the benefit of the Empire that it
should meet at intervals not exceeding four years for the
discussion of questions of common interest affecting the
relations of the Mother Country and the King's dominions
over the seas.

In 1907 the fourth Colonial Conference met. The Prime *Fourth Colonial Conference.*
Minister of the United Kingdom assumed its presidency,
and was declared to be its *ex-officio* President. The Secretary of State was also declared to be an *ex-officio* member,
taking the chair in the absence of the President. Ministers
such as their Governments might appoint were also constituted members. The Federal principle of equality of
State was acknowledged by each Government being allotted
one vote in the Conference.

At this Conference the permanent Secretarial Staff *The Secretariat.*
came into existence, under the direction of the Secretary of
State, to obtain information for the use of the Conference
to attend to its resolutions and conduct correspondence on
matters relating to its affairs. An additional power was
now given to call subsidiary Conferences.

In 1909 and 1910 subsidiary Conferences discussed *Subsidiary Conferences.*
Imperial military and naval defence, and copyright.

In 1911 the fifth Conference, like the others, met in *Fifth Conference.*
London, and for the first time the statesmen of the Domin-
ions were admitted into the secrets of Imperial policy.
A quarter of a century had only just elapsed since the

meeting of the first Conference of 1887. During these years Australia and South Africa had become federated and all the Dominions had reached manhood, and were growing strong in numbers, wealth, and strength.

Gain to the Empire.

What has been the gain to the Empire during this quarter of a century ? Imperial co-operation and Imperial defence, assimilation of laws, copyright, trade marks and patents, and partial co-operation in company law ; administrative changes, appointments of Trade Commissioners in the Dominions performing largely the duties of consuls in foreign countries, the recommendation of an Imperial Court of Appeal, naturalisation, with a recognition that after a period of five years' residence that the Imperial citizenship would follow. These have all either come into existence or are being effected, but this has not been all discussion, and intimacy have brought about a truer idea of the Empire amongst all concerned.

Committee of Imperial Defence.

Another body whose activities have been manifest during the last twenty-five years has been the Committee of Imperial Defence. For practical purposes this body superseded the joint naval and military committee established in 1890. The composition of this committee is very elastic, and admits of the presence of members of the Dominions to its deliberations. In 1905 Mr. Lyttleton, then Colonial Secretary, referred to it in his proposals for an Imperial Council.

Difficulties of creating Constitutional body.

It is extremely difficult to suggest any constitutional body on any scheme of Imperial Federation which would absolutely preserve the autonomy of all the self-governing Dominions and yet fulfil the purposes for which it was created. The position taken up by Mr. Chamberlain was

Mr. Chamberlain's position not now true.

that the United Kingdom was in the position of a trustee administering the Empire for the benefit of the Dominions, her *cestuis que trustent*. This, when he spoke, was comparatively speaking, true, but now the beneficiaries are coming of age, admitting their responsibility to the Empire, and preparing to take their share in its Government. It is clear that their request must be granted.

What is the Committee of Imperial Defence but a com- mittee to advise the Cabinet. The Cabinet is a committee which has been evolved from the Privy Council. Once the Government of the Colonies was carried out by the Privy Council and by a Committee of Trade and Plantations, who advised the Privy Council on all matters relating to trade and the Plantations, obtained expert advice, and executed the delegations of the Privy Council. It may possibly be found that as the Cabinet was evolved from the Privy Council, that an Imperial Cabinet may spring from an Imperial Privy Council, the members of which would be severally responsible for their share in the administration of the Empire to their own Parliaments and peoples.

The King is part of the Legislature of every Dominion, as well as of the Imperial Parliament ; as part of the Legislatures of the Dominions he is a separate Jurassic person, but every member of a Dominion Ministry is a member of an Executive Council, which advises him in the government of the Dominions as the Cabinet does in the United Kingdom. As the King was King of England and Duke of Normandy, so on the old theory that found favour with James I and Charles I, the King was King of England and of all and each of the Plantations. The theory is not now true in law, yet it must always have a fascinating attraction to the Imperialist, in view of the modern claim put forward by the Dominions to be sister States and sister nations. The powers of the Cabinet of the United Kingdom, which is a Sovereign State, exceed the powers of any of the Cabinets of the Dominions, since with Sovereign State rests the power to declare peace or war. To make an United Empire all the people of the Dominions must participate in the exercise of the Sovereign powers, and receive as a necessary result a representation, not in regard to the domestic affairs of the United Kingdom, but in regard to those common spheres of action which concern them equally as much as they do the people of the Mother Country. This they could exercise through an Imperial Cabinet, which would include in its Imperial membership all the members of the Cabinets of the

Dominions, and in practice could work through ministers for external affairs. Since such a representation would not interfere with the autonomy of the Mother Country, neither would it interfere with the autonomy of the Dominions.

The domain over which the Government of the United Kingdom exercises sole control would then be entrusted to the Dominions, in conjunction with the Mother Country. Instead of the Empire having only one trustee, as at present, there would be several trustees appointed by all the Dominions to execute the Imperial trust for the common benefit.

The Imperial Cabinet or Imperial Council, in its functions, must necessarily be mainly a consultative body, but it would work through its different legislatures. The first stage of Empire must be a Government of Consultation.

In surveying the many agencies that have assisted of recent years in so marked a way Imperial development, regard must be paid to the part played by the High Commissioners and the Agents-General, the official representatives of their Dominions or States in London. The duties of these high functionaries partake partly of the diplomatic and partly of the commercial character. In their first mentioned capacity they form a channel of negotiation on the spot with the Secretary of State for the Colonies on matters affecting their particular Governments. They are also able by reason of their position to inform their own Governments of matters not only particular to it, but also generally of the trend of thought in the heart of the Empire.

Of the Agents-General, those of Australia are of the greatest constitutional importance owing to the position that their States occupy under Federation. They represent States which possess considerable powers of Government, which they did not surrender by Federation. As their Governors, unlike the Lieutenant-Governors of Canada, who communicate with the Secretary of State for the Dominion, communicate directly with the Secretary of

Marginal notes:

No interference with autonomy.

Additional trustees.

Imperial Cabinet or Council.

Agencies bringing about Imperial development. High Commissioners' and Agents-General diplomatic capacities.

Importance of Australian Agents-General, Reasons for.

State for the Colonies, so the Agents-General are entitled
on behalf of their Governments to make representations
directly to the Secretary of State for the Colonies. It may Direct representa-
be said that, from the point of view of the Imperial Govern- tions to
ment, they are not official mediums. This is no doubt Secretary of State.
officially true, but nevertheless as the accredited mediums Official
of their Governments, they are entitled to express their channel.
views to the Home Authorities.

The Governors' communications are by letter or telegram, Negotiating.
but neither letters nor telegrams are always required. In
negotiating, as Lord Bacon says, it is generally better to
deal by speech than letter, and in all negotiations of difficulty
a man may not look to sow and reap at once, but must
prepare business and so ripen it by degrees.[1]

The Agents-General of the Provinces of Canada and Consuls of Trade.
the States of Australia may also be termed in a sense consuls
of trade, but their functions are not exactly the same in
other respects.

The Agents-General for Canada are necessarily of less Distinction between
importance, since the powers of the Provinces are less than Australian
the powers of the Australian States. In matters of trade and Canadian Agents-
the Australian Agents-General occupy as important a General.
position as they do in matters of emigration, for throughout
Australia, except in the Northern Territories, the lands
belong to the States. It has been previously explained that
the State Governments still exercise such of the concurrent
powers of legislation of the Government of Australia as
have not been assumed by the Commonwealth Parliament,
and that in addition they possess very considerable residuary
powers of legislation. For this reason the Agents of the
Government, the Agents-General, are generally chosen out
of the ranks of Ministers who possess both ministerial and
commercial experience.

The agencies in London of the High Commissioners and Organisation of agencies.
Agents-General comprise excellent Secretaries and perma-
nent officials trained by long experience in the duties Permanent Secretary and Staff.

[1] Bacon's *Essays*, No. XLVII, on Negotiating.

of their office. Whilst High Commissioners and Agents-General, on the one hand, are generally appointed for a fixed term by their Governments, the officials are, like the permanent officials, under Parliamentary government in the United Kingdom, who by their permanency supply an experience, which is very advantageous. A system which benefits the Mother Country by sending to her shores distinguished representatives from the Dominions, has not been without lasting benefit. The offices of the High Commissioners and Agents-General form so many secretariats of information of an accessible character, and which are without the traditional distinguishing features of aloofness common to so many public departments.

Distinguished
Australians.

Secretariats
for
information.

The veteran Lord Strathcona is High Commissioner for Canada ; Sir George Reid for Australia ; whilst the Union of South Africa has as its High Commissioner Sir R. Solomon. By the retirement of Sir John Taverner, the Agent-General for Victoria, Mr. T. A. Coghlan, the Agent-General for New South Wales becomes the Senior Agent-General of the States of Australia.

The Press.
In the work of Imperial Development and Co-operation the Press has taken its share. An uncensored press spreads the light of freedom, and the necessity for freedom is expressly or impliedly recognised in all the four Constitutions. The meeting of the Press Conference in London has taught its representatives, who are the intelligence service of the people, by the interchange of ideas, the necessity for the great task of welding the Empire together. They have not failed, but have looked from the heights of an Imperial Pisgah and seen afar off the promised land. To describe all the many agencies of Empire that are now at work would be by reason of their numbers too great a task. All are contributing to form that irresistible force known as public opinion.

Evolution
of the Empire.
In surveying the historical developments of the Empire, it has been shown how slow has been its growth. In the process of evolution it has passed from one stage to another,

but nevertheless always preserving its Anglo-Saxon Fashioned by the people characteristics—hatred of oppression and the love of freedom.

The Empire has not been fashioned by kings or princes, but by the Empire's common folk : the soldiers, the sailor, the workman, the pioneers of woods and forests, the restless toilers on land and sea, the shepherd, the ploughman, the smith, the farmer and the agricultural labourer. Consequently it is not an Empire of privilege or caste.

In the main the Empire is democratic, and it will probably Tendency of the Empire. become more so ! Will this tend to disruption ? The tendency is all the other way. No possible benefit can be promised from disunion that can counterbalance the greater attractions of a closer union. The democracy in all times and in all countries has rejoiced in strength.

It may be asked, but what will the Empire mean to the Peace. millions ; the people of the United Kingdom, the Canadians, the Australians, and South Africans ? Peace is the best of all benefits that may be assured by the protection of an Imperial Fleet. In the consciousness of a giant strength the peoples will be able to develop their lands and riches for the benefit of one and all. The Empire is immeasurably rich in everything that man desires, and when the Imperial citizenship is realised in fact its resources will become more easily developed, and its riches better distributed by the Resources more inevitable results of co-operation. available.

In concluding the history of these four Constitutions and Conclusion. their development, there are but a few words to add. The United States broke away from their Mother Country, introduced a Federal system, and has prospered amazingly under it, there seems no reason therefore why the three Imperial Federations should not meet with at least as great a measure of success.

The existence of Federal systems in a system of Imperial Federalism a benefit. Federation may prove to be of the greatest possible advantage in forming a yet greater one. In Canada and Australia the Provinces and States may be likened to pillars, on which the Arches of Federation rests.   The Empire in turn may rest secure upon the arches of Federation.   The success that has hitherto accompanied Federation as a working principle for the government of large areas by the Anglo-Saxon race may render its application ultimately possible to the Empire as a whole.   It has been proved to be the surest and most effective political system ever devised for forming unions that have afforded scope for that love of justice, fair play, and free discussion, which from the remotest times have been the glory and distinction of the people of the race.

Success of
Federalism.

INDEX

St. Germain, Lord, 160
Story, Dr., on taxing power of United
States, 91 ; on powers necessary
and proper, 102 ; on sovereignty of
States, 106 ; on Constitution
supreme law, 126
Subsidies to Alberta and Saskatche-
wan, 272
Suggestion, power of, 295, 318
Supreme Court, Canada, 245-8
Sydney Conference, 286

TANEY, Chief Justice of United
States, 88
Tacking, 319, 410
Tasmania, Representative Govern-
ment in, 164 ; formation of, 282
Tendency of Empire, 445
Territories, United States, position
of, 118
——, reservation of State rights,
119
Thompson, Deas, 284
Tilden, Democratic candidate for
Presidency, 65
Titles of nobility, 109
Toronto, Convention of, 189
Townsend, Charles, 161
Transvaal, introduction of Responsi-
ble Government, 372
Treaties of United Kingdom, 69
—— of United States, 68
—— (See also Commercial Treaties)
Trek, the Great, 370
Triennial Parliaments, 313
Tupper, Sir Charles, 189, 191

UNICAMERAL legislatures, Canada,
269
Uniformity, rule of, 327
Union of South Africa, nature of
Constitution, 423-6
United Empire Loyalists, 176
—— Kingdom, changes in Govern-
ment of Colonies after Rebellion,
160
—— States, Republican form of
Government, 131
Utrecht, treaty of, 187

VETO, political, value of, 218-23
Vice-president, United States election
of, 63-6
—— ——, functions of, 66
—— —— disqualifications, 66
Victoria, alteration of Constitution
of, 355
——, formation of, 282
Virginia, 29
——, Convention of, 145-6

WASHINGTON, Federal District of,
118
——, George, 24, 25, 70, 118
Webster on United States Con-
stitution, 82
Wentworth, Pioneer of Federation,
284
Westminster Palace Hotel Confer-
ence, 195
Western Australia, formation of, 282
Wolfe, Capture of Quebec, 172
Wyoming, 110

THE END

Printed by Sir Isaac Pitman & Sons, Ltd., Bath
(2125)

———— PITMAN'S ————
CATALOGUE OF GENERAL LITERATURE

ART

GREAT PAINTERS OF THE 19th CENTURY AND THEIR PAINTINGS. By Léonce Bénédite, Keeper of the Musée National de Luxembourg. With over 400 illustrations and 13 coloured plates. In large demy 4to, cloth gilt, gilt top, 10s. 6d. net.

" It is a splendid survey of the progress of painting in Europe and America during the nineteenth century, and combines art criticism with biography in a scholarly and instructive manner. —*Western Mail.*

THE HISTORY OF MUSIC : A Handbook and Guide. By Waldo Selden Pratt. With 130 illustrations and three maps. In demy 8vo, cloth gilt. 7s. 6d. net.

" A most convenient and valuable work of reference . . . the book may be said to cover the whole extensive field to which it is devoted, in a remarkably thorough and comprehensive fashion." —*Westminster Gazette.* " Indispensable in the music-lover's library."—*Pall Mall Gazette.* " A book which for terseness and inclusiveness has never been equalled in music literature."— *Sheffield Telegraph.*

COLOUR PRINTING AND COLOUR PRINTERS. By R. M. Burch. With a chapter on Modern Processes by W. Gamble. With 23 colour prints and 8 half-tone illustrations. In super royal 8vo, cloth gilt. 12s. 6d. net.

" In his excellent work recently published on this subject—a work which is to be heartily commended for the thorough knowledge it displays of colour printing in all its phases as well as for the clear and pleasant style in which this knowledge is communicated— Mr. Burch has traced the history of the colour print from the first doubtful experiments of the Fifteenth Century down to the present day."—*Morning Post.*

WHO'S WHO IN THE THEATRE. A Biographical Record of the Contemporary Stage. By John Parker. In demy 8vo, cloth gilt, 750 pp., 6s. net ; leather, 8s. 6d. net. In addition to the biographical section, the book contains many other interesting features, including a calendar of notable theatrical events ; full details of the new play productions and important revivals of the year in London, the Provinces, New York, and Paris ; Genealogical Tables of famous theatrical families, compiled by Mr. J. M. Bulloch, the Editor of *The Graphic ;* a most exhaustive Dramatic and Musical Obituary ; full particulars of the principal theatres in London, New York, Paris, and Berlin, with the seating plans of the leading London theatres, etc.

WHO'S WHO IN MUSIC. A Biographical Record of Contemporary Musicians. Compiled and Edited by H. SAXE WYNDHAM and GEOFFREY L'EPINE. Large crown 8vo, cloth, 6s. net ; Leather, 8s. 6d. net.

The first edition of the work contains about 1,000 biographies of the leading British, American, Continental, and Colonial Musicians, including Concert and Opera Singers, Concert Agents, Critics, Managers, with detailed accounts of their careers. There are many other features of interest and value.

BIOGRAPHY

JOHN BUNYAN : His Life, Times and Work. By the Rev. JOHN BROWN, B.A., D D. With portrait and illustrations by WHYMPER. Cheap edition. In demy 8vo, cloth gilt, 7s. 6d.

" The best life of John Bunyan."—*Literary World.*

(*See also* Dainty Volume Library, page 4.)

MRS. GASKELL. Haunts, Homes, and Stories. By Mrs. ELLIS H. CHADWICK. New, revised and cheaper edition. In demy 8vo, cloth gilt, 37 illustrations. 5s. net.

" The volume is certain of an enduring place among those which deal with the literary history of this country, and it is certainly indispensable to any who wish to understand the woman of whose life it tells, or the value of her work and influence . . . indeed a sympathetic and faithful picture not only of Mrs. Gaskell, but also of the days in which she lived."—*Manchester Daily Despatch.*

THE LIFE OF DANTE. By the late E. H. PLUMPTRE, D.D., Dean of Wells. Edited by ARTHUR JOHN BUTLER. In fcap. 8vo, lambskin gilt, 2s. 6d. net. Also in cloth, 1s. 6d. net.

THE LIFE OF SAMUEL JOHNSON, LL.D. By JAMES BOSWELL, Newly edited with notes by ROGER INGPEN. With 568 illustrations, including 12 photogravure plates, fully indexed. In two vols., crown 4to, half morocco, 21s. net. (Also in two vols., handsome cloth gilt, 18s. net.)

" A singularly complete and attractive edition. The greatest judgment has been shown in selecting pictures which should illustrate Johnson's period, and bring before the reader's eye the actual features of the men and women among whom he moved. Altogether the New ' Boswell ' is one which will be certain to secure a fresh band of admirers for a work which will ever remain one of the treasures of our literature."—*Westminster Gazette.*

BISHOP WALSHAM HOW. A Memoir. By his Son, FREDERICK DOUGLAS HOW. Cheap Edition. In crown 8vo, cloth gilt, 6s.

" Extremely well done . . altogether a book which cannot be read without profit and encouragement."—*Guardian.*

GEORGE MACDONALD. A Biographical and Critical Appreciation. By JOSEPH JOHNSON. In crown 8vo, cloth gilt 2s. 6d. net.

THE LIFE OF SIR ISAAC PITMAN (Inventor of Phonography). By ALFRED BAKER. " Centenary Edition." In demy 8vo, cloth gilt, with about 50 illustrations, including photogravure and steel plates. 2s. 6d. net.

" The book is very well done. It gives a life-like picture of a strenuous reformer, an original personality, an inventor to whom every newspaper, every public body, and every great business house owes an incalculable debt."—*Christian World.*

LIFE OF REGINALD POLE. By MARTIN HAILE. Second, Revised, and Cheaper edition. In demy 8vo, cloth gilt, with eight illustrations, 7s. 6d. net.

" An excellent book, based on a first-hand acquaintance with documents, some of which are here utilised, for the first time. It gives a vivid and most faithful picture of the last Archbishop of Canterbury who acknowledged the See of Rome."—*Daily Chronicle.*

THE LETTERS OF PERCY BYSSHE SHELLEY. Containing about 480 letters. Collected and edited by ROGER INGPEN. With 42 illustrations and two photogravures. New and cheaper edition, with corrections and additional matter. In two volumes, large crown 8vo, cloth gilt, gilt top, 12s. 6d. net. Hand-made paper *édition de luxe*, half leather, large demy 8vo, 21s. net.

" Mr. Ingpen has done all that can be done to provide us with a perfect edition of one of the most interesting series of letters in English literature. The edition is worthy of the magnificent material with which it deals."—*Daily News.*

REMINISCENCES OF MY LIFE. By Sir CHARLES SANTLEY. In demy 8vo, cloth gilt, gilt top, with 15 illustrations, 16s. net.

" Not a trace of the weary veteran is discernible in this entertaining volume."—*The World.*

COLLECTIVE BIOGRAPHIES

GREAT ASTRONOMERS. By Sir ROBERT BALL. Illustrated. In demy 8vo, cloth gilt, gilt top, 3s. 6d. net

THE HEROIC IN MISSIONS. Pioneers in six fields By the Rev. A. R. BUCKLAND, M.A. In crown 8vo, cloth gilt, 1s. 6d.

MODERN PAINTERS AND THEIR PAINTINGS. By SARAH TYTLER. For the use of Schools and Learners in Art. In crown 8vo, quarter cloth gilt, 4s. 6d.

MUSICAL COMPOSERS AND THEIR WORKS. By the same Author. For the use of Schools and Students in Music. Revised. In crown 8vo, quarter cloth gilt, 4s. 6d.

THE OLD MASTERS AND THEIR PICTURES. By the same Author. For the use of Schools and Learners in Art. New and enlarged edition. In crown 8vo, quarter cloth gilt, 4s. 6d.

THE ORGAN AND ITS MASTERS. A short account of the most celebrated organists of former days, and of the present time, together with a brief sketch of the development of organ construction, organ music, and organ playing. By HENRY C. LAHEE. In large crown 8vo, cloth richly gilt, gilt top, with 14 full-page plate illustrations. 6s. net.

MODERN COMPOSERS OF EUROPE. Being an account of the most recent musical progress in the various European nations with some notes on their history, and critical and biographical sketches of the contemporary musical leaders in each country. By ARTHUR ELSON. In large crown 8vo, cloth gilt, gilt top, with 24 full-page plate illustrations. 6s. net.

PITMAN'S
DAINTY VOLUME LIBRARY

Each in fcap. 8vo, limp lambskin gilt, gilt top, with Photogravure Frontispiece, 2s. 6d. per volume net.

DANTE. THE DIVINA COMMEDIA AND CANZONIERE. Translated by the late DEAN PLUMPTRE. With Notes, Studies, Estimates, and Life. In five volumes.

THE LIFE OF DANTE. By the same Author. In one volume.

THE TRAGEDIES OF ÆSCHYLOS. Translated by DEAN PLUMPTRE. In two volumes.

THE TRAGEDIES OF SOPHOCLES. Translated by DEAN PLUMPTRE. In two volumes

BOSWELL'S LIFE OF JOHNSON. (Abridged.) With an Introduction by G. K. CHESTERTON In two volumes.

THE POETRY OF ROBERT BROWNING. By STOPFORD A. BROOKE, M.A., LL.D. In two volumes.

TENNYSON: HIS ART AND RELATION TO MODERN LIFE. By STOPFORD A. BROOKE, M.A., LL.D. In two volumes.

JOHN BUNYAN; HIS LIFE, TIMES AND WORK. By JOHN BROWN, D.D. In two volumes.

CLOUGH, ARNOLD, ROSSETTI, AND MORRIS: A Study. By STOPFORD A. BROOKE, M.A., LL.D. In one volume, with four illustrations, 306 pp., 3s. 6d. net.

FICTION

BY WHAT AUTHORITY ? By ROBERT HUGH BENSON. **6s.**

THE LIGHT INVISIBLE. By ROBERT HUGH BENSON. **3s. 6d.**

RICHARD RAYNAL, SOLITARY. By ROBERT HUGH BENSON, 3s. 6d.

THE KING'S ACHIEVEMENT. By ROBERT HUGH BENSON. **6s.**

THE QUEEN'S TRAGEDY. By ROBERT HUGH BENSON. **6s.**

THE SENTIMENTALISTS. By ROBERT HUGH BENSON. **6s.**

A MIRROR OF SHALOTT. By ROBERT HUGH BENSON. **6s.**

LORD OF THE WORLD. By ROBERT HUGH BENSON. **6s.**

MY LADY OF AROS. A Tale of Mull and the Macleans. By JOHN BRANDANE. Coloured frontispiece. Cheaper Edition 2s. net.

MEN OF THE MOSS-HAGS. By S. R. CROCKETT. Illustrated. **6s.**

A DAUGHTER OF THE SNOWS. By JACK LONDON. **6s.**

ANNE OF GREEN GABLES. By L. M. MONTGOMERY. **6s.**

ANNE OF AVONLEA. By the same Author. Coloured frontispiece. 6s.

KILMENY OF THE ORCHARD. By the same Author. With four coloured illustrations. 6s.

THE STORY GIRL. By the same Author. Coloured frontispiece. **6s.**

THE GLORY OF THE CONQUERED. The Story of a Great Love. By SUSAN GLASPELL. 6s.

THE UNDER TRAIL. By ANNA ALICE CHAPIN. With illustrations. 6s.

THE PLEASURING OF SUSAN SMITH. By HELEN M. WINSLOW. With illustrations. 3s. 6d. net.

THE ISLAND OF BEAUTIFUL THINGS. A Romance of the South. By W. A. DROMGOOLE. With four coloured illustrations. 6s.

POLLYANNA. The "Glad" Book. By ELEANOR H. PORTER. Illustrated, 6s.

HISTORY

THE ENGLISH IN CHINA. Being an account of the Intercourse and Relations between England and China, from the year 1600 to the year 1843 and a summary of Later Developments. By J. BROMLEY EAMES, M.A., B.C.L. In demy 8vo, cloth gilt, gilt top, with maps and illustrations. 20s. net.

OUTLINES OF THE ECONOMIC HISTORY OF ENGLAND. A Study in Social Development. By H. O. MEREDITH, M.A., M.Com. In demy 8vo, cloth gilt, 5s. net.

THE BRITISH MUSEUM : ITS HISTORY AND TREASURES. A view of the origins of that great Institution, sketches of its Early Benefactors and Principal Officers, and a survey of the priceless objects preserved within its walls. By HENRY C. SHELLEY. Author of *Inns and Taverns of Old London.* With fifty illustrations. Size 6¼ in. by 9¼ in., elaborate cloth gilt, gilt top, 12s. 6d. net.

5

PRINCE CHARLES EDWARD. His Life, Times, and Fight for the Crown. By J. CUTHBERT HADDEN. In demy 8vo, cloth gilt, with illustrations, 7s. 6d. net.

THE ROMANTIC STORY OF THE MAYFLOWER PILGRIMS AND ITS PLACE IN THE LIFE OF TO-DAY. By A. C. ADDISON. With numerous original illustrations. Size 6½ in. by 9⅝ in., cloth gilt, gilt top, 7s. 6d. net.

INNS AND TAVERNS OF OLD LONDON. Setting forth the historical and literary associations of those ancient hostelries, together with an account of the most notable coffee-houses, clubs, and pleasure gardens of the British metropolis. By HENRY C. SHELLEY. In large crown 8vo, cloth gilt, gilt top, with coloured frontispiece and 48 other illustrations. 7s. 6d. net.

OLD COUNTRY INNS. By HENRY P. MASKELL and EDWARD W. GREGORY. With 50 illustrations by the authors. In large crown 8vo, cloth. New Edition with Lists of Old Inns, " Trust " Inns, and Glossary of Signs. 3s. 6d. net.

"Messrs. Maskell and Gregory have written this history of theirs very well indeed. They classify the inns of England according to their origin, rating them as manorial, monastic, Church inns, and so on. They discourse in a pleasant gossipy strain on coaching inns, wayside inns, haunted inns, the inns of literature and art, historical and fanciful signs and curious signboards ; of inn furniture, etc."— *Bookman.*

FLEET STREET IN SEVEN CENTURIES. Being a History of the growth of London beyond the Walls into the Western Liberty and of Fleet Street to our time. By WALTER GEORGE BELL. Author of *The Thames from Chelsea to the Nore.* With a Foreword by Sir Wm. P. Treloar, Bt. With 46 illustrations. Drawings by T. R. Way, Hanslip Fletcher, R. Anning Bell, T. E. Knightley ; reproductions of old prints, original documents, maps and photographs. In demy 8vo, cloth, gilt top, 15s. net.

"Mr. Bell has chosen the picturesque and episodic method for is history, yet it is, *par excellence*, an antiquary's book. Records, rolls, inventories, the proceedings of wardmotes have been laboriously ransacked ; but the result is never tedious, and we have seldom taken up a book of this kind which has had such a power of leading the reader on from page to page."— *Athenæum.*

THE FRANCO-PRUSSIAN WAR AND ITS HIDDEN CAUSES. By ÉMILE OLLIVIER, *of the Académie Française.* Translated from the French with an Introduction and Notes by G. BURNHAM IVES. In demy 8vo, cloth gilt, with eight illustrations, 558 pp., 8s. 6d. net.

A HOSPITAL IN THE MAKING. A History of the National Hospital for the Paralysed and Epileptic (Albany Memorial), 1859-1901. By B. BURFORD RAWLINGS, Author of *The Chronic Indigence of Hospitals*, etc. In crown 8vo, cloth, with illustrations, 5s. net.

A HUNDRED YEARS OF IRISH HISTORY. By R. BARRY O'BRIEN
With Introductions by JOHN E. REDMOND, M.P. New Edition.
In crown 8vo, cloth, 184 pp., 1s. 6d. net.

THE DISSOLUTION OF THE MONASTERIES. As illustrated by the
Suppression of the Religious Houses of Staffordshire. By FRANCIS
AIDAN HIBBERT, M.A., of St. John's College, Cambridge; Head-
master of Denstone. In crown 8vo, cloth gilt, 5s. net.

JOHN PYM. By C. E. WADE, M.A., Barrister-at-law. With
frontispiece. Demy 8vo, cloth gilt, gilt top, 7s. 6d. net.
" Mr. Wade gives a fresh and effective picture of this statesman's
career, keeping throughout in touch with his authorities ; and his
graphic narrative will fill the gap in the bookshelf made by the
disappearance of Forster's Life written nearly 80 years ago, and long
obsolete."—The Times.

MAKERS OF NATIONAL HISTORY. Edited by The Ven. W.
H. HUTTON, B.D. Each volume in this series—the aim of which is
to do fuller justice to men whose lives have not hitherto been adequately dealt with—is in crown 8vo, cloth gilt, with a frontispiece,
3s. 6d. net.

CARDINAL BEAUFORT. By the Rev. L. B. RADFORD, D.D.
" Studiously impartial . . . carefully written."—Glasgow Herald.

VISCOUNT CASTLEREAGH. By ARTHUR HASSALL, M.A.
" It is brilliantly written . . . exceptionally clear and vivid . . .
a book which was needed."—The Morning Leader.

ARCHBISHOP PARKER. By W. M. KENNEDY, B.A.
" Exceedingly well conceived, clearly expressed, and compiled
with great care."—The Guardian.

GENERAL WOLFE. By EDWARD SALMON.
" A picture and an estimate of Wolfe which could not be more
complete."—Canada.

FRANCIS ATTERBURY, Bishop of Rochester (1662-1732). By the
Very Rev. H. C. BEECHING, M.A., Litt.D., Dean of Norwich.
" A most delightful as well as a most valuable book."—Guardian.

EDWARD THE FOURTH. By LAURENCE STRATFORD, B.A.

THOMAS BECKET, Archbishop of Canterbury. By The Ven. W.
H. HUTTON, B.D., Canon of Peterborough, and Archdeacon of
Northampton.

NATURAL HISTORY, ETC.

THE A B C OF POULTRY. By E. B. JOHNSTONE. In crown 8vo,
cloth, cheap edition, 1s. net.
" A capital addition to the many books devoted to the outdoor
life."—World.

CATS FOR PLEASURE AND PROFIT. By Miss FRANCES SIMPSON. Third Edition. In crown 8vo, with 25 beautifully reproduced photographs of famous prize-winning cats. 2s. net.
" The author explains that her object has been ' to help those who desire to combine pleasure with profit.' This aim is very successfully achieved."—*Pall Mall Gazette.*

REPTILES OF THE WORLD. Tortoises and Turtles, Crocodilians, Lizards and Snakes of the Eastern and Western Hemispheres. By Professor RAYMOND L. DITMARS. With frontispiece in colour, and nearly 200 illustrations from photographs taken by the author. In royal 8vo, cloth gilt, gilt top. 20s. net.

BRITISH FERNS. A pocket help for the Student and Collector (comprising all the native species and showing where found). By FRANCIS G. HEATH. Size 6¼ in. by 3½ in., cloth, with 50 illustrations. 2s. net.

PEEPS INTO NATURE'S WAYS. By JOHN J. WARD. Being chapters on insect, plant and minute life. Illustrated from photographs and photo-micrographs taken by the Author. Cheaper Edition. In demy 8vo, cloth gilt, gilt top, 3s. 6d. net.

MISCELLANEOUS

THE DREDGING OF GOLD PLACERS. By J. E. HODGSON, F.R.G.S. With 17 illustrations. In demy 8vo, cloth gilt, gilt top, 5s. net. Principally intended for Company Directors, Property Managers, Prospectors, and the investing public.

ASTONISHING ANATOMY. An anatomical and medical skit profusely illustrated. Letterpress consisting of Imaginary Interviews, Free Medical Advice (after the style of the Weekly Press), etc., etc. By " Tingle." Crown 8vo, 1s. net.

ATHLETIC TRAINING FOR GIRLS. Compiled and Edited by C. E. THOMAS. In crown 8vo, cloth gilt, with many illustrations. Illustrated. 3s. 6d. net.
" A book that every schoolmistress, every mother, and every girl should be compelled to read, for it is full of the best advice and thoroughly practical hints."—*World.*

COMMON COMMODITIES OF COMMERCE. Each handbook is dealt with by an expert writer. Beginning with the life history of the plant, or other natural product, he follows its development until it becomes a commercial commodity, and so on through the various phases of its sale on the market, and its purchase by the consumer. Each is in crown 8vo, cloth, about 120 pp., with map, coloured frontispiece, chart and illustrations, 1s. 6d. net. Tea, from Grower to Consumer, by ALEXANDER IBBETSON. Coffee from Grower to Consumer, by B. B. KEABLE. **Cotton.** From the Raw Material to the Finished Product. By R. J. PEAKE. **Oil** ; Animal, Vegetable, Essential and Mineral. By C. AINSWORTH MITCHELL. Sugar—Cane and Beet. By GEO. MARTINEAU, C.B., Rubber. Production and utilisation of the raw material. By C. BEADLE and H. P. STEVENS, M.A., Ph.D. Iron and Steel. Their production and manufacture. By C. HOOD. Silk. Its production and manufacture. By LUTHER HOOPER. Wool. From the Raw Material to the Finished Product. By J. A. HUNTER. Tobacco. From Grower to Smoker. By A. E. TANNER. Coal : Its Origin, Method of Working, and Preparation for the Market. By FRANCIS H. WILSON, M.Inst., M.E., *Editor of Mining Engineering.*

Other Volumes in preparation

DICKENS IN YORKSHIRE. Being Notes of a Journey to the Delightful Village of Dotheboys, near Greta Bridge. By C. EYRE PASCOE. In foolscap 4to, with four illustrations in colour and 11 black and white illustrations. 1s. 6d. net.

THE FEDERAL SYSTEMS OF THE UNITED STATES AND THE BRITISH EMPIRE. Their Origin, Nature, and Development. By A. P. POLEY, B.A., *of the Inner Temple and Midland Circuit, Barrister-at-Law.* In demy 8vo, cloth gilt, 12s. 6d. net.

FRENCH PROSE WRITERS OF THE NINETEENTH CENTURY AND AFTER. With Biographical and Critical Notices in French, and Literary and Bibliographical Notes in English. By VICTOR LEULIETTE, B-ès-L., A.K.C. In crown 8vo, cloth gilt, 350 pp. 3s. net.

FOR HOME SERVICE AND OTHER STORIES. By LYDE HOWARD. With coloured frontispiece and black and white illustrations. In foolscap 4to, cloth, decorated, coloured top, and end papers, 2s. 6d. net.

HOME GYMNASTICS FOR OLD AND YOUNG. By T. J. HARTELIUS, M.D. Translated and adapted from the Swedish by C. LÖFVING. With 31 illustrations. Fifth Edition, revised. With a prefatory note by ARTHUR A. BEALE, M.B. In stiff boards, 1s. 6d.

HOW TO CHOOSE A HOUSE. How to Take and Keep it. By CHARLES EMANUEL, M.A., and E. M. JOSEPH, A.R.I.B.A. In crown 8vo, cloth, with illustrations. Cheap edition, 1s. net.
" This book seems to us to contain well nigh all the information that a person desiring to acquire a property could desire."— *Record.*

HYPNOTISM AND SUGGESTION. In Daily Life, Education, and Medical Practice. By BERNARD HOLLANDER, M.D. In crown 8vo, cloth gilt, 6s. net.
" We specially welcome the book before us. It is the work of a man of established reputation, who has devoted himself for years to the subject, and whose aim is to tell the English-speaking world what Hypnotism really is, what it can do, and to what conclusions

it seems to point. It is written in a thoroughly scientific spirit. No fact is shirked, and no evidence is either suppressed or rated above its real value."—*Globe.*

LIGHTER MOMENTS. From the note-book of BISHOP WALSHAM HOW. Edited by his son, FREDERICK DOUGLAS HOW. In small crown 8vo, cloth gilt, gilt top, 2s. 6d.

OVERHEARD AT THE ZOO. By GLADYS DAVIDSON. With 2 coloured plates and 26 black and white illustrations. In foolscap 4to, cloth, 2s. 6d. net.
The author has catered for all children who love animals. Her aim has been to present the animals' own point of view, so far as it may be divined by sympathetic study.

OVERHEARD IN FAIRYLAND, or The Peter Pan Tales. By MADGE A. BIGHAM. With coloured illustrations by RUTH S. CLEMENTS. In large crown 8vo, cloth, 2s. 6d. net.

PUBLIC SCHOOL LIFE. Each in foolscap 8vo, cloth, with 32 full page plate illustrations. 2s. net.
WESTMINSTER. By W. TEIGNMOUTH SHORE.
ETON. By AN OLD ETONIAN.
HARROW. By ARCHIBALD FOX.
RUGBY. By H. H. HARDY.

THE ROYAL HIGH SCHOOL, EDINBURGH. By J. J. TROTTER. With 32 illustrations. In crown 8vo, cloth gilt, 3s. 6d. net.

THE REVERIES OF A BACHELOR: Or, A Book of the Heart. By the late IK MARVEL. With an Introduction by ARLO BATES. In foolscap 8vo, gilt top, limp lambskin, 2s. 6d. net. Also in cloth, 1s. 6d. net.

ROODSCREENS AND ROODLOFTS. By F. BLIGH BOND, F.R.I.B.A., and The Rev. DOM BEDE CAMM, O.S.B. With over 88 full-page collotype reproductions, and upwards of 300 other beautiful illustrations. In demy 4to, two vols., handsome cloth gilt, gilt top, 32s. net.
"A magnificent work."—*Evening Standard.*

THE BOOK OF THE CHILD. An Attempt to Set Down what is in the Mind of Children. By FREDERICK DOUGLAS HOW. In foolscap 8vo, leather, with dainty cover design, gilt corners, 3s. 6d. net ; cloth, 2s. net.

MYSTICISM AND MAGIC IN TURKEY. An Account of the Religious Doctrines, Monastic Organisation, and Ecstatic Powers of the Dervish Orders. By LUCY M. J. GARNETT, Author of *Turkey of the Ottomans.* In crown 8vo, cloth gilt, gilt top, with illustrations. 6s. net.

THE PERSIAN PROBLEM. By H. J. WHIGHAM. With maps and illustrations. In demy 8vo, cloth gilt, 12s. 6d.

SCIENCE AND THE CRIMINAL. By C. Ainsworth Mitchell, B.A., F.I.C. In crown 8vo, cloth gilt, 250 pp., with 28 illustrations, 6s. net.
" The systems of personal identification are discussed, and the uses of photography, anthropometry, and finger prints are indicated. The selection of the cases and the manner in which the whole book is written show good judgment."—*Lancet.*

SYMBOLISM OF ANIMALS AND BIRDS Represented in English Church Architecture. By Arthur H. Collins, M.A. [Oxon.]. With 120 illustrations. In demy 8vo, cloth gilt, gilt top, 5s. net.

THE SUNLIT ROAD : Readings in Verse and Prose for Every Day in the Year. By the Rev. W. Garrett Horder. In demy 16mo, cloth gilt, gilt corners, 3s. net ; leather gilt, gilt corners, 4s. net.
" A dainty and delightful little ' day book ' for quiet moments. It is the most charming book of its kind we have seen for a very long time."—*Lady.*

PITMAN'S STUDIES IN ELOCUTION. A guide to the theory and practice of the art of public speaking and reciting, with over 100 selections for Reciters and Readers. By E. M. Corbould (Mrs. Mark Robinson). In crown 8vo, cloth gilt, gilt top, silk register, 2s. 6d. net.
" This treasury of prose and verse will appeal to all who cultivate the art of elocution or appreciate a choice store of literary gems." —*Educational News.*

THE BEGINNINGS OF THE TEACHING OF MODERN SUBJECTS IN ENGLAND. By Foster Watson, M.A. (Professor of Education in the University College of Wales ; Aberystwyth). In crown 8vo, cloth, 7s. 6d. net.

THE INNER LIFE OF GEORGE ELIOT. A Study of the Mental and Spiritual Development of the Novelist. By Charles Gardner, M.A. In crown 8vo, cloth gilt, gilt top, 5s. net.

POETRY, CRITICISM, & LITERARY HISTORY

THE POETRY OF ROBERT BROWNING. By Stopford A. Brooke. Original issue. In demy 8vo, cloth gilt, 10s. 6d.
" The most satisfactory and stimulating criticism of the poet yet published."—*Times.*
(*See also* **Dainty** Volume Library, page 4.)

TENNYSON : HIS ART AND RELATION TO MODERN LIFE. By the same Author. Original issue. In demy 8vo, cloth gilt, 7s. 6d.
" Will make a strong appeal to all lovers of our great Laureate."— *Quarterly Review.*
(*See also* **Dainty** Volume Library, page 4.)

A STUDY OF CLOUGH, ARNOLD, ROSSETTI, AND MORRIS. With an Introduction on the Course of Poetry from 1822 to 1852. By the same Author. In demy 8vo, cloth gilt, 6s. net.
(*See also* **Dainty** Volume Library, page 4.)

EXPERIMENTS IN PLAY WRITING. Six plays in Verse and Prose with an Introductory Essay. By JOHN LAWRENCE LAMBE. In demy 8vo, cloth gilt, 5s. net.

THE POEMS OF JAMES HOGG. The Ettrick Shepherd. Selected and edited, with an introduction, by WILLIAM WALLACE, LL.D. With photogravure portrait frontispiece. In crown 8vo, cloth gilt, gilt top, 5s.

WITH THE WILD GEESE. Songs of Irish Exile and Lament. By EMILY LAWLESS. With an Introduction by STOPFORD A. BROOKE. In square 8vo, cloth gilt, 4s. 6d. net.

THE WOOING OF A GODDESS. By B. BURFORD RAWLINGS. In foolscap 8vo, leather, 2s. 6d. net.

MODERN FRENCH LITERATURE. By B. W. WELLS, Ph.D. In crown 8vo, cloth gilt, 520 pp., 6s. net.

MODERN ITALIAN LITERATURE. By LACY COLLISON-MORLEY, Author of *Guiseppe Baretti and his Friends*. In crown 8vo, cloth gilt, 360 pp., 6s. net.

A SHORT HISTORY OF GREEK LITERATURE. From Homer to Julian. By WILMER CAVE WRIGHT, Ph.D., late of Girton College, Cambridge. In crown 8vo, cloth gilt, 544 pp., 6s. net.

GREEK INFLUENCE ON ENGLISH POETRY. By the late Professor JOHN CHURTON COLLINS. Edited with Introduction, by Professor M. MACMILLAN. In crown 8vo, cloth gilt, with portrait. 3s. 6d. net.

POLITICS, ETC.

THE CASE AGAINST WELSH DISENDOWMENT. By J. FOVARGUE BRADLEY. Third impression. In demy 8vo, 1s. net.

NONCONFORMISTS AND THE WELSH CHURCH BILL. By the same Author. 2nd impression. Crown 8vo, 1s. net.

THE RISE AND DECLINE OF WELSH NONCONFORMITY. An Impartial Investigation. By VIATOR CAMBRENSIS. Demy 8vo, 1s. net.

FAMOUS SPEECHES. First Series. From Cromwell to Gladstone. Selected and Edited with Introductory Notes by HERBERT PAUL. In demy 8vo, cloth, 470 pp., 7s. 6d. net.
"A book of selections such as this is delightful reading. Mr. Herbert Paul has chosen discreetly in the wide field from Cromwell to Gladstone, and has prefaced each orator with a judicious criticism."—*Spectator.*

FAMOUS SPEECHES. Second Series. From Lord Macaulay to Lord Rosebery. Selected and Edited with Introductory Notes by HERBERT PAUL. In demy 8vo, cloth, 398 pp., 7s. 6d. net.

THE TRUTH ABOUT HOME RULE. By PEMBROKE WICKS, LL.B., *Barrister-at-law*. With a Preface by the Rt. Hon. Sir EDWARD CARSON, K.C., M.P. In crown 8vo, cloth gilt, with illustrations, 3s. 6d. net.

SCIENCE

GREAT ASTRONOMERS. By Sir ROBERT BALL, D.Sc., LL.D., F.R.S. With numerous full-page and other illustrations. In demy 8vo, cloth gilt, gilt top, 3s. 6d. net.

" Sir Robert Ball's gifts as a narrator are very great. He is, of course, a master of his subject .. . . The most earth-bound mortal who opens this book must go on with it."—*Daily Chronicle.*

IN STARRY REALMS. By the same Author. The Wonders of the Heavens. With numerous full-page and other illustrations. In demy 8vo, cloth gilt, gilt top, 3s. 6d. net.

" The style of popular exposition adopted throughout is indeed admirable, the illustrations are excellent, the binding is tasteful, and the print good."—*Saturday Review.*

IN THE HIGH HEAVENS. By the same Author. A popular account of recent interesting astronomical events and phenomena, with numerous full-page and other illustrations. In demy 8vo, cloth gilt, gilt top, 3s. 6d. net.

" It has," says *The Scotsman,* " the freshest knowledge and the best scientific thought."

ASTRONOMY FOR EVERYBODY. By Professor SIMON NEWCOMBE, LL.D. With an Introduction by Sir ROBERT BALL. Illustrated. A popular exposition of the wonders of the Heavens. In demy 8vo, cloth gilt, gilt top, 3s. 6d. net.

BY LAND AND SKY. By the Rev. JOHN M. BACON, M.A., F.R.A.S. The Record of a Balloonist. With four illustrations. In demy 8vo, cloth gilt, gilt top, 3s. 6d. net.

SOCIOLOGY

SOCIALISM. By Professor ROBERT FLINT, LL.D. New, Revised and Cheaper Edition. In demy 8vo, cloth gilt, 6s. net.

" A new, revised and cheaper edition of Professor Flint's masterly study will be generally welcomed. References show that the additional notes are well up to date."—*Daily Mail.*

THE PEOPLE OF THE ABYSS. By JACK LONDON. A study of the social and economic conditions of life in the East End of London. By the author of *The Call of the Wild.* With 24 illustrations from actual photographs. In crown 8vo, cloth gilt, 6s.

" . . . Mr. Jack London, who is already known to the British public as a fine descriptive writer, has done for the East End of London what he did for the Klondyke—has described it fully and faithfully, looking at it as intimately as dispassionately."—*Daily Chronicle.*

WHAT IS SOCIALISM ? By " SCOTSBURN." An attempt to examine the principles and policy propounded by the advocates of Socialism. In demy 8vo, cloth gilt, 7s. 6d.

THE SOCIAL WORKER'S GUIDE. (See page 20.)

THEOLOGICAL

THE PRAYER BOOK DICTIONARY. An Indispensable Volume of Reference dealing with the origins, history, use, and teaching of the several authorised editions of the Book of Common Prayer within the Anglican Communion. Its scope embraces all accompanying ceremonies and supplementary rites, the ornaments of the Church and of all ministers, Church structures and fittings in their relation to worship, ecclesiastical persons and bodies, and the legislative judicial or administrative authorities now or heretofore empowered or exercising powers in regard to the above. Edited by GEORGE HARFORD, M.A., *Vicar of Mossley Hill, Hon. Canon of Liverpool;* and MORLEY STEVENSON, M.A., *Principal of Warrington Training College, Hon. Canon of Liverpool.* Assisted by J. W. TYRER, M.A., *Formerly Vicar of St. Luke the Evangelist, Walton.* Preface by THE LORD BISHOP OF LIVERPOOL.

Articles by nearly 150 Contributors, including :—The Bishop of Ossory ; Lord Hugh Cecil ; Dr. Hermitage Day ; The late Dr. Dowden (Bishop of Edinburgh) ; Canon Driver ; The Bishop of Ripon ; The Provost of King's College, Cambridge ; The Bishop of Lichfield ; The Rev. T. A. Lacey ; The Bishop of Moray and Ross ; The Bishop of Aberdeen ; Bishop Montgomery ; The Bishop of Durham ; The Bishop of Exeter ; Canon Simpson ; Chancellor P. V. Smith ; Canon Staley ; Dr. Eugene Stock ; The Dean of Canterbury ; Canon Bullock Webster ; The Rev. James Baden Powell ; Professor H. B. Swete ; Dr. H. P. Allen ; Professor Du Bose ; Dr. Guy Warman ; Dr. St. Clair Tisdall ; Mr. Robert Bridges ; Mr. Francis Burgess ; Mr. Edwin H. Freshfield, F.S.A. ; Mr. J. A. Fuller Maitland, M.A., F.S.A. ; Sir T. Sydney Lea, Bart. ; Sir Charles Nicholson, F R.I.B.A. ; Mrs. Romanes ; Professor J. E. Vernham. The work is complete in One Volume, crown 4to, half leather gilt, gilt top, 850 pp., 25s. net. *Write for 16 pp. Prospectus containing lists of Contributors and articles, specimen pages, etc.*

" A very successful attempt to meet a real want."—*Guardian.* " Thorough and scholarly."—*Church Times.* " The book will take its place at once amongst our indispensable works of reference . . . a great and scholarly achievement."—*The Churchman.* " We do not think that any Clergyman can afford to be without this highly scholarly volume."—*Church of Ireland Gazette.* " Its contents answer practically every question that we can ask about the book. It will make for itself a place on our reference shelves next to Hastings."—*Record.*

THE BOOK OF ISAIAH. NEWLY TRANSLATED WITH INTRO-DUCTIONS, CRITICAL NOTES AND EXPLANATIONS BY G. H. BOX, M.A. Together with a Prefatory Note by S. R. DRIVER, D.D Regius Professor of Hebrew in the University of Oxford, and Canon of Christ Church. In demy 8vo, cloth gilt, with two maps, 7s. 6d. net.

The Athenæum says it " deserves high commendation," and that " the advantage of having the prophecies placed before us in something like the original grouping of lines far outweighs the drawback of what might here and there be regarded as arbitrary or unnecessary alterations . . the book recommends itself by its scholarly character, its clearness of exposition, and the fearless, yet reverent spirit of investigation by which it is animated."

THE EZRA-APOCALYPSE. Being Chapters 3—14 of the Book commonly known as IV. Ezra (or II. Esdras). Translated from a critically revised text, with critical Introductions, Notes, and Explanations ; with a General Introduction to the Apocalypse, and an Appendix containing the Latin text. By G. H. Box, M.A., Author of *The Book of Isaiah,* etc. Together with a Prefatory Note by W. Sanday, D.D., LL.D., Litt.D., *Lady Margaret Professor and Canon of Christ Church, Oxford.* In demy 8vo, cloth gilt, 488 pp., 10s. 6d. net.

" Already known to the student by his excellent edition of *Isaiah,* Mr. Box has now ventured successfully as we think, into a field which Dr. Charles had almost made his own ; and Dr. Charles, we are sure, will not be backward in greeting him as a worthy *confrère.* Mr. Box's treatment of the various problems presented by the book is marked by the same clearness and thoroughness which characterised his *Isaiah* . . . Mr. Box has laid the readers of 2 Esdras under the highest obligations, and has produced a work, the only thorough English work on the subject, which does honour to English scholarship and will be indispensable to all students of this portion of the Apocrypha."—*Spectator.*

THE RELIGION AND WORSHIP OF THE SYNAGOGUE. An Introduction to the Study of Judaism from the New Testament Period. By W. O. E. Oesterley, D.D., and G. H. Box, M.A. In demy 8vo, cloth gilt, with eight illustrations. Second, Revised, and Cheaper Edition, 7s. 6d. net.

" It is not often that a large book can be written on a large subject in the field of religion, which is so entirely new and fresh as this important volume. . . . Its novelty and freshness lies in its point of view. It is a study of Judaism by Christian scholars of the Church of England, written for a Christian public, and it is a sympathetic, even a loving study."—*Church Times.*

" Its authors have written with good will and with quite exceptional knowledge."—*Jewish Chronicle.*

THE EVOLUTION OF THE MESSIANIC IDEA. A Study in Comparative Religion. By the Rev. W. O. E. Oesterley, D.D. In crown 8vo, cloth gilt, 3s. 6d. net.

" Dr. Oesterley's new work deserves the serious consideration of students. . . It is stimulating, earnest, frank, full of interesting information. . . . Likely to prove very useful to a wide circle of readers."—*Athenæum.*

THE FUTURE LIFE AND MODERN DIFFICULTIES. By F. Claude Kempson, M.B. In crown 8vo, cloth gilt, with diagrams, 3s. 6d. net.

" The author shows the simplest educated reader that there is nothing whatever in scientific discoveries to weaken our faith in Christianity."—*The Record.*

15

THE SAMSON-SAGA AND ITS PLACE IN COMPARATIVE RELIGION.
By the Rev. A. SMYTHE PALMER, D.D. In crown 8vo, cloth gilt,
with two illustrations, 5s. net.

THE KINGDOM WITHIN. Being Teaching for our Day Recorded
Exclusively by St. Luke. By AGNES STANLEY LEATHES. In crown
8vo, cloth gilt, gilt top, 3s. 6d. net.
" Her studies are thoughtful and yet simple ; they relate the
primary teachings of Christ to the facts of modern life. There
are useful chapters on spiritual healing, and on the value of the
results of psychic research, a value often over estimated by the
apologist for Christianity."—*Church Times.*

THE GOSPEL OF JOY. By the Rev. STOPFORD A. BROOKE, M.A.,
LL.D. In crown 8vo, cloth gilt, gilt top, 6s.

THE OLD TESTAMENT AND MODERN LIFE. By the same Author.
In crown 8vo, cloth gilt, gilt top, 6s.
THE LIFE SUPERLATIVE. By the same Author. In crown 8vo,
cloth gilt, gilt top, 6s.

THOUGHTS ON SOME OF THE MIRACLES OF JESUS. As MARKS
OF THE WAY OF LIFE. By the Right Hon. and Most Rèv. COSMO
GORDON LANG, D.D., Lord Archbishop of York. In crown 8vo,
cloth gilt, gilt top, 6s.
" A delightful book, full of helpfulness and cheer."—*Methodist
Times.*

THOUGHTS ON SOME OF THE PARABLES OF JESUS. By the same
Author. In crown 8vo, cloth gilt, gilt top, 6s.
" We can only express our wonder at the freshness of treatment
which he has been able to bring to a familiar subject."—*The Times.*

FAMOUS SERMONS BY ENGLISH PREACHERS. From the VEN-
ERABLE BEDE to H. P. LIDDON. Edited with Historical and Biographical Notes by Canon DOUGLAS MACLEANE, M.A. In demy
8vo, cloth gilt, 6s. net.
" This is a delightful collection, and the reading public owe a
debt of gratitude to Canon Macleane. Canon Macleane's Introductions to the Sermons are by no means the least valuable part of
the work . . . it deserves, and will no doubt receive, a hearty
welcome from all reading men interested in the history of our
Church."—*Record.*

LAY SERMONS FROM " THE SPECTATOR." By M. C. E. With
an introduction by J. ST. LOE STRACHEY. In crown 8vo, cloth
gilt, gilt top silk register, 5s. net.
" . . . The prime merit of these essays is their simplicity—a
quality which should commend them to many who instinctively
reject sermons as sermons are too often preached."—*Pall Mall
Gazette.*

THE PRESENCE OF CHRIST. By the late Bishop THOROLD. In crown 8vo, cloth gilt, 3s. 6d.

THE TENDERNESS OF CHRIST. By the same Author. In crown 8vo, cloth gilt, 3s. 6d.
" Deals with questions of universal and abiding import. His style, too, has a rare charm."—*Pall Mall Gazette.*

THE GOSPEL OF CHRIST. By the same Author. In crown 8vo, cloth gilt, 3s. 6d.
" May well take its place amongst the classics of experimental religion."—*Record.*

ON LIFE'S THRESHOLD : TALKS TO YOUNG PEOPLE ON CHARACTER AND CONDUCT. By the same Author. Translated by EDNA ST. JOHN. In crown 8vo, cloth gilt, gilt top, 3s. 6d.

THE SIMPLE LIFE. By the same Author. Translated from the French by MARIE LOUISE HENDEE. With biographical sketch by GRACE KING. New Edition. In foolscap 8vo, cloth gilt, 1s. net.

THE COMMANDMENTS OF JESUS. By the Rev. R. F. HORTON. Popular edition. In crown 8vo, cloth gilt, 2s. 6d. net.

THE TEACHING OF JESUS. By the same Author. Popular edition. In crown 8vo, cloth gilt. 2s. 6d. net.

HELP FOR THE TEMPTED. By Professor AMOS R. WELLS. With an Introduction by the Rev. F. B. MEYER, B.A. In foolscap 8vo, cloth gilt, gilt top, 2s. 6d. ; also in paper covers, price 1s. 6d.

THE GOSPEL AND THE AGE. By the late W. C. MAGEE, D.D., Archbishop of York. In large crown 8vo, cloth gilt, gilt top, 3s. 6d.
" Will arrest the attention of the world."—*Spectator.*

THE INDWELLING CHRIST. By the late HENRY ALLON, D.D. In large crown 8vo, cloth gilt, gilt top, 3s. 6d.
" Worthy to take their place among the masterpieces of the old divines."—*Daily Telegraph.*

CONSIDERATIONS FOR LENT. Readings for the Forty Days' Fast. By The Rev. VERNON STALEY, Hon. Canon of Inverness Cathedral. Author of *The Catholic Religion*, etc., etc. In foolscap 8vo, cloth, 1s. 6d. net. Leather gilt, gilt top, 2s. 6d. net.
The plan of the work is to give the reader food for reflection founded on Christian doctrine, in the best sense of the term, and to turn each day's reading, or portion, to bear upon character and practical religion.

CONSIDERATIONS FOR ADVENT. Devotional Readings for the Season. By the same Author. Cloth, 1s. 6d. net ; leather, 2s. 6d. net.

A BOOK OF THE LOVE OF JESUS. By Mgr. R. H. BENSON. In foolscap 8vo, leather gilt, gilt top, 3s. 6d. net ; cloth 2s. net.
" An anthology of some old Catholic devotions, slightly modernized, which will appeal to many by reason of its simplicity and beauty."—*To-day.*

A BOOK OF THE LOVE OF MARY. By F. M. GROVES. Preface by HIS EMINENCE CARDINAL BOURNE. In foolscap 8vo., cloth, with frontispiece, 2s. net. Leather gilt, gilt top, photogravure frontispiece, 3s. net.

" We give a cordial and grateful welcome to this beautiful little book about Our Lady, and her churches, pictures, images, shrines, guilds, wells and salutations, and the poems, prayers and days that honour her."—*Catholic Times.*

A LITTLE HISTORY OF THE LOVE OF THE HOLY EUCHARIST. By the same Author. In foolscap 8vo, leather gilt, gilt top, 3s. 6d. net.

In a previous work Mrs. Groves traced the history of the devotion to Our Lady in these islands, showing the various forms it took and the traces it has left in the language and the social customs of the country. In the present work she renders a like service to the history of the devotion to the Blessed Sacrament of the Altar in England during the centuries between the planting of Christianity here and the reign of Mary Tudor.

IN OUR LADY'S PRAISE. An Anthology of Verse. Compiled by E. HERMITAGE DAY, D.D., F.S.A. With Preface by the RIGHT HON. VISCOUNT HALIFAX. In foolscap 8vo, cloth, with photogravure, 2s. net ; leather gilt, gilt top, with photogravure frontispiece, 3s. net.

IN ANSWER TO PRAYER. Testimonies of Personal Experiences. By BISHOP BOYD-CARPENTER, the late DEAN OF SALISBURY, Canon KNOX LITTLE, M.A., the late Rev. Dr. JOHN WATSON (" IAN MACLAREN "), Rev. Dr. R. F. HORTON, the late Rev. HUGH PRICE HUGHES, and others. Cheaper edition. In crown 8vo, cloth gilt, gilt top, 2s.

THE LITERARY STUDY OF THE BIBLE. An account of the leading forms of literature in the Sacred Writings. By Professor R. G. MOULTON, M.A., Ph.D. Cheaper Edition. In demy 8vo, cloth gilt, 6s. net.

" A valuable help to the study of the Sacred Writings. . . We heartily recommend this book."—*Daily Chronicle.*

THE PRACTICAL WISDOM OF THE BIBLE. Edited with an introduction by J. ST. LOE STRACHEY (Editor of *The Spectator*). In demy 16mo, cloth gilt, gilt top, 2s. 6d. net ; leather 3s. 6d. net.

" No one, after reading the elegant and carefully produced volume can doubt that Mr. Strachey has done a good work in a thoroughly good manner."—*Standard.*

THE ST. PAUL'S HANDBOOKS. Edited by E. HERMITAGE DAY, D.D., F.S.A. Each in crown 8vo, cloth gilt, 2s. 6d. net.

This new series makes a strong appeal to the large number of busy Churchpeople who desire to obtain clear guidance for themselves upon those questions of faith and practice which emerge from time to time into the field of controversy. The volumes will be written by Priests and Laymen who have received the Faith from the Catholic Church in the English Provinces.

THE MINISTRY OF THE CHURCH. By E. HERMITAGE DAY, D.D., F.S.A.

Other Volumes in preparation.

THE SOCIAL RESULTS OF EARLY CHRISTIANITY. By C. SCHMIDT. Translated by Mrs. THORPE. With Preliminary Essay by R. W DALE, LL.D. In crown 8vo, cloth gilt, 3s. 6d. net.

" An easy book to read, and the educated layman will find it full of vital interest, while the more exacting student will have the further satisfaction of being provided with full and precise references to the original authorities in which many startling assertions are made."—*Nottingham Daily Express.*

EDUCATION AND SOCIAL LIFE. By the Rev. J. WILSON HARPER, D.D. In crown 8vo, cloth, 4s. 6d. net.

MODERNISM. A RECORD AND REVIEW. By the Ven. A. LESLIE LILLEY, M.A., *Archdeacon of Ludlow.* In demy 8vo, cloth gilt, 6s. net.

" Mr. Lilley is admirably suited, both by knowledge and sympathy, to be the medium through which the modernist position may be made known to the English public."—*Church Times.*

BODY AND SOUL. An Enquiry into the effects of Religion upon health with a description of Christian works of healing from the New Testament to the present day. By PERCY DEARMER, D.D. Ninth impression. Cheaper Edition. In crown 8vo, cloth gilt, 2s. 6d. net.

" Here is the book for which we have so long waited. . . We may say at once that the work could hardly have been better done. It takes a comprehensive survey of the main question, and of matters related to it. It is arranged with an admirable clearness." —*Church Times.*

THE CHURCHMAN'S GUIDE. A Handbook for all persons, whether Clerical or Lay, who require a Book of Reference on questions of Church Law or Ecclesiology. Edited by ARTHUR REYNOLDS, M.A. In crown 8vo, cloth, 368 pp., 3s. 6d. net.

" The work is extremely well done. Within the space of 333 pages, well and clearly printed in double columns, the editor has managed to include nearly a thousand articles and definitions. The articles on various legal points are lucid and authoritative ; those on ecclesiology interesting and practical ; those on historical points are commendably free from bias. In fact it is a trustworthy and convenient guide on the many matters on which the churchman constantly finds himself in need of information."—*Church Times.*

CHURCH ACCOUNTS. A Simple, Concise Method of Account Keeping, for use by the Clergy, Churchwardens, and other Officials. With Model Accounts. Compiled by the Rev. W. G. DOWSLEY, B.A. Size 15½ in. by 9½ in., half-leather, 106 pp., with interleaved blotting-paper, 6s. 6d. net.

" An exceedingly useful volume. . . . As to its thoroughness there can be no doubt ; . . . for large and highly organised parishes it would be difficult to devise anything better."—*Guardian.*

THE SOCIAL WORKERS' GUIDE. A Handbook of Information and Counsel for all who are interested in Public Welfare. Edited by the Rev. J. B. HALDANE, M.A., Secretary of the Southwark Diocesan Social Service Committee, with assistance from Fifty Experts. In crown 8vo, cloth, 500 pp., with over 500 articles. 3s. 6d. net.

" A book of reference of more than average value. The need of such a book is patent, and we do not know of any other publication which attempts to supply it. The notes are arranged in alphabetical order, and, generally speaking, they are wonderfully exhaustive."—*Guardian.*

HOW TO TEACH AND CATECHISE. A Plea for the Employment of Educational Methods in the Religious Instruction of Children. By the Rev. J. A. RIVINGTON, M.A., formerly Second Master at St. Paul's Cathedral Choir School. With a Preface by the LORD BISHOP OF GLOUCESTER. Cheaper Edition. In crown 8vo, cloth gilt, 1s. 6d. net.

" This is an invaluable little book . . . it might well be put into the hands of every Sunday School teacher."—*Churchman.*

A POPULAR HISTORY OF THE CHURCH IN WALES From the Beginning to the Present Day. By the Rev. J. E. DE HIRSCH-DAVIES, B.A. In crown 8vo, cloth gilt, 356 pp., 5s. net.

" It shows wide reading no less than special study. It is written with the simplicity befitting a popular history, and its interest never flags. It makes the Welsh Church, in strength and weakness, depression or re-awakening, live before our eyes."—*Church Times.*

THE LONDON CHURCH HANDBOOK. Being a Compendium of Information upon Church Affairs in the County of London [Dioceses of London and Southwark]. In crown 8vo, cloth, 412 pp., 2s. net.

THE SPRING OF THE DAY. SPIRITUAL ANALOGIES FROM THE THINGS OF NATURE. By the late HUGH MACMILLAN, D.D., LL.D. In crown 8vo, cloth gilt, 3s. 6d. net.

THE CLOCK OF NATURE. By the late HUGH MACMILLAN, D.D., LL.D. In crown 8vo, cloth gilt, 3s. 6d. net.

An attempt to bring out the wise lessons which the objects of Nature teach, and to illustrate the spiritual revelation of God in Christ by the revelation of God in Nature.

THE POETRY OF PLANTS. By the late HUGH MACMILLAN, D.D., LL.D. In crown 8vo, cloth gilt, 3s. 6d. net.

A collection of popular studies, showing the many points of beauty and interest about some of the commonest of our trees and wild flowers.

TRAVEL, TOPOGRAPHY, AND SPORT

THE ADVENTURER IN SPAIN. By S. R. CROCKETT. With 162 illustrations by GORDON BROWNE and from photographs taken by the Author. In large crown 8vo, cloth gilt, 6s.

WANDERINGS ON THE ITALIAN RIVIERA. The Record of a leisurely tour in Liguria. By FREDERIC LEES. With coloured plate, and 60 illustrations, map. In large crown 8vo, cloth gilt, gilt top, 7s. 6d. net.

"The Italian Riviera . . . is practically unknown to the majority of visitors, and Mr. Lees has done it and the public a service in writing this very readable and pleasant volume. All intellectual people will appreciate the description of local customs, art and architecture, literature and folk lore, which Mr. Lees has set himself to expound."—*World.*

THE IMMOVABLE EAST. Studies of the People and Customs of Palestine. By PHILIP J. BALDENSPERGER. With Biographical Introduction by FREDERIC LEES. With 24 full-page plate illustrations and map. In demy 8vo, cloth gilt, gilt top, 7s. 6d. net.

"Nothing so intimate has yet appeared upon the subject as this book. To those who know already something of the people and the life described, there is no book we should recommend more strongly to enlarge their knowledge."—*The Athenæum.*

Countries and Peoples Series

Each in imperial 16mo, cloth gilt, gilt top, with about 30 full-page plate illustrations, 6s. net.

ITALY OF THE ITALIANS. By HELEN ZIMMERN.

"The knowledge and judgment displayed in the volume are truly astounding, and the labour the author has expended on it has made it as indispensable as Baedeker to the traveller, as well as invaluable to the student of modern times."—*Daily Telegraph.*

FRANCE OF THE FRENCH. By E. HARRISON BARKER.

"A book of general information concerning the life and genius of the French people, with especial reference to contemporary France. Covers every phase of French intellectual life—architecture, players, science, and invention, etc."—*Times.*

SPAIN OF THE SPANISH. By Mrs. VILLIERS-WARDELL.

"Within little more than 250 pages she has collected a mass of ordered information which must be simply invaluable to any one who wants to know the facts of Spanish life at the present day. Nowhere else, so far as we are aware, can a more complete and yet compendious account of modern Spain be found."—*Pall Mall Gazette.*

SWITZERLAND OF THE SWISS. By FRANK WEBB.

" Mr. Webb's account of that unknown country is intimate, faithful, and interesting. It is an attempt to convey a real knowledge of a striking people—an admirably successful attempt."—*Morning Leader.*

GERMANY OF THE GERMANS. By ROBERT M. BERRY.

" Mr. Berry abundantly proves his ability to write of *Germany of the Germans* in an able and informing fashion. What he does is to state, so far as can be done within the scope of a single handy volume, particulars of all aspects of life as lived in Germany to-day."—*Daily Telegraph.*

TURKEY OF THE OTTOMANS. By LUCY M. J. GARNETT.

" There could hardly be a better handbook for the newspaper reader who wants to understand all the conditions of the ' danger zone.' "—*Spectator.*

BELGIUM OF THE BELGIANS. By DEMETRIUS C. BOULGER.

" A very complete handbook to the country."—*World.*

HOLLAND OF THE DUTCH. By the same author.

SERVIA OF THE SERVIANS. By CHEDO MIJATOVICH.

" It is a useful and informative work and it deserves to be widely read."—*Liverpool Daily Courier.*

JAPAN OF THE JAPANESE. By Professor J. H. LONGFORD. With map.

" A capital historical résumé and a mine of information regarding the country and its people."—*London and China Telegraph.*

Other Volumes in preparation.

The " All Red " Series

Each volume is in demy 8vo, cloth gilt, with 16 full-page plate illustrations, maps, etc., 7s. 6d. net.

THE COMMONWEALTH OF AUSTRALIA. By the Hon. BERNHARD RINGROSE WISE (formerly Attorney-General of New South Wales).

" The ' All Red ' Series should become known as the Well-Read Series within a short space of time. Nobody is better qualified to write of Australia than the late Attorney-General of New South Wales, who knows the country intimately and writes of it with enthusiasm. It is one of the best accounts of the Island Continent that has yet been published. We desire to give a hearty welcome to this series."—*Globe.*

THE DOMINION OF NEW ZEALAND. By Sir ARTHUR P. DOUGLAS, Bt., formerly Under-Secretary for Defence, New Zealand, and previously a Lieutenant, R.N.

" Those who have failed to find romance in the history of the British Empire should read *The Dominion of New Zealand.* Sir Arthur Douglas contrives to present in the 444 pages of his book an admirable account of life in New Zealand and an impartial summary of her development up to the present time. It is a most alluring picture that one conjures up after reading it."—*Standard.*

THE DOMINION OF CANADA. By W. L. GRIFFITH, *Secretary to the Office of the High Commissioner for Canada.*

" The publishers could hardly have found · an author better qualified than Mr. Griffith to represent the premier British Dominion . . . an excellent plain account of Canada, one of the best and most comprehensive yet published . . trustworthy."—*Athenæum.*

THE BRITISH WEST INDIES. Their History, Resources, and Progress. By ALGERNON E. ASPINALL, *Secretary to the West India Committee.*

" . . . hence the value of such a book as Mr. Aspinall has compiled so skilfully. Its treatment of current topics is copious, up-to-date, and full of varied interest . . . every visitor to the West Indies will be well advised if he takes Mr. Aspinall's book as his guide."—*Times*

THE UNION OF SOUTH AFRICA. With chapters on Rhodesia and the Native Territories of the High Commission. By W. BASIL WORSFOLD, *Sometime Editor of the " Johannesburg Star."*

" . . . The promoters of ' All Red Series ' got the right man for the work. Mr. Worsfold's considerable experience of the making of the country from within, combined with his training as a journalist, have enabled him to cope with the task in a way that would have been impossible to a less skilled and well-informed annalist. Into 500 pages he has compressed the main outlines of the history and geography of that much-troubled dominion, the form of its new Constitution, its industrial developments, and social and political outlook. The volume is an encyclopædia of its subject." — *Yorkshire Post.*

THE EMPIRE OF INDIA. By SIR J. BAMPFYLDE FULLER, K.C.S.I., *Formerly Lieutenant-Governor of Eastern Bengal.*

" Sir Bampfylde Fuller was well qualified to write such a book as this which will serve admirably for an introduction to the study of Indian conditions and politics. Sir Bampfylde Fuller presents a complete picture of the Indian Empire—the country, its people, its government, and its future prospects."—*Times.*

"No western mind more practically versed in and sympathetic with the Indian spirit could be found than his, and his long administrative experience could not fail to lead him to compile a well balanced volume."—*Times of India.*

WINTER LIFE IN SWITZERLAND. Its Sports and Health Cures. By Mrs. M. L. and WINIFRED M. A. BROOKE. In crown 8vo, cloth, 290 pp., with coloured frontispiece and many full-page plates, maps, and other illustrations, 3s. 6d. net.

" This book is so full of description and useful information on all points as to be an indispensable possession to anyone intending a winter visit to Switzerland . . . this invaluable little book."—*Throne.*

Sir Isaac Pitman & Sons, Ltd., London, Bath, and New York.

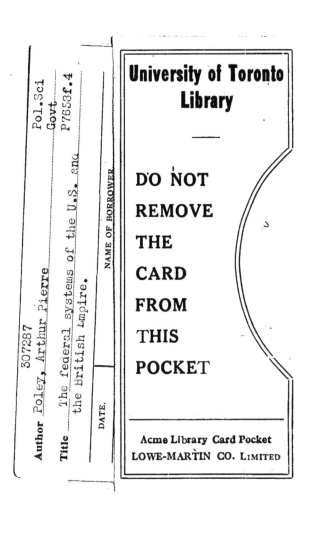

Lightning Source UK Ltd.
Milton Keynes UK
UKHW022231280119
336364UK00008B/937/P